CRIMES

AND

CRIMINALS

CRIMES
— AND —
CRIMINALS

MetroBooks

2004 MetroBooks

This edition published by MetroBooks by arrangement with
Time Warner Books UK

ISBN 0-7607-6542-1

M 10 9 8 7 6 5 4 3 2 1

MetroBooks
122 Fifth Avenue
New York, NY 10011

Printed in Spain

CONTENTS

Introduction

WHAT CAUSES our universal fascination with stories of crime – even, if not especially, amongst the most respectable and law-abiding citizens? Is it the thrill of seeing how others dared to flour society's conventions? . . . the spice of a dash of controlled horror? . . . or even the fascinating insights into human psychology and behaviour that they provide?

The tales of crimes of all types collected together in this volume provide all these facets of fascination . . . and more! From the gruesome stories that inspired the Vampire legends and the terrifying accounts of witchcraft – and the way society dealt with so-called witches – to classic crimes of jealousy like that of Ruth Ellis, the last woman to be hanged in Britain, and the contemporary accounts of the 'big-business' of organized crime and gang warfare.

There are sections of the book devoted to the less sensational aspects of crime, such as the stories of pitiful victims and how their lives are changed by the criminal act, the painstaking police work that has gone into solving some of the great crimes and scandals of recent times, and the often lengthy and engrossing trials that have resulted, and, in many cases, changed the course of legal history.

Perversion

The 'Baby-faced Beast' of Coatesville, Pennsylvania,
has never been forgotten in his home town,
such was the brutal nature of his crime.
Pink-cheeked Alexander Meyer was just twenty
years old when he knocked down sixteen-year-old
Helen Moyer in his truck, carried her off
unconscious, raped and finally killed her.

THE BABY-FACED, pink-cheeked youth who drove
along a quiet road near Coatesville, Pennsylvania,
did not look like a killer, but when he set out in
his green Ford truck that afternoon of February
11, 1937, he had killing on his mind – and rape.

It was just after 3.30 p.m., when the children
came out of high school. He passed several girls,
but there were always other people around, or
other cars on the road. Then he saw, far ahead, a
solitary female figure on a lonely stretch of road.
Without hesitation, he swerved the truck and
struck her, knocking her down. The truck went
over her body. The youth jumped out, picked up
the unconscious girl and dumped her in the back.

He drove to a deserted farmhouse and carried
the girl inside. There he stripped her and raped
her. The schoolgirl seemed to be dead – or so the
attacker later claimed. He carried the naked body
to the well outside and threw her down it. After

that he went home and ate a good dinner. Two days later he returned to the farm with a stick of dynamite, which he threw down the well. The ensuing explosion partly covered the body with rubble.

Obsessional Neurosis

The police who were confronted with the disappearance of 16-year-old Helen Moyer were at first baffled. They found her shoes and schoolbooks close to the spot where she had been knocked down. The shoes had been split open, and the shattered glass of a headlight suggested that she had been the victim of a hit-and-run driver. But where was she?

When the news of the girl's disappearance became known two people contacted the police. One was a scrapyard worker, and it seemed possible that he had actually seen the 'accident' from a distance. At least, he had seen a green truck swing across the road and hit a telegraph pole. It backed, turned, and hit another pole. Then it had driven off fast.

Helen Moyer's next-door neighbour, a fifteen-year-old schoolgirl, also came forward. Six days before Helen's disappearance she had accepted a lift from a young man in a green truck; he had a 'baby face' and wore dirty overalls. He pulled up in a quiet lane and tried to undress her. However, the girl fought back, and he hit her with a wrench. She had managed to jump out of the truck and run towards a house, and the man drove off.

Police examined the telegraph poles and found flakes of green paint – the same type of paint they had found on Helen's shoes. They began tracing and questioning the owner of every Ford truck in Chester County, and when the Philadelphia police discovered that twenty-year-old Alexander Meyer was the owner of a green Ford truck they realized suddenly that this might be their man.

Three years before, Meyer had been given an indeterminate sentence for firing at two Philadelphia girls with a rifle. He was the son of a well-to-do coal broker from Downington, twelve miles from where Helen had disappeared. The medical report from the reformatory said he was a 'constitutional psychopathic inferior, the victim of his own retarded mentality, insensible to pain . . . sadistic and slightly effeminate'.

Meyer was arrested as he was driving his milk truck – the green Ford – and taken in for questioning. At first he denied all knowledge of the girl. Then, when the police pointed out that dents on his truck corroborated the scrap-man's story, and that the paint matched that found on the schoolbooks, he admitted that he *had* knocked Helen down, but said it was an accident. Finally, he told the true story of the attack and the rape, and led the police to the well. There the body was dragged to the surface – minus a leg torn off by the blast. Medical evidence revealed that the girl had been alive when she was thrown in, and that she died by drowning.

Meyer went to the electric chair in April 1937. More than a quarter of a century later the 'Baby-faced Beast' has still not been forgotten in Coatesville.

The horror of the story drives us to ask: why do such things happen, and how can they be prevented? There is no simple answer to either question. Meyer was a 'pervert', like Jack the Ripper, like Peter Kurten, like Harvey Glatman, who indulged his sadistic fantasies by tying up his female victims and photographing them as they struggled before he finally choked them to death. In psychological terms these men were suffering from 'obsessional neurosis'. One idea dominated their minds to the exclusion of all others.

Most of us have to make a considerable effort to concentrate on a particular subject for more than a fairly short period; we are distracted by things that happen around us. A child may be watching television, but if someone brings him a new toy, he will instantly forget the programme to play with the toy. The older child or a teenager might well finish watching the programme, then examine the toy, deciding to take one pleasure at a time.

This is sensible – but not entirely desirable, for people who 'take life as it comes', and enjoy the pleasure of the moment spontaneously, are often healthier and happier than more 'sensible' people. An obsessional sense of duty often produces ulcers. We all have to learn to balance our sense of purpose with the ability to just 'open up' and enjoy the present moment. This is something the 'obsessional' cannot do.

An obsessional is *not* necessarily a pervert.

Some women are obsessed with cleanliness in the home. Many patients in mental homes wash their hands every time they touch something. Obsession is what happens when the sense of purpose gets wildly out of hand. But if the obsession happens to be sexual, then the community has reason for concern.

Freud's explanation of the obsessional type was that it represented: 'the outstripping of libidinal development by ego development' – which means simply that a child's 'ego' – his sense of his own importance – grows faster than his 'sense of pleasure'. The word 'libido' does not refer only to our 'love energies' but to *all* kinds of enjoyment, from playing football to eating an ice cream, but Freud's definition only *describes* the obsessional, without explaining him.

One thing is clear, however, the pervert is essentially immature. All babies want their own way, and see no reason why they shouldn't have everything they want. If the family background involves a great deal of love and security they soon begin to learn to give – and to give way. They recognize that having their own way in everything would give pain to those they love. So one basic answer to the problem of the obsessional is lack of love in childhood.

Love has the same effect on the personality as sunlight on vegetation – it causes it to grow and ripen. Without love the obsessional sees no need to 'ripen', or to try to grow up. Perhaps his parents denied him many things he wanted in childhood, so he harbours a deep feeling of resentment. Later, he feels that society is denying him many things he wants; and so he is prepared to grab it when society is off its guard. The result is behaviour like that of Alexander Meyer, where another human being is treated purely as a dispensable object, like a throwaway handkerchief.

The Remorseless Ego

In his book *Sex Perversions and Sex Crimes* Dr. Melvin Rheinhardt describes the temperament in two words: the 'remorseless ego'. The characteristics are always the same – a completely self-enclosed state of mind in which the other person is unreal. The California rapist Harvey Glatman kidnapped models, spent hours – sometimes days – raping them, then killed them.

In 1953 a middle-aged pervert named Carl Folk 'hi-jacked' a trailer containing a man and his wife, Raymond and Betty Allen. He tied up the husband, then spent a whole night raping and torturing the wife, who finally died. Folk was so preoccupied that he did not notice the husband's escape, and was startled when Raymond Allen pulled open the door and shot him in the stomach. But it was too late, unfortunately, to save Betty Allen. When Raymond Allen shot him, Folk was about to drench the caravan in petrol, to burn the Allens and their baby. He treated them as 'throwaways', whose sole purpose was to provide him with pleasure.

In a sense such perverts are insane. They have allowed their obsession to dominate them until it becomes their sole aim. Yet to call them insane is to evade the central issue. There is undoubtedly an element of *free will* in all this. The pervert *chooses* to be 'insane'.

This can be seen in one of the grimmest cases of 'compulsion' on record, the murder of Alice Porter by Donald Fearn near Pueblo, Colorado, in 1942. Fearn was a 23-year-old railway mechanic, a mild-looking, bespectacled little married man. He was fascinated by stories of the Pueblo Indians and their capacity to bear pain. In an adobe church out in the desert, members of an Indian sect called the Penitentes had tortured, and sometimes crucified, one another.

Fearn began to spend a great deal of time in the adobe church, fifty miles outside Pueblo. He was particularly obsessed by the bloodstained altar. It appeared that he was 'taken over' by the spirits of the Penitentes. The explanation, however, is simpler. By brooding on thoughts of torture he brought a flash of intensity into his otherwise dull life, and he dreamed of kidnapping a girl and taking her to the adobe church. 'Ever since I was a young boy I have wanted to torture a beautiful young girl.'

He put his fantasy into practice on April 22, 1942, when his wife was in hospital having their second baby. Seventeen-year-old Alice Porter, a pretty student nurse, was walking home from evening classes at 9.30 in the evening. Fearn jumped out of his car, pointed a gun at her and ordered her to get in. She screamed, and a nearby resident looked out in time to see a blue car driving away.

Fearn drove Alice Porter to the adobe church and then proceeded to put his sadistic fantasies into practice. He bound her, undressed her, then placed her on the altar and tortured her in a manner that has never been fully reported. It involved binding her with red-hot wires. Fortunately she lost consciousness long before Fearn had finished. Finally, he raped her and, like Meyer, threw her body down a well.

Driving home through a storm, his car became bogged down in the mud. He had to find a local farmer to haul it out with his tractor, and then he returned to Pueblo to visit his wife in hospital. The baby had been born the day before. When the police finally searched the adobe church the burnt remains of the girl's clothes and the 'torture kit' convinced them they had found the site of the murder. They soon located her body in the well, her head having been battered with a hammer.

There were fingerprints on the awl which had obviously been used in the killing, but they were not of any known sexual offender. Routine investigation led police to the farmer who had hauled Fearn's car out of the mud. He told them it was an old Ford sedan. The detectives eventually located it in a Pueblo garage. Fearn's fingerprints matched those on the awl. When details of the murder came out, mobs gathered and there was talk of a lynching. Fearn was taken away to jail in Canon City for his own safety. On October 22, 1942, he was executed in the gas chamber there.

It is worth making one purely practical point

about this case. If Alice Porter had screamed and run it is possible that Fearn might have shot her, but the chances are that he would not have killed her. Rape cases reveal this basic truth: that girls who refuse to allow themselves to be forced into having sex, escape without harm more often than girls who submit, hoping to 'get it all over quickly'.

As in the case of Alexander Meyer, the girl who fights and tries to escape stands a good chance of survival. This is not always true, of course, in certain circumstances a girl may escape more serious injury if she submits to her attacker. But in innumerable cases involving rapist *killers*, it is the girls who have fought who have lived to identify their attackers. It seems to be partly a question of 'victimology'. The question is not simply how to prevent people like Donald Fearn from becoming possessed by sadistic obsessions, but also to prevent girls like Alice Porter from making it too easy for them.

It is true that cases like the ones described above produce a certain feeling of helplessness, and that there is absolutely nothing that doctors or criminologists can do about perverts like Glatman, Meyer and Fearn. It would be a mistake, however, to allow this feeling to paralyse our sense of balance and logic. To start with, when we study such cases we begin to see the emergence of an over-all pattern. And to see a pattern is to begin to understand a thing *scientifically*. And that is the first and most difficult step in solving any problem.

For example, we see that men like Harvey

Glatman, Peter Kurten and Donald Fearn are not exactly a 'modern' phenomenon. Krafft-Ebing describes the 'girl-stabber of Bozen', a case from 1829, which involves a young soldier with violently sadistic impulses. 'Gradually, the thought came to him how pleasurable it would be to stab a young girl in the genitals, and take delight in the sight of blood running from the knife.' After several attacks on girls he was arrested.

In 1867, at Alton, in Hampshire, a clerk named Frederick Baker, 'a young man of great respectability', spoke to three small girls who were playing in a meadow and offered one of them, Fanny Adams, a halfpenny to go with him into a hollow. He led her away, crying. Later that evening, searchers found the child's head in a hop garden. Other parts of the body were scattered about the garden.

I Don't Know What I'm Doing

After Baker's arrest his diary was found, with an entry: 'Killed a young girl today. It was fine and hot.' He was hanged in December 1867. In 1880 a four-year-old child named Louise Dreux vanished from her home near the Tuileries, Paris. The following day neighbours reported to the police the foul black smoke that was issuing from the chimney of a retarded twenty-year-old youth named Louis Menesclou, who lived on the top floor of the same house.

The police burst in and searched Menesclou; they found the child's forearms in his pockets, and parts of her body half burned in the stove. He admitted luring the child to his room with sweets, where he violated her, then killed her. In his pocket the police found a poem by Menesclou that ended: 'In my blind fury, I don't know what I'm doing.' He admitted sleeping on the corpse on the previous night. He was executed.

In Manhattan, in February 1961, a four-year-old girl named Edith Kiecorius vanished from outside her home. The uncle who had been keeping an eye on her had gone off to buy some cigarettes. There was a massive police search. Police finally looked into the recently vacated room of an alcoholic dishwasher, 34-year-old Fred Thompson, and found the child's body hidden there. Thompson was caught in Tom's River, New Jersey. He was an electronics expert, but he had been in and out of sanatoriums many times for alcoholism.

These killers all have one thing in common: they are outcasts, men living alone without real social contact. The American psychologist William Glasser had said that before he can start to cure a patient, the patient needs to have one real 'contact' with another person; without such a contact there can be no cure. Thompson, Menesclou, Baker, Fearn and Meyer all lacked this contact. They were living in modern civilization like hermits in the desert.

This is the foundation of the problem – Karl Marx's 'alienation'. And this once again suggests immediate grounds for optimism. Marshall McLuhan, the 'communications expert' who is the author of the best-seller *Understanding Media*

(1964), has pointed out that the various forms of alienation were the outcome of the invention of printing, and of other mechanical devices – like the wheel and the radio – that became extensions of man and produced a new environment. People felt 'cut off', like a child lost in an engineering factory.

Television is again changing the world into a 'global village' and is bringing all kinds of people into other people's homes. The smallness and lack of definition in a TV picture means that children 'scan' it for meanings in the same simple way that an African tribesman might scan it. They do not 'follow' it, as a literate adult follows a cinema film or reads a novel. So McLuhan believes that some of the basic effects of 'alienation' will wear off. We shall again have a society of non-alienated people who communicate directly with one another.

McLuhan may be over-optimistic, but his ideas suggest that these new mass media – TV, pop records and so on – might be used in some purposeful way to bring people closer together, to educate at a partly unconscious level. His most famous assertion – that 'the medium is the message' – means that it doesn't matter whether television is showing gangsters shooting each other or Mickey Mouse. It is the medium itself, not what it 'says', that has the really important *subliminal* effect. If this is true it suggests new and interesting approaches to the increasing problem of crime.

It is, admittedly, difficult to see how a McLuhanized criminology could do anything about the real perverts – for example, about a man like the Hungarian Sylvestre Matushka, a 'company director' who needed to see a train crash in order to achieve full sexual satisfaction, and dynamited a number of trains in the early 1930s. On Saturday, September 12, 1931, as the Budapest-Vienna express was crossing a viaduct near Torbagy station, there was a tremendous explosion, and part of the train plunged into the abyss. Twenty-two people were killed. It had been detonated by an electrical device.

One of the 'passengers' who sued the railway company for injuries was Matushka. However, when the police began to investigate his background, they could find no one on the express who had actually seen him – although he had undoubtedly been at the scene of the explosion. Further investigation revealed that Matushka had bought dynamite. He was arrested, and finally confessed that the Bia-Torbagy explosion was his third attempt on a train.

He had also been responsible for an unsuccessful attempt to derail the Vienna-Passau train near Ansbach on New Year's Day 1931, and for the derailing of the Vienna express near Berlin on August 8, 1931, in which sixteen people were injured. Matushka was tried several times, the juries being unable to agree on his sanity. Matushka explained that a spirit called Leo had ordered him to wreck trains. He was finally sentenced to hang, but appeals led to his sentence being reduced to life imprisonment.

It may ultimately be impossible even for the most highly skilled 'social engineering' to eliminate madmen like Matushka. But it *could*, undoubtedly, do a great deal to reduce the 'alienation-level' in our society. In so doing it could not only reduce the number of sadistic perverts, but also have decisive effects in lowering the crime rate. This is an aim well worth the deepest consideration of all criminologists and social workers.

The Underworld

Poverty and overcrowding are the fertile soil
in which the underworld roots and flourishes . . .
from the highwaymen of old England to the
smooth Mafiosi of today.

JAMES ISLAND is a half square mile of territory out
in Chesapeake Bay and, apart from being a US
quarantine station, its inhabitants are mostly Sika
deer. It was in 1956 that a scientist named John
Christian went to study the deer. Five of them had
been transported from the mainland in 1916, and
forty years later they had increased to a herd of
three hundred.

Then, two years after Christian's arrival, a very
strange thing happened. The deer started to die
off at an astounding rate – more than half of them
died within three months. By the middle of 1959
there were only about eighty deer left on the
island. Then, just as strangely, the deaths stopped.

What was so puzzling was that there appeared
to be no obvious reason for their deaths. They
looked healthy and well-fed. Christian had shot a
number of deer when he first arrived on the
island and made a detailed study of their internal
organs. The only obvious difference between
these and the more recent deaths was that the
animals that died in 1959 and 1960 had enlarged

adrenal glands – in some cases nearly twice as big as in the shot deer. The adrenals are glands that flood the system with the hormone adrenalin when confronted with a crisis.

Christian's observations indicated that the deer had died of stress due to overcrowding. Yet in realistic terms they were not overcrowded at all, in fact around one to an acre. All the same, that was enough to produce a condition of continual stress that caused haemorrhages of the glands, brain and kidneys. It was nature's way of controlling the population.

Rapists and Cannibals

The deer is a non-aggressive animal, and its response to over-crowding is to 'give up' and die. One writer on ethology noted that the same thing affected some American prisoners in Korea. They would become dull and lethargic and die of convulsions – it became known as 'give-upitis'. In more aggressive species the response to over-crowding is crime – violent and often pointless aggression. The researcher John Calhoun observed that overcrowded rats became rapists and cannibals.

When slum areas of cities become overcrowded a certain proportion of their inhabitants – usually about 5 per cent – develop a kind of 'alternative society'. This is a way of life that is based on crime, and which is taken completely for granted as a social norm – in other words, an 'underworld' develops.

It is an interesting observation that the 'under-world' of a city seems directly related to its population. Before the 1917 revolution the Russian port of Odessa had a flourishing underworld, and it is described, somewhat humorously, in stories by the writer Isaac Babel. By comparison modern Russia has no underworld, and this is only partly due to the totalitarian system, which reduces crime by reducing the freedom of the individual. The basic cause is the fact that, as the Russian population expands, a new city is built in the wilderness to house the overflow.

Russia has well over 200 cities with populations of over 300,000. By American, or even English, standards these are little more than villages. Consider, on the other hand, that New York has a population of more than 19 million, that Hong Kong has more than 7 million, and Calcutta more than 10 million. Also consider that these cities which are crammed into a relatively small area, also have the highest crime rates in the world. If you stop to consider that Calcutta is currently expanding at the rate of over a million every three years, eventually it will be one immense seething hotbed of crime.

Anti-climactic

It is necessary to understand all this if we are to understand the frighteningly steady growth of the 'underworld' in the twenty-first century. In the 1850s a sociologist named Henry Mayhew undertook an enormous study of the habits of the

London poor and produced four big volumes describing them. If we turn to the sections on London's underworld, they seem absurdly anticlimactic compared with modern organized crime.

There are accounts of prostitutes and their 'bullies', pickpockets, shoplifters and thieves. Types of robbery described include stealing from street stalls, stealing from clotheslines, breaking shop windows, and child-stripping – enticing a child into a dark alleyway and stealing its resalable clothes. This 'underworld' was run on a strictly amateur basis. The real professionals, it seemed, were the 'fences' who bought the stolen goods.

The last real attempt to organize crime had been made more than a century earlier by the notorious 'thief-taker' Jonathan Wild, who was basically a highly successful fence. Wild had been executed in 1725, in the days when the commonest crime in England was highway robbery. By half-way through the nineteenth century a fairly efficient police force had made the highways safe. Besides, the great majority of travellers now went by rail. So crime had contracted again into the heart of the great cities – Glasgow, Liverpool and London.

But it sprang out of poverty rather than from any anti-social resentments. The same was true of most of the great crime cities of the world, including Paris, Berlin and New York. In these cities there was no room for a 'crime explosion', for the police knew most of the habitual criminals.

Sheer Cunning

In Paris the Sûreté was even *run* by an ex-convict, Vidocq, and when he began work as a police-informer, around 1809, Paris had a number of gangs of efficient thieves. By sheer cunning and skill Vidocq broke up most of these. On one occasion he joined the gang run by a man called Constantin, posing as an escaped galley-convict from Toulon. When the gang arrived back from a burglary Vidocq had the police waiting for them.

It was America that gave birth to the first truly organized crime. This was the Chinese tongs, which originated in the gold fields of California in the 1860s. They were originally intended as protection societies for the Chinese, who were hated by the white Americans, as were the Mexicans. Inevitably they began to live off their own people, and 'protection' took on its modern meaning – extortion. There were plenty of gangs of desperadoes in all the major cities – New York, San Francisco, Chicago – but they usually controlled a small area, perhaps only a single street.

Then in the 1870s the Italians began to create their own secret societies – or, rather, they brought them from Italy. In Italy, societies like the Camorra had been formed for the protection of citizens, since the police were underpaid and subject to political pressures.

In America the Camorra became the Black Hand, then the Mafia. It began an organized despoliation of the Italian community. New Orleans was one of its major breeding grounds. After the murder of police chief David Hennessy in 1890, and the subsequent acquittal of the nine accused, the irate citizens rose up, broke into the jail and lynched the malefactors. For the time being the power of the Mafia in America was broken.

It soon revived, however, this time in New York. In 1902 and 1903 there was a sudden wave of murder in the Italian colonies of New York City. Bodies were found in sacks, barrels and boxes. In many cases the tongues had been slit in two, indicating that this was a gang murder whose aim was to impose silence. The victims had been 'talkers', and the gangs' code of conduct was harsh and brutal. Giuseppe Morello, a Sicilian gang-leader, had his own eighteen-year-old step-son kidnapped and tortured to death because the boy had let slip some of his stepfather's secrets. Most of Morello's large income came from a counterfeiting ring whose products went out all over the United States.

The downfall of the Morello gang occurred shortly after this. Its most feared members were Morello himself and two lieutenants, known as Lupo the Wolf and Petto the Ox. On April 13, 1903, a woman strolling past a lumber pile on the edge of the Italian sector of the lower East Side saw a barrel – with an arm and leg protruding from it.

Powerful Slash

When the police opened the barrel, they found the body of a man whose head had been almost severed with one powerful slash of a razor. The fact that his ears had been pierced suggested that he was a Sicilian. He wore a watchchain, but no watch. A detective who saw a photograph of the murdered man, recognized him as an 'unknown' who had been seen in the company of the Wolf and the Ox in an Italian restaurant run by Pietro Inzarillo. The detective had been shadowing the Wolf and the Ox.

Good detective work soon led them back to the Italian restaurant. The barrel, with sawdust in the bottom, scattered there to soak up the blood, had contained onion skins and butts of Italian cigars. It was traced through the manufacturer to a wholesale grocer, who had supplied it to Inzarillo's restaurant.

A brilliant Italian operative, Joseph Petrosino, was assigned to the case. He went to Sing Sing to interview a convict named de Priemo, an ex-member of Morello's gang, now serving time for counterfeiting. When de Priemo saw the photograph of the murdered man he wept. It was his brother-in-law, Beneditto Madonia. Mrs. Madonia later identified her husband's body.

Detectives went to question Lupo at his wine shop. Lupo instantly pulled a stiletto, and was about to plunge it into the throat of a detective when another policeman grabbed his arm and dragged him to the floor. Lupo was arrested, and so were Petto the Ox, Morello, Inzarillo and several other suspects. In Morello's house the police found a letter, written to him by Madonia shortly before his death, saying that he was tired of this dangerous work of distributing counterfeit money and intended to return to his family in Buffalo. It was clear he had been killed because he knew too much.

But the inquest on Madonia revealed something of the power of Morello and his Black Hand. Madonia's son was asked to identify his father's watch. There was an ominous shuffling of feet in court, and a man rose to his feet and placed his finger to his lips. Madonia's son stammered and was suddenly unable to swear that the watch was his father's. Mrs. Madonia also seemed to lose her memory when the shuffling began. De Priemo was brought from Sing Sing to testify, and he declared with an air of apparent frankness that he was certain the Ox had *not* killed his brother-in-law because the Ox was one of his oldest friends.

And so all the suspects went free. However, the New York police were determined to get them behind bars. Not long after, Morello and the Wolf were arrested and charged with counterfeiting. Although the evidence seemed thin, a judge sentenced them to 25 and 30 years respectively. Inzarillo was picked up on a charge of altering his citizenship papers and sent to prison for a longer term than the offence warranted. In fact, reading between the lines of the account given by ex-Deputy Inspector Arthur Carey, it looks as though the police stretched the letter of the law to get the killers of Madonia behind bars.

Unknown Intruder

Petto the Ox moved to Browntown, Pennsylvania,

but in October 1925 he stepped into his back yard and was cut down by five shotgun blasts. Coincidentally, de Priemo, the man who had sworn to get the killer of his brother-in-law, had recently been released from Sing Sing, his term of imprisonment commuted for exemplary conduct. When Inzarillo came out of prison he opened a pastry shop, and shortly afterwards was also killed by an unknown intruder.

It became increasingly clear to the American police – and politicians – that the problem of organized crime started in Italy. A member of the committee from Congress was told by the police chief of Palermo that Sicily had very little crime. He asked why, and was told seriously: 'Most of our criminals have gone to America.' In 1907 Joseph Petrosino went to Palermo to see what could be done about close co-operation between the Sicilian and American police. On the day of his arrival he was shot down in broad daylight outside the Palazzo Steri, the court of justice, by the head of the Sicilian Mafia, Don Vito. Vito, of course, had an unshakeable alibi and was never charged with the murder. That round of the fight had definitely gone to the Mafia.

Ever since the 1870s America had been convulsed by violent labour disputes. In many ways this is understandable. The accounts by Jack London of his own early days as a stoker make it clear that labour was ruthlessly exploited. The American 'success ethic' meant that an employer had no pangs of conscience about keeping a man on a starvation wage, and dismissing him and allowing his wife and children to starve, if he could get someone at an even cheaper rate.

The commercial world was a jungle – the title Upton Sinclair gave to his great novel of corruption in the Chicago stockyards. With fighters like Sinclair, Jack London, Clarence Darrow and Eugene Debs, organized labour slowly began to make some headway against the big corporations, although strikes were often long and bloody, and imported strike-breakers were sometimes ambushed and murdered by angry workers.

As organized labour finally began to establish its right to exist, the thugs moved in. In New York all the major industries were controlled by gangs – the docks, the garment industry, the gambling houses and the brothels. The 'protection racket', which had developed in New Orleans in the 1870s, was now a recognized and established business. The gangs fell into three clear groups: the Jews, the Irish and the Italians. The Chinese, who had once been New York's leading racketeers, had long ago been forced into a minor position.

In the autumn of 1912 East Side clothing workers went on strike – at least, most of them did. Some, however, were not militantly inclined and continued to work. Labour leaders, who were always hand-in-glove with racketeers, approached a Jewish gangster, Dopey Benney Fein, to send some strong-arm boys over to persuade these recalcitrants to join the strike.

However, the clothing bosses had also bought 'protection' from a couple of gang leaders named

Tommy Dyke and Harry Lenny, an ex-prize fighter. It was an absurd situation, with both sides of labour represented by mobsters. Dopey Benney's chief lieutenant was an Irishman named Joe Miller, who, to demonstrate his freedom from racial prejudice, had renamed himself Jew Murphy. Murphy was told to interview Dyke and Lenny and order them to withdraw their protection from the clothing bosses.

One of Dyke's men punched Murphy in the face and threw him out. Murphy swore revenge. A month later, at the opening of the six-day bicycle race at Madison Square Garden, shooting started between the two gangs. Luckily only one of Lenny's henchmen was injured. Commissioner Arthur Woods, who had recently been installed in office, realized that next time the innocent bystanders might not be so lucky.

He proved to be an accurate prophet. Trouble came on the evening of an annual ball given by the Dyke and Lenny gang at Arlington Hall, near St. Mark's Place. As Dyke and Lenny were about to swagger up the steps of the hall to meet a respectful reception committee, firing suddenly broke out behind them. They leapt up the steps and into the hall. For the next ten minutes the air was full of bullets. And when the shooting stopped a man lay dead on the pavement: Frederick Strauss, a court official.

No Police Allowed

Woods was furious. The gangs were going too far.

Not long before, he had had to send in whole contingents of police to the Car Barn district on the East River because the Car Barn Gang had put up notices declaring that no police would be allowed in the area. The Car Barn Gang had been broken up; now he was determined to do the same for the Dopey Benney Mob and the Dyke and Lenny Association. His first problem was to find out how the Fein mob had managed to get hold of guns.

Most of them were known to the New York police and were likely to be stopped at any hour of the day or night. If they were found in possession of a hidden weapon it usually meant at least a year in jail, so Woods was reasonably sure that they had not gone to Arlington Hall carrying guns. The underworld grapevine brought him his answer: a girl named Annie Britt had carried seven guns in her handbag. She was one of the first 'gun molls' on record.

Woods ordered the arrest of seven members of Fein's gang, including Annie Britt. The trial was a complete fiasco. Most of the testimony came from gangsters and it conflicted so much that the accused men were acquitted. Nevertheless, police harassment had its effect. During Woods' administration the gangs almost disappeared. Dopey Benney's gang broke up as a consequence of the case. Woods had proved that the police *could* break this new kind of organized crime if they simply harassed enough.

Then America entered the First World War. Many of the gangsters went off to fight, and New

York crime dropped. When the soldiers came back home there was a crime wave – there usually is after a war – but the police proved that they were able to cope. For a while it looked as if the pattern of organized crime in America might be broken.

Unfortunately for America there were powerful forces at work in support of crime – forces that believed themselves to be on the side of law and order. The Temperance Movement began in America as long ago as 1770, when a member of a Quaker meeting in Philadelphia protested that he was 'oppressed by the smell of rum' from his fellow Quakers. Rum was one of the most popular medical remedies of the time.

By the 1930s 'Temperance' had become a powerful movement in England as well as America. Dramas like *The Drunkard* and *Seven Nights in a Bar Room* brought in massive crowds in the 1840s and 50s. But England, with its usual genius for compromise, declined to embrace strict Temperance; the Americans, as usual, preferred to do things the hard way. Hot gospel revivals had always been an American speciality, now the Anti-Saloon League, represented at national level by Senator Andrew Volstead, succeeded in declaring all forms of alcoholic liquor illegal in the United States as from January 17, 1920.

Prohibition had arrived – and with it America's last chance, in the twentieth century at least, of being organized. The story of Johnny Torrio, Al Capone, Dutch Schultz and the other gangleaders of the bootleg era has been told many times. The problem was that they had the average American citizen on their side, that the man in the street thought it was stupid that his democratically elected government should deny him his finger of whisky or gin. In effect Capone and Shultz were voted into office by the people. Organized crime gained the stranglehold that it has held ever since.

Joseph Pistone

An FBI agent, Joseph Pistone, spent six years working undercover in the Mafia as jewel man Donnie Brasco. He was a well-liked 'family' member and rose high in the organization's ranks. He managed to infiltrate the organization so deeply that even when the sting operation was over in 1981, and the Mafia was informed that Pistone was working for the other side, they just wouldn't believe it. They were very wrong indeed, for Pistone's efforts resulted in more than one hundred, mostly highly ranked, Mafia officials being convicted. The Mafia has even changed its rules of enrolment because of this agent who now has a $500,000 contract on his head. He has since written a book, *Donnie Brasco, My Undercover Life in the Mafia*. The Hollywood movie *Donnie Brasco*, based on his memoirs, stars Johnny Depp as Pistone and Al Pacino and Michael Madsen as the two under-world men whom he befriended.

Sex Scandals

Indecent disclosure, particularly when it involves
politicians, is a feverish obsession of the British.
'Kinky' spanking or flogging is known in Europe
as 'the English Vice'. The case involving MP
Lord Lambton and prostitute Norma Levy,
whipped the public into a prurient frenzy.

'THERE IS a rich old banker in Broad Street who
has arranged with the headmistress of two girls'
schools, one in Hackney, one in Stratford, to pay
them a large weekly sum each for a most peculiar
entertainment. At the time of his weekly visits at
each school, the children receive their accumulated punishments. The old man stands in the
adjacent room and watches through an aperture
while the girls, one after another, are brought in,
bared behind, and chastized with the rod.'

This extract from a book published in 1792 –
The Cherub or Guardian of Female Innocence –
pinpoints one of the more curious aspects of the
psychology of the English. For some reason the
strong element of *voyeurism* seems to be part of
the national character. Ivan Bloch, the German
sexologist, makes the same point at considerable
length in this classic *Sexual Life in England*,
where he also remarks that the English taste for
flogging and spanking is so well-known on the
Continent that it is referred to as 'le vice anglais'.

Masochistic Pleasure

Both obsessions find expression in the peculiar English love of sex scandal. Most countries are inclined to hush-up the sexual indiscretions of their public men. The English seem to take a masochistic pleasure in displaying them to the whole world. In 1825, a high-class prostitute named Harriette Wilson wrote an indiscreet volume of memoirs in which the Duke of Wellington figured prominently. When she offered to let him buy his way out, the duke made the celebrated remark 'Publish and be damned'. She did, and became rich on the proceeds.

Nearly a century and a half later, the public displayed the same voracious and morbid interest in the divorce proceedings of the Duchess of Argyll, which had all the ingredients that delight the British press: aristocracy, political scandal (most of it carefully suppressed, but these things leak out), lots of promiscuity and even dirty photographs showing the duchess in compromising positions. A Sunday newspaper bought the duchess's memoirs at a record price.

And then, overnight, everyone forgot her – the headlines were occupied with more important matters. International crises? The moon rocket? No, merely the saga of an indiscreet Cockney named Christine Keeler, who had not only slept with a cabinet minister, but also with a diplomat from the Russian embassy.

The rest of the world saw it as a storm in a tea-cup. Nobody believed for a moment that the minister had disclosed state secrets to Miss Keeler, who had then passed them on to the Russians. But the British public were not willing to take this *blasé* attitude. They wanted their scandal, their indecent disclosures, and the press saw to it that it got them – for month after month, ad nauseum.

Why *are* the English so obsessed by sex? There are two reasons: the basic puritanism of the English character, and sexual frustration. It is true that the Americans are also puritanical, being Anglo-Saxon in origin, but America is always in some kind of violent ferment. The latest political scandal, the latest mass murder, provides plenty of material for the headlines.

England is a quieter country. It is also a small, crowded country, where everybody tends to know everybody else's business – particularly in working-class areas. The teenager who gets herself pregnant, the youth who gets into trouble with the police for carnal knowledge of a girl under sixteen, is likely to remain the subject of gossip for months. In this atmosphere of scandal and disapproval, sexual desires become repressed.

The English attitude to sex can be seen most clearly in the music-hall joke, with its endless *double entendres* and the Blackpool dirty post-card, with its henpecked little husbands casting longing glances at bosomy blondes in bikinis. A number of Sunday newspapers cater for this desire for scandal. The headlines and tone of the stories are full of moral disapproval – 'Should This Beast Have Been Allowed Out of Jail?' They take care to report every shocking detail – 'He placed one hand over my mouth, and tore at my panties with the other . . .'

For various reasons, sexual attitudes on the Continent of Europe have always been more candid and uninhibited. The English schoolboy who reads *The Three Musketeers* finds it startlingly unlike the romances of Henty and Rider Haggard. Dumas simply takes it for granted that his heroes have love affairs with married women. As to the Scandinavians, they seem to take a healthy, almost sterile attitude to sex that the English find repellent. If sex isn't rather wicked, surely you lose half the fun . . . ?

Unscrupulous Opponent

The result of this outlook is that, in England, sex scandal has become the ideal weapon for ruining political opponents. The Duke of Wellington could afford to say 'Publish and be damned', as a result of the battle of Waterloo, he was a national hero. Besides, a soldier is allowed his love affairs. But later politicians discovered just how deadly a weapon British public opinion can be when used by an unscrupulous opponent.

Charles Stewart Parnell was one of the most remarkable Irishmen ever to shake the foundations of the British government. Inspired to become a politician by the execution of the 'Manchester martyrs' in 1867, he soon became the most powerful advocate of Home Rule for Ireland in the British House of Commons. He forced Parliament to listen to him by 'filibustering' – talking for hour after hour to prevent a debate being wound-up.

The British government tried accusing him of provoking political crime in Ireland and had him put in prison, which only proved to make him even more powerful. After the Phoenix Park murders, when two British diplomats were killed by Irish patriots, *The Times* published the facsimile of a letter, purporting to have been written by Parnell, condoning the murders. For a while, it looked as if Parnell was ruined – until he was able to prove, in court, that the letter was actually forged by a man named Richard Pigot, who subsequently committed suicide. Parnell emerged from the case more influential than ever.

Challenged to Duel

And then, in 1889, an old friend and colleague of Parnell's – Captain O'Shea – cited Parnell as co-respondent in a suit for a divorce. O'Shea had known about his wife's adultery with Parnell since at least 1881, eight years earlier, when he had challenged Parnell to a duel. Subsequently O'Shea acted as Parnell's agent, and in 1885 Parnell got him elected Member for Galway. So it was, to say the least, highly convenient for the British Government that O'Shea should suddenly decide to cite Parnell in his divorce case.

The divorce took place, Parnell married Kitty O'Shea, and his Irish party declared they would stand by him. But his English supporters, including Gladstone, hounded him out of office. His fall broke Parnell, who died a year later. In Ireland, his own party divided into those who regarded him as a martyr, and those who found his adultery too shocking to accept. This dispute split the party for many years.

The techniques that destroyed Parnell proved equally successful a quarter of a century later against another Irish rebel, Sir Roger Casement. Casement had been granted his knighthood for his services to the British government – he had been in the consular service, and investigated atrocities in the Belgian Congo and in the Putumayo, South America. During this period, Casement kept diaries that seem to indicate that he was homosexual. By modern standards of frankness, however, the entries seem mild and discreet: 'Gave [medicine] to [Indian servant] and rubbed it over his lovely body, poor boy . . . After dinner spoke to steward Indian Cholo about frejot and he got some for me and then another thing. It was huge and he wanted awfully.'

The entries, which were interspersed among much other material, showed that Casement was obsessively interested in male sexual organs. 'Steward showed enormous exposure after dinner, stiff all down left thigh.' The native loincloths gave him full opportunity to indulge his curiosity.

There are many entries mentioning money given to the Indians, and cryptic references which seem to refer to orgies: '0 14$. A 10$ and beer . . . Olympio first at Big Square, then Polvoro and followed and pulled it out and to Marco when in deep.' Casement obviously took advantage of his position, but it was a known fact that in the

Congo or the Putumayo most white men did the same. Casement merely happened to prefer the native men to the women.

Condemned to Die

In 1912, he left the consular service, returned to Ireland, and became increasingly involved in Nationalist politics. What he wanted, quite simply, was for the Irish not to get involved in the war that was obviously looming over Europe. On the contrary, he saw it as an opportunity for Ireland to make the break with England. He went to America as a Nationalist propagandist, and then, in 1914, to Germany, where he tried to persuade Irish prisoners of war to fight for Ireland, and to persuade the Germans to send an expeditionary force to Ireland.

They were not interested, so Casement returned to Ireland in a German submarine, escorting a ship with arms to help the rebellion. The rebellion took place in Easter, 1916. A British patrol boat captured the ship; Casement landed near Tralee, but was captured and taken to London.

Now clearly, the British had a perfectly fair case for executing him as a traitor. Eire was then part of Great Britain, and Casement had been prepared to let in the Germans. On the other hand, as his friend Bernard Shaw recognized, Casement was only trying to do what Parnell had tried to do. He had failed. With luck – and British justice – he might escape with a term in jail.

Shaw advised Casement not to defend himself,

but to make a rousing speech about Irish nation-
alism – Shaw even offered to write it for him.
Casement, however, was too discouraged even to
try. His defence confined themselves to the argument that Casement had not technically committed 'treason', since treason involves being in the
King's realm at the time, and Casement was in
Germany. It failed, and Casement was condemned
to die.

Even so, there was a strong body of opinion in
favour of a reprieve. Influential Americans were
on Casement's side. Bishop Henson, a friend of
King George V, was also known to be in favour
of a reprieve. But there were just as many influential men who wanted to see him hanged;
among them, F. E. Smith (later Lord Birkenhead),
who prosecuted Casement. Casement's diaries
had been found in his London lodging, and Smith
realized this was what he needed. The 'pornographic' sections were copied or photographed,
and secretly shown to anyone who might be
inclined to support a reprieve – Bishop Henson,
the King, influential Irishmen and Americans.

Sexual Degeneracy

Sir Ernley Blackwell, legal adviser to the Home
Office, wrote disgustingly: 'Of late years he seems
to have completed the full cycle of sexual degen-
eracy, and from a pervert has become an invert –
a woman or pathic, who derives his satisfaction
from attracting men and inducing them to use
him.' His memorandum was circulated among

members of the government. This, and the diary excerpts, served their purpose, and the movement for a reprieve was stopped in its tracks.

In those days, it was only necessary to whisper the word 'homosexual' to arouse memories of the trial of Oscar Wilde, in 1895, on charges of indecent behaviour with males. Until that time, many Victorians had never even suspected the existence of such a vice. Wilde became a symbol of something unutterably evil and perverse, that must be suppressed and forgotten as soon as possible.

And now Casement was raising the spectre all over again. To reprieve an Irish patriot was one thing, but to reprieve a 'moral invert' was another. So Casement was executed in Pentonville prison on August 3, 1916.

But he was not to be forgotten, as Blackwell had predicted. He became an Irish martyr, and one of the names that inspired the uprising of 1921, which led to the independence of Eire. Casement's defenders alleged that the British government had forged the diaries, but this was unfair. They were published in America in 1959, and their authenticity is clear on every page. What is equally clear is Casement's basic decency and honesty. It seems strange, somehow, that such a man should have been executed for a genetic peculiarity over which he had no control.

It might be supposed that the 'permissive society' has produced some basic changes in the English attitude to sex scandal. In fact, this is not so. It is something too deep to be easily eradicated. In the early months of 1973 there was every sign that something like the Christine Keeler scandal was about to be repeated. A Sunday newspaper announced that it had evidence that a government minister was involved with a prostitute.

For the next ten days there was feverish speculation, which ended abruptly when the Prime Minister announced the resignation of Lord Lambton. He had been paying regular visits to a call girl named Norma Levy. The call girl's husband had taken secret photographs, which he had offered for sale to the newspaper. In this case, there was no possibility of official secrets being involved; in fact, some newspapers had the courage to say that it was Lord Lambton's private life, and therefore nobody's business but his own.

But it would have been politically impossible for a man who frequents prostitutes to remain a member of a government whose attitude towards sex is definitely conservative. Lord Lambton made public apologies, and vanished out of the political limelight. Norma Levy, an Irish nurse who specialized in 'kinky' clients with a penchant for being beaten, fled to Spain with her husband at the time of the resignation, and the British public was cheated of its revelations of high life.

Dressed in Leather

When Norma returned a few months later, a 'girly' magazine, *Alpha*, immediately ran a long interview with her, showing her dressed in black leather and holding a whip. She spoke quite frankly of her life as a prostitute. *This* is what would have been impossible in the mid-sixties – the open discussion of her activities in a magazine. It is an interesting example of the double standard in British society. The conservative majority, shocked that a minister should have an extra-marital sex life, and the sophisticated minority, who take it for granted that some men like to be beaten by girls dressed in black leather. How long it will take for the minority attitude to percolate through to the majority is a question of considerable sociological interest.

Although it is difficult to generalize about a country as big as America, it would be safe to say that, in most parts, the transition took place many years ago. In the 19th century, America was as puritanical as Victorian England. Its attitudes can be gauged from the famous Beauchamp tragedy, the great *cause célèbre* of 1826. In the nationwide interest it inspired, the Beauchamp affair could be compared to England's Red Barn murder, which took place in the following year.

In Frankfort, Kentucky, a prominent lawyer named Colonel Solomon P. Sharp had a love affair with Ann Cooke, a woman in her early thirties. When she became pregnant there was no question of Sharp marrying her – he was already married – so she retired to her family's farm near Bowling Green, where she bore a stillborn child.

Kill the Seducer

The scandal was a nine days' wonder, and it fascinated an eighteen-year-old law student, Jereboam

Beauchamp, who came from the area. When he returned to Bowling Green, he persuaded his sisters to introduce him to Miss Cooke. He fell in love with her, and asked her to marry him. She agreed, but only on one condition – that he killed her seducer, Colonel Sharp. However, in Beauchamp's confession later, he asserted that the murder was *his* idea.

Beauchamp agreed. He met Colonel Sharp in the street, slapped his face and challenged him to a duel. Sharp, however, declined. Then Beauchamp and Miss Cooke plotted to lure the Colonel to her farm, where he could be murdered. He accepted the invitation, then became suspicious and changed his mind. Four years went by, and Beauchamp married Miss Cooke, but this did nothing to reduce his morbid obsession with the 'seducer'. In the early hours of Sunday, November 6, 1825, Beauchamp knocked on Colonel Sharp's door at two in the morning, claiming to be an acquaintance. The Colonel let him in and Beauchamp stabbed him in the solar plexus. The Colonel died a few hours later, and Beauchamp was arrested. A court found him guilty and sentenced him to death.

In his confession, Beauchamp declared that his death would serve the purpose of causing seducers to 'pause in their mad career' and think about retribution. His wife was allowed in his cell. On the day of the execution, July 17, 1826, both took opium, and then stabbed themselves. Mrs. Beauchamp died, while Beauchamp, half dead, was dragged to the gallows and hanged.

To our own age, it seems clear that Beauchamp was possessed by a mixture of envy and sexual repression. The very thought of 'seduction' filled him with violent emotions, which he mistook for moral indignation. The interesting thing is that the rest of America felt the same. The Beauchamp tragedy became the subject of endless sermons, newspaper articles and even popular ballads. Ten years later it was to inspire a play by Edgar Allen Poe, *Politian*, and as late as 1842 was turned into a novel by William Gilmore Simms. The idea of illicit sex fascinated everybody, in a country where morality was still as rigid as in the days of the Pilgrim Fathers.

By the turn of the century, this attitude was slowly changing. Sensational journalism was virtually invented by one man: William Randolph Hearst. When he discovered that stories about love nests and vice dens would sell a million copies, he made sure that his newspapers featured them prominently. The result was that the American public gradually became *blasé* about sex scandal, assuming, usually correctly, that it was being blown up out of all proportion. J. Edgar Hoover talked angrily of the 'public apathy and moral deterioration of our population'.

A typical example can be seen in the case of a scandal which erupted in June 1955, when the Massapequa Farmers' Market in Long Island burned down. The market also contained the luxury apartment of a well-known millionaire. In the burned-out rubble, firemen found rolls of 16-mm film, which, when examined, proved to contain shots of various young girls engaged in obscene acts. Their ages ranged from eleven to seventeen, and they were local schoolchildren.

Unsuspecting Parents

It became clear that, for several years, the millionaire had been luring young girls to his apartment and holding orgies with them. In some cases, the unsuspecting parents had given their children permission to go to the home of the 'nice millionaire', who was regarded as eminently respectable. There were more than twenty girls on the film, and they were obviously just a fraction of the total.

In England, the man would have been locked up, and the Sunday newspapers would have spent the next year detailing the life stories of every girl involved. The American court, while indignant, felt no such morbid curiosity. He was allowed free on a $100,000 bail, and promptly vanished to Latin America, and has not been heard of since.

No doubt it is a pity he escaped the penalty. On the other hand, the American public escaped being bombarded with sordid details that might have inspired even more attacks on children. Hoover may be right about moral deterioration, but there are times when there is a great deal to be said for public apathy.

SEX SCANDALS: CASE STUDY

The 'Powerful Perverts' Mystery

Beautiful dancer Maud Allen was a sensation on the London stage during the First World War. She played 'Salome' in Oscar Wilde's play, produced by J. T. Green. But the fanatical Noel Pemberton Billing accused her of being the head of a 'Cult of the Clitoris' . . .

NOT EVEN Charlie Chaplin at his most maniacal could have reduced a courtroom to such a shambles. The Old Bailey in London – normally a scene of sombre dignity, rigid tradition, and measured words – had turned into a madhouse. A preposterous charlatan held the stage with a mixture of threats, abuse, innuendo and audacity. A motley collection of witnesses paraded through the witness box with stories so fantastic they had virtually tongue-tied Prosecuting Counsel. Interrupted at almost every other sentence, the Judge banged his gavel in a hopeless attempt to restore order to a trial that had lost all contact with reality.

COURTROOM CARNIVAL

But then, what could one expect? The whole case had begun with a crackpot allegation that no person in his right mind could have taken seriously. From there it had escalated into a full-dress courtroom carnival, with a cast of clowns, conmen, liars and lunatics.

Right in the centre was one of the biggest frauds ever thrown up by a country rich in eccentrics – Noel Pemberton Billing, independent Member of Parliament for East Hertfordshire. Patriotism, rather than politics, was Pemberton Billing's big drum – and the mighty whack he had given it a few months earlier had reverberated round Britain.

The year was 1918 and victory seemed further away than ever. All the early optimism had evaporated in the face of the appalling death-toll on the Western Front – where an advance of a yard was measured in thousands of lives. The British public, unused to the spectre of defeat, had reached a stage of fear and desperation where they were willing to believe that some sinister force was working against them, and that some weakness or corruption in high places was sabotaging every effort. What they yearned for, above all, was a scapegoat, someone on whom the blame could be fastened.

Noel Pemberton Billing, part-time inventor, professional patriot, witch-hunter, and rabble-rouser, had found one . . . or rather, 47,000 of them. In his magazine *Imperialist* – founded to promote 'purity in public life' – he revealed the evil force that was sapping Britain's energy. It was that old friend of professional puritans, sexual vice. And not the good, old-fashioned variety, either, but perverted and unnatural vice, which had left 47,000 of the country's leading figures open to blackmail by German agents.

What's more, the names were all on record in a shameful 'Black Book', kept under lock and key by a high German official. Under the heading 'THE FIRST 47,000', the magazine's anonymous informant wrote:

'There exists in the *Cabinet Noire* of a certain German prince a book compiled by the Secret Service from the reports of German agents who have infested this country for the past twenty years, agents so vile and spreading debauchery of such a lasciviousness as only German minds could conceive and only German bodies execute.

The officer who discovered the book while on special service outlined for me its stupefying contents. In the beginning of the book is a precis of general instructions regarding the propagation of evils which all decent men thought had perished in Sodom and Lesbos.

The blasphemous compilers even speak of the Groves and High Places mentioned in the Bible. The most insidious arguments are outlined for the use of the German agent in his revolting work. Then more than a thousand pages are filled with the names of 47,000 English men and women. It is a most catholic miscellany. The names of Privy Councillors, youths of the chorus, wives of Cabinet Ministers, dancing girls, even Cabinet Ministers themselves, while diplomats, poets, bankers, editors, newspaper proprietors and members of His Majesty's household follow each other with no order of precedence.'

However, the *Imperialist* was a cranky magazine with a small circulation, and only a handful of Britons slept uneasily in their beds that night. What was clearly needed to inflame public opinion was a recognizable symbol of moral decadence, someone around whom fear and prejudice could crystallize. The unlucky person appeared right on cue, in the shapely form of Maud Allen, the celebrated dancer and aesthete.

According to newspaper advertisements, Maud Allen had agreed to give two private performances at the Royal Court Theatre of Oscar Wilde's play, *Salome*, including her famous rendition of the Dance of the Seven Veils. The climax of the dance, with the artiste kissing a wax model of Jokaanan's head, had already horrified some local authorities, and one had insisted on her substituting a dish of gravy. The Sunday performances, for subscribing members only, were being promoted by Mr J. T. Grein, a respected ballet critic and entrepreneur.

It was a gift for Pemberton Billing. Here was a man with a German name defiling the British Sabbath with a noxious play by a known pervert, and starring a licentious dancer who had received her training in Germany. In the stifling atmosphere of Edwardian Britain Maud Allen had certainly asked for trouble. She had defied prudish convention, dancing in bare feet, dressed in what some critics had described as 'a wisp of chiffon'.

SCANDALOUS ADVERTISEMENT

Her sensual image had been heightened by the purple and panting prose of her publicity hand-outs. These handouts told how she was in 'artistic sympathy' with those Latin races whose volup-tuous bodies and acute passions had brought about the greatest 'crimes of passion'; how she was perfectly made, with slender wrists and ankles; how her skin was satin-smooth, crossed only by the pale tracery of delicate veins that laced the ivory of her round bosom; how her naked feet beat a sensual measure while the pink pearls slipped amorously about her throat and bosom; how the desire that flamed from her eyes and burst in hot gusts from her scarlet mouth infected the very air with the madness of passion; how she was such a delicious embodiment of lust that she might win forgiveness for the sins of such wonderful flesh.

Maud Allen's forthcoming appearance contained all the elements upon which Pemberton Billing could capitalize. In one stroke he could appeal to philistinism, patriotism and popular prejudice, and ensure a wave of public acclaim which could make him a national hero.

Under the headline 'The Cult of the Clitoris' – a sentence many people would have regarded as far more obscene than any of Maud Allen's cavortings – Pemberton Billing reprinted the advertisement for the performance in full, adding the comment: 'If Scotland Yard were to seize the list of subscribers to these performances I have no doubt they would secure the names of several thousand of the First 47,000.'

This time the response was instantaneous. There was a public outcry, and Maud Allen instituted proceedings for criminal libel. Pemberton Billing's 'smokescreen' defence, which hid the fact that he had no defence at all, was that *Salome* was 'an open representation of degenerated sexual lust, sexual crime and unnatural passions', and its performance would attract many of the 'easy victims of pressure' whose names were listed in the Black Book. The result would be 'highly deleterious and prejudicial to public morality and to the interests of purity in the public life of this country generally'.

The Judge was the light-hearted Mr. Justice Darling, whose constant stream of witticisms from the Bench had endeared him to the public and earned him the undying animosity of every advocate at the Bar. From the moment the trial opened, however, the jocular Judge was to be reduced to the position of stooge.

Almost before counsel had taken their seats, Pemberton Billing – conducting his own defence – was on his feet, objecting to being tried by Mr Justice Darling. 'My reason,' he explained, 'is that I have, in my position as a public man and as a Member of Parliament, on many occasions criticized Your Lordship's administration of justice in this country. I have referred to both in the columns of the Press and in a book I have written and on public platforms to the atmosphere of levity which Your Lordship has frequently introduced into cases you have tried.'

'NO HINT OF VICE'

For once the Judge didn't have a merry riposte to cover the situation. Casting the objection aside, he commented snappily that he had never read any of Pemberton Billing's criticisms. Falling over backwards to prove his impartiality, the Judge invited the defendant to step down from the dock and conduct his case at a table in front of the Bench. It was Mr Justice Darling's first mistake. Never a man to be satisfied with an inch when he could snatch a yard, Pemberton Billing was to take advantage of the Judge's extraordinary latitude time and again, until the entire courtroom became his soapbox.

With the supercilious disdain with which only the British can reduce poetry to banality, Pemberton Billing read passages from *Salome* to illustrate that it was 'evil and corrupt'. He dwelt at length on the kissing scene at the end of the Dance of the Seven Veils, and in the stilted courtroom atmosphere the prose sounded more over-heated than ever . . .

'Ah! thou wouldst not suffer me to kiss thy mouth, Jokaanan. Well! I will kiss it now. I will bite it with my teeth as one bites a ripe fruit. Thy body was a column of ivory set on a silver socket. It was a garden full of doves and silver lilies. Thy voice was a censer that scattered strange perfumes . . . I love ye yet. I am athirst for your beauty. I am hungry for thy body; and neither wine nor fruits can appease my desire.'

There were disapproving mumbles from the court – memories were stretching back to the homosexual scandal of Oscar Wilde 23 years earlier – but Mr Ellis Hume-Williams KC, Prosecuting Counsel, argued that there was no hint of unnatural vice in *Salome*. There was nothing but 'the straightforward passion of a woman for a man'.

With unwordly innocence, Maud Allen claimed that Salome's love of Jokaanan was 'the awakening of her soul to the voice of God' – a lofty interpretation that provided Pemberton Billing with an excuse for quoting more of Wilde's exotic rhapsodizing . . .

'Thy mouth is redder than the feet of those who tread the wine in the winepress. Thy mouth is redder than the feet of the doves who haunt the temples and are fed by the priests. It is redder than the feet of one coming from a forest where he hath slain a lion, and seen gilded tigers.'

Judge: Gilded tigers?
Pemberton Billing: Yes, gilded tigers.
Judge: Go on.

Pemberton Billing: 'It is like the Bow of the King of the Persians, that is painted with vermilion, and is tipped with coral. There is nothing in the world so red as thy mouth.' Before we go any further . . .

Hume-Williams: Let us go no further.

Maud Allen: She would not have been the first woman who has asked to kiss a man's mouth.

Judge: But, gentlemen, that is hardly the question. She is the first woman who has talked about the gilded tiger!

Maud Allen: Not as an Oriental, I do not think. Besides, it is her fantasy; I think her imagery is very great. It is quite uncustomary for a Westerner to understand the imagery of the Oriental people.

Judge: Do you think that Oscar Wilde understood it?

Maud Allen: He may have understood it and written it down. I do not understand Oscar Wilde, because I did not know the gentleman.

At this, Pemberton Billing snapped shut *Salome* and turned to a far more explosive volume, the infamous Black Book. The time had come to relegate Maud Allen to the wings and introduce the depraved 47,000. It needed all Billing's unscrupulous cunning and barefaced effrontery to use the courtroom as the platform for his campaign. For there was one awkward obstacle to be overcome. Despite all the wild claims of his witnesses, the Black Book could not be produced.

If the trial was like a scene from a farce, then Mrs Villiers Stuart was undoubtedly the female comedian. Her haughty and piercing cries of 'It's in the book!' were to convulse the court and make Mr Justice Darling speechless. She mounted the witness box with aristocratic aplomb, and launched into a bizarre tale of an evening when two Army officers took her – for no apparent reason – to a remote lakeside inn called The Hut Hotel. Over a calming cup of tea she was shown the perfidious Black Book. It contained the names of some of the highest people in the land. The two officers, she hinted darkly, had been 'put out of the way'.

'IT'S IN THE BOOK!'

The story was too much for Mr Justice Darling. He turned to Pemberton Billing and ruled that nothing more could be said about the Black Book unless the volume could be produced. With a wild gleam in his eye Billing turned to the bristling Mrs Villiers Stuart.

Pemberton Billing: Is Justice Darling's name in that book?

Mrs Stuart: It is, and that book can be produced!

Judge: It can be produced?

Mrs Stuart: It can be produced; it will have to be produced from Germany, and it can be, and it shall be. Mr Justice Darling, we have got to win this war, and while you are sitting there we will never win it. My men are fighting – other people's men are fighting . . .

Pemberton Billing: Is the Prime Minister's name in the book?

Mrs Stuart: It's in the book!

Pemberton Billing: Is his wife's name in the book?

Mrs Stuart: It is! It is!

Pemberton Billing: Is Lord Haldane's name in the book?

Mrs Stuart: It's in the book!

Judge: I order you to leave the witness box!

For an hour after this incredible exchange the court echoed with abuse, accusations and applause, with Pemberton Billing in the centre, inflaming the mood of hysteria like some mad magician. The following morning a procession of advocates appeared, representing the famous people slandered in the Black Book. 'My client wishes to disclaim the completely unfounded allegations made in court' became a daily refrain throughout the trial.

If Mrs Villiers Stuart's story had been barely credible, then Captain H. S. Spencer's account of the Black Book aspired to an entirely different level of fantasy. Captain Spencer, it turned out, had been the author of the original article exposing the 47,000 in the *Imperialist*. He was also the unnamed officer who, while working as *aide de camp* to the German Prince William of Wied, had been shown the dreaded Black Book at the Palace of Durazzo in 1913.

'It was,' he said, 'a list of names of people who might be approached, and the method in which they could be approached, to obtain information.'

That was just about the only coherent sentence in his testimony. From there the Captain rambled off on a tortuous story about a secret mission he had undertaken to the Balkans, which had been thwarted at every turn by mysterious forces. 'An attempt was made to silence me by the military authorities because I knew too much,' he claimed. He eventually found himself locked in a small hut with another man, who got up after a while, held out his hand and said, 'Goodbye, old chap. They are shooting me at three o'clock.'

Certain nasty suspicions which had been germinating in the minds of the spectators seemed to be confirmed when Captain Spencer went on to describe how Army doctors had told him he was suffering from 'unusual hallucinations'. However, this was merely another plot to prevent him telling the truth to the British public. 'The doctors put me in a room in an old orphan asylum,' he said, 'but I escaped in the uniform of a medical orderly. After further medical examination I was maliciously invalided out of the service.'

WHERE ARE YOUR NOTES?

It was with some trepidation that Mr Hume-Williams rose to cross-examine. As it turned out, he had every reason to be nervous. Counsel tried to unravel a statement by the Captain that he had seen the book three times, and had taken some notes. Slowly, Counsel became enmeshed in the witness's vague and meandering answers.

Counsel: What has become of the notes?

Spencer: I put them in another book, a book of Albanian personalities, with their failings and vices.

Counsel: What did you do with your notes?

Spencer: The whole thing was cabled for and given to Commander Cozens-Hardy, of Naval Intelligence. I put everything in a trunk. It was all I took out of Durazzo, with the exception of a toothbrush.

Counsel: What did you do with your notes when you got to Rome?

Spencer: I put them in a small steamer-box or trunk.

Counsel: What became of the steamer trunk?

Spencer: I cannot trace it. I do not know.

Counsel: Did you lose it?

Spencer: I do not know what became of it. I was ordered on special service. If you communicate with Commander Cozens-Hardy you might find the notes.

Counsel: Did you say he found the trunk?

Spencer: He cabled, and got all the papers.

Counsel: In whose care did you leave the notes?

Spencer: I did not leave them in anybody's care.

Counsel: Then how did Commander Cozens-Hardy get them?

Spencer: I do not know. It is hearsay evidence.

Counsel: Then you do not know he got them?

Spencer: Yes, I know he got them because I saw them at his office at the Admiralty.

Counsel: Did you examine them?

Spencer: I did not.

Counsel: Did he tell you he had got the notes?

Spencer: He told me he had received what he

was trying to get.

Counsel: Did he tell you he had your notes?

Spencer: He did not specify notes; it was a packet of papers and books.

GERMANY AT WORK

The ultimate incredulity came when the Captain tried to involve Mr Hume-Williams in the impenetrable cloud of conspiracy surrounding the Black Book. The Captain had claimed that British secret agents were 'marooned on Greek islands' when they got to know too much.

Spencer: The agent is ordered to an island, and then kept there.

Counsel : And he is sometimes shut up as mad?

Spencer: Yes.

Counsel: When he is not?

Spencer: Yes.

Counsel: And that is the English system?

Spencer: No, it is a German system, practised in England. It is Germany working in England.

Counsel: So that the people who are able to get Secret Service agents marooned by the orders of the British government are in the German service?

Spencer: Yes, I think I told you that privately. Do you remember meeting me at dinner, and my talking to you?

Counsel: I? Never!

Spencer: When I came back from Albania you met me at dinner at a house, and we had a conversation together.

Counsel: I never met you before!

Spencer: I expected you to say that.

Counsel: Because it is the truth!

Spencer: You were never at the Clitheroes?

At this point Mr Justice Darling threw a lifebelt to the struggling advocate. 'At this rate,' he quipped, 'I expect one or other of you will get marooned.'

After Pemberton Billing had shepherded a collection of priests and doctors into the witness box – including a physician who maintained that it would have been impossible for Maud Allen to have played the part of Salome as Oscar Wilde had intended 'without her being a sadist herself' – there burst through the doors one of the most familiar figures in British litigation. It was Lord Alfred Douglas, Oscar Wilde's former boyfriend 'Bosie', now a repentant sinner and professional witness, without whom no British libel trial of the time was complete.

In the eighteen years since Wilde had died Lord Alfred Douglas had lost no opportunity to condemn or denigrate his former lover. Confident that everyone in court – and outside it – sympathized with his new role as moral guardian, Lord Alfred Douglas gave full vent to his bitterness on the subject of Wilde and *Salome*.

'I think Wilde was the greatest force for evil that has happened in Europe during the last 350 years,' he said. 'He was a man whose whole object in life was to attack and sneer at virtue and to undermine it in every way by every possible means, sexually and otherwise. I do not think he ever wrote anything which had not got an evil intention, except perhaps a stray poem or two. But if you take the whole of his poetry, it is inspired by evil intention. It is the same with his plays and books. He was studying Krafft-Ebing when he wrote *Salome*, which he intended to be an exhibition of perverted sexual passion. Whenever he was going to do anything particularly horrible it was always disguised in the most flowery language and always referred back to Art.'

Mr Hume-Williams approached cautiously and read out a complimentary review of the play which Lord Alfred Douglas had written at Oxford.

Counsel: Is that your opinion of *Salome*?

Lord Alfred: It is exactly the same opinion as *your* witnesses now have about it. The only difference is I have escaped from the influence and your witnesses are still under it!

If was the fifth day of the trial, and Pemberton Billing was still parading his witnesses like a circus ringmaster. Some were coming round for the second time – like the formidable Mrs Villiers Stuart, who provided a grand finale by imitating the witness box technique of the fanciful Captain Spencer. According to her, the Black Book, though still unobtainable, had moved a little nearer the Old Bailey. It was now lying in the former British Embassy in Berlin.

Pemberton Billing: Had you mentioned this book to anyone before this trial?

Mrs Stuart: Yes. I mentioned it to a prominent public figure. I described it as a dangerous state of affairs, but the man advised me that there were too many people involved to make a personal sacrifice to expose it.

Pemberton Billing: Who was this man?

Mrs Stuart: Mr Hume-Williams KC!

But it was left to Mr Justice Darling – roaring back into form as one of the biggest buffoons on the British Bench – to give the whole travesty of a trial its punchline. Five days too late he decreed that all the evidence concerning the Black Book had been 'irrelevant'. Pemberton Billing's comment that 'If Scotland Yard were to seize the list of subscribers I have no doubt they would secure the names of several thousand of the First 47,000' had not been defamatory in itself. The charges rested on the headline, with its imputations against Maud Allen.

Pemberton Billing, however, was almost dancing with delight. He had achieved his object and used the court as a vast megaphone for his own self-promotion. In his final speech he crowed: 'I am a libeller. I have libelled public men for the last two and a half years. I have libelled them in the Press; I have libelled them on public platforms; I have libelled them in the House of Commons.' He finished with a sinister warning note. 'There is an influence, a mysterious influence, which seems to have dogged our footsteps throughout the whole conduct of this war campaign. Gentlemen of the jury, I assure you there must be some reason for all the regrettable incidents of this war!'

The bewildered figure of Maud Allen – who had almost forgotten why she was there – heard Mr Hume-Williams try to inject some reality into the last few minutes of the trial.

'Almost the only person of whose personal honour nothing disparaging has been said has been Miss Allen,' he said. 'But I fear it is in vain. If you are going to return a verdict in this case which shall clear the character of Maud Allen I confess it will take some courage. The defendant has created a sort of atmosphere, by his friends in the gallery and his followers outside, calculated to intimidate the jury if he can do it.'

When, an hour and a half later, the jury returned a verdict of Not Guilty there was uproar in the court. A jubilant crowd surged towards Pemberton Billing. Above the pandemonium the defendant smiled wolfishly at the Judge and made an enquiry about costs. 'You have nothing to pay, sir,' snapped Mr Justice Darling, out of humour for once. 'You are discharged!' Grim faced, the Judge stalked from the court as the news of Pemberton Billing's acquittal spread to the crowds waiting outside the Old Bailey. The cheers were deafening.

It was a victory only for the blind and the bigoted. The following day the *Daily Mail* reported scathingly, 'The proceedings in court constituted nothing less than a libel on the nation. A weak Judge, a feeble counsel and a bewildered jury combined to score for the defendant a striking and undeserved success.'

In a statement a few days later the Foreign Secretary disowned Captain Spencer as a secret agent. 'He had not been entrusted with any special mission,' he said, 'nor had he made any special confidential reports.' Even the Germans disclaimed all knowledge of the dashing Captain. Prince

William of Wied denied ever having heard of him.

And the unspeakable Black Book? The Germans admitted that they would have loved to have compiled a list of 47,000 high-ranking perverts who might be open to blackmail. But no such list ever existed, and they were at a loss to explain how the rumour ever came about.

One German official, however, worried about the mystery for years. Long after the war had ended he came up with an explanation. Far from being a record of degenerates who 'practised evils which all decent men thought had perished in Sodom and Lesbos', the Black Book had merely been a pre-war list of potential British customers for Mercedes cars.

SEX SCANDALS: TRIAL

The Mad Mudslingers

A girl is washed up on a beach . . . in life she had been unknown, and now she is gone for ever. But the name of Wilma Montesi is about to burst on to every front page for many weeks. She will rub shoulders with the rich, glamorous and powerful, and play the lead in a tragi-comedy which brings Italy to the verge of civil war.

THE WILDLY dramatic case which became known as the 'Montesi Affair' began with the sad but un-remarkable death of a 21-year-old girl, washed up one morning on the beach at Tor Vaianica, fifteen miles south of Rome. Fed by gossip and specula-tion, the affair swelled into a resounding political scandal. By the time the cloud of rumour drifted away, reputations had been wrecked, a senior government official had resigned and the govern-ment itself faced accusations of corruption and demands for its resignation. It was Wilma Mon-tesi's misfortune to die at exactly the right time.

Wilma Montesi, a dark, attractive girl, had left her home in Rome on the afternoon of April 9, 1953, apparently to visit the Ostia lido only thirty minutes from the capital. She was never seen alive again. Thirty-six hours later – at dawn on April 11 – her body was found at Tor Vaianica, ten miles further down the coast. Her stockings and suspender-belt were missing.

SECRETLY DESTROYED

A post-mortem indicated that she had been having her period at the time and a routine police inquiry concluded that she had fainted while paddling and her body had been carried down the coast to Tor Vaianica by the wind. Her suspender belt, it was assumed, had been removed by the friction of water and sand. That was where the pathetic story of Wilma Montesi should have ended. But, in fact, it was only just beginning.

A few weeks later, a Rome scandal-sheet dropped a vaguely-worded hint that Wilma's suspender-belt had been secretly destroyed by the police after being handed in by the son of an influential government Minister. With its whiff of scandal in high places and government corruption, the idle piece of tittle-tattle was a gift to the Communists, ever eager to seize a chance of embarrassing the right-wing Christian Democrat party.

This was election year and Rome – like the rest of Italy – was governed by the Christian Democrats. Social reforms had ground to a standstill, corruption was widespread and there had been a series of scandals implicating the government. Riots had broken out all over Italy, the grossly underpaid Southern workers were campaigning for better pay and conditions, and the whole political future of the country was in the balance. The Montesi Affair couldn't have happened at a more propitious moment.

In January 1954, the scandal broke. Writing in

the weekly newspaper *Attualita,* a journalist named Silvano Muto linked the death of Wilma Montesi with 'goings-on' at a hunting-lodge called Capocotta, only a short distance from where her body was found. Capocotta was owned by a syndicate consisting of some of Rome's most illustrious names. There were heavy-handed hints about degenerate parties, drugs, girls and orgies. In time-honoured fashion, the readers were left to draw their own conclusions.

However reluctant they may have been to re-open the Montesi case, the authorities had no alternative. On January 28, Muto appeared in court charged with 'publishing falsehoods likely to disturb the public peace'. The first 'Montesi Trial' had started.

Muto lost no time in hurling mud around. In reply to the Judge's first questions, he offered to produce witnesses who would testify that Wilma Montesi had been taken ill after experimenting with drugs during a party at the Capocotta hunting lodge. She had died and her body had been taken away in a car and dumped on the beach. According to Muto's informants, the lodge had been the scene of drug orgies.

Shaken, the Judge adjourned the hearing for five weeks for Muto to produce his witnesses. The balloon was up. The Left-wing Press hurled itself into a frenzy of speculation and condemnation. The government was branded as decadent and corrupt. The police were accused of suppressing evidence. Ugo Montagna – named in court as the head of the Capocotta syndicate – was hounded by reporters.

Unita, the Communist party daily, ran a story alleging that, a few days after Wilma Montesi's death, 'a famous film star' had telephoned Piero Piccioni, son of the Italian Foreign Minister, and said: 'What sort of a mess have you got yourself into this time? So you knew her, did you? Well, what are you going to do now? And what does Ugo think about it?'

DECLINE IN MORALITY

By the time the trial was resumed on March 5, the whole of Italy was agog to hear the evidence of Muto's witnesses, Adriana Bisaccia and Anna Caglio, two aspiring young actresses. They were in for a disappointment with Adriana Bisaccia. She was recovering from barbiturate poisoning and answered every question with a numb 'I am in no condition to remember'. But Anna Caglio – who admitted to being Ugo Montagna's mistress – gave much better value.

Anna Caglio's testimony was long and detailed, and delivered with verve and relish. She alleged that Montagna and Piero Piccioni had conspired with government officials to hush up the whole affair. According to Caglio, Piccioni had telephoned Montagna a few days after Wilma Montesi's death and pleaded with him to intervene with the Chief of Police.

Together, Caglio and Montagna drove to the Cabinet Office, where they met Piccioni. They were inside for half an hour and when they reappeared Piccioni looked agitated but Montagna appeared calm and satisfied. 'Now everything's fixed up,' Montagna had said. When Caglio commented, 'If Piero Piccioni has slipped up, he ought to pay for it even if he is the son of a Minister,' Montagna became angry and shouted at her. When he calmed down, he told her, 'Look here, old thing, you know too much. It's time you had a change of air and went to Milan.'

After that Caglio frequently used to wake up in the middle of the night to find Montagna awake and staring at her, as if he had been listening to her talking in her sleep. On one occasion, Montagna had told her 'before they arrest me, I'll let them know about twenty other people'.

Anna Caglio claimed that Montagna's money came from drug-trafficking and that there was frequent talk of 'orgies' among his circle of friends. A few weeks after the rendezvous at the Cabinet Office, Montagna had shown her round a flat which, he said, had been bought for Tommaso Pavone, the Chief of Police, 'for services rendered'.

TESTIMONY OF MISTRESS

Anna Caglio's evidence was sensational and the repercussions were immediate. Newspapers beat their breasts about the decline in national morality. Angry crowds besieged the law courts. In Parliament, the Communists accused the Christian Democrats of being 'pimps and spies'. Montagna sued Muto for libel and on March 13 Police Chief Tommaso Pavone resigned. Three days later,

Foreign Minister Piccioni tendered his resignation, only to have it turned down.

In her first big dramatic role, Anna Caglio – the aspiring TV starlet – had almost succeeded in toppling the government. But the trial of Muto wasn't yet over, and the most startling development was yet to come.

While the hearing was still going on, Signora Marri – Anna Caglio's landlady – told the press that Anna had written the name of the person responsible for Montesi's death in a letter and handed it to her. There was pandemonium. The landlady was hauled to court and ordered to produce the letter. 'Impossible,' she replied, 'Anna asked me to post her back the letter, which I did this morning.'

The Judge immediately suspended the sitting and ordered the police to find the letter at all costs. With sirens wailing, squad cars raced through the streets to the letter-box where Signora Marri had posted the letter. It had been cleared. The cars roared on to the Rome sorting office, and the police began sifting every letter posted that day. After an hour, they found it. With motor-cycle escorts clearing the way the police cars screamed back to the courtroom, where the hearing was resumed.

Dramatically, the judge held up the envelope. 'We have in our hands an envelope,' he said. 'We tear it open along the top. We take out a plain sheet of white paper, we unfold it and we read: "Do not believe any other letter I may have written, only this one. All the others have been extorted from me. My Christian principles are too strong for suicide but because I know the character of Ugo Montagna and Piero Piccioni, I am afraid of disappearing and leaving no trace behind. Alas, I know that the head of the gang of drug-traffickers is Montagna. He is responsible for the disappearance of many women. He is the brain of the gang, while Piero Piccioni is the murderer . . ."'

As the riot squad formed up in a solid cordon round the Law Courts, the Judge adjourned the trial of Muto indefinitely and ordered the authorities to prepare criminal charges against Montagna and Piccioni and any others suspected of being involved in Wilma Montesi's death. The investigations, and interrogation of witnesses, were placed in the hands of Raffaello Sepe, the respected President of the Instruction Section of the Court of Appeal. Two-and-a-half years and 92 volumes of evidence later, the trial opened in Venice under the distinguished Judge, Mario Tiberi. It had been decided not to hold the trial in Rome, as the risk of public demonstrations was too great. Piero Piccioni was charged with culpable homicide. Ugo Montagna and Saverio Polito – a top police official – were charged with complicity in Piccioni's crime and all three were charged with conspiracy.

Piccioni, a 35-year-old jazz musician, denied ever having met Wilma Montesi. 'The first I ever heard of her was the day her death was reported in the newspapers, like everybody else.' He did know Anna Caglio, however. She went to him for singing lessons.

MODEST IN EVERYTHING

Polito, the former police boss, now bent and aged, cut a pathetic figure. 'They have embittered the last years of my life and sought to destroy me,' he told the Judge. 'You know, Mr President, to go from the chair of the *Questore* of Rome of the dock is a terrible thing. It is an intolerable burden and there is nothing against me; nothing, nothing, nothing. Do you understand, Mr President? Forgive me this outburst.'

Montagna, a large, striking-looking man, with a smooth, sophisticated manner, told the court: 'I proclaim my innocence with all my strength!'

Rodolfo Montesi, Wilma Montesi's father, took the stand next, and launched into a passionate defence of her honour. 'Wilma was a good girl, religious, respectful and modest,' he said. 'It angers me that newspapers say she used to be out at night with men. When I went to the police station to report her disappearance and when I told them she was a good and honest girl, the officer said to me, "You say that because you're her father", and began to consult the register of prostitutes. I thought I would die of shame and anger. I deny that my daughter had a double life. She was modest even to her clothes, as in everything else.'

That Wilma had, in fact, been a virgin was one of the few points on which the parade of expert medical witnesses agreed. The other was that she had drowned. From then on, each doctor stuck to his own theory. One said she had been murdered. Another claimed she had committed suicide. The third plumped for accidental death.

None of the witnesses pushed harder than Anna Caglio, making her triumphant return to the witness stand. This time, she got off to a shaky start.

Judge: You have already said too many things that have nothing to do with the trial. In this place, you must only refer to the Montesi Affair. Now, what did Montagna tell you about the affair?

Caglio: Immediately after the death of the girl, he told me that Piccioni was very depraved and that he'd had an accident, but that it was nothing to do with him and that if anybody tried to push him aside, he'd let them have twenty names first.

Public Prosecutor: When you speak of the disappearance of a lot of women, what do you mean?

Caglio: One was Montesi, another would have been me, if they'd killed me. And then Muto told me about the other women.

Public Prosecutor: So the source of this information was Silvano Muto?

Caglio: Well, partly, yes.

After the efforts of the aspiring actress, it was the turn of an established star to take the stage.

Alida Valli had been identified as the 'famous star' who was alleged to have telephoned Piero Piccioni after the death of Wilma Montesi. She quickly knocked the bottom out of any sinister implications the conversation might have had.

Judge: When you were talking to Piccioni, did you mention the Montesi Affair?

Valli: I have already told Dr Sepe that, if any reference to the affair was made, it was with regard to the news that had already appeared in the papers.

Judge: Do you remember saying, 'What have you done? What has happened to that girl? So you knew her, and what are you doing to do?'

Valli: As I have already said, if I did refer to the affair at all, it was only on the basis of what I read in the papers.

Public Prosecutor: Do you deny having uttered the phrase 'And now look what a fix that idiot's got himself into', in the bar?

Valli: I do deny it. I never talk to myself.

METHODICAL ALIBI

Far from piling up, the evidence against the accused seemed to be getting thinner and thinner. Piero Piccioni's brother swore that on the night Wilma Montesi disappeared, Piero had been in bed with tonsillitis. There was no doubt about the date. 'My brother is very methodical,' said the witness. 'He even has a file with "Health" written on it, where he keeps the results of analyses, prescriptions and X-rays on himself.'

The alibi was borne out by a procession of doctors and nurses, along with a policeman on duty at the house that evening who had given Piero injections to relieve the discomfort.

It was at this point that the most preposterous character in the entire cast burst upon the court in a blaze of innuendo . . . Gianna la Rossa, or Red Jenny, a figure straight from the pages of a melodrama. She first appeared in a letter to the investigator, Dr Sepe:

'I know all about the events of April 1953 and the death of Wilma Montesi. Since I was horrified at the cruelty of Montagna and Piccioni, I tried to get in touch with the drug traffickers who operate in the province of Parma, at Traversetolo, and I tried to make a big purchase from them, while keeping the police informed at the same time, so that they could be arrested.

'But the Parma police pigeon-holed it and wouldn't act. A few months before, while I was preparing to do this, I deposited a letter with the priest of a little village near Traversetolo. He is a priest who is qualified as an engineer. I knew him at the university. I was almost certain that if I were found out I should end up the same way as poor Wilma. The priest will hand over the letter if you give him the torn-off half of a ticket which I enclose. The other half is with the letter.

'I will only come forward if I have adequate guarantees for my personal safety. Montagna's money and Piccioni's contacts could be my ruin, even if I were protected by the police. My skin is not worth much, but it is all I have.'

There was no problem in tracing the priest with the other half of the ticket. He was Don Tonin Onnis, the thirty-year-old parish priest of a small village called Bannone di Traversetolo. The two halves were exchanged in true cloak-and-dagger fashion and Dr Sepe read the second letter from Red Jenny:

'When these lines are read, I shall be dead. I wish it to be known that I have not died a natural death, but have been done away with by the Marquis Montagna and Piero Piccioni. I ask God's pardon for my life, and I hope that men also will pardon me. I have been drawn into a whirlpool against my will. I wish these things to be known so that other poor girls may not meet my end. I have found that it is impossible, or at any rate very difficult, to do anything to avoid this evil. I live from moment to moment under the threat of ending up like poor Wilma, and I know that human justice can be bought with the money and the contacts that those two have. Poor people like us just have to suffer in silence and then, when we are no longer useful, or become dangerous to them, they do away with us with such monstrous ease.'

BIZARRE SITUATION

Red Jenny repeated her determination to set a trap for the drug traffickers by acting as a go-between with the police, and ended:

'I have no one to say goodbye to, because no one in the world has ever loved me. I ask pardon once more from God.'

For a humble parish priest, Don Onnis seemed to have a knack for finding himself in bizarre situations. He told Dr Sepe that, in August 1953, he was going to Parma on his motor-scooter when he was stopped by a man who asked him to carry a package into town. Luckily for him, Don Onnis refused, for as soon as he reached the city, he was waved down by police. At the police station, Don Onnis was told that the police had received a letter which said that, during the day, a man of 'irreproachable character' would try to smuggle a packet of drugs into the town on a motor-scooter bearing the priest's number plate.

It seemed that Don Onnis had unwittingly found himself in the centre of a vast and sinister conspiracy. Nor was its baleful influence confined to the priest. A few days after the Bishop of Parma, Monsignor Evasio Colli, had taken Don Onnis aside to ask him to behave with greater decorum, he received a threatening letter from Red Jenny.

NATIONWIDE SEARCH

If Dr Sepe suspected there was more than a hint of greasepaint about the whole Red Jenny affair, he didn't show it. A nationwide search was conducted for her but, to nobody's surprise, Red Jenny remained elusive. In court, it was the hapless Don Onnis's task to pluck Red Jenny from the pages of imaginative fiction and clothe her in flesh and blood.

After describing how Red Jenny came into his

sacristy and borrowed his typewriter to write her letters, he was questioned by the Judge.

Judge: How was she dressed, this woman?

Don Onnis: She was a woman of about thirty, dressed in a decent manner. She was educated, spoke without any noticeable accent. She was tall, had a good figure, her hair was fair or light brown and she had an oval face.

Judge: Yes, but how was she dressed?

Don Onnis: I don't know exactly how to say. She had a leather bag and hung it on her chair by a strap. Her suit was perhaps brown or rust colour. I don't know much about these things. I remember she had a car key with a lucky charm.

Public Prosecutor: Why did you ask her name and address?

Don Onnis: I wanted to know who she was.

Public Prosecutor: But when she went out, you weren't interested enough to follow her?

Don Onnis: I thought perhaps she was a woman in trouble, that she might have done something silly.

Francesco Carnelutti (Piccioni's counsel): Did you think of anybody who Red Jenny might have been?

Don Onnis: I did name two or three people; people who might have done it to harm me.

Judge: But you didn't know the woman who came into your sacristy?

Don Onnis: She might have been sent by them.

Carnelutti: But what harm could he have done you with this letter?

Before Don Onnis could reply, Defence

Counsel Augenti chipped in with the thought that had already begun to surface in many minds: 'People might have thought he was Red Jenny himself.'

DECENTLY BURIED

There were more sarcastic asides as Don Onnis floundered through his account of the drug-carrying incident.

Public Prosecutor: Did anybody else know that you were going to Parma on the morning of August 27?

Don Onnis: Only my mother.

Public Prosecutor: You realize that, because of the letter to the police, at least one other person besides you *must* have known you were going?

Don Onnis: I don't understand.

Public Prosecutor: What do you mean? Surely you tried to find out who wrote that anonymous letter?

Don Onnis: No, I didn't try to find out. I guessed.

Question by question the parish priest sank deeper below the surface of credibility.

Judge: Did you go back to the police in Parma after this occasion?

Don Onnis: They had told me to come back to hear how the affair was going on. Once I went on my own accord, but there was an official I didn't know. I told him the story of the packet of drugs all over again and he said to me, 'Go home and don't worry. The packet has been confiscated. Don't think any more about the whole affair.'

Public Prosecutor: You have described Red Jenny and have told us that she wore strong perfume. I don't suppose you know the names of perfumes?

Don Onnis: What do you think?.

Public Prosecutor: Do you know that the day after your talk with the Bishop of Parma, he received a letter?

Don Onnis: I have heard it. My Bishop talked to me about it in a general way but I have only recently seen a photostat of the letter and seen that it was signed 'Red Jenny'.

Public Prosecutor: And what do you think about it?

Don Onnis: That there is some brainless person who is trying to get between me and my Bishop.

Public Prosecutor: Well then, explain the coincidence of the signature.

Don Onnis: What can you expect? Everybody was talking about Red Jenny by then.

Public Prosecutor: But did you tell anybody about your talk with the Bishop?

Don Onnis: Certainly not. I told nobody.

Public Prosecutor: Then there is a little devil stealing your thoughts. You have to go to Parma and the little devil goes and warns the police. You have a talk with your Bishop and the little devil tells Red Jenny, who writes a threatening letter.

Carnelutti: Was it a nice talk you had with the Bishop?

Don Onnis: Talks with one's superiors are always nice.

Judge: Did the Bishop rebuke you?

Don Onnis: What do you mean by rebuke? It was simply a clarification. We informed each other.

And so, with good humour all round, Red Jenny was decently buried and the court turned to more serious matters. Slowly, the whole tone of the trial was changing. As the earlier, wild allegations were knocked down one by one, the atmosphere began to clear. Even the three defendants started fading into the distance, particularly when the various members of the Montesi family began following each other into the witness box. What had begun as a national scandal was contracting into a typical Italian family feud. The first hint that all was not well in the Montesi family came when Wilma's aunt, Ida Montesi, was giving evidence:

'I remember that when she was a child Wilma was playing one day in the water on the beach at Fregene. She was five and I was twelve. At one moment, she slipped in deep water and disappeared. I ran up and pulled her out of danger and helped her back to the beach. She was quite lost. My sister-in-law told me that Wilma often remembered that episode and said "If Ida hadn't pulled me out, it would have been a good death. The water is beautiful".'

Public Prosecutor: Why have you not said all these things before today?

Ida Montesi: Originally my sister-in-law didn't want anybody to mention her fear that Wilma had committed suicide, but I thought that she herself would talk about it sooner or later.

The uneasy feeling that somebody, somewhere, was hiding something was heightened by the appearance of Giuseppe Montesi, Wilma's thirty-year-old uncle. On the day Wilma disappeared, he had left work early. At first, he denied this, but his story floundered when he was confronted with Leonelli, the Chief Compositor of the printing firm where he worked.

First, the Public Prosecutor asked Leonelli: 'Did Montesi tell you that he was having an affair with a girl who would sleep with him the day before her marriage?' 'Yes,' replied Leonelli. Then the two men faced each other.

CHANGE OF STORY

Leonelli: On April 9, you went out shortly after five and you said you were going to Ostia, where you boasted that you had a *pied-à-terre*.

Giuseppe: Ask the witness if he has a criminal record!

Judge: That doesn't concern us. You tell us whether you went out of your office on April 9 in the afternoon.

Public Prosecutor: Listen, Montesi. We are not accusing you of anything. We only want to know where you were between 6 and 11 on the evening of April 9. There are certain moments in one's life when one has to admit things that one would rather keep quiet.

Giuseppe: I am sure you are not accusing me, but I still say that I was at the printing works.

Judge: Did you go to Ostia?

Giuseppe: I did not.

Public Prosecutor: Then where did you go?

Giuseppe: I don't know.

Counsel: He had better say, for his own good.

Giuseppe: I can't say!

This was too much for the Judge; Giuseppe was clearly trying to conceal something. The court was cleared and Giuseppe was pressed again on the events of April 9. Without the embarrassment of the public hanging on every word, Giuseppe changed his story. Yes, he admitted he had left early; for some time he had been having an affair with his fiancée's sister, Rossana Spissu. On April 9, she had phoned him and they had driven to a lonely spot in the Via Flaminia and made love. Rossana had subsequently borne his child.

The Public Prosecutor still wasn't satisfied and Giuseppe was charged with perjury, on the basis of his first version of the story. The Public Prosecutor was determined not to let Giuseppe off the hook. He savaged Rossana Spissu, who rather lamely supported Giuseppe's alibi. Then he turned again on Giuseppe.

COLLAPSED IN TEARS

Public Prosecutor: You've invented all this business afterwards, but you've invented it badly. And so what did you do that evening?

Guiseppe: As usual, we went along the bank of the Tiber and we had a coffee in one bar and a brandy in another, and then we went to our usual place, out along the Via Flaminia.

Public Prosecutor: You've cooked up this version with Rossana, but you've forgotten to put the lid on the pot. Why did you need to see each other so urgently, if you met every day?

Giuseppe answered limply that, on this occasion, he hadn't seen her for two days and felt a desire to take her to the Via Flaminia.

Public Prosecutor: On the evening of April 9, you did not go home before 11 o'clock, and that is a very suspicious circumstance. You are not telling the truth this time, either. Perhaps there is a third truth, and of course it may have nothing to do with the disappearance of your niece. Perhaps you went to a place or with a person you don't want to be known, but we must make it clear to you that we have absolute proof you are not telling the truth today either.

Overcome by the cross-examination, Giuseppe could barely croak 'But I am telling the truth! I have never been subjected to such an examination!'

Day after day, the grilling of Giuseppe continued. Repeatedly accused of lying, Giuseppe jumped to his feet and bellowed: 'This is the last time I shall repeat that I know nothing! I know nothing of the death of Wilma Montesi. I don't know how Wilma died. Perhaps her father knows, or her mother or her sister, but I don't know anything!' At the end of one interrogation, he clutched his head and shouted, 'No, no, no!'

When he wasn't facing the Public Prosecutor, Giuseppe was confronted with other witnesses who challenged his evidence, like the journalist Luciano Doddoli:

Doddoli: Look in my eyes! You told me that you often saw your niece!

Giuseppe: What are you insinuating, 'saw'?

Doddoli: This. When we spoke of a man in Wilma's life, I said to you: 'Signor Montesi, you are that man.'

Giuseppe: You are lying. You are lying in a completely barefaced manner!

Doddoli: And you were afraid and said: 'For God's sake don't bring my name in! I'll help you in any way I can.'

The same heat was turned on Rossana.

Public Prosecutor: Signora Rossana, tell the truth!

Rossana: But I have told it! I swear on the head of my child!

Public Prosecutor: Leave your child alone. Do not bring innocence into this room! Tell the truth and stop crying! Tears are useless. Tell us why Giuseppe did not recognize the child at first.

Rossana: He will.

Public Prosecutor: But why has he waited so long?

Rossana: That doesn't come into it.

Public Prosecutor: It does come in. Why has he decided now to recognize the child? Perhaps his recognition of his son is tied up with your evidence?

By now, the Judge and Prosecutor between them had screwed the tension to screaming-point with their highly-charged combination of machine-gun questioning and dramatic confrontation of witnesses. Every day, the court was packed with spectators, their emotional reactions mirroring the moods of the witnesses . . . anguished, outraged, defiant, downcast.

When it seemed that nothing more could be squeezed out of Giuseppe and Rossana except further tears, the prosecution produced two surprise witnesses whose evidence destroyed the 'Via Flaminia' alibi.

Mr and Mrs Piastra swore that, on the evening of April 9, Rossana Spissu was with them at Rome Central Station, seeing off Mrs Piastra's mother. They produced a marked book of concessionary railway tickets to prove it. Rossana denied going to the station, but faced with the implacable Piastras, she collapsed in tears.

'Tell me, Signor Piastra, why you want to harm me?' she pleaded. 'You know I was not at the station.' The whole courtroom sobbed with her as her shoulders rose and fell. The Public Prosecutor, as usual, was made of sterner stuff.

'Rossana,' he intoned, 'perhaps you are afraid that if you tell the truth you will do a great deal of damage. Giuseppe Montesi is not accused of anything. He has chosen you as his shield, but the shield has failed him.'

It was a relief to see the pressure lifted from Giuseppe and Rossana – there was nothing more they could say and it was useless baiting them any further – and on the last day, a parade of picturesque witnesses entered the court for the 'grand finale'.

Wilma Montesi's fiancé turned out to be a rather simple-minded policeman who referred to the girl throughout as 'this Wilma Montesi'. He did not appear the most inspiring lover and the Public

Prosecutor couldn't resist commenting that Wilma used to put on two coats of lipstick to prevent him kissing her. A furious row broke out between two witnesses – punctuated by shouts of 'Scum!' and 'Liar!' – and an elderly Fascist who volunteered to give evidence ended up hitting everyone in sight and having to be restrained by two policemen.

It was a fitting conclusion to a trial that had started as a national sensation and ended in family recrimination.

DEFTLY DEFUSED

On May 20, the Public Prosecutor made his final speech. He maintained that Wilma Montesi had indeed gone to the beach, not at Capocotta but Ostia, and with a man, though there was no evidence to show it had been Piccioni. He added darkly, 'There is the possibility of finding out in the future who this man was.' After defence counsel had made their pleas, the Judge and his two colleagues retired for seven hours to consider their verdict. The result was hardly a revelation. Piero Piccioni was acquitted for 'not having committed the crime', and Ugo Montagna and Saverio Polito were also acquitted, 'as there had been no crime'.

The 'Montesi Affair' was right back where it started from, but at least it had shed the hysterical atmosphere of witch-hunting fermented by the press and the politicians. Outside Italy, observers wondered how all the half-baked witnesses and ramshackle evidence ever got as far as the court-room.

But sophisticated Italian analysts of the political scene knew that the truth was subtle. To have refused to hold a trial on the grounds of insubstantial evidence would have left the Christian Democrats wide open to accusations of corruption and suppression. As it was, Italy was almost on the brink of civil war and the Communists were baying for blood.

By taking a chance and allowing the Montesi Affair to take its own course, the situation had been deftly defused and the rumours exposed for the nonsense they were. If there was any political conspiracy at all in the entire Montesi Affair, that was it.

Con-Men

They prey on 'mugs' and 'suckers', their
bait is greed. They have sold the Eiffel Tower
and Brooklyn Bridge and even conned
Henry Ford himself . . .

WOULD YOU believe that a car could be run on
water instead of gasoline? Before you answer No,
consider the incredible case of the inventor Louis
Enricht. In the year 1916, the world was gripped
by an oil crisis. One April morning, New York's
reporters were invited to call at a house in Farmingdale, Long Island, to witness a demonstration
which, they were assured, would be spectacular.
The few reporters who turned up found a big,
grey man with an impressive face and foreign
accent, who introduced himself as Louis Enricht,
and explained that he had invented a cheap sub-
stitute for gasoline. The reporters yawned, and
looked bored.

Enricht led them to a small European car,
pointed out that the gas tank was empty, and
asked the reporters to examine it closely to see
that there was no supplementary fuel tank. They
weren't experts, but it certainly didn't look as if
Enricht was deceiving them. Enricht then asked a
reporter to fill a bucket at the tap. When the man
returned with the water, the inventor produced a

bottle full of a green liquid. He told the man to empty it into the bucket – warning him that the stuff was deadly poison.

The reporter poured the bucket into the gas tank, and Enricht asked the driver to try the engine. After a few splutters, it started, and a smell of almonds pervaded the air. Enricht offered each of the reporters a ride around Farmingdale. If there *was* a concealed gas tank – which is the obvious hypothesis – then it must have been large, for the car trips went on for at least an hour.

The next day, the story made the front pages, and Enricht was besieged with letters, phone calls and reporters. He declined to see them. A Harvard professor declared sourly that no possible combination of chemicals could turn water into a combustible fuel, but Enricht declined to comment. His next visitor was Henry Ford himself. Ford examined the car carefully, and since he was one of the world's leading experts, he was pretty thorough. He watched Enricht mix his green liquid with water, and then went for a ride in the car.

Enricht admitted that the smell was cyanide, but said it had been put in to conceal another smell. His process was absurdly simple, he said, and until his lawyer had devised a way to patent it, he wasn't dropping any hints.

Ford was so impressed that, even when the *Tribune* printed a story revealing that Enricht had been a fake company promoter, Ford ignored it. The evidence of his own eyes assured him that the car had run on water, and he gave Enricht a cheque for $10,000 on account.

When this news was leaked to the papers – by Enricht – Hiram P. Maxim, son of the inventor of the Maxim gun, offered Enricht a million dollars, and offered to build him a laboratory for further research. In fact, Enricht received only $100,000; he was to receive the rest when he handed over the formula – which, Maxim agreed, should not be until he had patented his discovery.

Penny-a-gallon Fuel

Ford was infuriated, but since Enricht had returned his cheque, there was nothing much he could do. Then America came into the First World War, and Maxim was so busy making munitions that he agreed to call off the whole thing. He had more than recovered his investment in the upward-turn taken by his company's shares when his deal with Enricht was announced.

The man who decided to take over from Maxim was a rich banker named Yoakum. He also gave Enricht $100,000, accepting a sealed envelope which was supposed to contain the formula. Yoakum told President Wilson that he intended to present the secret penny-a-gallon fuel to the American people, and Wilson was delighted. But Enricht launched delaying tactics, and Yoakum hired the Pinkerton Detective Agency to investigate him.

He was flabbergasted to discover that Enricht had been seen consorting with Von Papen, the German military attaché, before the outbreak of war, and that the 'inventor' was suspected of being a German spy. Then Yoakum opened the envelope that was supposed to contain the formula – and found only a few liberty bonds. But there was no way to get Enricht into a court of law.

Yoakum had broken his own undertaking by opening the envelope. Talk about trying Enricht for treason dragged on until Yoakum died, and Enricht was once again in the clear.

At the age of 75 Enricht was still a man of restless imagination. In 1920, he announced that his continued experiments in the manufacture of gasoline had led him to conclude that the easiest and cheapest way was to distill it from peat. Such was the magic of his name that investors again rushed to thrust cheques into his hand, and he may have received as much as a quarter of a million dollars.

But the Nassau County District Attorney decided it was time someone brought Enricht's career to an end. The District Attorney examined Enricht's bank accounts until he found a cheque for $2,000, handed over by an investor and promptly endorsed to pay a bookmaker. That was fraud, since he was a limited company, and all money was supposed to benefit other investors. At the age of 77, Enricht received seven years in gaol for grand larceny. Paroled after a few years, he died at the age of 79 without revealing to anyone the secret of his formula for cheap gasoline.

The Formula

How did he do it? The answer may lie in a

formula discovered by Thomas Edison. He found that a mixture of acetone and liquid acetylene *will* drive a car if mixed with water. If cyanide is added, it hides the very distinctive nail-varnish smell of acetone. The mixture costs more to make than gasoline, and it also had the disadvantage of corroding the engine after a while. But this is probably the answer to the enigma.

Greatest Con-Man

Undoubtedly, the most remarkable con-man of them all was the Scotsman, John Law. Born in Edinburgh in 1671, Law had no need to work. His father, a successful goldsmith and moneylender, had left him two estates. But Law was immensely ambitious. Besides, he was driven by another itch that characterizes many of the great con-men: the passion for beautiful women. At 23 he went to London where his success in love became as legendary as his success at cards. He packed more experience into the next five years than most men in a lifetime. Then his luck turned: he killed a man in a duel, was tried and fled to the Continent.

There he continued to gamble and seduce, but he also became a fascinated student of high finance. It seemed to him that the secret of wealth was a perfectly simple one. All businesses run on credit, and the more money they make, the more they borrow in order to expand. But in those days, money was made of gold or silver, and there was a limited amount of it to go round. The answer, said Law, was to print paper money instead – which could be instantly redeemed for gold merely by walking into a bank.

But so long as the customers trusted their paper money, why should they demand gold instead? And in that case, the government could issue any amount of paper money, and use it to increase trade. So long as there was no sudden panic, it was a foolproof way of increasing credit and prosperity.

Law returned to Scotland – which at the time had its own government, so that he was safe from arrest – and tried hard to persuade his fellow countrymen of the value of a national bank that would issue paper money. He was ignored, and when Scotland discussed union with England, he decided it was time to return to the Continent. In 1708 he went to Paris, and found it the most exciting capital in Europe. Everyone gambled. Soon Law was known in the most exclusive drawing-rooms in Paris, and the size of his stakes made him famous.

He met the Duc d'Orleans, and convinced him of his financial genius. For a while it looked as if he would get his opportunity to print paper money. Then the police began investigating him. D'Argenson, lieutenant of the Paris police, had received hundreds of complaints from losers who doubted Law's honesty. Law was driven out of France.

In 1715, Louis XIV died. Law could hardly believe his luck when he heard that his old friend the Duc d'Orleans had been appointed Regent of the young king, and was virtually dictator of France. He hurried back to Paris, and this time the Duke allowed him to put his schemes into effect.

To begin with, he gave Law permission to open a private bank and to print his own money. Law had built up a fortune of eighty thousand pounds, so he had the gold to back his notes – to begin with. He started out cautiously, aiming to create confidence. He lost money, but people came to feel that his notes were as safe as gold.

By 1718, Law's bank was making so much money that the Duke transformed it into a Royal Bank. Law could print as much money as he liked.

Now obviously, this was a very dangerous game. It is true that money makes money, but if there is a slump or sudden panic, a bank must have enough money to change all its notes into gold – or collapse. In theory, Law had all the money he needed; it was now time to use it to make more money – real money. The answer lay across the Atlantic, in Louisiana, which belonged to the French.

Louisiana consisted of thousands of square miles of swamps and uncultivated land. Law set himself to persuade the French people that it was full of gold, silk and valuable minerals, and that all they had to do to double their money was to invest it in Louisiana bonds. The money flowed in, Law cornered the Canadian fur market, and made huge profits.

But he was now aware of the dangers of this incredible game of confidence. As the money poured in, share prices rose; speculators could make fortunes overnight. Everything went faster and faster – and Law had to keep running faster than anybody, always making sure he had the gold to meet all demands. If Louisiana was to make money, he had to persuade emigrants to go there. Law hired men to go throughout France, telling stories of the wealth of Louisiana.

From the government he purchased the right to collect taxes, and made a vast fortune that way. He bought trading companies in the Far East. He cornered Virginia tobacco. The money kept flooding in. His office in the narrow Rue Quincampoix was besieged by crowds day and night. Any shares he deigned to sell could be resold within minutes for twice their price. Moneylenders nearby lent their money at one per cent *per hour*, and their customers still made a fortune.

Soon there wasn't enough gold to go round. The Duc d'Orleans had to be persuaded to pass laws forbidding goldsmiths to make gold articles weighing more than a few ounces. Confidence slumped, and the rush came. At first the bank would only cash one hundred livre note per person; soon this was reduced to ten livres. In December 1720, two years after he had become head of the Compagnie d l'Occidente, Law decided it would be safer to flee the country.

For the next few years he lived quietly in London. His old skill as a gambler had not deserted him; when he had only a thousand pounds left, he staked it all on a bet that he could throw six double sixes one after the other: he won.

But his luck turned, perhaps due to the curses of thousands of Frenchmen whom he had ruined. He remained on friendly terms with the Duc d'Orleans to the end. The Duke had remedied the bankruptcy by the simple expedient of burning every paper connected with the Royal Bank. But when Law finally died in Venice, in 1729, he was once again a pauper.

In the year of the collapse of Law's Compagnie de l'Occidente, England was having its own grave financial crisis, the bursting of the South Sea Bubble. The full details of the dealings of the South Sea Company are even more complex than those of Law's Royal Bank; but the parallels are otherwise very close. Law needed the permission of the Regent to start his company; the directors of the South Sea Company got their permission for their vast dealings by offering to take on the English National Debt – the money the government owes investors in government stocks.

Their equivalent of Louisiana was Peru and the South Seas. Between 1711 and 1720, millions of pounds changed hands, and fortunes were made. All kinds of other schemes swept to success on the tail of the South Seas comet: a scheme for making a 'wheel of perpetual motion', a scheme for making a soft metal out of mercury. One speculator even launched a scheme 'for great advantage, but nobody to know what it is', and made two thousand pounds in one morning.

The South Sea directors had to take legal action against these other companies, and in doing so, they started the panic slide that led to the crash.

In this case, some investors got back at least some of their money, for the government seized part of the assets of the directors of the Company.

The Eiffel Tower

The classic 'con' case of modern times is undoubtedly that of Count Victor Lustig's sale of the Eiffel Tower – not once, but twice. Like John Law, Lustig came from a respectable middle-class family, and he too loved gambling and women. Some time before the First World War, he left his home in Czechoslovakia and moved to Paris. Lustig was only one of two dozen aliases that he used at different times. He learned the techniques of confidence trickery from the gambler Nicky Arnstein.

Lustig was in Paris when he saw a newspaper item reporting that repairs to the Eiffel Tower would cost thousands of francs. Some days later, several rich financiers received letters from a government department inviting them to a secret conference at the Hotel Crillon. The 'director deputy-general' who received them was actually Victor Lustig. He began by assuring them that this business was classified as top-secret – hence the hotel suite instead of his office.

The government has decided, he told them, that the Eiffel Tower is too expensive to maintain; it is to be sold for scrap metal . . . They gaped. 'Would you gentlemen care to submit your bids to me?' He had already noted the man who was the obvious 'mark', Andre Poisson, a man who clearly felt socially inferior to the others. A few days later, Lustig rang him and told him that his bid was the highest – several million francs – and that if he would bring a certified cheque to the hotel, the deal could be concluded. Poisson was not entirely happy, until Lustig apologetically asked for a bribe, to ensure that negotiations would go smoothly.

That convinced Poisson that this was a genuine government official; he handed over the cash. When it became clear, later, he had been swindled, he was too ashamed to go the police and make himself the laughing stock of France. The result was that Lustig was able to repeat the same trick a few years later.

The second part of Lustig's life was an anti-climax – an observation that applies to most confidence tricksters. In America in the early 1930s, he turned to the distribution of counterfeit money. The FBI finally caught up with him, and he was sentenced to twenty years in gaol, dying in Alcatraz in 1947. The Federal agent mainly responsible for his capture, James P. Johnson, wrote the classic book on his career under the title *The Man Who Sold the Eiffel Tower.*

It is a saddening book, for it underlines the strange romanticism that leads brilliant and imaginative men to become confidence swindlers.

CON-MEN: CASE STUDY

Willie the Actor

If ever there was a frustrated Thespian, it was Willie. Right from the start of his career as America's most successful bank robber, he had been fascinated by make-believe and impersonation.

THE WAVERLEY School of Drama could be proud of its star pupil, Willie Sutton. He had studied hard for the part, paying particular attention to the make-up. He had flattened his nose, puffed out his cheeks with cottonwool, heightened his complexion. His costume of a bank messenger had been selected with great care. He was word-perfect.

Willie Sutton was about to make his acting debut in a dramatic role which would bring in probably the highest-ever fee for a single perform-ance. His opening line: 'I've got a telegram for the boss,' was perfectly timed. It was 8 a.m. and the sleepy doorkeeper of the bank at Jamaica, Long Island, took the familiar-looking Western Union yellow envelope and started to sign. With both the doorman's hands occupied, Willie deftly lifted the revolver from the man's holster and told him, 'Now be a good boy and you won't get hurt.'

The man was flabbergasted. Raising his hands, he backed into the bank while Willie's accomplice,

Jack Bassett, slipped in and shut the door. One by one, the bank staff arrived for work. With Willie's gun prodding him from behind, the doorkeeper followed his usual routine and let them in. Jack Bassett lined up half a dozen chairs against the wall and each employee was forced to sit down with his hands in the air. With the arrival of the manager at 8.30 a.m. Willie's first-night audience was complete.

'All I want you to do,' he told the manager, 'is to open your vault. It would be very silly of you to refuse. If you do, nothing will happen to you but I promise you that the lives of your employees here will be jeopardized.'

POLISHED PERFORMANCE

The line of clerks looked at their manager imploringly. It was a cunning move. With a gesture of resignation, the manager unlocked the vault. Inside was $48,000 in new banknotes, which Willie dropped into his 'messenger's' briefcase.

It was 9.40 a.m. – only twenty minutes before the bank was due to open for business – and Willie Sutton's meticulous dress rehearsals had already shown that there would probably be a few early customers waiting outside.

But the actor had his audience exactly where he wanted them. 'We're leaving now,' he told the seated employees. 'But I have a third man outside. If anyone goes through this door in the next five minutes, he will be shot.'

There was no third man, but Willie Sutton

knew his threat would keep them glued to their chairs for at least a minute, and that was all the time he needed to make his escape.

He and Jack Bassett slipped out of the door and melted into the crowds hurrying to work along Jamaica Avenue. It was a polished performance and one which was to be repeated many times to stunned audiences all over the east coast of America. Willie the Actor, the prize – indeed, the only graduate – of the Waverley School of Drama, had arrived.

The Waverley School was one of Willie's most inspired inventions. A few weeks before the bank robbery, he had had imposing notepaper printed with the name and address of the non-existent college. With a contrived story about a college drama production, he had been able to get his bank messenger's uniform from a theatrical costumier. Obtaining the second important 'prop' – the Western Union cablegram – had been easy. He merely wired one to himself, steamed it open and inserted the bank manager's name behind the cellophane window.

It was detailed planning like this, coupled with a genius for make-up and disguises, that earned him the title of Willie the Actor. 'I thought of it all as a drama with myself as the director and lead actor.' he once said.

CHARACTER SKETCHES

Willie was totally fascinated by make-believe and impersonation. He learned to put corks in his nostrils to flatten his nose and pads in his cheeks to broaden his face. He dyed his hair or powdered it to make himself look older. He altered his appearance with wigs and moustaches and increased his height with built-up shoes. In an extraordinary series of 'character sketches' – policeman, postman, messenger, railwayman, window cleaner – he cleaned up more than $2,000,000 and became the most wanted man in America. Beneath all his disguises, his real face was such a mystery that he once stood underneath his own 'Wanted' poster without being recognized.

CONSTANT TEMPTATION

Yet the strange truth about Willie Sutton was that the man of a thousand faces really *was* faceless. Somehow, his own character became swallowed up in his disguises. A mild-mannered and often lonely man, he enjoyed nothing more than reading and gardening.

Girlfriends knew him as gentle and rather diffident. On the run in the 1940s, he worked for two years at an old folks' home, where his sympathetic manner endeared him to the nurses and inmates.

The flaw to his character was that he just couldn't resist robbing banks. Other people's money stuck to his fingers. Some men cannot resist drink, drugs, women or even gambling. Willie Sutton's constant temptation was the door to a bank or a jewellery store. Every one was a challenge that made his eyes light up. Even passing a bank on a stroll, he automatically sized up its potential and calculated its risk.

It wasn't always the money that fired his compulsion. He once robbed a bank with $40,000 already in his pocket. Although hardly a consolation to his victims, he just couldn't help it.

In the end, he paid a crucifying price for indulging his obsession. So did his friends – for there was a jinx on Willie.

PERFECT CRIME

Although non-violent himself – he never fired a shot in his whole career – nearly every person whose path he crossed met a violent end. Some were shot evading arrest, while others were gunned down by gangsters. Suicide, madness, blindness, the living death of life imprisonment, the voodoo of Willie Sutton touched almost all who knew him. There was also a succession of pathetic, trusting women who discovered, too late, that life with a fugitive is measured in days, not years.

The inevitability of Willie Sutton's rise to big-time crime – from the day in 1908 when, aged only eight, he stole 50 cents from his mother's purse – has a theatrical touch to it, like one of those old Warner Brothers gangster movies, with James Cagney in the leading role.

Born in the rough Irishtown quarter of Brooklyn . . . as a child, progressed from shoplifting to breaking into stores after dark . . . during the First

World War gave up a secure job to earn big money in a munitions factory . . . with the fat pay-packet, a taste for natty suits, silk shirts, fast cars and faster women . . . then the Depression and unemployment . . . the 'easy money' lure of organized crime . . . and the apprenticeship, working as a collector for racketeers like Arnie Rothstein, 'Dutch' Schultz and 'Legs' Diamond.

Willie's solution to any problem was to put his fingers in the till. At seventeen, he fell in love with Bessie Hurley, daughter of a Brooklyn shipyard owner. They eloped to Poughkeepsie, a romantic adventure financed by $16,000 he had stolen from her father's wages-office. They were hauled back, but Mr Hurley's influence saved him from a jail sentence. He was never to see Bessie again.

So far, Willie had only hovered on the fringes of the underworld. It was a 'doctor' who finally provided the prescription for the perfect crime, and who unerringly set him on the path to being Willie the Actor.

Eddie 'Doc' Tate had studied science at Chicago University and now employed his formidable knowledge in a way which would have amazed his professors. He was America's top safebreaker, a perfectionist who disdained vulgarities like oxy-acetylene and dynamite, relying entirely on his sensitive fingers, which he protected by white gloves during off-duty hours. The most fiendish locks melted like butter in his hands.

'Doc' Tate's motto was 'Plan every detail in advance' and among his golden rules for safer safe-breaking was 'Always use ordinary tools and leave them all behind when you finish a job, except for your jemmy. Keep that with you until you are clear. Never overlook the possibility of locked doors barring your escape. If you have your jemmy with you, no door is locked against you.'

Tagging on to the cutaway coat-tails of the elegant Doctor, Willie embarked on a series of spectacular break-ins. On their first combined effort, they looted four shops in two hours, netting more than $10,000. As a sign that the evening's work was over, the Doctor sportingly left his jemmy on the window-sill of a nearby police station.

TIP-OFF

Willie was a star pupil, his skill soon rivalling that of 'Doc' Tate. Gradually, the character of Willie the Actor was taking shape. His girl-friend was Adeline 'Atchie' Rao, a Broadway showgirl. Sitting in her dressing room before a performance, he discovered how make-up could completely alter a person's appearance. Fascinated, he watched actors mould their faces like putty, saw them grow younger or age before his eyes.

But it was a chance walk down Broadway that provided the final inspiration. He noticed two uniformed security guards ringing a bell outside a locked store. They were immediately admitted, with barely a glance at their faces. It wasn't only a jemmy that opened all doors, he realized, but a uniform. Quickly checking through a classified telephone directory, he found dozens of theatrical costumiers who specialized in providing convincing uniforms of all kinds. It was better than being handed a key.

The opportunity to put his theory into practice came quicker than Willie expected. 'Doc' Tate decided to take off for a long holiday in California. 'You don't need me any more,' he told Willie. 'You've learned about all I can teach you.' It was time for Willie the Actor to take the stage.

Willie Sutton was now twenty-four, but it was to be another six years before he could make his debut. From 1925 to 1929 he was a 'guest artiste' at Sing Sing and Dannemora jails. Following a tip-off by an informer, he had been arrested and sentenced for burglary. It was in Sing Sing that Willie met Jack Bassett and together they achieved Willie the Actor's first great coup, the robbery of the bank at Jamaica, Long Island, in 1930.

After the robbery, Willie returned home to his wife, Louise. The sudden appearance of $24,000 needed some explaining, but Willie's 'training' with the Waverley School of Drama saved the situation. 'You'll never guess what has happened,' he told her. 'My rich Uncle William has died in Ireland and left me all this money. I've just collected it from his lawyers.'

Using one disguise after another – but never the same one twice running – Willie went on a rampage of robbery. 'Uncle William's legacy' was boosted by the proceeds of fourteen break-ins within a few months. At the Rosenthal jewellery store on Broadway – where Willie used the Western Union messenger trick again – the manager was so terrified that he forgot the combination of his own safe. At the point of a gun, they forced the negro porter to phone the proprietor at his home and ask for the combination – using the flimsy explanation that the manager hadn't turned up. The result was $130,000 of gems . . . and another prison sentence.

The trap they hadn't foreseen was Jack Bassett's love life. Jack's wife, Kitty Bassett, found out about his string of mistresses and in revenge betrayed him to the police. Under third-degree interrogation, Bassett confessed to the Rosenthal break-in and thirteen other jobs, implicating Willie Sutton. As 'Doc' Tate had said years earlier in one of his homilies, 'Women, whisky and work don't mix.'

STEEL DOORS

Willie was a tougher nut to crack, however. For five days, police beat him with rubber hoses until his entire body, except for his face, was deep purple. Fearing that they might extract a confession under delirium, Willie tore open the roof of his mouth with his fingernail and started spitting blood. He convinced the prison doctor that he had sustained internal injuries and the beating stopped. But his kidneys had been so badly damaged that he passed blood and urine for five months.

Willie's skill at make-up and disguise paid dividends at an identification parade, where victims of nearly all his robberies were asked to pick him out. Nobody recognized him. One victim shook his head and said, 'No, the guy who robbed me had a flat nose.' Another laughed and said, 'This skinny fellow? The man who took my stuff had fat cheeks. I remember it clearly.' A third victim was even more impatient. 'Don't waste my time,' he said. 'The man who grabbed my jewellery must have been sixty. This fellow is just a kid.' For a moment, Willie the Actor thought he had fooled them all. Then the negro porter at Rosenthal's jewellery store stopped in front of him. 'That's the man,' he said.

Willie went to Sing Sing for a year. Actually, the judge sentenced him to thirty years, but in December 1932, Willie picked four steel 'escape-proof' doors in quick succession, climbed over the wall on a ladder hidden by another prisoner and drove off in a car left by an outside accomplice. He was in business again.

A one-man crime wave hit New York. Robbery after robbery bore Willie the Actor's fingerprints. Disguised as a policeman, he took $18,000 from one bank. At a Fifth Avenue jewellery store, a fireman turned up and asked to inspect the premises to check if there were any violations of the city fire-prevention laws. When the proprietor, Mr Isadore Wiatre, recovered consciousness, diamonds worth $45,000 were missing. Posing as an impatient postman whose package was too big to go through a bank's letterbox, he persuaded the caretaker to open the door. Within five minutes, the bank was lighter by $160,000.

But, despite these huge hauls, Willie's life had

become furtive and deprived. By a quirk of irony, the one thing Willie the Actor could never achieve was recognition. A fugitive afraid of voices, shadows, and footsteps, his money melted as he flitted from bolthole to bolthole.

The more notorious he became, the more he was rejected as an outcast. He could never return home, although his wife had had a baby daughter. In his search for superficial and safe companionship, he mingled with the crowds at the Roseland dance-hall, where for a dime you could dance with one of the hostesses. After buying a few dollars' worth of companionship, he would return to his lonely apartment and go to bed with a book.

His jinx had already started to cast its shadow. 'Dutch' Shultz had died, victim of a gangland killing. Johnny Eagan, one of his partners, had been slain by hoodlums. Another partner, Eddie Wilson, was blinded by a police bullet. Jack Bassett was to spend thirty-two of his fifty-two years behind bars and 'Doc' Tate choked out his last breath in a prison infirmary. In every way, Willie the Actor was a dangerous man to have around. But not for long. For the law was catching up with him again.

SOLITARY CONFINEMENT

The police had picked up Joe Pelango, one of Willie's accomplices in the $160,000 Philadelphia bank robbery. They worked him over and he talked. At breakfast a few days later, Willie Sutton was reading newspaper accounts of Adolf Hitler's accession to power in Germany when there was a knock at his door. He found himself staring into the muzzle of a police tommy-gun. On February 4, 1934, he walked through the gates of the Eastern State Penitentiary – one of the toughest jails in America – to begin a 25–50 year sentence.

If there was one thing Willie prided himself on more than getting into a place, it was his skill in getting out. The prison officers knew that, and for eighteen months he was kept in solitary confinement before being transferred to the top-security '7th Gallery'. Alert guards, stone walls and thick steel doors weren't the only obstacles to escape. The prison was riddled with informers out to curry favour with the parole board. There wasn't a chance . . . but Willie the Actor still started working on his first plan to 'Exit, left'.

It almost ended in disaster. Using a man slipped to him by another prisoner, Willie managed to get into the underground sewage system. After crawling 200 feet, he reached a second conduit full of water and refuse, with a steel door at the end. He plunged into the sewage and swam underwater for fifteen feet, his hands groping for the handle of the door. But it was automatically operated – and immovable. Willie's lungs were bursting and there was not room to turn round. As he pushed himself backwards from the door, he could feel himself beginning to black out. Then his head broke the surface. Staggering back along the 200-foot main conduit, he picked up his clothes, climbed into the prison cellar and got back into his cell. Thirty second later, the guards started making the roll-call.

FACE MASK

Two years dragged by before Willie tried again. With materials smuggled into his cell by fellow-prisoners, he made a plaster of Paris mask of his face and hand. Again, his make-up skill proved useful. He pulled hairs from his head to make eyebrows and a moustache. He fashioned a wig from cord salvaged from his cell-mops. He tinted the mask's cheeks and pencilled in details of eyes, nose and mouth. When friends smuggled in some rope, a grappling hook and a hacksaw blade, he was ready.

On a wet and chilly night, he hunched up his bedclothes, placed the mask on his pillow and let the hand peep from under the blanket. He had already sawed through most of the bars and it only took a few minutes to finish the job. Squeezing on to the window-ledge, he waited for the hoot of a nearby factory whistle which coincided with the change of guard. In the few minutes while the guards were handing over their duties, all he had to do was throw out the grappling hook and haul himself over the prison wall.

ISOLATION BLOCK

However, instead of the expected whistle, the prison alarm suddenly sounded and the whole place was alive with guards, shouts and searchlights. Willie had picked the very moment when another group of prisoners had tried to stage a breakout.

Feeling uncomfortably like a figure in a French farce, Willie scrambled back off the freezing window-sill, replaced the bars, hid his tackle, mask and plaster hand and tumbled into bed. 'What's going on?' he asked innocently as a warder flashed his torch into the cell. 'Two damn fools tried to go over the wall,' the man replied.

The most immediate result of the escape attempt was an all-round tightening of security. The following morning, a routine search in Willie's cell uncovered his getaway kit and he was committed to the isolation block for two years.

Willie used the time to learn shorthand, typing and Spanish, eventually being allowed to act as secretary to the prison psychiatrist. The work interested him, and he was deeply affected by the letters to the doctor from former prisoners who had been successfully rehabilitated.

'What about me?' he once asked the doctor. 'I've been here ten years now. Don't you think I have learned my lesson?' The doctor's reply was evasive.

'I don't know, Willie. Every time you see a bank, it appears to present a challenge you can't resist.

Willie pressed on. 'You don't think I can ever be a useful member of society?' Again the doctor wouldn't give a straight answer.

'Only you can answer that, Willie.'

FREEDOM TURNED

Willie knew his life was slipping away. Outside

117

the penitentiary, the world had changed. Prohibition had been repealed. President Franklin D. Roosevelt had been elected President, served and died. Hitler had come and gone. The Second World War had been fought and won. In the year Willie was arrested, the latest weapon had been the tommy-gun. Now it was the atom bomb.

Towards the end of 1945, Willie and twelve other prisoners – each one with little hope of parole – started digging a tunnel to freedom.

The plan called for backbreaking work. A 30-foot shaft had to be sunk from a cell occupied by a forger named Clarence Kliney, followed by a 97-foot tunnel and an upwards shaft leading to the street on the other side of the prison wall. Yet six months later, it was finished.

The break-out was timed for just after breakfast. One by one, the men lowered themselves into the tunnel and crawled the 120 feet to the end. Only 24 inches of earth separated them from street level. The remaining rubble and tarmac were hacked away and then men burst out, scattering in all directions.

Willie leaped from the hole . . . and ran straight into the arms of two policemen.

'Put your hands up or I'll shoot!' one of them shouted.

'Go ahead then, shoot!' cried Willie in despair. All the men were rounded up and Willie found himself once more in the isolation block, with 10 to 20 years added to his original sentence.

Incredibly, Willie Sutton still clung to his dream of escape, strengthened by the knowledge that he now had nothing to lose. The first glimmer of hope came in August, 1946, when he and four others were transferred to Homesburg County Prison, near Philadelphia. After eighteen months, an outside accomplice managed to smuggle in a ·38 revolver in a vegetable-delivery lorry. Friends in the prison machine-shop obtained hacksaws and blades, and Willie and the others started sawing slowly through the bars of their cell doors. On February 9, 1947, Willie Sutton was ready for his fourth and most desperate escape bid.

At ten minutes before midnight on a wild, snowy night, Willie cut through the last threads of his bars and joined the others in the centre of the cell-block. They crouched outside the steel door to the guardroom, set in the hub of the star-shaped prison complex. Every night, the door opened for a few seconds to allow one of the armed guards to slip out and patrol the corridors.

Their only chance was to force their way in the instant the door opened. They heard the key turn in the lock, followed by a knife-edge of light as the door began to open. Together, they hurled themselves into the guardroom so quickly that the guards didn't have time to reach for their guns. Covering the officers with the ·38, they carried on to the engine-room, where ladders were stored.

Using the guards as a shield, and partly obscured by the swirling snow, they carried the ladders across the prison yard. As the officers were placing the ladders against the wall, a trigger-happy sentry in a watchtower let off a burst of machine-gun fire. With presence of mind, one of the convicts shouted, 'Stop it! Can't you see we're guards?'

The sentry walked forward to get a closer look, shielding his eyes against the snow, but the convicts shinned up the ladder and dropped over the wall. They raced to a spot three blocks away where a getaway car should have been waiting. It wasn't there. Luckily, a milk-delivery lorry lurched round the corner and they commandeered it. As the lorry rattled towards Philadelphia, the convicts toasted their escape in milk. At his fourth attempt in thirteen years, Willie the Actor was free.

The others were quickly recaptured, but Willie had long practice at keeping one step ahead of the law. He scanned the 'Situations Vacant' columns of the newspapers, searching for the kind of low-paid, anonymous job where you almost merged into the wallpaper, and where board and accommodation were included. One vacancy was made to measure – a hospital porter at Farm Colony, an old folks' home on Staten Island. The New York City authorities had provided the perfect hideout, and under the name of 'Edward Lynch', Willie signed on for his £20 a week job and simply evaporated.

Willie enjoyed working at the home and a strange and touching relationship grew up between the fugitive who sought anonymity and the old people who craved company. Lonely, frequently disabled and virtually waiting for death, their plight was worse than his. He listened to their stories, comforted and fussed over them. Willie was so highly regarded by the staff that he was 'promoted' to the main women's ward. 'I was completely happy there,' Willie recalled later, 'and I felt humble before the low-paid dedication of those nurses.'

ASHEN TINT

For once, it looked as though Willie the Actor had turned his back on crime and was playing a useful role in life, the part of 'Eddie Lynch'. Maybe the prison psychiatrist had been wrong all those years earlier, and he *was* capable of rehabilitation. Encouraged by favourable reports from the patients, one of the nurses. Mary Corbett, took him in as a lodger. For the first time since 1931, he had a home. He started going to church.

But there was one profound difference between Willie and the old folk he tended. Their past life was gone, finished, almost beyond recall, while Willie's was waiting to catch up with him.

The sense of security he created so carefully was shattered one day in August, 1949, when a voice behind him in the ward suddenly boomed, 'Hello, Willie Sutton!' No feat of make-up could have captured the ashen tint that spread across his face as he turned around. But he still retained his composure. 'Willie Sutton? Who's that?' he asked.

Gertrude Horgan, one of the nurses, handed him a copy of that day's *Daily News*. Every time a bank was raided, the newspaper cried: 'Willie Sutton strikes again!' This time, they had used a picture. 'You must admit, it looks just like you,' laughed the nurse. 'You're right,' said Willie. 'Only if I were Willie Sutton, I wouldn't be working here for $80 a month.' They all laughed the incident off. But it had shaken Willie to the soles of his shoes.

He decided to leave Farm Colony. Mary Corbett was enthusiastic. 'I always knew you could do better for yourself if you tried,' she said. Willie brushed up his typing and shorthand and went the rounds of the employment agencies. The answer was the same in each one: 'Sorry, but you're too old.' At fifty, the normal life which had never begun was already over.

Years earlier, Willie had hidden $18,000 in a buried jar in a field near Laurenton, Long Island. He dug it up, intending to use the money to start his own little business. But his past life was now on his heels. One afternoon, he just happened to walk past Manufacturers' Trust Company Bank, in the New York City suburb of Sunnyside. Like a long-disused combination lock suddenly manipulated by sensitive fingers, his mind started automatically clicking into place. Almost unconsciously, it registered the entrance, the condition of the roof, the number of people going in and out. Willie walked inside and noted the position of the cages, the alarm system, the number of employees. The old compulsion had not died. He visited the bank several times, mentally photographing vital details. It was vulnerable and he knew it.

FATAL COMPROMISE

Willie was torn in a cruel mental struggle. Everything in him rebelled against returning to crime, yet he knew he could crack that bank. In the end, he made a fatal compromise. He passed on his information to a gang of cracksmen. A few weeks later, the bank was robbed of $64,000 in a 'carbon copy' of one of Willie's operations. Once again, the papers were filled with Willie the Actor's picture and he was back on the run, with nowhere left to run to.

On February 18, 1952 – two years after the Sunnyside robbery – 24-year-old Arnold Schuster, a salesman working in his father's clothing factory, was sitting in a New York subway train. The man opposite seemed familiar and Schuster looked at him for a long time.

Then it dawned on him. It was the same face that he had seen staring out a hundred times from the warning leaflets the police had distributed to every clothing store in the city. Leaflets which said: 'If this man tries to hire a uniform or costume from you, contact the police immediately.' It was Willie the Actor.

Willie had noticed the way young Schuster had been watching him and got out at Bergen Street station. Schuster followed him as far as a garage, then went to tell the police.

Willie Sutton was tinkering with his car battery – it refused to start – when the two policemen loomed over him. At first, they just asked to see his licence. But they returned with a detective.

'You'd better come along to the station with us,' one of them said. 'You look like Willie Sutton.' Desperately, Willie insisted it must be a case of mistaken identity. His shoulders drooped and he looked like a tired old man. 'I might as well be dead now,' he said. 'You can kill me for all I care.'

The first public reaction to Willie's arrest – except among those he had robbed – was a tinge of regret. The law had finally caught up with a colourful character who had become a legend in his lifetime. On Sunday, March 9, the public mood abruptly changed to revulsion. While walking home to his father's store, Arnold Schuster was ambushed by an underworld trigger-man and shot in each eye – the ritual form of killing for an informer. Willie's jinx had claimed another victim. Although he disclaimed all knowledge of the crime – and there was no proof that he was connected in any way with the killing – he instantly forfeited all public sympathy. It was a tragic way to bring home the lesson that, for all his non-violence, Willie still belonged to the brutal and degenerate world of the professional criminal.

Willie Sutton was charged with the robbery of the Manufacturers' Trust Bank at Sunnyside. Throughout the trial, he vehemently protested his innocence, sticking to his story that he had merely passed on the information.

Was Willie innocent? Or deep down, was he just ashamed to admit that he had failed himself. That after attempting to go straight, he had finally been unable to control the criminal urge, and that in the end he had confirmed the prison psychiatrist's conclusion that he would always be an habitual thief?

Several witnesses testified that he had led the

gang which raided the Sunnyside bank, but he claimed they had been 'conditioned' to recognize him after seeing so many pictures in the newspapers.

It could be the ultimate irony that, after 32 successful robberies, Willie the Actor was convicted for the one crime he didn't commit. The point is academic. At 52, Willie Sutton was sentenced to thirty years to life. Taking into account sentences still outstanding, it meant he would be behind bars until the year 2087. 'They said I was the best,' he told the court sadly. 'But what is the result? I'm 51, I've spent most of my adult life in prison or in hiding and now I haven't a penny.'

But there was still a flash of the old humour. When the suit he was wearing at his arrest was searched, $7,000 in cash was found in the pockets. Asked why he hadn't banked it, Willie replied laconically, 'It's never safe in a bank'.

CON-MEN: TRIAL

The Trials and Tribulations of Horatio Bottomley

Horatio Bottomley was one of the most colourful characters ever to appear in the dock of the Old Bailey. He was a Member of Parliament, financier, company promoter, journalist, public orator, newspaper and magazine proprietor, theatrical backer, racehorse owner, gambler and bankrupt.

HORATIO BOTTOMLEY was twice acquitted in spectacular trials in which he was charged with fraud and conspiracy, and in another trial the magistrate refused to convict him of promoting an illegal lottery, in spite of the evidence.

It was the fourth and final trial, which opened at the Central Criminal Court before Mr Justice Salter on May 18, 1922, that proved his undoing. This time he was accused on 24 counts of fraudulently converting to his own use more than £150,000, entrusted to him by members of the public for investment in his so-called Victory Bond club and three other enterprises.

Mr Travers Humphreys, perhaps the greatest criminal lawyer of his time in England, led the prosecution. Bottomley, as usual, conducted his own defence.

By this date, the 62-year-old defendant looked bloated and dissipated. 'In truth, it was not I who floored Bottomley,' said Humphreys after the trial. 'It was drink. The man I met in 1922 was a drink-sodden creature, whose brain could only work on repeated doses of champagne.'

Both Bottomley's parents died when he was a child and in consequence he was placed in an orphanage school. He ran away from the school to become successively an errand boy, a clerk in a solicitor's office and a shorthand reporter in the Law Courts, where he acquired considerable legal knowledge as well as forensic skill.

For many years he pretended to be the illegitimate son of the celebrated atheist Charles Bradlaugh, whom he strikingly resembled. Actually, his father was a tailor's foreman who ended his life in a lunatic asylum. But he did have a somewhat tenuous connection with Bradlaugh through his mother who was a sister of Bradlaugh's friend George Holyoake, the founder of the Co-operative Movement.

His first business venture, a small suburban weekly newspaper, ended in bankruptcy and prosecution for fraud. He was acquitted and the judge who tried the case was so impressed with his conduct of it that he advised him to become a barrister. As an undischarged bankrupt, however, he was unable to obtain admission to any of the Inns of Court, so he turned instead to the shadier occupation of promoting Australian gold mining companies.

RECKLESSLY EXTRAVAGANT

By the time he was 37, it was estimated that Bottomley had made £3 million in this way. However, his companies failed regularly, and in the first five years of the twentieth century he was served with no less than 67 bankruptcy petitions and writs. At the same time Bottomley was recklessly extravagant on his personal expenditure. He started a racing stable, and although he won the Cesarewitch and other prizes on the turf, he squandered large sums on various theatrical enterprises, besides a luxurious flat in London, a large country house in Sussex, where he kept his racing stables, and a villa in the South of France.

He posed as a philanthropist and this helped to secure his election to Parliament as Liberal MP for South Hackney in 1906. Three years later he was again charged with fraud and acquitted. But shortly afterwards he was made bankrupt for a second time and therefore had to resign his seat in Parliament.

The outbreak of war in 1914 provided Horatio Bottomley with a fresh opportunity for self-advancement and, incidentally, self-enrichment. He told his friends he would break with his 'sordid past', in which he had latterly been involved in the organization of gigantic lotteries and sweepstakes. He now became a recruiting officer for the armed forces and stomped the country making patriotic speeches – for no less than £50 a time – exhorting the young men to join the colours.

These speeches, along with a series of propaganda articles which he wrote for the *Sunday Pictorial*, for which he was likewise well remunerated, made him a nationally known figure. He was thus able to pay off his old creditors and to obtain his discharge from bankruptcy.

At the General Election in 1918 he got back his old parliamentary seat in South Hackney, this time as an Independent. Shortly afterwards the government floated a Victory Loan, in which the smallest bonds were of a nominal value of £5 and were issued at £4 5s. Bottomley conceived the brilliant idea of forming a club, so that the 'little man' and the 'little woman' could share in the loan by subscribing smaller sums; with these Bottomley would buy Victory Bonds or National War Bonds in the club's name.

Interest on the club's holding of stocks, and the bonuses, represented by the government's annual redemptions, were to be combined in a fund which would be distributed by lot among the subscribers; and the subscribers would also be entitled to withdraw their subscriptions at any time and get their money back in the same way as Government Premium Bond holders can do today. Bottomley invited the public to subscribe in units of 15s 6d, which represented the purchase price of a £1 share, the proceeds of which he would incorporate in the club's funds.

DEFAMATORY PAMPHLET

The public fell for the scheme in a big way. Between June 1919 and the end of the year,

Bottomley received subscriptions to the amount of nearly half a million pounds. Some of this he handed over to the Treasury Department, but much of it – so it was alleged – Bottomley applied to bolster up various companies in which he was interested, or else bare-facedly transferring to his own pocket.

In October 1921 the Chancery court appointed a receiver to examine Bottomley's enterprises. At the same time he quarrelled with an associate named Reuben Bigland, who proceeded to publish a defamatory pamphlet about him in which he described the Victory Bond Club as Bottomley's 'latest and greatest swindle' and told how he 'gulled poor subscribers to invest one pound notes' in the Club. Bottomley replied by prosecuting Bigland for criminal libel.

Bigland put in an elaborate written plea of justification, but in the event he was not called upon to prove his accusations, since Bottomley abandoned the prosecution and Bigland was formally acquitted. This made Bottomley's own prosecution inevitable.

Since Bottomley was still an MP, the normal practice would have been for the Crown to be represented by one of the Law Officers. But such was the legend of Bottomley's invincibility in the courts that Mr Lloyd George's government, which was highly nervous about the proceedings, declined to instruct either the Attorney-General or the Solicitor-General. They offered Humphreys any KC he might choose to lead him, however, but Humphreys declined. Though he had no specialized knowledge of accountancy, he put aside all other work to prepare the prosecution case, had an extra table brought into his chambers in the Temple, and worked for weeks with the government accountants, so that he eventually became as familiar with the questioned figures as Bottomley himself.

TWO FAVOURS

The preliminary proceedings took place in March 1922 at Bow Street Magistrates' Court. On his way to the court, Bottomley waylaid the prosecutor's clerk and asked for a few minutes' interview with his master. Humphreys consented provided his junior counsel was present.

Bottomley asked for two favours at the interview. First, he wanted a short adjournment each day at 11.30 a.m., so that he could have a pint of champagne, which he said he simply could not do without if he was to get through the morning. He added that he would call it his 'medicine' to the magistrate. Humphreys agreed provided that the magistrate had no objection, and this was conceded.

Secondly, Bottomley wanted Humphreys to suppress the name of a certain lady into whose account, which he had opened for her in the same bank, he had paid various Victory Club subscriptions. Humphreys agreed provided Bottomley would state that the account was his own private one. If there was any attempt at prevarication, said the prosecutor, the lady would be put into the witness box. In the event the hearings before the magistrate went according to plan, and Bottomley was duly committed for trial.

In his opening speech to the jury at the Old Bailey, Humphreys showed how very large sums from the Victory Bond Club had passed to its founder. For example, there was a payment of £5,000 for the upkeep of racing stables in Belgium, and another to a wine merchant for over a hundred dozen bottles of champagne, while a company which was merely an alias for Bottomley benefited by £20,000.

Many thousands more went to one of his numerous lady friends who acted as another go-between. Altogether over £150,000 in cheques drawn on the Club's account had been diverted in this way. Books dealing with the Club accounts were absent, there were never any Club trustees except Bottomley, and there was never any regular audit.

Since the Club's affairs had been taken over by the Receiver, 85,000 persons had written in claiming back their money, but of course it was impossible to call these people as witnesses. But the fraction Humphreys did put into the witness box could be taken as a fair cross-section of the whole.

A colonel who said he was a regular reader of Bottomley's weekly *John Bull*, in which the attractions of the Victory Bond Club were extensively puffed, stated he had lost £10,000 which he had invested in it. At the other end of the scale were domestic servants, the unemployed, needy widows and the like who had been persuaded to part with a few pounds, amounting sometimes to all their savings. Many were deluded by the following advertisement:

A New Road to Fortune
£1 gives you an opportunity of
winning £20,000

One woman, named Mrs Alice Twichett, said she sent £10 to Bottomley after reading the advertisement. In April 1921, she wanted her money back. She wrote four letters and eventually forwarded the certificates. But she never got a penny back. Another woman witness who had invested £5 eventually received a letter giving the result of the draw, after she had asked to have her £5 returned.

'You did not get a prize?' asked Humphreys.

'No,' replied the witness.

Only one witness, a retired naval officer, who was also a regular reader of *John Bull*, admitted when cross-examined by Bottomley, that he had no grievance against him, and that he did not charge him with the fraudulent conversion of the £4 he had invested in the bonds. But this witness also admitted that he had been asked to subscribe for a French Premium Bond, although he had not parted with any more money. This was a new scheme of Bottomley's by which Victory Bonds could be exchanged for French Government Bonds, Bottomley making a profit on each exchange.

PERTINENT QUESTION

A stockbroker gave evidence to the effect that Bottomley had owed him £10,000 since 1912 and that eventually the debt had been settled through an arrangement by which Bottomley gave the broker scrip of National War Bonds for that amount.

'In exchange for the £10,000,' Bottomley asked the witness in cross-examination, 'did I claim against you a considerable number of shares?'

'Yes, under the settlement,' the broker agreed.

'On very favourable terms, as it happened?' Bottomley continued.

'I should think so, undoubtedly.'

Humphreys asked the witness one extremely pertinent question on re-examination: 'Just tell me the name of the company in which those shares were?'

'John Bull Limited.' This was, of course, Bottomley's magazine company. By that time *John Bull*, though still edited by Bottomley, had been taken over by Odhams Press.

SUBSCRIPTIONS OR NOT?

An official of the Midland Bank, who had been employed by Bigland to make investigations gave particulars of the Victory Bond account and the account of another Bottomley concern, the Northern Territory Syndicate. A cheque for £25,000 drawn on the Victory Bond account was paid into the Northern Territory account, and shortly afterwards the sum of £5,000 was withdrawn from the latter to purchase Belgian francs in order to defray the expenses of Bottomley's racing stable at Ostend.

'Are you satisfied,' Bottomley asked this witness, 'that considerable sums of money, other than subscriptions were paid into the Bond Club's account?'

'The bank would not know whether the credits were or were not subscriptions to the club,' replied the bank official. 'Considerable sums were paid into the Victory Bond Club account which were cheques drawn in your name.' He added that the bank would know nothing of the ins and outs of the account. The cheques were simply paid in.

Bottomley went on to ask the witness whether he could say from his investigation of the Victory Bond Club account how many debits represented repayments to subscribers for their money. The reply was that he had not totalled them up, but there were a large number of small items.

'I suggest that they came to nearly £50,000?'

The witness said he could not accept or deny that, but on being pressed by Bottomley he admitted he should have thought they were quite £50,000.

EMOTIONAL APPEAL

'Do you say,' Bottomley went on, 'it is or is not wrong to draw on a trust account, assuming that the monies you draw out were due to you?'

'I think that is a lawyer's question and not a

banker's question,' was the cautious reply. 'A great deal would depend as to whether the bank was suspicious.'

'Take the £25,000 transferred from the Victory Bond Club to the Northern Territory account. Would that appear a suspicious transaction?'

'It would all depend. I don't say it would be.'

At this point the Judge, who was well nick-named 'Drysalter', broke in. 'Is it a question for the witness to say what he suspects? Is it not rather a question for the jury?'

Before opening his defence, Bottomley asked the judge to say if he was entitled to call 100,000 members of the Victory Bond Club, if necessary, to prove that they had had their money back in full, by way of rebutting the few witnesses called by the prosecution. Mr Justice Salter refused to give any ruling but contented himself with saying that he would listen to any evidence and objections placed before him. He then directed Bottomley to proceed with his opening, which the defendant did with a strongly emotional appeal to the jury.

SHADY FINANCIAL TRANSACTIONS

'You may have entertained a great opinion of me,' he said, 'and thought that, whatever my faults in days gone by, I have endeavoured to do my duty to my King and country. Now you are asked to change your opinion, and to say that all the time I was an arrant humbug and scoundrel.' The only question for the jury, he went on, was whether he had dealt fraudulently with the funds and securities of the Victory Bond Club.

'You have got to find,' he declared, 'that I had the intention to steal the money of poor devils such as ex-soldiers who subscribed to the Club. You have got to find that Horatio Bottomley, editor of *John Bull*, Member of Parliament, the man who wrote and spoke throughout the war with the sole object of inspiring the troops and keeping up the morale of the country, who went out to the front to do his best to cheer the lads – you have got to find that that man intended to steal their money. God forbid!'

'I swear before God,' he concluded, 'that I have never fraudulently converted a penny of the Club's money.' But this in effect was just what Travers Humphreys's searching cross-examination revealed. Even his 'patriotism' was financially rewarding. 'Were you not paid for your patriotic speeches during the war?' the prosecutor asked him.

'Never a farthing for my recruiting meetings,' answered Bottomley. 'But later on, as lecturer on the war, I got certain remuneration.' He was a bankrupt at the time, he added, and had to get his living. Pressed for details, he agreed that his lecture receipts for a time averaged between £300 and £400 a week. In fact he had made £27,000 out of his speaking campaign.

'So the war did you pretty well?' queried Humphreys.

'No, it did not,' replied Bottomley angrily. 'As a professional journalist and lecturer, I delivered a large number of lectures, as distinct from attending a large number of recruiting meetings. I was most desirous of clearing off my liabilities and getting back into Parliament. I am not at all ashamed of my work as a professional lecturer . . . I think it is rather unfair to introduce this.'

There was, however, nothing unfair about the way the prosecutor took Bottomley through the tangled web of his shady financial transactions, in which there was an occasional gleam of humour. For instance, his friend the eccentric Independent MP Pemberton Billing had bought the captured German submarine *Deutschland* for £5,500 and sold it to *John Bull* for £15,000 paid out of the Victory Bond Club account. But it did not become the property of the Club, since at that time the Club owed him (Bottomley) more money than the submarine cost.

'They could have the vessel now, if they liked,' Bottomley added amid laughter. The *Deutschland* was to be taken round the country on exhibition, but before she was ready an explosion took place on board injuring several people. The exhibition when it was mounted resulted in a considerable loss.

AT A LOSS FOR A REPLY

Questioned about a meeting of Club members he had called in the Cannon Street Hotel in January 1920 for the purpose of explaining the position to them, Bottomley said about 200 were present. 'Did they all speak?' asked Humphreys.

'Many of them at the same time,' said Bottomley, and his reply raised a laugh.

At the same time Bottomley had circulated a report in which it was stated that the stock of the Club consisted of £500,000 in bonds.

'Was that true?'

'Well,' said Bottomley, 'it is not quite the phrase I should have used myself.' Nevertheless he admitted responsibility for the report, in which it was also stated that the bonds were held by the Club's bank. In fact, those left had been transferred to Bottomley's private account with the Credit Lyonnaise in Paris.

It was practically the same thing, said Bottomley. Yet by February 1921 all the remaining stock had been sold. 'Is that practically the same thing as remaining with the Club's bankers?' For once Bottomley was at a loss for a reply.

GUILTY ON ALL ACCOUNTS

In his defence Bottomley called two former members of his staff to prove that £3,500 had been repaid to Victory Bond subscribers. But not a single one of the 100,000 people whom Bottomley had stated had been repaid their subscriptions in full appeared in the witness box.

In his final speech to the jury, Bottomley again reached the height of his characteristic rhetoric. 'You will not convict me,' he fulminated. 'The jury is not yet born who would convict me on these charges. It is unthinkable.' He then pointed to the large sword suspended above the Bench.

'The sword of justice will drop from its scabbard

if you give a verdict of Guilty against me,' he went on. 'I say it with a clean conscience. I say it without one thought of fear or misgiving. I know my country and my country's people, and knowing you, and knowing myself, and knowing the truth about this matter, without one atom of hesitation, one atom of fear . . . I know by the mercy of God and the spirit of justice you will liberate me from this ordeal.' He thereupon burst into sobs, so affected was he by his own oratory.

But the jury was not impressed when they heard the Judge's scrupulous fair summing up of the evidence. In less than half an hour they found Bottomley guilty on all accounts, except one which was withdrawn on the Judge's direction. Meanwhile, the sword of justice remained securely in its scabbard.

'Horatio Bottomley,' said the Judge to the man in the dock, 'you have been rightly convicted by the jury of a long series of heartless frauds. These poor people trusted you, and you robbed them of £150,000 in ten months. The crime is aggravated by your high position, by the number and poverty of your victims, by the trust which they reposed in you. It is aggravated by the magnitude of your frauds and by the callous effrontery by which your frauds were committed. The sentence of the Court upon you is that you be kept in penal servitude for seven years.'

EXPULSION FROM THE HOUSE

'I was under the impression, my Lord,' said the

prisoner, 'that it was sometimes put to an accused person, "Have you anything to say before sentence is passed upon you?"'

'It is not customary in cases of misdemeanour,' replied Mr. Justice Salter.

'Had it been so, my Lord,' observed Bottomley, 'I should have had something rather offensive to say about your summing up!'

With that remark Bottomley was taken to the cells below and thence to Wormwood Scrubs prison. A few days later he was formally expelled from the House of Commons, after he had apologized, in a letter to the Speaker, for the slur he had brought upon it. His expulsion, he wrote, was 'a punishment far greater and more enduring than any sentence of any Court of Law . . . But I have myself to blame, and all I can do is to ask Members of the House to judge me as they knew me'.

After serving just over five years of his sentence, Bottomley was released on licence. A Sunday newspaper paid him £12,500 for a series of articles on his prison experiences, a considerable sum for those days. Some old friends, mostly money lenders who had done well out of him in the past, rallied round with more money, and he started a magazine which he called *John Blunt*.

A PATHETIC END

It was a failure from the start, as were his other journalistic ventures at this time. He was again made bankrupt and had to part with 'The Dicker', his large country house near the Sussex Downs. He was eventually driven to applying for the Old Age Pension, which was granted and then for some reason immediately withdrawn.

His wife died, and in his last days he was cared for by an ex-musical comedy actress named Peggy Primrose, whose shows he had backed in more prosperous times. Finally, he made a pathetic series of appearances at the Windmill Theatre, but after a few days he collapsed and was admitted to Middlesex Hospital. He died in May 1933. 'What a wasted life,' commented Travers Humphreys when he heard the news. 'What a pity!'

The Mass Murderers

In 1966, 25-year-old Richard Speck was
already familiar with violence, drugs, and alcohol.
Following his marriage break-up he methodically
murdered eight student nurses in a Chicago
hostel.

BETWEEN JUNE 1918 and April 1926 the district of
Rudraprayag in northern India was terrorized by
a savage killer who despatched his victims by
tearing their throats out . . . he claimed 126 lives.
Yet when the man who finally shot him saw the
body, he was surprised.

The deadly killer was only an old leopard, whose
muzzle was grey and whose lips lacked whiskers.
Yet over a period of eight years he had brought
more terror to Rudraprayag than Jack the Ripper
had brought to Whitechapel, or Peter Kürten to
Düsseldorf. The hunter Jim Corbett ended the reign
of terror with a single bullet through the shoulder.

Why is it, then, that we feel no horror when we
read of the man-eater? Because, as Jim Corbett
said: 'This was the best-hated and most feared
animal in all India, whose only crime – not
against the laws of nature but against the laws of
man – was that he had shed human blood, with
no object of terrorizing man, but only in order
that he might live.'

Beasts of Prey

This goes to the heart of the matter. When killing is performed in this clean, natural way, we feel no horror, because there is no *evil* involved. It is the human capacity for evil, for cruelty, that frightens us. And here we face a strange paradox. The worst modern criminals, from Jack the Ripper to Richard Speck and Dean Corll, *are* beasts of prey, in the most precise sense. They stalk through modern cities like a hungry tiger, completely indifferent to the fear and sufferings of their victims. Their only desire is to satisfy an appetite.

A typical case is that of Jerry Thompson, who was not a mass murderer, but simply a rapist. His one and only murder victim was found on the morning of June 17, 1935, in a ditch in the cemetery at Peoria, Illinois. She was a pretty girl, and her white dress had been pulled up under her armpits; her torn underwear lay nearby. The medical report revealed that she had been raped and strangled. She was identified as 19-year-old Mildred Hallmark, a waitress, who had vanished the evening before, shortly after leaving the cafeteria where she worked. When the police appealed for information, several girls came forward, and disclosed that they had also been raped. The attacker was a good-looking young man who had offered them a lift, then driven them to a quiet place and forced them to submit.

The police decided to make a general appeal through the newspapers, asking for all women who had been attacked to come forward, with a promise of complete anonymity. They hoped that one of these women might be able to give them some clue to the identity of the rapist. The response startled them. More than fifty women came forward, and it became clear that the police were looking for a highly successful sex-maniac.

In many cases he had stopped beside a girl walking along a lonely street and dragged her into the car. If she resisted or screamed, he silenced her with a violent punch on the jaw or in the stomach. He would drive to a lonely place, undress the girl, and commit rape. Then he would take out a camera, and take photographs of her naked, sprawled in obscene positions. He would tell the girl that if she told the police her name would appear in the newspapers, and everyone would know what had happened to her. There are few girls who do not prefer privacy to revenge.

Five days after the discovery of Mildred Hall-mark's body the police had the break they needed. A girl named Grace Ellsworth told them that she had been picked up by a clean-cut, well-spoken young man who had offered her a lift. In an empty road, he stopped the car, and tried to kiss her. When she slapped his face, he hit her on the jaw, then beat her up so viciously that she was incapable of resisting as he undressed her. Afterwards, he dragged her into the headlights of the car, took photographs of her with a box camera, and warned her that if she reported him to the police the pictures would be sent to her friends and relatives.

And then, some weeks later, a man had been

introduced to her at a dance. She was certain this was the rapist. When she asked him if they hadn't met before, he denied it. But *she* was sure. The man had been introduced to her as Jerry Thompson. The police had no way of tracking down Jerry Thompson, but they suspected that Mildred Hallmark had known her killer. She was a shy girl who would never get into a car with a stranger. They went to her father, who worked in a tractor factory in East Peoria, and asked him if he knew a Jerry Thompson: he did. Thompson worked in the machine shop, and was a neighbour of theirs.

Ripped Underwear

Thompson proved to be a handsome young man in his mid-twenties, who was engaged to be married. He flatly denied being the rapist; but Grace Ellsworth picked him out from a line-up, and a lie detector test revealed that he knew more than he would admit about the murder. The detective in charge of the case shocked a confession out of him by throwing Mildred Hallmark's ripped underwear into his lap.

Thompson broke down, he confessed to picking up Mildred, offering her a lift, and taking her to the cemetery. She had resisted, and he had struck her under the chin and throttled her into unconsciousness before tearing off her clothes and raping her in the back seat. Then, he said, he realized she was dead. In his room, police found dozens of photographs of the naked women he had raped, and a diary detailing dozens of rapes that he had committed since he was sixteen. He was electrocuted on October 15, 1935.

The Thompson case is interesting because we can see that he was living by the 'law of the jungle'. *All* healthy young men, particularly the 'dominant 5 per cent', would like to be able to make love to dozens of pretty girls. No doubt it is partly fear and caution that prevents them from becoming Jerry Thompsons. But it is also, perhaps, a sense of decency; they do not want to *hurt* another human being, any more than they would want to set fire to a haystack or torture a cat. So desire is outweighed by revulsion.

Jerry Thompson was obviously a man of exceptionally strong sexual desires; but his cold eyes and slightly cruel mouth, reveal that he lacked the human warmth that would have led him to restrain these desires. He may not have been evil or cruel by nature, but after the first few rapes he would begin to *think of himself* as a criminal, a lone beast of prey, and so develop this aspect of his personality.

Thompson's rapes were committed between the mid-1920s and 1935. This was the 'Age of Sex Crime', especially in America. During the Second World War, the rate of sex crime rose steadily – which is to be expected when thousands of men are away from home, deprived of their wives. But it continued to rise after the war. Why? Because men who thought they were coming home to a new world where they would be treated like heroes found themselves in the same old ruthless mechanized civilization, where they were mere cogs in a wheel.

Such a civilization produces the effect which Karl Marx called 'alienation', the feeling of not belonging. The mass murderers of the fifties and sixties were all 'alienated men', 'outsiders': Haigh, Heath, Christie, Richard Speck, Howard Unruh, Charles Manson, Charles Whitman and Ian Brady.

Not all these men were sex criminals; Haigh was motivated by money. Unruh and Whitman and Manson by paranoid hatred of society; but the sense of alienation meant that they had no fellow feeling for their victims. And the Richard Speck case shows something even more disturbing: the alienation turning into cruelty. *Not* sadism; Speck did not actually torture any of his victims; but he took pleasure in terrorizing them.

Speck's orgy of murder came to light at just after 5 a.m. on Thursday, July 14, 1966, when a girl rushed out on to the balcony of a nurses' hostel on the south side of Chicago and began screaming. Two patrolmen who rushed into the building found a nauseating scene. In various rooms there were the naked bodies of eight women. Most of them had been strangled, and also stabbed many times. Their hands had been tied behind them. None of them had been raped, but a perverted sexual attack had been made on one of them, Gloria Davy.

The one survivor, a Philippino girl named Corazon Amurao, told how there had been a knock on her bedroom door sometime after midnight. She opened it, and found herself facing a man who smelt of alcohol and held a gun. He had a pockmarked face and blond hair. This was Richard Speck, a 25-year-old seaman. Speck rounded up six girls into one dormitory bedroom, and tied their hands with sheets that he cut up with a knife. He kept explaining that he needed money to get to New Orleans, and promised not to hurt them.

This indicates that, in spite of his intention of committing murder, he still maintained some 'fellow feeling' for the intended victims. Three more nurses came home late; Speck took their money, and tied them. Finally, Speck took one of the girls out of the room. A few minutes later he took another, and they heard a cry.

Corazon Amurao was a courageous girl more 'dominant' than the others. She urged them to free themselves and try to 'jump' the man. They replied that he didn't appear to be violent, and that they had better sit still. Miss Amurao decided to roll under a bed, where she hid. The man continued to come in and out for hours. Then all was quiet. When an alarm clock went off at five o'clock, Miss Amurao rolled out from under the bed, crawled on to the balcony, and began to scream for help.

A Sultan with his Harem

Speck had left his fingerprints all over the place, and Corazon Amurao was able to give an exact description of him, even to a tattoo on his arm, with the words, 'Born to raise hell'. From the seaman's knots that bound the dead girls, the police guessed that the man was a sailor. There was a labour exchange much used by sailors not far away. The police soon established the identity of the man they were seeking, and half an hour past midnight, on the following Sunday, Speck was taken into the Chicago Cook County Hospital, his wrists slashed in a suicide attempt. The doctor who attended him saw the tattoo, and called the police.

Psychiatrists who examined Speck learned that he had been known at school as a 'sulky loner' who hated his stepfather. He drifted from job to job – labourer, garbage collector, truckdriver and seaman. At the age of twenty he married a fifteen-year-old girl, and they had a baby daughter, whom he adored. But after five years of fighting, they divorced.

He drank heavily, and took drugs – yellow jackets, red-birds – amytal and seconald drugs that can cause hallucinations. In Dallas, Texas, earlier in 1965, he had attacked a young girl as she was parking her car, holding a carving knife to her throat. Sentenced to eighteen months in prison, he was soon released on parole – which he instantly skipped. To drinking companions he was known as a braggart who boasted about all the women he had slept with, but who never seemed to be able to date a girl.

In April 1966, when Speck had returned to Monmouth, Illinois, where his relatives lived, a barmaid named Mary Pierce vanished from a tavern where Speck drank. Her naked body was later found in a hog house behind the tavern.

Speck had often asked her for a date. After leaving Monmouth, Speck had worked on Great Lakes ore boats, but had been rushed into hospital for an appendix operation in early May.

He began to date a nurse there; she found him gentle, but full of hatred of society. He talked vengefully of two people in Texas he wanted to kill, and he told someone else that he intended to return to Texas and kill his ex-wife Shirley. Significantly, the only Chicago nurse who was sexually assaulted closely resembled his wife. On the day before the murders, he had been drinking heavily in Chicago bars.

Chicago was in the midst of a heat wave, and there were riots when negro children turned on fire hydrants to bathe and police tried to stop them. Towards midnight, drunk and drugged, Speck approached the hostel that he had often passed – the building that was full of young girls. He was like a fox creeping into a chicken house. And the length of time he took to kill eight girls suggests that he was enjoying every moment of it: for a few hours he was a sultan with absolute power over a harem of girls.

It was two years after Speck had been sentenced that the police of Salem, Oregon, realized that they were dealing with another sex killer who had claimed several victims. Linda Slawson, of Aloha, vanished in January, 1968; Jan Susan Whitney, 23, had vanished from McMinnville in November, 1968; 16-year-old Stephanie Vilcko, who vanished in July 1968, was found in March 1969, on the banks of Gales Creek, her body so decomposed that the cause of death could not be established.

An Ordinary Transvestite

On April 23, 1969, Linda Salee, 22, vanished when she was out shopping for a birthday present for her boyfriend, and on May 10 a fisherman on the bank of the Long Tom River, near Corvallis, saw a body floating below the surface. It proved to be female, half clothed, without bra or panties, and had been held down by a heavy car-part. It was Linda Salee, and she had been raped and strangled. Not far away, the police found another body, 19-year-old Karen Sprinker, who had vanished on March 27. Her underclothes were also missing; she had been raped and strangled, and was held down by part of a car engine.

In April, a 15-year-old schoolgirl had been grabbed by a man who tried to force her into a car, but she managed to break away. Not long after, two schoolgirls had seen a man dressed in women's clothes in the car park of a big store. The police thought it possible that he was an ordinary transvestite – a man who dresses in women's clothes because he wants to be a woman. However, soon after the finding of the two bodies, the police had a break.

A girl student from Oregon State University told them of a date she had had with a strange man. He had claimed to be a Vietnam veteran, who spent an evening with her in the lounge of her dormitory, and had told her she ought to be 'sad' on account of the girls who had been killed. He seemed a gentle, quietly spoken man, and it was only afterwards that she began to wonder if it was worth telling the police. It was one of hundreds of tips, but they checked it.

It led them to a mild, 30-year-old married electrician and photographer named Jerry Brudos, and they were soon convinced that this man, who made a habit of telephoning girls and claiming to be a Vietnamese veteran, knew something about the murders. He had a police record for stealing women's underwear, and for trying to force two girls to strip by threatening them with a knife. He had been caught near the women's dormitory of the Oregon State University carrying stolen women's clothing, and wearing a bra and panties.

Suspended from the Ceiling

The police searched his home, near the State Hospital, to which he had been committed after the sexual charges. Brudos's wife seemed to have no suspicion that her husband had been leading a double life – her time was taken up tending to their two children – but she admitted that he spent much time in the photographer's dark room adjoining the house. In this dark room the police found what they were looking for – photographs of the dead girls.

It became clear that Brudos had kidnapped them, taken them to the studio, and there suspended them from the ceiling by their wrists while he had committed sexual assaults and photographed them. Brudos confessed to killing the four missing girls, though the death of Stephanie Vilcko, the 16-year-old, is still unsolved. He was sentenced to life imprisonment.

Comparing these three cases – Thompson, Speck, Brudos – we immediately note the violence and sadism of the more recent ones. Thompson, a typical killer of the 'Age of Sex Crime', only wanted to possess attractive girls, with or without their consent. Speck and Brudos had a deep, psychopathic hatred of women.

It would not, of course, be true to say that torture murders were unknown in the 'Age of Sex Crime'. One of the grimmest cases on record is that of Donald Fearn, a 23-year-old railway mechanic of Pueblo, Colorado, who in 1942 kidnapped Alice Porter, drove her into the desert to an old adobe church used by the Indians, and whipped and bound her with red-hot wires. He killed her with a hammer after raping her and threw the body into a well – he was executed in the gas chamber.

There was the mysterious 'Moonlight Murderer' of Texarkana, Texas, who in 1946 attacked courting couples, and in two cases killed the man and then spent hours torturing and raping the girl before killing her.

A burnt-out car found near the murder scene suggests that the murderer destroyed the evidence – police had tyre tracks of the murderer's car – and then committed suicide by flinging himself under a train. However, crimes like these are solitary examples of sick perversion which stand out from the general pattern of crime as exceptions. The murders of Richard Speck fit all-too-neatly into a pattern of crime that is becoming increasingly familiar in our time.

Seen and Not Heard

There is a strange sense of *lack of motivation*. We are confronted with patterns of crime that would have baffled criminologists of the old school, like Lombroso or Ivan Bloch. In February, 1968, the bullet-riddled body of August Norry, a landscape gardener, was found on a hillside in San Mateo County, California. A few months later, a pretty 18-year-old pony-tailed blonde named Penny Bjorkland confessed that she had killed him 'for fun'. He was a stranger who had offered her a lift, and she had suddenly felt the urge to shoot him – for apparently no reason.

In June, 1972, Santa Barbara police arrested a man in connection with a supermarket hold-up. He was 47-year-old Sherman McCrary, and the investigation led police to arrest McCrary's wife Carolyn, his daughter Ginger, and his son Danny and his son-in-law Carl Taylor.

And as the police investigated the itinerant family, they came to the conclusion that they had been, jointly, responsible for murdering more than twenty young women, mostly waitresses and shop assistants, who had been abducted and raped over the past two years. The women were apparently aware that their husbands were involved in orgies of robbery and rape, but felt that a housewife should be seen and not heard.

And so the mass murders continue: after Manson, John Linley Frazier, Juan Corona, Herb Mullin, the McCrarys, Edmund Kemper, Gerry Schaefer, Dean Corll. In all these cases there can be no doubt that the fundamental problem is 'alienation'. Karl Marx would have smiled grimly. But if he was still alive, he would have to admit that *Das Kapital* holds no solution to this most baffling and disturbing problem of our time.

Stranglers

Albert DeSalvo, better known as the Boston Strangler, wrote this poem a few years before his death in 1973:

Here is the story of the Strangler, yet untold,
The man who claims he murdered
thirteen women, young and old.
The elusive Strangler, there he goes,
Where his wanderlust sends him, no one knows
He struck within the light of day,
Leaving not one clue astray.
Young and old, their lips are sealed,
Their secret of death never revealed.
Even though he is sick in mind,
He's much too clever for the police to find.
To reveal his secret will bring him fame,
But burden his family with unwanted shame.
Today he sits in a prison cell,
Deep inside only a secret he can tell.
People everywhere are still in doubt,
Is the Strangler in prison or roaming about?

THE WORD 'strangler' has a brutal ring: like 'slasher' and 'ripper', it conveys an idea of physical violence, and this is no linguistic accident. In fact, most stranglers have been violent and brutal men. The act of strangling suggests a deliberate savagery.

A man who kills with a gun wants to get it over as quickly as possible, and a man who kills with a knife may be possessed by a vindictive fury, his basic aim being to destroy, to extinguish the spark of life. But the strangler is a man who takes pleasure in close contact with his victim. It takes several minutes to kill someone by strangulation, and during that time the strangler holds the choice of life or death; by simply relaxing his grip, he can allow the victim to breathe again. So strangling is a more wilful and deliberate form of murder than most, and it is never free from a touch of sadism.

It is therefore not surprising that in the great majority of cases stranglers are motivated by sex. Christie, the rapist of Notting Hill, chose to strangle his victims after he had rendered them unconscious with a coal-gas 'inhaler', and then stripped and assaulted them. It would have been just as simple to have smothered them with a pillow, or even to gas them; he preferred strangulation because it was another form of 'rape'.

Life of Murder

Earle Nelson, the 'Gorilla murderer', strangled and outraged 22 women during his incredible career of murder in North America and Canada. The word 'outraged' here has a certain frightful accuracy, since he tore open some of the bodies with his bare hands. Peter Kürten, the Düsseldorf sadist, often grabbed women in dark streets and throttled them until he achieved a sexual climax. If he achieved the climax while the victim was still alive, he left her, and, strangely enough, some girls who went out with him more than once actually allowed him to throttle them as they had intercourse. Kürten told one who protested, 'that's what love's all about.'

It follows then, that female killers seldom commit murder by strangulation. The very few known cases involve highly dominant women, and the sexual *motif* is usually present somewhere. There was Nina Housden, who lived near Detroit: a passionate, violent and neurotic woman who was pathologically jealous of her bus-driver husband Charles. In 1947 he left her. Just before Christmas that year, she invited him over for a drink 'for old times' sake', got him drunk, then strangled him with a clothes line.

The next day, she dismembered him and wrapped the parts of the body in newspaper. But from then on, luck was against her. She set out with the parts of the body in the car, intending to dispose of them in the Kentucky Hills. The car broke down in Toledo, Ohio, and the garage proprietor was surprised when the woman said she would wait in the car, even if it took a week to repair.

A garage mechanic looked into one of the evil-smelling parcels on the back seat while Nina slept, and discovered a human leg. She was sentenced to life imprisonment. Then there was Mrs. Stylou Christofi, who strangled her daughter-in-law, stripped her naked, and tried to burn the body on a bonfire in the back garden of her Hampstead home in London. The motive was sexual jealousy of her son's wife, and this is underlined by the stripping of the body.

Pathetic Case

Perhaps the most pathetic case of a female strangler was the Scotswoman, Susan Newell, who, in June 1923, strangled the 13-year-old boy who brought her newspapers. Her husband had deserted her, and she was living alone. The following morning, together with her eight-year-old daughter, Janet, Mrs. Newell took the body to Glasgow in a go-cart.

As she climbed out of a lorry that had given her a lift, the cart slipped, and a head and foot protruded from the wrapped bundle inside it. A woman who saw this from an upstairs window called the police. Mrs. Newell was found guilty, and in due course hanged. A psychiatrist had declared that she was not insane. It seems probable that the motive for the crime was sexual. Sex-starved women have often been known to approach young boys. He may have struggled or threatened to tell, and she strangled him.

There is no complex Freudian reason for this association of strangling with sex. It is simply that, of all forms of killing, strangulation is the one that most directly expresses resentment. And, as police officers know, there is usually *some* sexual motive concealed in a strangling case, even if it is not at once apparent. For example, when the strangled body of 35-year-old John Mudie was found in a chalk pit near Woldingham in Surrey, the police were at first inclined to believe that the motive was robbery.

Letters in the victim's room led them to Thomas

Ley, ex-Minister of Justice for New South Wales, Australia, and to John Smith, a foreman builder who had been hired by Ley to help murder John Mudie. It eventually transpired that Ley had been insanely jealous of Mudie, believing that he was the lover of Ley's ex-mistress, Mrs. Maggie Brook. The belief had no foundation whatsoever, but when Ley succeeded in luring Mudie to his house in Kensington, he administered a brutal beating, then strangled him.

Even in the case of the death of a woman, the sexual motive may not at once be apparent. When the body of 21-year-old Mary Moonen was found in a driveway in a fashionable quarter of Minneapolis in April 1955, there was at first nothing to suggest a sexual attack. Her red coat, black skirt and white blouse were untorn, and the skirt had been pulled well down over her thighs. Her panties were apparently undisturbed, the autopsy revealed no sexual attack.

A handbag underneath the body contained five dollars, so the motive was clearly not robbery. But Mrs. Moonen had certainly been strangled, and had had intercourse not long before her death. At her home in East 17th Street the police discovered that she was the mother of a nine-month-old daughter, and that she was living with her father, an elderly retired man in poor health. Her husband was in the army in Korea.

Mystery Lover

This offered the police their first real lead, for

Matthias Moonen had been overseas for six months, and Mrs. Moonen was found to be three months pregnant. Who, then, was her lover? Here they seemed to encounter a dead end. Her father seemed certain that she had no lover. She was a good Catholic, deeply in love with her husband and devoted to the baby. She was a regular churchgoer, and it seemed impossible that she could be having a secret affair.

Dentist's Pill

The police questioned the victim's sister, Mrs. Donald Newton, a pretty girl in her mid-twenties. At first, she could provide no clue. Then, when the police told her that her sister had mentioned a dental appointment on the day of her murder, Mrs. Newton looked thoughtful. She was able to tell them the name of Mary's dentist: it was Dr. Arnold Asher Axilrod. He was a well-known figure in Minneapolis, having served as mayor during the war, and since then taken an active part in civil affairs.

He *had* been Mrs. Newton's dentist, but she had walked out one day and never gone back. Why? Because Axilrod had given her a pill that had knocked her out for six hours. When she had woken up, he had 'talked suggestively', and on a later occasion he had made a pass at her. But that had not prevented her recommending Axilrod to her sister when she needed a dentist. And the sister knew that Axilrod had given Mary the same 'knock-out pill' on a number of occasions, and had to drive her home afterwards.

When the police called on Mary Moonen's doctor, the case suddenly began to simplify. The doctor told them that Mary claimed Axilrod was the father of the unborn child. He had given her a pill that made her groggy, laid her on the couch and had sexual intercourse with her. Dr. Axilrod, a middle-aged man with dark hair and dark moustache, was brought in for questioning and quickly admitted killing Mary Moonen. He claimed that she had often visited him and accused him of being the father of the child, which he denied.

Wait in Car

On the day of the murder she had again accused him of fathering the child. He had asked her to wait for him in his car, then driven off with her. She threatened that she would expose him; then, said Axilrod, he blacked out and when he came to, he was alone in the car. 'I guess I did it,' said Axilrod, sighing. 'No one else was there.'

The police now discovered that they already had a complaint against Axilrod on file. Three weeks before the murder a 17-year-old schoolgirl had called at his surgery for treatment. He had given her a pill. When she woke up, six hours later, Axilrod was sitting beside her. She had no idea whether any assault had taken place, but she was angry at being kept in his office until the early hours of the morning. Axilrod drove her home, and she had reported the matter by phone. The police found that Axilrod seemed to prefer female patients – he had few males on his books, and at least twenty women told of being put to sleep with a knock-out pill, and waking many hours later, lying on the couch. Newspapers talked openly of Axilrod's 'love pills' – the laws of libel being less stringent in America than in Europe.

The prosecutor at his trial described him as an amorous philanderer who drugged his pretty victims so they could not resist his sexual advances. The defence confined itself to trying to show that the police had not proved their case against Axilrod: for example, the victim's clothes had not been properly examined, but had been left in a damp morgue for five months. They also called a surprise witness – the victim's brother-in-law, Donald Newton.

Newton was serving a three-month sentence for indecent exposure, and had told a cell-mate that he would crack the case wide open. However, he only added to the confusion; when asked whether he had been at work on the evening of the murder, he replied that he must decline to answer the question 'because it might incriminate me'.

This naturally gave rise to speculation about whether he meant he had some connection with the murder – although, on balance, it seems more likely that he was referring to the crime for which he was serving a sentence. Another witness, a taxi driver, declared that he had seen Mrs. Moonen get out of Axilrod's car and drive off with two men. But the jury remained unconvinced. They found

Axilrod guilty of manslaughter, and he was sentenced to between five and twenty years in the State prison.

Aggressive Impulse

This final ambiguity about the Axilrod case is characteristic of many strangulation murders. When a man seizes a woman by the throat, his intention may only be to silence her. Alternatively, he may be expressing some aggressive impulse that intends to stop short of murder. This means that, in many cases, the real solution should perhaps be in the hands of a psychologist rather than a policeman. The following case of Frederick Field may be taken as a typical example.

On October 2, 1931, the almost naked body of a young woman was found in an empty shop in Shaftesbury Avenue, London. She had been strangled. It did not take the police long to identify her as a prostitute, 20-year-old Norah Upchurch, who was well known in the area. Suspicion quickly came to rest on the man who had the keys to the empty shop, an electrician, Frederick Field, who claimed he had given them to a man who wanted to rent the shop.

The police could establish no obvious motive for the crime – why should anyone kill a prostitute for sex? So although both the police and the coroner were convinced Field was lying, a verdict of murder by persons unknown was returned. On the whole, robbery seemed the likeliest motive. In 1933, Field, now in the Royal Air Force, walked into a newspaper office and said he wanted to confess to the murder of Norah Upchurch. It soon became clear that, if Field *was* guilty, his confession was basically false.

For example, he said he had strangled the girl with his hands; but she had been strangled with a belt. It seemed likely that he had confessed to get money out of the newspaper, which had treated his story as an 'exclusive' and talked to him for hours before informing the police. Field went on trial, and now withdrew his confession, saying he made it only because he was 'fed up' and he was having trouble with his wife. The judge instructed the jury to find him Not Guilty.

Prostitute's Body

Then, in April 1936, the body of a prostitute was found in her room in Clapham; she had been suffocated. She was identified as Mrs. Beatrice Vilna Sutton, but no one had seen her with her killer. That evening, Frederick Field, who had deserted from his unit, called on a girlfriend and told her mysteriously that she would soon read something interesting in the newspapers. The girl's mother, thinking Field looked insane, telephoned the police.

The deserter was arrested, and at the police station he suddenly confessed to the murder of Mrs. Sutton. His description of her room was circumstantial – and nothing had yet appeared in the newspapers. At his trial, Field tried the same trick as before: repudiating his confession, declaring he had made it because he was 'fed up', but it was obvious that this time he knew too much about the crime to be innocent. The jury found him guilty, and he was sentenced to death. Police suspected that he may have been responsible for the murder of at least four more prostitutes in the Soho area.

The Lucie Berlin murder investigation, which took place in 1904, certainly deserves a high place among epics of forensic detection. Lucie Berlin was a nine-year-old girl, well developed for her age, who lived in a slum tenement in Berlin. On June 11, 1904, a boatman on the River Spree saw a bundle floating in the river and pulled it out. It contained the headless and limbless torso of a child, who was soon identified as Lucie Berlin, who had been missing for two days.

It was definitely a sex murder. The child had been raped, and her parents declared that she had been told repeatedly never to go off with a strange man. This led the investigators to wonder if she had been killed in the slum tenement at 130 Ackerstrasse. They questioned all the other tenants. On the floor above Lucie's parents lived a prostitute named Johanna Liebestruth. A man who was also in her room identified himself as Theodore Berger, and gave another address.

It was only days later that the police discovered that Johanna had been in prison for three days – for insulting a client – at the time of the murder, and that Berger, her lover and pimp, had lived in her room during that time. They also learned that Berger was proposing to marry Johanna – which caused some remark among their neighbours, since he had been steadfastly refusing for the past eighteen years.

More parcels, containing the missing head, arms and legs, were found in the ship canal. Berger was taken to view these remains, but he continued to insist that he knew nothing about the child's death. Johanna Liebestruth was taken to police headquarters and questioned. She had nothing to hide, and she was even frank about the reason Berger had finally agreed to marry her. On the day Lucie's body had been found, she had come home from gaol and had discovered that a wicker suitcase was missing.

Making Love

Berger had admitted that he was responsible. He had taken a prostitute back to the room, and only after lovemaking had he admitted that he had no money. He gave the woman the suitcase instead. And to placate Johanna for his infidelity, he had agreed to marry her.

The police asked Berger about the suitcase, and he instantly denied knowing anything about it. A few days later, a bargeman handed the case to the police. The stains in the basket proved to be of human blood; so did certain spots on the floor of Johanna Liebestruth's room, and Berger was charged.

What had happened was pieced together at the trial. One day not long before the murder, Lucie had been in Johanna's room, standing on her head, and Berger had noticed how well formed her legs were. When Johanna was in prison, Berger became sex starved. He invited Lucie into the room and attempted indecent assault on her, but she struggled. He strangled her, raped her, then dismembered the body and transported it to the river in the wicker suitcase, which he then threw away. Berger was executed.

STRANGLERS: CASE STUDY

The Boston Strangler

Even though the Boston Strangler killed thirteen women many people cannot even remember his name. Perhaps it is because they have a strange fascination for the actual crime rather than the strangler himself.

ALBERT DESALVO strangled thirteen women in Boston, in the USA, between the months of June 1962 and January 1964. DeSalvo wasted little time in getting to know his victims and managed to gain access to their homes by pretending to be an official who had been authorized to carry out repairs in the unsuspecting women's homes. He seemed to be driven by uncontrollable sexual desires, but had a kindly manner and seemed able to talk his way easily into the homes of women living on their own. As soon as he had gained access he wasted no time in raping his victims, and then strangled them, usually using a piece of their own clothing – for example, stockings or tights. He left his own particular trademark in that he would tie a bow under the chin of his victim, using whatever article he had obtained to carry out his ugly deeds. As if that was not enough, he would always position the the body, after killing them, in very obscene positions, meaning that whoever found the body was in for a nasty shock.

His victims were usually middle-aged women, and the first one was a 55-year-old divorcee by the name of Anna Slesers. Her son discovered her naked body in June 1962, and was horrified when he saw her lying on the floor of her home with her legs spread wide apart. She had been raped and strangled with her own dressing gown cord. There appeared no to be no other motive than pure sexual frenzy.

As murder after murder happened in the vicinity of Boston, terror spread among women who lived on their own, and as soon as it became dark they remained behind locked doors fearing for their safety.

The police questioned many well-known sexual offenders, and as is usual in a case of this nature, many false confessions were received. The police enlisted the help of forensic psychiatrists to try and assist them in tracking down the Boston Strangler who was committing such dreadful atrocities against women. They built up a profile of a youngish man, aged between 18 and 40, someone who was suffering from delusions of persecution, and possibly someone who had a hatred of their own mother.

This last theory, however, went out of the window when the Strangler struck again on December 5, raping and killing 20-year-old Sophie Clark, followed by 23-year-old Patricia Bissette on December 31.

Once again the police built up a new 'psychofit' picture of a man, now considered to be around 30, strongly built, of average height, clean shaven and a mass of thick, dark hair. He was definitely a paranoid schizophrenic and possibly of Mediterranean origin. As it turned out later this latest picture of the murderer was remarkably accurate.

In January 1964 the spate of murders inexplicably stopped. Despite all the efforts of everyone involved to solve the case, it was DeSalvo himself who eventually brought about his own capture.

On October 27, 1964, the strangler struck again. He gained entry into the home of a newly-married woman who was still asleep in bed. Her husband had already left for work, and she suddenly awoke to find a man inside her bedroom. DeSalvo put a knife to her throat and threatened her with, 'Not a sound or I'll kill you'. He stuffed underwear into her mouth to keep her quiet and proceeded to tie her to the bedposts using her own clothing, spreading her legs were spread wide apart. He kissed her and molested her, but then, something which was completely out of character, he apologized for what he had done and fled the apartment.

Once she had managed to free herself from her bonds, the girl immediately called the police and was able to give a very accurate description of her assailant. He was immediately identified as Albert DeSalvo, who had been released from prison in April 1962 following a conviction for indecent assault. The police arrested him at his home and then asked him to take part in an identification parade. His last victim was able to identify him, and at last the police had got their man.

When he was arrested DeSalvo was said to be mortified by the fact that his wife had had to see him in handcuffs. His wife, however, said she was not surprised that her husband had turned out to be the Boston Strangler, as he was totally obsessed by sex, and that no one woman would ever be enough for a man like that. Although DeSalvo denied any involvement in the murders, he did admit to breaking into over four hundred houses and committing rape. Also, when his photograph was distributed by the police, they received numerous reports from women who claimed that DeSalvo had assaulted them.

DeSalvo was assessed by psychiatrists and was judged to be a schizophrenic and therefore not competent to stand trial. He was committed to Boston State Hospital. Even to this day there is no conclusive evidence that Albert DeSalvo was the Boston Strangler, but while he was in hospital he did confess to killing thirteen women, and even described in detail how he killed them and described the insides of their homes.

DeSalvo was never actually charged with being the Boston Strangler, but he was sentenced to life imprisonment in 1967 for sex offences and robberies that were committed before the crimes. He was found dead in his prison cell on November 26, 1973 at Walpole State Prison, Massachusetts – the cause of death, stab wounds to the heart.

Cop Killers

Sergeant Mike McNeil was a careful cop. He always
frisked his suspect thoroughly. However, when he
tried to arrest three at the same time, he slipped up
. . . and even as he died, a colleague was
being buried. It's total war – and war is hell.

THE LONDON Metropolitan Police Force came into
being in the year 1829. It was the brainchild of the
Home Secretary, Sir Robert Peel – and consequently the new policemen became known as
'bobbies'. The nickname was not totally affectionate, however, for the people of London hated
them. The old watchmen and parish constables
who had kept order were just public employees,
like rat-catchers and street sweepers. These uniformed men were 'officials', whose business was
to smell out offences against the law and put the
offenders in jail. As a consequence, it was a risky
job to be a policeman in the 1830s.

On June 29, 1830, Police Constable Grantham
saw two drunken Irishmen quarrelling over a
woman in Somers Town, north London. He tried
to separate them and the men *and* the woman
turned on him and knocked him down. The men
'put in the boot', kicking him brutally on the
temple. He died shortly afterwards, thus becoming
the first English policeman to die in the course of

execution of his duty. The murderers walked off and were never brought to justice.

Six weeks later there was an incident that must have confirmed the London poor in their view that they were better off without the police. On August 16, Police Constable John Long accosted three suspicious-looking characters in Mecklenburgh Square, Grays Inn Road. One of them pulled a knife and stabbed Long to death. There was a hue and cry. A police constable who came on the scene saw a man running and grabbed him; the man protested that *he* was chasing one of the murderers.

A youth who was sitting on a doorstep was arrested by a police inspector. The youth protested that he was waiting for a friend, whereupon the police arrested the friend too. All three were taken into court, but the magistrate, reasoning that it was unlikely that a murderer would be sitting on a doorstep, discharged two of the defendants. But a tradesman's boy and a prostitute identified the remaining man as one of the policeman's assailants. No one asked the boy why, at an earlier stage, he had admitted that he had not even seen the murder. The accused man – almost certainly innocent – was hanged. One has a feeling that the early police force felt it was better to hang the wrong man than nobody at all.

In May 1833, a rather mildly revolutionary group called the National Political Union called for a public meeting of 'anarchists and revolutionists' in Coldbath Fields, not far from the site of Constable Long's murder. Their 'revolutionary' programme was hardly extreme, they simply wanted votes for the working man. The Home Secretary didn't like the idea; he told the Commissioner of Police to ban the meeting. The ban was ignored. A crowd gathered, and a speaker on a soap box asked the crowd to be orderly and peaceable.

Revolution and Sedition

They had little alternative, being surrounded by about 800 policemen and troops. Other speeches were made and a police spy slipped away to report that revolution and sedition was being preached. The man in charge of the police, Lieutenant-Colonel Charles Rowan, who had fought at Waterloo, ordered his men to advance slowly, holding their truncheons, and to halt frequently to allow 'innocent' bystanders to get away. The police advanced – and were booed and pelted with stones.

This angered the Force, and they began hitting out wildly, knocking down women and children as well as men. Police Constable Robert Culley tried to capture one of the anarchist's banners, and hit the man with a truncheon. The man drew a knife, and stabbed Culley in the chest. He staggered a few yards and fell dead. Culley was a married man of 27 whose wife was about to have a baby.

The Coroner's jury that met to consider how Culley met his death were not disposed to sympathize with the police. They were mostly respectable tradesmen, and they felt that the police should have minded their own business, and permitted the traditional British right of free speech. They asked the police witnesses impertinent questions; then, when they were sent out to reach a verdict, told the Coroner they were unable to agree.

The Coroner did what was quite common in those days – told them that they would stay in the room without food or drink until they *did* agree. The result was that the angry jury produced a verdict that enraged the police and delighted the British public: that the man who had killed Constable Culley – and who had never been caught – was only guilty of justifiable homicide. The spectators in the court cheered. The jury were treated as heroes, and found themselves wined and dined for their defiance of the 'bobbies'.

This raises again the fundamental question: were the public simply protesting against this frightening new innovation, a police force? Or was it rather the expression of something deeper – that idealistic anarchism which is perhaps a profound and permanent part of human nature? For it is not only, for instance, 'primitive' and peaceable societies such as the South Sea islanders who feel they have no need for civil authority. Slum dwellers in London's East End and country dwellers in tiny rural villages feel the same. The poor may fight among themselves, but they also help one another.

'Kill Them Like Dogs'

In the poverty of Whitechapel and the Ratcliffe

Highway there was a strong community spirit, which could be seen occasionally when a whole street hired a horse bus for an expedition to the country, or families went hop-picking to the fields of Kent, sleeping rough under hedges. As to country people, anyone who has ever moved from a city into a quiet country district has noticed the friendliness and warmth, and how a total stranger may go out of his way to offer help.

This is what had convinced nineteenth-century 'peaceful anarchists' such as the Russians Kropotkin and Malatesta that men are good at heart, and that to subject them to the harsh processes of the law is an indignity to human nature. To some extent, it is undoubtedly the modern commercial metropolis, with its fairly well-to-do inhabitants living in flats, that has eroded this spirit of co-operation among ordinary people. No doubt Kropotkin, Bakunin, Proudhon and the rest were being absurdly idealistic when they imagined that a whole modern state could be run without the police, army or government. Yet they had grasped something about human nature that many people have lost sight of: that man is basically gregarious and prepared to help his fellow-creatures, because he needs help from them.

This explains some of the deep and widespread hostility to the police that persists even in our crime-ridden society. It is, of course, due partly to a kind of stupidity, to the confused reasoning of socially immature individuals, but it is more than that. There is also the obscure longing for a more innocent form of society, where the brotherhood of man is a reality. Many anarchists would agree that society needs law and order, because there are always people who may commit violent crimes.

But the answer, according to them, is to have police purely as guardians of the peace, like the sheriff of an old Wild Western town, whose business was to chase rustlers and stop visiting cowboys from shooting up the local saloon – not to go around looking for people who have parked their horse on double yellow lines.

This view actually offers a ray of hope in a society where the killing of policemen has become an increasing problem. (In America, more police are killed every year than have been killed in England since the beginning of the twentieth century.)

If the police killing is pure anti-social viciousness, then this is a reason for gloom. But if it also springs from some distorted impulse of defiance and human dignity, then a little intelligent thinking may provide some of the answers.

The outline of some of these answers can be seen in the subsequent history of the police force. In America, on the continent of Europe, and especially in Russia, the police continued to be regarded by most ordinary people as an instrument of oppression. 'Police and militia, the bloodhounds of capitalism, are willing to murder!' declared a headline in the *Arbeiter-Zeitung*, the Chicago German-language anarchist daily.

On May 4, 1885, police moved in to break up a strikers' meeting in the Haymarket Square when someone threw a bomb into the police ranks. The explosion was terrific, and when the bleeding and screaming confusion died down, seven policemen were lying dead. In the following year, eight anarchists – arrested at random from the crowd – were sentenced to death for the killings.

It started a chain reaction of shootings, explosions, strike-breaking and the deliberate starvation of workers and their families, and the violence continued intermittently for nearly half a century. The execution of Sacco and Vanzetti in 1927 marked the end of this phase of militant anarchism in America.

Shot Through the Neck

On May Day, 1891, French anarchists were dragged into the police station at Clichy and beaten viciously. At their trial, one of them shouted: 'If the police come, do not hesitate to kill them like the dogs they are . . .' On November 8, 1892, a bomb exploded in the police station in the Avenue de l'Opéra, Paris, blowing six policemen to fragments, including the one who had been rash enough to carry it, and once again there were explosions, assassinations, executions that continued for decades.

In 1922, anarchists robbed a train travelling from Paris to Lyons, and one of them murdered an army officer who resisted. A few days later police arrested an anarchist called Jacques Mecislav Charrier, who had been overheard boasting of the robbery in a bar. Seven days after the robbery, acting on information forced from Charrier, police ambushed two men in the Rue des Ternes, Paris. Both men were killed; so was a police inspector.

Charrier declared in court: 'I am a desperate enemy of society and I defy you to take my head.' And although he screamed and pleaded for mercy as he was dragged to the guillotine, other French anarchists felt that the great war against the 'bloodhounds of capitalism' was going on.

In England, however, the situation had changed in favour of the police. To begin with, the English have always been traditionally lenient towards political offenders. When Karl Marx fled to England in 1850, he was amazed that the English police were unarmed, and that the authorities did not seem particularly concerned about the 'dangerous revolutionaries' in their midst. Anarchist and socialist clubs met openly, yet no one seemed worried. Jack the Ripper actually committed one of his murders – of Elizabeth Stride – in the backyard of one of these revolutionary clubs for foreign immigrants in 1888.

Marx was also astonished to find himself in a country where people seemed to quite like their policemen. The British bobby was usually an easy-going, kindly sort of man, and although there were still plenty of streets in London's East End where a policeman would never venture alone, no one actually regarded them as 'capitalist bullies'. Anybody who *wanted* to express that opinion was welcome to stand up on a soap box in Hyde Park and say so, while several bobbies looked benevolently on in case the crowd felt like attacking the speaker.

Two-hour Chase

A number of violent incidents actually caused widespread sympathy and support for the police. For example, there was the Tottenham outrage of 1909, when two young anarchists from the Baltic states tried to take a payroll from the men delivering it to Schurmann's rubber factory. The wages clerk struggled; shots were fired, and the two men fled. Unarmed policemen chased them. The first victim of the gunmen was a small boy, who fell dead. Next, a policeman named Tyler was shot through the neck and killed. The chase pounded on through back gardens and across allotments; more policemen were wounded.

In the Chingford Road, the men leapt on to a passing tram, and forced the conductor to drive it. An elderly passenger lost his nerve, and was shot in the throat. As the gunmen leapt off the tram, a milkman who ran towards them was shot in the chest. The men stopped a horse-drawn grocer's van and ordered the teenage driver to whip up the horse. Policemen on bicycles – one of them carrying a cutlass – hurtled after them.

Passing a policeman, one of the men fired, hitting him in the foot. The policeman blew his whistle and despite his wound joined in the chase. The anarchists leapt out of the van as their pursuers gained ground, and raced across fields again; at a fence, one of them fell. Before the police could reach him, he had shot himself through the brain, and he died later in hospital. Finally, the police cornered the other man in a cottage; two policemen burst into the child's bedroom where he was hiding, and shot him through the head. The chase had lasted two hours, and covered six miles. A policeman and a child had been killed, seven more policemen shot, and fourteen other people injured.

It was this kind of incident that rallied warm support around the British police. So did the shootings in Houndsditch a year later, when three policemen were killed and four more were injured by a gang of foreign burglars. When the Houndsditch affair culminated in the famous Siege of Sidney Street, everyone in England was delighted that the foreign desperadoes had been trapped. On the whole, the British public had decided that its police force was to be trusted.

Climate of Violence

The situation in America is different. The high incidence of police-murders is due less to public hostility than to the general climate of violence, and the permissive American gun laws. Two typical cases of 1971 – one in England, one in America – will serve to underline the difference between the two countries.

On the evening of June 27, 1971, Detective Constable Ian Coward, 29, was driving through Reading when he noticed a white Morris that was swinging across the road in a manner that suggested the driver was drunk. When the car stopped in front of a restaurant, he got out and approached it. There were two men inside. He asked the driver for his identification and the driver, a young, unshaven man, got out to look for it. Coward went back to his own car, got into the driver's seat, and told the man to get in beside him.

At this moment, the other man approached the police car, pulled a gun, and fired nine bullets into Coward. As the policeman fell across the seat and through the open passenger door, the other man kicked him. Then both ran back to their car and drove off. Incredibly, Coward was still alive. He was rushed to hospital, but on July 23 he died.

Witnesses to the shooting were able to pick out the two men from the 'rogue's gallery' of mug-shots. They were identified as Arthur Skingle, 25, and Peter Sparrow, 28. Both had criminal records, and Skingle, the gunman, had been released from prison – where he served a sentence for robbery with violence – only ten days earlier. The men drove the white Morris to a spot a few miles away, and set it on fire with petrol. It was a routine matter for the police to pick up the murderers, who were both sentenced to full life terms.

On November 29, 1971, Sergeant Mike McNeil of Albany, New York, pulled in a car driver for questioning. His driver's licence did not corres-pond to the car's registration number. While the driver was being interrogated at the section house, his three companions, who were waiting outside in the car, escaped.

Shot by a Woman

McNeil went after them, caught them up a block

away, and ordered them into his car. Before they climbed in, he frisked them. Even so, he missed a revolver in the pocket of Joseph Guerin, and when McNeil climbed into the driving seat Guerin shot him several times in the back of the head.

The killer ran off. The other two – a man and a woman – remained, and were able to give the police a lead that eventually led to Guerin's arrest. It was then discovered that Sergeant McNeil's killer was also wanted for grand larceny and robbery. He was sentenced to 'life'.

McNeil was the second Albany officer to die in three days. On the 26 November, Patrolman Edward Stevens was detailed to collect a woman and escort her to a mental home – where a court had ordered her to have treatment. As he knocked on her door, she fired through it with both barrels of a shotgun, killing him instantly.

Notorious Women

Who are the outrageous, sensual women whose
lust for life carries all before them? What makes them
thrive on wild passion, intrigue . . . and danger?

THE ORIGINAL scarlet woman was hardly a seductive siren. When she first makes her appearance, in the Book of Revelation, she has seven heads and ten horns – it is not clear how the horns are distributed among the heads – and is drunk with the blood of martyrs and saints. This makes it fairly clear that what Saint John the Divine had in mind was not some Babylonian Mae West, but the city of Rome. After the coming of Luther, Protestant theologians insisted that it was the Roman Catholic Church. It was a singularly unpromising beginning for what has become one of the great basic myths of the western world – and it is, essentially, a modern myth.

The ancient world experienced no feeling of morbid interest in the courtesan or prostitute. On the contrary, she was regarded as one of the foundation stones of a healthy society. The Babylonians took the view that every woman ought to have some experience of prostitution, so every woman in the land had to go to the temple of Venus – known as Mylitta – once in her life, and prostitute herself to a stranger.

The rule applied to everyone, from peasant girls to kings' daughters; in Phoenicia all virgins had to be ritually deflowered by a stranger before marriage. The inhabitants of Heliopolis, in Egypt, were so enraged when the Christian emperor Constantine put a stop to this custom that they burst into the temple, stripped the holy virgins naked, deflowered them, then disembowelled them, and encouraged the pigs to eat food from their stomach cavities.

In Cyprus a girl prostituted herself to earn money for her marriage portion, and her husband took great pride in a wife who had earned him a small fortune. Early European travellers in Africa were shocked to discover that the tribal whore was regarded as an almost sacred figure. Such a girl would be bought in the slave market and ritually initiated into her trade in a public ceremony. After that, she was given a hut on the edge of the village and had to give herself to any man, youth or child who wanted her.

If she was exceptionally young or desirable there was a queue at her door for the first week or so, and she might have to satisfy a hundred men a day. Working at that pace, she inevitably lost her good looks, and then the demand dropped off. Most of these tribal prostitutes died in a very short time of venereal disease, yet they were regarded as so essential to the well-being of the community that a tribal overlord who wanted to punish a village only had to confiscate the village whore to reduce everybody to total subjection.

The explanation, obviously, is that in primitive

societies there is no *idealization* of women. They are child-bearers, beasts of burden; the male's attitude towards her is thoroughly realistic, and this is how the women expect to be treated. But as a society becomes more 'civilized' a new class of woman develops. Her hands remain white, because she has servants; her body remains attractive well into middle-age, because she is not worn out with childbearing and drudgery. To a large part of the population such aristocratic ladies become remote, glamorous creatures; and the idea of romantic chivalry develops.

In Europe this happened some time around the age of King Arthur – about the 7th century AD – and, significantly enough, the stories of King Arthur involve one of the first of the legendary Scarlet Women, the sorceress Morgan Le Fay, King Arthur's wicked sister. She is beautiful – she never looks more than sixteen – and has had a convent education, but she studied magic under Merlin – who, in some versions, she seduces. She also tries to seduce Sir Lancelot, and generally spends her time making trouble and mischief.

These legends of King Arthur began to crystallize out around the thirteenth and fourteenth centuries. At roughly the same time Boccaccio was writing his famous – and scandalous – work *The Decameron*. In *The Decameron* the women are healthy and down-to-earth, and even Mother Superiors of convents are capable of seducing young gardeners. Yet a few centuries later *The Decameron* was a 'dirty book', banned in most countries. The old, carefree sexual morality of the

Middle Ages had given way to something more rigid and puritanical. 'Woman' was idealized. Consequently, the prostitute was regarded with a kind of horror.

Looking back on it, we can see that this was a thoroughly unhealthy state. Society was becoming sex-obsessed, in the worst possible way. A prostitute could be ducked in a wooden cage until she was half drowned, or made to walk through the streets in a half-shift, while 'respectable women' were allowed to slash and prick at her thighs. This clear division between 'respectable women' and 'loose women' was a product of a morbid attitude towards sex.

The Babylonians were altogether healthier when they made every woman prostitute herself once in a lifetime. This new obsession with respectability was really based on the notion that sex was a wicked activity that could only be disinfected by marriage, and that people who indulged in it without proper sanction were headed for damnation.

Dirty Books

Boccaccio had an amusing story in *The Decameron* about a randy monk who seduces an innocent girl by telling her that her vagina is Hell, and that his penis is the Devil, and that he will show her how to please God by putting the Devil in Hell. But in the seventeenth century people really believed it; a man who entered a strange vagina was headed straight for Hell. Not surprisingly, the very fact that sex was forbidden gave it an unhealthy attraction.

It is significant that there was very little pornography before the eighteenth century. There were plenty of books that were *later* considered pornographic, like *The Decameron, The Heptameron* by Queen Margaret of Navarre, and the *Lives of Gallant Ladies* by the Sieur de Brantôme. But real 'dirty books', written for sexually frustrated people – rather than people with a sense of humour – only started to appear in the mid-eighteenth century. John Cleland's famous *Fanny Hill* was one of the first of these, and Cleland was promptly offered a pension by the government if he would promise to write no more dirty books. The 'establishment' obviously felt that pornography was a real menace to the state.

Now anybody who has ever read *Fanny Hill*, which is now quite easily obtainable, will realize why it caused so much alarm. Fanny is unashamedly a Scarlet Woman. In those days women were supposed to be sternly virtuous. The most popular novel of the day was Samuel Richardson's *Clarissa*, in which the virtuous heroine is kidnapped by wicked Lovelace and finally drugged and raped; but she refuses to yield her virtue, or even to marry the villain, and when she escapes she eventually dies for her lost honour.

On the other hand, young Fanny Hill cheerfully allows herself to be seduced – admittedly by a man she loves – then to become an older man's mistress, then starts seducing handsome young lads for the pleasure of it . . . It was more than just pornography. It was a deliberate jeer at the current idea of female virtue. Cleland was saying: most women enjoy sex just as much as men, and if they 'lose their honour' they don't commit suicide; they make the best of it.

In 1761 Jean Jacques Rousseau created an even greater scandal with a book called *The New Heloise*, in which the pretty, virtuous heroine falls in love with her handsome young tutor and yields her virginity to him because she believes that when people are truly in love sex is no longer sinful. It is difficult now to understand the universal sense of shock caused by Rousseau's dangerous thesis. Less than two centuries earlier, Shakespeare's Antony and Cleopatra hopped into bed together without causing Queen Elizabeth any concern; but now the idea of female respectability was regarded as the bedrock of society.

Triumphant Vice

It is also significant that the vilest and most sickening pornography ever written was produced in the final years of the eighteenth century by the Marquis de Sade, a French nobleman who spent most of his life in prison because of his sexual misdemeanours. De Sade is absolutely obsessed by this 'virtuous' society that refuses to allow him to indulge his sexual inclinations as freely as he thinks he deserves, and the wickedest people in his works are always judges, priests and other pillars of society – who are invariably engaged in practising incest with their daughters, or raping convent girls.

De Sade wrote the ultimate attack on the idea of the virtuous woman: *Justine*, in which, from the first page onward, the chaste and innocent heroine is raped, sodomized and beaten. And at the end, just as her misfortunes seem to be over, she is struck by lightning. De Sade then followed up this tale of injured virtue with a story of triumphant vice, *Juliette*.

Juliette is Justine's sister, and she is undoubtedly the most scarlet of all scarlet women. There is no vice or wickedness that she doesn't enjoy. She even seduces her own long-lost father, and then has him murdered; and at the end of the book she is rich and happy. It is not surprising that they kept De Sade in a lunatic asylum – though his sanity was never in doubt – until he died. The 'virtuous society' had produced a man who rejected everything about it, who derided all its standards, and who insisted on trying to make it see its own face in a cracked distorting mirror.

Nausea of Lust

The nineteenth century – the age of ultimate respectability – produced a non-stop flood of pornography. One of its most remarkable characters was a mystery man who is known to posterity only as 'Walter'. He was a 'gentleman'; that is to say, he had enough money to devote most of his life to the untiring pursuit of sex.

He wrote the story of his endless sexual adventures in an astonishing document called *My Secret Life*, which is some 3,000 pages long. It is instructive to compare this remarkable book with the famous *Memoirs* of Casanova, written a century earlier. Casanova also spends his life in seduction, but he regards it as one of the legitimate pleasures of life, and is interested in many other subjects – magic, philosophy and literature, for example. Walter, on the other hand, broods morbidly and single-mindedly on sex. He cannot see a woman without wondering what she is like without her clothes on, and if she is a working-class girl he always makes an effort to find out.

During the course of the book he possesses some hundreds of women, describing most of them in detail: whores, married women, virgins, even a 10-year-old girl. A phenomenon like Walter would not have been possible two centuries earlier. Men simply took sex more for granted; it was like drinking or hunting or falconry, one of the pleasures of life, not something that produced a kind of nausea or lust. The German psychologist Ivan Bloch wrote a famous *History of English Morals* in the early twentieth century, and it is mostly a description of the dozens of perversions that could be encountered in Victorian England.

More recently Ronald Pearsall's remarkable book *The Worm in the Bud* has done the same thing. What is abundantly clear is that it was the Victorian obsession with morality and respectability that produced this explosion of morbid sexual obsession. In fact the Jack the Ripper murders were almost inevitable. The killer was undoubtedly some typical Victorian who had been brought up to think of sex as wholly sinful, and of prostitutes as an evil, degraded race. The truth, as we now know, is that most of the Ripper's victims were toothless, pathetic down-and-outs, and the only young one among them, Mary Kelly, was a strapping, boozy Irish doxy who could have knocked most men flat with a blow of her fist.

But for the average Victorian these women lived deliciously sinful lives. They even called them 'daughters of joy'. And the whores paid for their wicked pleasures with their horrible death at the hands of a satanic madman with a long knife . . . Jack the Ripper, like Dracula, has become an archetypal figure of world mythology.

But even in the time of the Ripper things were changing. The puritanical sex-morality had exerted its stranglehold on European society for about two centuries, and it was time for something new. It began on the Continent, notably in France. Because of their political upheavals – the Revolution, Napoleon, the Second Empire – the French had always been less conventional than their luckier neighbours.

While Dickens, Thackery and Trollope were writing novels for the Victorian family, Balzac and Dumas were writing about adultery and sexual intrigue, and their contemporary, George Sand – who was actually a woman – was shocking everybody by wearing men's clothes, smoking cigars and taking a succession of lovers. And in the second half of the century writers like Zola and Maupassant shocked even the French with their tales of adultery and prostitution. When an English publisher dared to issue a translation of Zola he was promptly thrown into jail.

Over Indulgence

Amazingly enough, the breath of scandal was also blowing from across the Atlantic. It was in 1855 that a thin quarto book called *Leaves of Grass* was printed in Brooklyn. The author was a journalist named Walt Whitman, and his 'free verse' celebrated the vastness of America – its many people, its rivers and cities – and also the sexual pleasures of healthy men and women coupling. No one could doubt Whitman's sincerity; yet this kind of frankness was almost frightening to the respectable Victorians, who even covered up table legs because the very mention of legs was enough to make ladies blush.

Whitman became a storm centre of controversy. His headquarters was a beer cellar beneath Broadway, run by a German called Pfaff. 'Pfaff's' became the 'bohemian' rendezvous of America. Everybody who visited New York in the 1860s looked in at Pfaff's, hoping to catch a glimpse of Walt Whitman – and also of the lady who was known as the Queen of Bohemia. Her name was Ada Clare, and she was beautiful, blonde, talented – and promiscuous.

She had begun her career, in the same year as the appearance of *Leaves of Grass*, by writing rather moving little love poems, devoid of literary merit, which were published in the New York weekly *Atlas*. Ada soon had a reputation as a fine poetess, and when she started coming to Pfaff's none of the male customers objected. She wrote a regular column in the newspapers. Now at this time one of the most sought-after males in America was a handsome young pianist called Louis Gottschalk. Women swooned at his recitals. He was also a composer, whose music is now once again becoming popular – his piano pieces in syncopated rhythms are said to be the true origin of jazz.

Louis was a Don Juan – in fact his early death was due to sexual over-indulgence. As soon as Ada Clare saw him she trembled with adoration. Gottschalk was never one to pass up an opportunity, and in no time at all he had made Ada pregnant. By the time her son was born, however, Gottschalk was giving concerts and seducing women at the other end of America. But Ada did not allow the disgrace to worry her. She continued to attend Pfaff's and to take lovers.

To begin with, she was in no way dependent on literature for her income – she owned property in the south. But she lost it in the Civil War, and from then on had to make her living by her pen – and also by stage appearances. She was not a good actress, but she was persistent. People streamed to see her because she had the reputation of being beautiful and wicked. She married an actor, and apparently settled down to becoming a faithful wife; but for her fellow-countrymen she remained the Queen of Bohemia, America's own Scarlet Woman.

Ada even wrote a novel describing her love affair with Gottschalk, and with Edwin Booth, the actor-brother of Lincoln's assassin. Then, in 1874, when she was 38 a tragic accident put an end to her career – and to her life. She was sitting in a chair at a dramatic agency when a small dog leapt into her lap. She continued to talk as she caressed the dog; suddenly it jumped at her face and bit her through the bridge of the nose.

The wound was not – apparently – serious or disfiguring, and it began to heal after being sterilized. But Ada was convinced the dog had rabies, and she died on March 4, 1874. The owner of the dog said it was not suffering from rabies; so it could be that Ada's death was due to fatigue and hysteria.

After Ada Clare, a series of scarlet women demolished the myth that women are innocent and sexless. There was Ada Mencken, the circus rider who rode in flesh-coloured tights that made her seem naked. On one occasion friends of the poet Swinburne decided that he needed a love affair, and paid Ada £10 to seduce him; but apparently the poet was overcome with nervousness and embarrassment, and remained a virgin. There was Lola Montez, the adventuress who caused the downfall of the Bavarian throne. There was the young French actress and novelist Colette, who not only wrote scandalously frank books but openly flaunted her lesbian love affairs.

There were actresses like Eleonora Duse and Sarah Bernhardt, whose love affairs were known all over Europe – Duse was known to be tragically in love with the Italian poet Gabriele D'Annunzio who, in true bohemian fashion, seduced and then deserted her. There was Isadora Duncan, the dancer, who bore a child to the actor Gordon Craig, and preached a fiery gospel of free love, and who also died tragically in 1927 when her scarf caught in the wheel of a car and strangled her.

But the woman who certainly did most to shatter the Victorian ideas on demure womankind was a pretty and voluptuous young woman called Marie Stopes. Born in 1880 of highly respectable parents, she was a brilliant student of science, and decided to become a doctor. In Japan, at the age of 27, she had an unhappy and unconsummated love affair with a Japanese professor. In America, in 1911, she met Dr. Reginald Gates and married him – then found he was impotent, and divorced him on the grounds that she was still *virgo intacta*.

Since she was a highly sensual and dominant young woman, this long frustration made her intensely unhappy, and out of this unhappiness she wrote a book called *Married Love*, which at once became a best-seller and made her famous. She married a rich man – a founder of the Avro aircraft firm – and launched a campaign for birth control. She sued Dr. Halliday Sutherland for libel when he declared that her methods were danger-ous. She was finally awarded a mere £100 dam-ages, but the case made her name known to every newspaper reader in England and America. Towards the end of her life she had the satisfac-tion of seeing many of her measures for birth control advocated by the Church of England – which had bitterly opposed her in earlier days – at the Lambeth Conference in 1958. She died later in the same year.

Women's Lib

We are now seeing the consequences of the work of Marie Stopes – and others like her. She may be regarded as the true founder of 'Women's Lib'; she certainly did more than anyone else to bring about our modern 'permissive society'. It is too soon to know whether all this will produce a happier society; but it will certainly produce a less frustrated – and therefore healthier – one.

NOTORIOUS WOMEN: CASE STUDY

Operation Madame Kitty

In its heyday the elegant building in Berlin's Giesebrechtstrasse enjoyed the rapt attentions of an endless stream of male visitors. This was Kitty Schmidt's kingdom, where she ruled over a bevy of the sexiest girls in all Germany. They had been chosen for their looks, their charms and their skill in the art of spying on their distinguished, but unsuspecting clients.

ACCORDING TO city records, Kitty Schmidt owned the 'Pension Schmidt', an anonymous-looking rooming-house at 11, Giesebrechtstrasse. Everyone in fashionable Berlin in the late 1930s, however, knew that the Pension was a front for the city's most luxurious and discreet brothel. At

57 Kitty was Berlin's most celebrated 'Madame'.

The Pension Schmidt was frequented by some of the most distinguished and influential figures in German society, by diplomats and government officials, by high-ranking officers, by famous names from the stage and movies.

They were catered for by the cream of the profession. Kitty's girls were trained to pander to every whim, to flatter, to flirt, sometimes just to listen patiently while their customers poured out their problems. Madame Kitty's fees were extremely high. What made it all worthwhile to the visitors who slipped in through the door of No. 11 was not the fine food and wines from her cellars, the expensive decor or even the all-embracing charms of the girls, but the atmosphere of absolute discretion which shrouded the establishment like the rich velvet curtains in Kitty's parlour.

TIME TO GO?

But, for some time, Kitty had seen the writing on the brothel wall. The rise to power of Adolf Hitler had been reflected in a subtle change in her type of clientele. Roughnecks from the Brownshirts and SS had gradually replaced her favourite Jewish bankers and industrialists. The police, who for so long had turned a benevolent eye to the Pension Schmidt – indeed, the Chief of Police was one of her most devoted customers – had begun to harass her. Somehow, Kitty felt, there was no longer any room for her individual kind of trade in the new regime.

That was why she had started to salt away her takings in Britain. By 1939 she had transferred hundreds of thousands of dollars to bank accounts in London – mainly through the aid of Jewish refugees she had helped from Berlin. On June 28 she decided it was time to slip out of Germany and join her money.

SUAVE AND DEVIOUS

She had got as far as the frontier between Germany and Holland when a hand fell on her shoulder. Kitty spun round, to stare into the unsmiling face of a secret agent of the SD – the Sicherheitsdienst, the Nazi Central Security Organization. She had been followed from the moment she left the capital.

It took two weeks of softening-up in the cellars of the Prinz Albrechtstrasse – the Berlin head-quarters of the Gestapo – before Kitty Schmidt was judged ready to meet the suave and devious head of the SD, SS-Obersturmführer Walter Schellenberg.

Schellenberg wasted no time on courtesies. 'You're in trouble,' he said icily. 'Big trouble.' He leafed through the dossier in front of him. 'You realize the crimes you have committed?' Helplessly, Kitty Schmidt shook her head.

Schellenberg spread the fingers of one hand and ticked off the incriminating litany on each finger. 'Helping Jews to escape – don't deny it, we have the evidence – illegally exchanging German marks for foreign currency, illegally transferring money out of the country, attempting to leave Germany without permission and travelling on a forged passport. I have no need to remind you of the penalties for such crimes?'

UNGOVERNABLE APPETITES

Kitty Schmidt had read the newspapers. She knew that the punishment for at least one of the offences was death, with a living death in a concentration camp for the others. So why the lecture? Kitty's intuition told her that there was more to it than that. Schellenberg drew slowly on a cigarette. 'Of course,' he said, 'if you can do something for me, I may be able to do something for you. Are you willing to co-operate?' Kitty knew she had no choice. 'Anything, Obersturmführer,' she said. 'Anything you say.'

Kitty Schmidt was a woman of the world. She had earned her money the hard way and in her long and lurid life she thought she had heard everything. But the proposition Walter Schellenberg proceeded to make caused even her hardened jaw to sag.

In exchange for her freedom, she was virtually to hand over her brothel to the SD. There were no explanations. Schellenberg pushed an 'Official Secrets' form across the desk and ordered her to sign it. The first clause read, 'Any attempt to divulge Classified Information will be punishable by death.' Trembling, Kitty signed. 'You can now go,' said Schellenberg, 'but report to my office every day.'

Operation 'Salon Kitty' had started. Later that day, Schellenberg marched briskly into the office of Gruppenführer Reinhard Heydrich – head of the entire Gestapo network – snapped 'Heil Hitler!' and saluted.

Reinhard Heydrich, later to achieve infamy as 'The Butcher of Prague', was one of the most frightening administrators thrown up by the Nazi Party. Ruthless, intelligent, and ambitious, he had all the warmth of an icefloe and – according to Schellenberg – 'ungovernable sexual appetites'. He was also a man of few words. 'Well?' he said. 'Everything went perfectly,' replied Schellenberg. 'We can now go ahead with our plans to – ah, reorganize – the Pension Schmidt.'

Heydrich twisted his features into a passable imitation of a smile. 'Excellent, Obersturmfuhrer!' he said. Operation Salon Kitty had been Heydrich's idea from the start. For some time the Gestapo had been concerned about careless security leaks in high places. With Germany rapidly nearing a war footing, it was essential to stem idle chatter, and – even more vital – to identify the chatterers. There was nothing like wine and beautiful women to loosen a man's tongue, Heydrich had concluded. So what better than to infiltrate an exclusive brothel and use the girls as intelligence agents, reporting back to the SD any items of value they overheard?

It was Schellenberg who had added the extra refinements. Why stop there? he had asked. Why not take over the brothel completely and use it as a vast intelligence clearing-house? Security-leak suspects, and persons under surveillance, could easily be steered unawares to the brothel. It could also be used to glean information from visiting dignitaries, foreign diplomats, and embassy staff.

There was no need to rely on Madame Kitty's girls. They could install a team of girls, specially trained in intelligence techniques, who would encourage the customers to talk freely, watching out for any indiscretions. The girls would file immediate written reports as soon as the customers left.

RACIAL PURITY

But as a final safeguard – unknown to anyone except the highest security officials – all the rooms would be bugged, the wires leading down to a nerve-centre in the basement. Here, a team of agents working in shifts could monitor, and record on disc every word uttered, confided, breathed, sighed, or exclaimed in the entire establishment. Schellenberg's electronic voyeurs could become the third ear of Nazi internal security.

Heydrich had given the go-ahead. Now the first stage in Operation Salon Kitty had been achieved. They had got their brothel. There was one monumental snag, however. They had not got the girls. That was the problem that landed on the desk of Untersturmführer Karl Schwarz of the SD – the luckless agent delegated to organize the complete transformation of the Pension Schmidt.

Schwarz's first recruiting drive was a disaster. In what struck him as a brilliant stroke, he enlisted the services of the Lebensborn, the much-vaunted organization which undertook to bring together superb specimens of Aryan manhood and womanhood for the purpose of breeding babies of undeniable racial purity. Schwarz's memorandum to the heads of the organization left little room for misconstruction.

'A situation has arisen.' he wrote, 'where we urgently need a group of women who are intelligent, attractive, have unwavering faith in the ideals of the Nazi Party and, preferably, possess a knowledge of foreign languages.' The main qualification, however, was a liking for members of the opposite sex. The unspecified – but unmistakable – job would, he said, 'be a wonderful opportunity for serving Führer and Fatherland'. There was not one reply. Breeding for the Führer was one thing, soliciting was another.

EYE-STOPPING AGENTS

Undismayed, Schwarz turned to the only other alternative. Since the amateurs weren't interested, he would have to try the professionals. During the next few weeks, the Berlin vice squad carried out an unprecedented number of raids on brothels, nightclubs, 'dance bars', and other known haunts of prostitutes.

Hundreds of girls were rejected outright as being 'emotionally unreliable'. Many others were closely questioned by teams of investigators. Eventually, the 'possibles' were winnowed down to a short-list of about ninety. Schwarz himself, aided by a group of psychiatrists, doctors, language consultants, and university professors, made the final selection.

The twenty girls who emerged successfully from the seven days of non-stop tests and interrogation were certainly the most eye-stopping agents ever to write their names in invisible ink. A few days later, the girls were transferred to the officers' Academy at Sonthofen – where a sealed-off wing had been set aside for their training.

For seven weeks they underwent arduous courses in foreign languages, unarmed combat, home and foreign politics, marksmanship, economics, the use of codes and ciphers, and general intelligence techniques. Experts in cookery, make-up, and hygiene gave lectures. They had to memorize posters and wall charts illustrating military uniforms and decorations. Interviewers from German radio demonstrated how conversation could be used to draw out information. There was even a grim, severe-looking woman to instil the rules of etiquette.

Meanwhile, Untersturmführer Schwarz was seeing to the 'redecoration' of the Pension Schmidt. The entire place was gutted. Under the pretext of renewing the electrical wiring, microphones were installed in all the bedrooms, corridors, and reception rooms – with the leads joining in a multi-core cable which ran along the guttering and down a drainpipe to the listening-post in the cellar.

The cellar was completely rebuilt and bricked off, and contained five monitoring desks, each housing two record-turntables. Conversations in all seven bedrooms, Kitty's 'reception' parlour, her own private room, and the kitchen could be recorded simultaneously on wax discs. On a tour of inspection, Walter Schellenberg was delighted. The place was as replete with bugs as a flophouse mattress. 'I only hope,' he said, 'that the Salon Kitty lives up to expectations.'

As it turned out, Operation Salon Kitty was to exceed their most audacious hopes. On March 25, 1940, Madame Kitty sat in the parlour of the magnificently refurbished Pension Schmidt and waited for Untersturmführer Karl Schwarz to reveal the part she was expected to play in the heady new life of the brothel.

'You will be told no more than is absolutely necessary,' he began. 'Business will carry on as before, and you will continue to welcome all your old customers as if nothing had changed. If they enquire about the redecoration, you can explain that the place was getting a little shabby. Your existing staff of girls can stay, but there will be one small difference.'

Schwarz reached into a mock-leather briefcase and pulled out a large album. It contained a selection of eyebrow-raising pictures of his twenty 'horizontal agents', each girl identified by a typed list of personal details.

UNWITTING CLIENT

'Every now and again, we will direct a certain customer to your premises,' he said stiffly. 'Under no account will you introduce him to one of your girls. You will show him this album, and when he makes his choice you will phone for the girl in question, and she will arrive within ten minutes. You will not discuss the client with her, and she will leave immediately the man has gone.'

Kitty Schmidt knew a set-up when she saw one, but she said nothing. 'How will I recognize one of your special clients?' was all she asked. 'Simple,' said Schwarz with a self-satisfied smirk. 'He will introduce himself with the code phrase "I come from Rothenburg". As soon as you hear that, you know what to do.'

The time had come to test the system. The un-witting test client chosen to 'launch' the Salon Kitty was Wolfgang Reichert, a young SS officer on leave in Berlin. Steering him to the salon was pimp's play. 'Just say you come from Rothenburg,' Schwarz winked. 'I can promise you an orgy of a time.' So, on April 8, 1940, Schwarz and other high-ranking SD officers listened-in gleefully to the 'opening performance' in the basement monitoring-room.

At first, Reichert was a disappointment. As the microphones followed his progress from parlour to bedroom, he babbled on about his home, his relatives, his friends in the SS, and his fervent regard for the Führer. It sounded more like a recruiting advertisement than a security leak. Then the girl got to work. 'I bet you want to see some real fighting soon . . .' she cooed. Reichert rose to the bait. To the horror of the eaves-droppers in the cellar, he started bragging about his unit's imminent transfer to Flensburg.

'If you ask me,' he boasted, 'the Führer's got his

eye on Sweden.' 'It works, it works!' cackled Schwarz, forgetting for the moment that the young officer had just let slip a vital piece of top-secret information. Salon Kitty was in business. Two hours later, the girl filed her written report, unaware that the entire conversation had already been recorded and forwarded to Gestapo head-quarters, and that her talkative companion was heading for court-martial.

STATUESQUE BLONDE

As more 'Rothenburgers' were fed into the pipe-line, Salon Kitty flourished as never before. Schwarz's twenty girls were soon loving round the clock. Shorter shifts were introduced as the monitoring teams slumped exhausted over their turntables. The attractions of the brothel were being increasingly touted among the country's high-ups, and Madame Kitty's guest-list read like an official reception for the Führer.

When the Rothenburgers started out-numbering the genuine customers, Kitty complained that not only was the place running at a loss, she could no longer keep up with the demand for rationed food and alcohol. 'Ignore the official rationing system,' said Schwarz blandly. 'We'll organize special supplies. As for money, put in your expenses for every Rothenburg customer.'

The customers, both contrived and genuine, poured in. In 1940, nearly 10,000 people climbed up to the third floor of No. 11 Giesebrechtstrasse. At its peak, the monitoring team were recording

3000 love-session discs a month. The 'stars' of the records were some of the biggest names in international diplomacy.

Sometimes the listening team got more than they bargained for. The Italian-speaking female agent who slid between the sheets with the Italian Foreign Minister, Count Galeazzo Ciano, was treated to a blistering tirade on the inadequacies of Adolf Hitler as a statesman, politician, soldier, lover, and family-man. In the basement, ears patriotically burned. Count Ciano then turned to Italy's prospects in the war, and scattered an incredible amount of vital information before he remembered his reason for getting into bed. Schwarz was alerted, and a transcript of the pillow talk was sent to Hitler. Relations between Germany and Italy were never the same again.

There was more embarrassment when the roistering, bucolic Major-General Sepp Dietrich – commander of the *SS Leibstandarte*, Hitler's private bodyguard – bounced into the Salon Kitty, bellowing the 'Rothenburg' code-word. 'Don't show me one tart,' he shouted jovially as Madame Kitty flipped through the album. 'Bring the lot! I want to see them on parade!'

While a maid plied Dietrich and his companions with beer, Kitty frantically phoned the number given to her by Schwarz. 'Round up as many of your friends as you can,' she said, 'we've got a party.' In the bedroom, the monitoring team were impressed by Dietrich's performance, particularly his sweeping command of sexual vocabulary, delivered in a thick Bavarian accent. But there were no dropped secrets. He fell asleep after an hour, the girl in one hand and a champagne bottle in the other.

The 'Rothenburg' password only slipped up once. One evening, a soldier appeared at the door and, after some preliminary mumbles, announced 'I'm from Rothenburg'. He didn't look as if he would know a secret if he tripped over one, but Kitty was taking no chances. The man thumbed through the album, eyes popping like wine corks. Eventually, he settled for Isolde, a statuesque blonde twice his size, who looked as though she had just stepped out of a Wagnerian opera.

The eavesdroppers in the basement were bewildered as the man revealed to the girl while undressing that he was a private in an infantry regiment on leave from the front. One banality followed another. However hard the girl tried, the only coherent sentence she could get out of him was, 'How wonderful it will be to get back to the farm after all this is over.' One of the monitoring team took off his earphones. 'Who on earth sent this idiot?' he demanded. Months later, the truth came out. The man was a cowhand named Krebs . . . from Rothenburg.

CRACKPOT PLAN

Nobody was too important to be funnelled into Salon Kitty. On September 23, 1940, a telephone call warned Kitty Schmidt to be ready for a party of distinguished guests. 'Make sure you pick girls who speak Spanish,' said the caller. Thirty minutes later, the bell rang. Standing at the door were the German Foreign Minister, Joachim von Ribbentrop, his Spanish opposite number, Don Ramon Serrano Suñer, and a group of Foreign Office officials. Kitty Schmidt had more important visitors than she realised, however. Down in the cellars, Walter Schellenberg himself had arrived to eavesdrop on the Foreign Minister. It was not a wasted hour. Locked in the parlour, Ribbentrop outlined a crackpot plan to Suñer involving the occupation of Gibraltar – which would have placed Germany under an impossible obligation to Spain.

Schellenberg scurried out of the building with the transcript and immediately telephoned his boss, Reinhard Heydrich. 'It's monstrous!' said the Gruppenführer, secretly delighted at being handed fresh weapons to use in his long vendetta against von Ribbentrop. Heydrich reported the conversation to Heinrich Himmler, Hitler's head of the SS, who took steps to have the plan squashed instantly.

With his highly sharpened sexual tastes, it wasn't long before Heydrich yielded to desire and started visiting Salon Kitty, usually in the guise of a 'tour of inspection'. The inspection invariably took in several of the girls. 'On these occasions,' Schellenberg recalled in his *Memoirs*, 'I was given special orders to turn off the listening and recording apparatus.'

BRITISH AGENT

It was towards the end of the year that their most unwelcome guest almost literally stumbled across the existence of Salon Kitty. Lljubo Kolchev, a junior press secretary at the Rumanian Embassy, chose to wander down Giesebrechtstrasse at the exact moment that Untersturmführer Karl Schwarz was supervising the re-routing of the monitor wires to a new listening post at the SD head-quarters at Meineckestrasse.

Kolchev almost tripped over the wires, and Schwarz involuntarily leaned forward to steady him. Kolchev took in the whole scene in a flash: the obvious SD man in civilian clothes, the workmen who looked more like soldiers, the multi-core cable running down the drainpipe, the general air of furtive hurry. He knew Salon Kitty was on the third floor of No. 11, and the 'Rothen-burg' password had already been bandied about the Rumanian Embassy.

'It's an intelligence set-up!' he thought. 'A love-and-listen centre.' He was well qualified to judge. For Lljubo Kolchev was in fact Roger Wilson, a British Intelligence agent operating in Berlin.

It was fortunate for Wilson that he was hand-some, and something of a sexual athlete. For Control in London ordered him to keep tabs on Salon Kitty without arousing any suspicion. 'We will be sending you a technician to see if there is any possibility of tapping the wires for our own use,' he was told.

Kolchev, alias Wilson, became a regular visitor

to the salon, keeping his eyes and ears open even at the most ecstatic moments. Eventually, his communications expert arrived. Under cover of darkness, he managed to tap two or three of the individual leads in the multi-core cable. Now the bugs had bugs, and from the end of 1940 the British Secret Service was supplied with titbits from Salon Kitty.

But the golden days of Madame Kitty's speak-your-fate machine were waning. As Allied bombing raids on Berlin became more frequent, the flood of customers dried to a nervous trickle, and the monitoring teams had little to transcribe except for ardent and climactic monosyllables. Heydrich was also using the recordings more and more as ammunition in his inter-departmental feuds at Gestapo Headquarters. In 1941, he ordered the monitoring centre to be moved to Prinz Albrechtstrasse, under his own control.

On July 17, 1942, the line from No. 11 went dead. The monitoring team tried everything, but they couldn't restore communications. Then the news was phoned in: 'A bomb has just hit Kitty's.' The indefatigable Untersturmführer Karl Schwarz raced to the scene, his main concern being to spirit away the bugging equipment before anyone discovered it. The upper floors of No. 11 had been demolished. Kitty Schmidt's elegant furniture, carpets, and curtains were scattered all over Giesebrechtstrasse. Schwarz threw an army cordon round the building, and ordered his men to retrieve anything in sight and store it in the cellar.

Soot-blackened and awry, Kitty Schmidt stood

watching as the firemen rolled up their hoses and the soldiers left the shell of No. 11. 'Report to me tomorrow,' said Schwarz as he climbed into his car. With a determined lift of his chin, he added, 'Salon Kitty will rise again!'

When Schwarz had a problem, everyone associated with him shared it. Before the day was out, squads of workmen arrived to convert the relatively undamaged ground floor into a new salon. For 48 hours they struggled non-stop. On July 19 Salon Kitty reopened for boudoir business. Even Schwarz had to admit, however, that it was no longer possible to use electronic equipment to monitor the rooms. He had to rely on written reports.

But Salon Kitty had outlived its usefulness. The Nazi hierarchy had learned that it was one huge megaphone, eager to amplify and transmit their innermost thoughts, for or against the Führer. The diplomats, the officials and the officers drifted away, leaving it to soldiers on leave and old friends of Kitty's. Discipline began to slacken among the 'Rothenburg' girls, and drunken parties – strictly forbidden by Schwarz – went on far into the night, to the sound of bombs, sirens, and anti-aircraft guns.

The salon had served its purpose. In the beginning of 1943 surveillance activities were officially wound up and the premises handed back to Kitty Schmidt, now 60, fat and haggard, and looking her age. Most of the 'Rothenburg' girls had come to like the place, and they agreed to carry on as her normal 'staff'. Before the salon was returned to her, Kitty Schmidt had to sign a second form, swearing not to divulge anything she had seen, heard, or understood of 'Operation Salon Kitty'. The penalty for betraying this was death.

EXTRAORDINARY STORY

Within two years the Russians were at the gates of Berlin, now reduced to a wilderness of smoking rubble. The precious discs, so carefully stored in indexed filing cabinets at Gestapo headquarters, vanished. In 1954 huge crowds turned out for the funeral of Kitty Schmidt. She had honoured her word. To her dying day she never spoke about the secret of No. 11 Giesebrechtstrasse.

But the rumours about the hidden microphones, the highly trained girls and the turntables in the cellar persisted. Only one man ever got on the right trail. For 25 years author Peter Norden investigated the extraordinary story of the love-nest-with-ears for his book, Madame Kitty (Abelard-Schuman). Only one thing eluded him: the whereabouts of the missing discs.

One day in 1963 he walked into a top-secret strongroom in the headquarters of the East German State Security Services in Communist East Berlin. And there they were, 25,000 of them . . . the silent graveyards of long-ago love, lust, and loose tongues.

Fireraisers

Prometheus stole fire from the Gods: his punishment
was to lie chained to a rock, while an eagle endlessly
tore at his liver. Some fireraisers suffer gnawing anguish,
mixed with sexual pleasure, while others, like Samuel
Furnace, use fire for gain . . .

'DURING THE FIRING of the haystacks, the thought
that human beings might be burnt added to the
sensations that I experienced. I always watched
the fires, usually from near at hand, so near in fact
that I have been asked to give a helping hand . . .
The shouting of the people and the glare of the
fire pleased me. During the big fires, I always had
an orgasm. If you see in my confession, sometimes several arsons in one night, then I had no
success with the first or the second. I also had an
orgasm when I fired the woods. It was a lovely
sight when one pine after another was consumed
in the flames fanned by a sharp east wind . . . that
was wonderful.'

This extract is from the confessions of the arch
sexual-pervert, Peter Kürten, the monster of
Düsseldorf, and it introduces us to the most
baffling of all sexual abnormalities: pyromania.
Even today, little is known of this frightening
urge. It is pointedly ignored in most textbooks of
clinical psychiatry. Perhaps this is understandable.

Anybody can understand a rapist or even a sadist, because there is a fragment of them in every one of us. But how can a normal human being understand someone who obtains sexual satisfaction from watching a fire?

We can obtain some insight into this complex process from a confession quoted by Dr. Melvin Reinhardt, in his classic study *Sex Perversions and Sex Crimes*. He cites the case of a 14-year-old boy who, with three other boys, was smoking cigarettes in a hay barn. Someone unintentionally tossed a cigarette butt into the hay; the barn caught fire, and all four ran away. The boy felt an odd compulsion to stop and watch; he stayed behind bushes, and observed the arrival of police and firemen. This *could*, of course, have been normal curiosity – most people like seeing a fire. But he also noted that he had vague sexual thrills from the sight of the flames. As he read about the blaze in the newspaper the next day, he again experienced the same excitement, and a compulsion to go and start another fire. This time the thrill was even stronger. Finally, by the time he was watching his fourth fire, the intensity was so great that he masturbated. He was caught and sent to a reformatory.

There *are* other psychological elements here that we can recognize: for example, his delight as he read the newspaper headlines, and thought that no one but he knew who was responsible. This is straightforward ego-satisfaction, and it undoubtedly plays a part in pyromania. The psychiatrist Dr. Wilhelm Stekel has commented that most pyromaniacs are unhappy, drifting individuals, who feel themselves rejected by society. They often suffer from strong feelings of inferiority. Even so, this fails to explain how or why fire is associated with sexual feeling.

It becomes somewhat clearer in another case cited by Reinhardt, involving an extraordinary, complex web of sexual emotions. The father of a family of three girls, all in their teens, had ceased to have sexual relations with his wife. His sexual desires became fixated on the 14-year-old daughter. One day, he met her out of school, drove her to a quiet lane, and had intercourse with her. The girl admitted in her statement to the police: 'For two or three times, Daddy removed my panties . . . then I began liking it.' Like many young girls she was infatuated with her father.

For the next three years they continued to have sexual intercourse two or three times a week, and he also encouraged her to stimulate him orally. One night, the mother heard her daughter going to the father's bed. There was a violent quarrel, and she threatened to report him to the police. It was after this that he began to brood on killing his wife and one of the other daughters. (The third was away from home.) He then enlisted the aid of the incestuous daughter, who alleged: 'He said he wouldn't interfere with me any more if I helped to poor gasoline on the floor.'

On the afternoon of the murder, he met his youngest daughter, Ruth (age 13), in the kitchen and hit her violently in the stomach, knocking her unconscious. When his wife came in, he also struck her with his fists; he was obviously a powerful man, for three blows laid her out, too. The eldest daughter then came in; they both soaked the kitchen (and the unconscious wife and daughter) in paraffin. As they left, the man tossed a match into the room. As the place burst into flames, he drove off, went shopping, went for a swim, and then returned home, and found the fire engines there and the house burnt out. The empty paraffin cans gave the police the clue to the fire.

In this case, it would seem as if the fire was started as an attempt to cover up the crime. Understandably, no policeman of 50 years ago would have assumed there was any sexual element in the case. On the other hand, there is one highly significant point. In a carefully planned murder, the killer does not leave empty paraffin cans to suggest that the fire was started deliberately. However, every criminologist has observed that there are many cases of murder in which the killer seems to *want* to get caught. He does something that will provide an obvious clue: for example, parks his car near the scene of a murder, or leaves some article of clothing behind. This desire to expiate guilt happens most frequently in cases of sex murder. It appeared to apply to the present case, and was undoubtedly the reason that led Dr. Reinhardt to classify it with other examples of pyromania. After three years of sexual intercourse with his daughter, the father felt a burden of guilt, and the fire was a strange, twisted attempt to *burn away* the guilt. This could well resolve the otherwise inexplicable relation between sex and fire. Fire is a symbol of purity, and the self-divided pyromaniac simultaneously longs for purity and is sexually excited by it. This is confirmed by another curious observation made by many criminologists: that the pyromaniac often feels the need either to urinate or empty his bowels when he sees the flames.

In *The Sexual Criminal*, Dr. Paul de River mentions two female pyromaniacs - middle-aged, sexually frigid women - who felt a compulsion to stoop down and urinate as they watched the fires they had started, and a burglar who had to hide in bushes and empty his bowels after he had watched a fire. In all these cases, the criminal confessed to an immense feeling of relief *and purification* after the act – all of which seems to suggest the psychological explanation of this mystery.

Most people know what it's like to feel thoroughly oppressed by their everyday life, and to want simply to run away from problems. The inadequate personality feels like that all the time – which explains why, as Stekel says, he is often a drifter; he keeps on running away. There is an exhilarating finality about a fire; for example, if you burn old love letters or diaries, it is like watching your own past go up in flames. In a weak, vacillating person, flames may become associated with a feeling of delight and relief – just as the Russian physiologist Pavlov taught dogs to salivate when he rang a bell, because they *associated* it with dinner.

So the pyromaniac starts fires because each one brings this sense of relief, of a new start – as well as satisfying a basic resentment against the civilization that oppresses him. (The pyromaniac burglar cited by de River did not *always* set fire to the apartment; sometimes he only lowered his trousers and defecated on the carpet; this seems to prove the association between fire and resentment.) Finally, it is easy to understand how two completely different forms of relief – fire and sex – can become associated, in the same 'Pavlovian' way.

This, then, is probably the basic psychology of the pyromaniac. There is evidence to suggest that, to some extent, it applies to *all* criminals who use fire as their 'final solution'. For some deep, atavistic reason, human beings have the feeling that fire can solve any problem whose solution seems to demand total destruction. This explains why witches and heretics were burned, and why the Nazis constructed ovens in their death camps. We can also see the same psychology at work in the case of Alfred Rouse, the English burning car murderer, and of the aptly named Samuel Furnace, whose crime was probably inspired by Rouse.

Numerous Clues

In January 1933, Furnace, a builder of Camden Town, north London, killed a rent collector named Spatchett, stole £40 he was carrying, and then incinerated the body by setting fire to a shed that served him as an office. The corpse was assumed to be of Furnace – until the pathologist noticed that it had been shot in the back of the head. A nationwide murder hunt for Furnace followed.

He wrote a letter to his brother-in-law, asking him to meet him in Southend-on-Sea, near London, and the brother-in-law informed the police. In prison, Furnace managed to poison himself by drinking a bottle of hydrochloric acid that he had sewn into the lining of his coat. A detailed study of the case reveals that Furnace was undoubtedly an 'inadequate personality'. To begin with, he was not (like Rouse) heavily in debt – only to the extent of £90. And his suicide revealed the same basic failure to face up to the consequences of his own actions.

This 'psychology of inadequacy' can be seen in an otherwise somewhat commonplace murder that took place in Ypsilanti, Michigan, in 1931. Three ex-convicts had been drinking moonshine whisky, and then decided to go out and rob someone. They found four 16-year-olds in a car in a lovers' lane, held them up, and robbed them of two dollars. One of the girls was then dragged out of the car and raped. The others resisted, and all were battered to death or shot. The robbers next set the car on fire. Because of numerous clues they left behind, they were placed under arrest within a few hours. A court tried the case and sentenced them to life imprisonment in record time – there was a howling mob outside the courthouse, hoping to lynch the men.

A more recent American case makes the link between incendiarism and inadequacy even plainer. Gerry Cornwell who was a 32-year-old mechanic, who lived in Oakland, California. Until a few weeks before Christmas, 1955, he had lived with his mistress, an ex-waitress, Alice Franklin, who was three years older than himself. Then Alice transferred her affections to a 27-year-old steelworker, Robert Hand. Cornwell quietly moved out of the apartment. He actually remained on fairly good terms with his ex-mistress and her lover, and on the night of the murder had been at a party with them.

He was drunk, and followed them back home to 5955 Telegraph Avenue; hiding outside the bedroom window, he watched them make love, then fall into an alcoholic slumber. He went to a nearby garage, bought three gallons of petrol, then walked into the bedroom – where the lovers snored on – and drenched the bed in petrol. As he went out, the pilot light of the stove ignited the petrol fumes. Firemen rushed the victims to hospital, but both died a few hours later. The police had no difficulty in locating Cornwell, who confessed. An interesting legal point arose at the trial – whether Cornwell could be charged with murder when he had not actually struck the match that ignited the petrol. The judge, however, pointed out that it was undoubtedly his intention to kill his mistress and her lover, and he was found guilty and sentenced to life imprisonment. Cornwell's inadequacy appears throughout: handing over the apartment to his rival, remaining friendly with the lovers, following them back to the apartment to watch them make love – a strong touch of masochism here – and the blind rage that is so typical of the inadequate personality when pushed too far.

No account of fire-raisers would be complete without some account of 'the German Rouse cases' – although, in many ways, they fail to fit into the general pattern or pyromania. The first case actually took place a year before Rouse murdered an unknown tramp on the Northampton road. Kurt Erich Tetzner was also a commercial traveller, but in 1929 business was poor. One day, his mother-in-law told him she had cancer, and that her only hope was an operation; her chances of surviving it were only 50/50. Tetzner dissuaded her – for just long enough to insure her life for the equivalent of £500. (Because of her cancer, he was unable to make it more.)

Then he persuaded her to have the operation after all. His gamble paid off; she died three days later. Tetzner was amazed and charmed at the ease with which one could get money out of the insurance companies. He discussed with his wife how they could repeat the *coup*. She suggested a plan that was virtually the same as Rouse's: to get a body from a graveyard and burn it in his own car. Tetzner disagreed about the graveyard. 'There must be blood around,' he said.

He tried advertising for a 'travelling companion'. A young man applied, but something in Tetzner's manner made him suspicious, and he changed his mind. Next, Tetzner picked up a hitchhiker on the road to Munich. The man's name was Alois Ortner, and he was an out-of-work mechanic. In a town called Hof, Tetzner gave him money to have a shave and buy himself a collar and tie. Then, outside the town, he asked the mechanic to check an oil leak under the car.

As soon as the man disappeared, Tetzner seized a hammer and an ether pad. If he had waited until Ortner's head appeared, and then hit him while he was still under the car, Tetzner might have succeeded. But in his excitement, he allowed Ortner to emerge before he attacked him. The mechanic fought back fiercely, then ran away into the woods. But apparently he failed to report the incident.

On November 25, 1929, Tetzner picked up another hitchhiker, a thinly clad youth of 21, whose name Tetzner never found out. The youth complained of being cold, so Tetzner wrapped him in the travelling rug. When his arms were tightly pinioned, he grabbed a piece of rope and strangled the youth. Near Ettershausen, he crashed the car into a tree, put the body in the driving seat, and sprinkled it with petrol. Then he laid a trail of petrol back to the car and set it on fire.

Phone Calls from Strasbourg

Tetzner was more fortunate than Rouse; he was not seen as he ran away. The burnt-out car was found; his wife identified the corpse as that of her husband, and it was buried. She now applied to the insurance company for the 145,000 marks for which Tetzner had insured his life (more than £50,000 in present-day terms).

However, the insurance officials were suspicious; to begin with, the slightly built corpse was not really like Tetzner. They contacted the Leipzig police, who kept a man on permanent duty watching Frau Tetzner. During the next few days, she was twice called to the telephone in a neighbour's flat. The neighbour told the police that the call was from Strasbourg and that the caller identified himself as 'Herr Stranelli'.

The police then asked their Strasbourg colleagues to check on a Herr Stranelli, who was probably thick-set, and had a podgy face with pig-like eyes. When a detective from Leipzig arrived, the Strasbourg police already had 'Stranelli' in custody. It was, as they had suspected, Tetzner.

Tetzner at first confessed to the murder, then withdrew the confession. His story in court was that he had accidentally knocked down the young man and killed him. He had placed the corpse in the boot of his car, and gone for supper. During the meal, he suddenly realized he could carry out his plan to disappear. . . . A forensic expert from Leipzig University supported his story, saying that injuries to the body suggested it had been run over. But the jury disbelieved it, and Tetzner was condemned to death. He was executed at Regenburg on May 2, 1931.

A young man named Fritz Saffran read about Tetzner's crime with great interest. He was manager of a large furniture store, Platz and Co., in Rastenberg. To all appearances, the store appeared to be prosperous. In fact, it was nearly bankrupt. Saffran had been selling the furniture on hire purchase, and during the depression his customers were simply not paying. Herr Platz, the owner, was perfectly happy to leave the management of the store in the hands of the brilliant young manager, for Saffran not only paid him a generous pension, but was also his son-in-law.

In fact, the plan was to insure Saffran's life heavily, plant a body in the store, and set the store on fire. The problem was, where to obtain a body? Their original plan – of digging one up from a grave – was rejected. The three of them then set up camp in the Nicolai forest, and every morning Kipnik and Saffran would each drive off in his car, looking for a victim.

At their trial it transpired that they had made several unsuccessful attempts. One man who got into the car with all three of them said he had six children, so they let him go. On another occasion, Ella lost her nerve while Kipnik was pounding a man with a life preserver, and allowed the person to go alive and free. Finally, they found a suitable victim, a young man on a bicycle – Saffran later said Kipnik had got out of the car and shot him, while Kipnik blamed Saffran. The corpse was duly taken to the store. For some reason, the conspirators delayed starting the fire.

The dead man – a dairyman named Dahl – was killed on September 12, 1930. But it was not until the evening of the 15th that a tremendous explosion shook the store. Many employees who were inside miraculously escaped safely. Kipnik, apparently in hysterics, declared that Saffran had rushed into the flames to try to save the account books. Later, a charred body was found.

Two weeks after the fire, a chauffeur named Reck was asked by Ella to call at her house and drive her mother to Kÿnigsberg. A man came out of the house, and the chauffeur recognized Saffran. He talked about this, and his gossip came to the ears of the police.

Their enquiries soon revealed the motive for the crime – that the store was nearly bankrupt. The manhunt for Saffran began. He was hiding in Berlin, with a relation of Ella Augustin's, a poor carpenter. In early November he stole the carpenter's identity papers, and boarded a train for Hamburg – from where he hoped to escape to America. However, an old army acquaintance recognized him at the Spandau station, and notified the police. Saffran was arrested, and he, Kipnik, and Ella Augustin appeared in the same dock in Bartenstein, East Prussia, in March 1931. They pleaded for sympathy, begged the victim's wife tearfully for forgiveness, and tried to blame one another. The two men were sent to prison for life; Ella received five years.One thing, however, that is not in doubt is that when Prometheus, in Greek mythology, stole fire from the Gods and brought it to earth, he did not live up to his name – which meant Forethinker. He literally did not know the conflagration he was starting, and for his crime he was riveted to a rock by Zeus, who daily sent an eagle to tear out the prisoner's liver – which was renewed each night. A cruel, but, in mythological terms, just punishment.

Secret Agents

Soviet agent Rudolph Abel, posing as a bohemian New York artist, ran one of the most successful spy rings of all time – until he was jailed. Then American U.2 pilot Gary Powers was shot down over Russian territory and the two men were exchanged. Is this spying by international agreement . . . ?

THE CORPSE that was dragged out of the icy waters of the Baltic Sea was still clutching two hefty books in its arms. The Russian captain of the vessel which found him was puzzled; why on earth should a sailor want to leap into the sea holding heavy books – and why hadn't he let go of them when he was drowning? The Russian was a novice in modern warfare; it was only September 1914, and most naval and military men were still naïve enough to believe that wars were fought only with soldiers. They knew little about spies and secret codes.

Coded messages

The captain's superiors in the Russian Admiralty were not much wiser. They recognized that they had captured German code books – handed by the captain of the sinking *Magdeburg* to one of his men, with orders to drop them into the sea.

But it did not strike them as a particularly exciting discovery. A few days later, the Russian attaché in London called on Winston Churchill, the First Lord of the Admiralty, and told him that they had found the German naval code books. If the English would care to send a ship, they were welcome to them.

Churchill immediately appreciated their value. He sent the ship, and rushed the books to Admiral Oliver, head of Intelligence. Oliver handed them to one of his best men, an ex-teacher named Alfred Ewing. Ewing knew all about codes: he had been trying to crack the German naval code for months.

He grabbed the latest batch of coded messages, picked up from radio signals sent out from the German naval base at Wilhelmshaven. Within a few minutes, he knew that fortune had presented him with a prize. It was possible for him to read the secret orders of Grand Admiral Tirpitz and other senior commanders.

Two months later, in November 1914, Ewing was given a new boss – Captain William Reginald Hall, known as 'Blinker' (because of a twitching eyelid). The new head of Naval Intelligence did not look in the least like a spy; he was one of the most brilliant spymasters in the history of espionage.

Tense wait

The first thing Hall wanted to know was whether the codes could tell them something useful. On

December 14, 1914, Ewing decoded a report that announced that the German fleet intended to sail. Quietly, Hall moved his own ships into position in the North Sea. Two days later, Britain suffered its first naval bombardment, as ships of the German navy pounded the north-east coastal towns of Scarborough and Hartlepool with their heavy guns. Hall signalled his own battle cruisers, lying near-by, and told them to move in for the kill.

All day, Churchill and Hall waited tensely for news. When it came, it was disappointing. Fog and rain had swept down over the North Sea as the British Navy moved in. There had been a few shots exchanged, and the Germans had vanished into the mist. Churchill was disappointed; but to his surprise, Hall was looking jubilant. 'There'll be a next time!' he cried. But that stoical reaction hardly explained his delight. He had been struck by a kind of vision. Modern warfare depended on *surprise*. The Germans had gained the element of surprise when they invaded Belgium. But ever since Marconi's discovery of radio in the 1890s, the surprise depended on a man with a transmitter and a code book. If he could find *all* the code books, it would be possible to anticipate every important move of the enemy. But how was he to do this? The two he had were important, but they were not the only ones.

For example, there were the strange signals coming from a transmitter in Brussels. Ewing had been working on the code for months, without success; Hall had a feeling it concealed important secrets. He ordered his spies to find out everything they could about the Brussels transmitter. This was not difficult; it had been there, in an office in the Rue de Loi, before the war. More inquiries revealed that it was operated by a young man called Alexander Szek. 'That name doesn't sound German,' said Hall thoughtfully.

He made some inquiries – and suddenly knew that he was close to a solution. Alexander Szek, he discovered, was an Austro-Hungarian subject who had been born in Croydon, in south London. Members of his family were still living in England. Hall persuaded Szek's father to write Alexander a letter, begging him to work for the British. A British agent in Holland smuggled it to Brussels – and soon discovered that Szek was not particularly pro-German. The Germans had persuaded him to work for them because he was a good radio engineer. But neither was he a born spy; the idea of stealing the German secret code terrified him. The British hinted that his family in England might be put in prison if he refused: so, finally, Szek agreed.

Szek was not himself in possession of the code; a German Intelligence officer worked with him, and showed it to him when he needed it. But he could memorize it – a few figures at a time – and write it out. In the early months of 1915, Szek began stealing the code. Every time he completed a page, he handed it over to the British agent. His nerve, however, was beginning to crack. He told the agent that he wanted to be smuggled to England as soon as he had finished copying the code. The agent pointed out that if he did that, the Germans would immediately change the cipher. But Szek was insistent.

Then, a short while afterwards, Szek was found dead in his room in Brussels. He appeared to have been killed by a burglar. The British later said he was a victim of the Germans. The truth, almost certainly, is that he was murdered by the British. Next, to their horror, the Germans suddenly discovered that their 'surprise' moves were no longer surprises. Their European armies found they were being outgeneralled because the enemy was able to anticipate their moves. The day of modern espionage, the espionage of the 'cold war', had arrived.

During the American War of Independence, there were some notable espionage exploits. Nathan Hale, spying for the Americans, was captured and executed in the first year of the hostilities. He died saying, 'I only regret that I have but one life to lose for my country' – the kind of sentiment that would make a modern spy snort cynically. Hale became a martyr; so did the British spy, Major John André, who liaised with the infamous traitor Benedict Arnold. Women spies also came into their own during the war – since no one could tell which side a woman belonged to, and the officers of both nations were far too gallant to search one of the 'gentle sex'.

Important battle

Belle Boyd, a 'rebel' spy, had Northern officers quartered in her house in Martinsburg, Virginia.

She was thus able to gather all kinds of information about troop movements, which she promptly relayed to General Stonewall Jackson. (On one famous occasion, she got through the Northern lines and delivered a message that enabled Jackson to win a battle.)

The most amusing thing about her career is that the Northern officers were soon convinced she was a spy, but were forbidden by chivalry to take any action. She was finally arrested, when one of her dispatches fell into the hands of a Union agent – but she was exchanged for a Northern prisoner, and became a heroine in the South. The careers of 'Rebel Rose' Greenhow and Pauline Cushman (a spy for the North) were equally remarkable, and now belong to American folklore.

Major industry

But it was under the Soviet regime that spying became the major industry we know today. The Russians always had their tradition of secret police; under the last of the Czars, it was called the Ochrana, and its chief business was to root out revolutionary activity. Trotsky's secret police, the 'Cheka', soon became the dreaded G.P.U. ('Gay Pay Oo'). But after Lenin's death, the congenitally suspicious Stalin felt uneasy about the increasing power of the secret police. Its head, Yagoda, was executed in the purges of 1937. It was fortunate for the Russian Intelligence Service that two of its greatest spies – Ernst Wollweber and Richard Sorge – were working abroad, out of Stalin's reach.

It is generally agreed by experts that Sorge was probably the greatest spy of all time. Born in Russia in 1895, his family moved to Germany when he was a child. As a student he became passionately left wing; he joined the German Communist Party, and eventually became its intelligence chief. He trained in Russia, then moved around Europe, building up spy rings in Scandinavia and Britain. (The British Secret Service spotted him fairly quickly; after that Sorge always maintained that it was one of the best in the world.)

Ardent womanizer

In Russia in the late twenties, he was involved in clashes between the Army Secret Service and the Secret Police (G.B.), and his fate might well have been the same as that of Yagoda. Fortunately for him, the Communists decided that he would be useful in the Far East, specifically Japan. His instructions were simple, the Soviets were firmly convinced that the great threats of the future would come from Germany and Japan.

He was well qualified for the job. A highly intelligent man, who spoke several languages, he also had the perfect cover. He was an ardent womanizer. With so many shreds of scandal attached to his name, and a reputation for being an incorrigible philanderer, who could believe that he was also a spy and a top level Communist official? He didn't seem to be serious enough.

Nevertheless, in Japan, Sorge began to recruit agents. These included Agnes Smedley, a well-known author of books on China, and a friend of Mao Tse-Tung; Ozaki, a Japanese correspondent; a Yugoslav pressman, Voukelitch. Methodically, Sorge also built up an intelligence network in China. Then, when Hitler came to power in 1933, he was given another task: to spy on the Germans in Japan. There was one important preliminary – he had to apply for membership of the newly-formed Nazi Party. Hitler's Intelligence system was so inadequate that Sorge was given a party card. Back in Tokyo, he then completed his own Japanese spy network with the addition of an American-Japanese, Miyagi Yotuka. Miyagi and Ozaki were ordered to form their own sub-network of Japanese spies.

Sorge's charm – and his cover as a correspondent for the *Frankfurt Times* – soon made him friends at the German embassy, among them a military attaché, Lieut-Colonel Eugen Ott. Meanwhile Ozaki became a leading member of a 'breakfast club' of Japanese intellectuals, with close connections with the cabinet. It was he who told Sorge in advance of Japan's projected attack on China: information which delighted the Kremlin, because while Japan was fighting China, it was unlikely to invade Russia.

Later, when Colonel Ott was appointed German ambassador, Sorge had sources of information about German and Japanese policies which made him the most important secret agent in the world. Sorge knew about the Japanese attack on Pearl

Harbor – in December 1941 – weeks before it happened. He knew the exact date when the Germans intended to invade Russia, and if it had not been for Stalin's complacency in ignoring his information, 'Operation Barbarossa' would have been defeated within days.

The head of Japanese Intelligence, Colonel Osaki (not to be confused with the agent, Ozaki), knew there was a major spy network in Japan; his radio receivers picked up their coded messages, but he could not read them. Finally, he became convinced that Sorge was his man. He asked a German attaché to arrange a meeting with Sorge at a nightclub. Over a bottle of sake, he told Sorge about a beautiful girl who danced in the cabaret – about how many men were in love with her. Sorge was curious – and his curiosity was increased by the mask the girl wore. He began to spend every evening at the club, until finally the girl became his mistress. But she was an agent of Colonel Osaki's – an aristocratic Japanese girl who had been asked to sacrifice her self-respect for her country.

One night while driving her home, Sorge stopped his car, and started to make love to the girl. Then he asked her to come back and spend the night with him. Before deciding, the dancer asked him for a cigarette. Sorge took out his case – and a tiny roll of paper fell from it. He carefully tore the paper up, and threw the pieces out of the window. The girl made an excuse to get to a telephone, and rang Japanese Intelligence. Almost as soon as the car had driven away, Japanese agents were collecting the torn fragments of paper. The next morning, as Sorge lay asleep beside the girl, Colonel Osaki walked into the bedroom. He handed Sorge a section of the message he thought he had destroyed. The spy stood up and bowed. He knew he was defeated.

According to one account, Sorge faced his executioners – in November 1944 – with complete nonchalance, smoking a cigarette. But there is no definite evidence that Sorge *was* executed. It is known that he claimed a reprieve on the grounds that he was a Soviet citizen, and that Russia was not at war with Japan. A British diplomat who knew Sorge claimed that he saw him in Shanghai in 1947. And it was at about this time that the girl who betrayed Sorge was murdered. So it seems possible that he ended his days behind a desk in the G.P.U. headquarters in Moscow. After the war, Soviet Intelligence suffered a heavy blow when the attaché Gouzenko defected to the West, and took with him a complete list of Russian spies and their contacts. The result was that Russia decided to reorganize her spy system in the United States. The man who was chosen for the job was Colonel Rudolph Abel.

Abel was, in fact, already in New York when Gouzenko's defection led to the arrest of the Rosenbergs and the rest of their network. He had been a veteran of the secret service ever since Trotsky had founded it after the 1917 Revolution. Now, in 1948, on the collapse of the Soviet spy network in America, Abel patiently set about rebuilding it.

The master spy established himself in an artist's studio in Fulton Street, Brooklyn. On the door was a notice: Emil Goldfus, Photographer. As well as film and cameras, the place was also full of radio equipment – Abel explained that he was a radio enthusiast, and supplemented his income repairing sets, which was true. His cover, like Sorge's, was almost perfect. A good-looking, intelligent, middle-aged man, he liked girls, played the guitar well, and was a more than passable painter. The artists who attended parties in his studio regarded him as a typical Bohemian with typical artistic activities.

In fact, he was busy contacting the remnants of Russia's spy ring in the United States, and putting them to work again. He also re-contacted various American embassy officials who had been blackmailed into aiding Russian Intelligence when they were stationed in Moscow. By 1953, the revitalized Russian spy ring was stronger than ever. The secrets that flowed to Moscow via Abel's transmitter included details of the American hydrogen bomb and atomic submarines.

Demoralized assistant

His downfall was a new assistant, Reino Hayhanen, a Russian Finn. Like many Finns, he was a heavy drinker. He was also unhappy about spying in a foreign country. Abel had Hayhanen's wife sent out to join him, but this proved to be a mistake. The couple quarrelled all the time, and Hayhanen became less efficient than ever. He resented his lack of contact with Abel; their meetings were often in public parks, or in the New York subway.

In 1955, Abel went to Russia; when he returned, he discovered that Hayhanen had been drunk for weeks. He told his demoralized assistant that it was time he journeyed to Russia for a holiday. Hayhanen was terrified; with his reputation as a drunk, it was a 50/50 chance that he would be eliminated. He travelled as far as Paris – then went to the American embassy, and explained that he wanted to defect. So one more Russian spy network collapsed. Abel was sentenced to 30 years in jail; but he spent only five there. In 1962, he was exchanged for the American pilot, Gary Powers. And Russia's greatest spy since Sorge returned after all to end his days in Moscow.

More and more the spy lives in a limbo between his employers and those whom he seeks to betray. In some cases – when the agent plays a double, or even treble, role – his life span can be calculated in terms of days rather than weeks, weeks rather than months. Ultimately, the spy finds himself with only one person left whom he can trust – himself. And when his own self-trust evaporates – as it eventually does – then he is as good as dead.

Express Murders

The train shrieks into a tunnel that seems endless . . .
and for some hapless travellers it is indeed a journey of
no return. Shrouded in darkness, train murders are
rarely easily solved – if at all.

ON JULY 25, 1814, a strange contraption with iron
wheels groaned and hissed into life, and dragged
eight wagonloads of coal along parallel iron tracks.
That first railway engine, christened 'Blücher' and
affectionately known as Puffing Billy, also
dragged its inventor into the limelight of world
history.

George Stephenson, the self-educated son of a
Northumbrian miner, was not only an inventive
genius; he also proved himself an inspired
prophet when he told the British House of
Commons: 'People will live to see the time when
railroads will become the great highways for the
King and all his subjects . . .' What he did not
foresee was that his great invention was inaugurating a new and fascinating chapter in the
history of murder.

Oddly enough, the classic cases of 'murder on
the railway' – Müller, Dickman, the Merstham
tunnel mystery, the Rock Island Express murder –
now have a nostalgic fascination for students of
crime. We can anticipate the day when railway

stations will disappear and give way to airports – as they have already disappeared in many parts of America – and the thought of a steam engine chugging between green fields has all the charm of a pleasant daydream.

A Run for his Money

England's first train murderer was Franz Müller: Müller may well be the world's first train murderer, for he killed Thomas Briggs in 1864, and it was almost another ten years before Jesse James committed the world's first train robbery and brought a new kind of risk into the lives of railroad passengers. At least Müller had a run for his money. This was not true of England's second train murderer, Percy Mapleton, alias Lefroy, who seems to have been one of those unfortunate young men for whom nothing ever goes right.

He had a beaky nose, a low forehead and a receding chin, and his ambition was to make a living as a writer. His short stories were heavily sentimental, and the one he finished in mid-June 1881 was no exception. It was about a music-hall comedian, whose wife, Nellie, leaves him for a life of gaiety and sin, and finally returns, dying 'of cold and want'. Her husband naturally forgives her.

' "At last – Joe – darling husband – goodbye –", and with a sweet and happy smile, Nellie went down with the sun.' Mapleton was a vain young man, and he liked to dress well. Short-story writing was obviously no way to a fortune, so on

June 27, 1881, Mapleton took a decision that had been reached by the hero of Dostoevsky's novel *Crime and Punishment*: he would commit one remunerative crime, and use the proceeds to finance a career devoted to the entertainment and betterment of humanity.

He was seen walking up and down the platform of London Bridge Station, peering into carriages. In those days, the corridor train was almost unknown; so once you were in a compartment, you stayed in it till the next station. Mapleton selected a compartment containing an old gentleman who looked rather well-to-do; he was, in fact, a retired merchant named Frederick Gold.

As the train was about to enter Merstham tunnel, between London and Brighton, passengers were startled by the sounds of revolver shots. At Horley, a village on the other side of the tunnel, several people in cottages near the line noticed two men struggling in one of the compartments as the train went by. A few miles farther on, at Balcombe tunnel, a door was heard to slam. When the train arrived at Preston Park, Brighton – where Mr. Gold lived – a young man climbed out, and his appearance attracted the attention of several passengers.

His face was blood-stained, his collar and tie missing, and he looked as if he had been in a fight. When the ticket collector noticed a watch-chain hanging from his boot, he stopped him and asked him his name. The young man said Lefroy. He explained that he had been attacked in Merstham tunnel. According to 'Lefroy', there had been two other people in his compartment: an old gentleman – Mr. Gold – and a rough-looking man of 'rustic appearance'.

In Merstham tunnel, said Lefroy, he had received a violent blow on the head. When he recovered consciousness, the other two passengers had vanished . . . The story was absurd; he was asking them to believe that the robber had first knocked him unconscious, then leapt out of the carriage with Mr. Gold. The ticket collector sent for a policeman, and Lefroy was arrested.

Not long after, the body of Mr. Gold was discovered in Balcombe tunnel – minus his watch and wallet: but his death was due to a violent blow on the head; there were no gunshot wounds. With some dignity, Lefroy asked if he could go to his lodgings to change his clothes. The policemen agreed. Lefroy took them to a ladies' boarding school in Croydon, which, he claimed, was run by his aunts. He asked the police to wait outside; and, amazingly enough, they did. Lefroy vanished inside. Half an hour later, the police realized he was gone; he had walked out by the back entrance.

But Lefroy's appearance was too distinctive for him to remain at large for long. A *Daily Telegraph* artist made a sketch of him according to the description of witnesses – the first identikit picture. When it appeared in the newspaper, a landlady in a cheap Stepney lodging recognized it as a strong young man called Park, who kept his blinds drawn and stayed indoors all day. He had told her he was an engraver and needed quiet to work.

But when the police arrived, Lefroy, whose real name was Percy Mapleton, gave himself up quietly. At his trial he strenuously maintained his innocence. He also asked permission to be tried in a dress suit, convinced that no English jury would sentence a 'gentleman' to hang. He was mistaken. Before his death, he confessed to killing Frederick Gold. He was hanged on November 29, 1881. Oddly enough, the revolver was never found.

The next railway murder was unsolved. At 8.25 p.m. on the evening of February 11, 1897, a cleaner who entered a railway carriage at Waterloo Station saw a pair of legs sticking out from under the seat. The compartment was heavily blood-stained, and the body proved to be that of 33-year-old Elizabeth Camp, a barmaid from the East End of London. The motive was robbery; she had been carrying a silver-handled umbrella and wearing a rather flashy brooch – actually made of paste diamonds. She had also carried £16 in her handbag – which, like the umbrella and the brooch, was missing. She had been battered to death.

A Blood-stained Pestle

The compartment she had been travelling in was second class; her sister, who had seen her off at Hounslow Station at 7.42 p.m. that evening, had remarked that first-class compartments were safer for women; Miss Camp had replied that she preferred the class of people she met travelling second. Her murderer – who must have killed her very quickly, since the train halted every few minutes – was never caught. The only clue, a blood-stained chemist's pestle found on the line, led nowhere.

In 1901, a Mr. Pearson was shot in a tunnel near Wimbledon; a third passenger had been present, and the killer, a man named Parker, was quickly found and executed. But the next British train murder remains an intriguing mystery. On Sunday, September 24, 1905, at eleven o'clock at night, a gang of workmen who were about to carry out repairs to Merstham tunnel – the same tunnel in which Mapleton had attacked Mr. Gold – found a body lying by the railroad track. It had been badly mutilated by a train, and closer examination revealed it to be a young woman. The first assumption was that this was suicide. The head was smashed, the face unrecognizable, the left leg cut off, and the arm crushed.

Two facts soon convinced the police this was murder. A gag had been forced into the woman's mouth; and on the sooty side of the tunnel there were long marks indicating that she had jumped – or been thrown – out of a train. She had rebounded under the wheels of the train. The next day, a young dairy farmer named Robert Money viewed the body and identified it as his sister, 22-year-old Mary Sophia Money. Mary was a book-keeper who worked for a dairy at Clapham and lived on the premises.

And now the police encountered an impenetrable mystery. Mary had been on duty that

Sunday. She had finished her work at seven o'clock, and told another woman, a Miss Hone, that she was going for 'a little walk'. Shortly after, she called at a confectioner's at Clapham Junction and told the man from whom she bought chocolates that she was going to Victoria. No other witnesses could be found who saw her after she walked towards the Victoria train at Clapham Junction.

But now a problem arises. There were only two trains from which Mary Money could have been pushed, and both of them ran from London Bridge to Brighton. Before Merstham tunnel, these trains both stopped at Croydon. So it seems that she went out from her lodging, claiming that she was going for a short walk, and had every intention of going to Victoria. Why? Almost certainly, to meet someone – a man. For some reason she then went on to London Bridge, or, possibly Croydon. A guard who walked along the platform at East Croydon noticed a young man and woman in one compartment – No. 508 – and they looked so 'intimate' that another passenger, for whom he opened the door, went into the next compartment.

At South Croydon, the same guard – who seems to have had the instincts of a Peeping Tom – looked into the compartment again and saw they looked even more 'intimate', having pulled up the arm-rest between them; they also looked guilty and furtive, as if they had been kissing. His description made the girl sound like Mary Money.

Altogether, then, the evidence suggests that Mary Money went off that evening to meet a male acquaintance at Victoria, intending to return to Clapham later the same evening. The man persuades her to get on another train to London Bridge or Croydon. Then he persuades her to take the train to Brighton with him. She is sufficiently infatuated with him to agree. They kiss and cuddle from Croydon to somewhere just before Purley Oaks; then the man gets carried away and tries to rape her. She screams; he forces a gag into her mouth – at which point he either decides to throw her from the train, or she opens the door and jumps.

In August 1912, the British press speculated about another possible solution after a sensational suicide case. A woman ran screaming from a room in a Brighton boarding house. Shortly after, there was a roar of flame, then the sound of shots. Firemen were called, and when they had extinguished the blaze, they found five charred bodies in the room: a man, a woman, and three children. In a vase there were twenty gold sovereigns, and a note saying: 'I am absolutely ruined, so killed all that are dependent on me . . .' It was signed C. R. Mackie, but Mackie was soon identified as Miss Money's brother Robert, the man who had identified her body.

The woman who had run from the room was his mistress; the dead woman was her sister. Robert Money, it seemed, was a weak, vain man and an inveterate liar. He posed as 'Captain Murray' and said his father was a barrister, although he was, in fact, a carpenter. He had lived with one of the sisters in Clapham, and given her two children, then ran away with the other and given her a child, too. He married her, but later left her to return to his original mistress.

The circumstances that led him to despair are not clear; all that is known is that he invited wife and mistress – separately – to the room in Brighton, together with the children, then pulled out a revolver and tried to kill them all. The mistress escaped, wounded. Money had time to soak the bodies in petrol, throw a match on it, then shoot himself.

Many journalists now asked in print whether he was the murderer of his sister. It seems possible but unlikely. What was his motive? Why should his sister go with him to London Bridge, then take the Brighton train? The tragedy of Robert Money only strengthens the possibility that Mary Money was murdered by a man with whom she was starting a liaison, for it suggests that brother and sister may have shared the same taste for 'forbidden pleasures'. Many leader writers at the time pointed out that railway murders could be stopped quite easily – by doing away with the old type of train in which the compartments are separate, and substituting corridor trains.

Baffling Features

As an increasing number of corridor trains came into service, train crimes became rarer, and murders almost ceased – although as recently as the 1960s rapes have taken place in the old type of railway carriage. A case that occurred in 1914 has some features as baffling as those in the murder of Mary Money. On January 9, a boy travelling in a train from Chalk Farm to Broad Street noticed a leg sticking from under the seat.

It proved to be that of a five-year-old boy named Willy Starchfield, who had been strangled. Willy had lived in Chalk Farm with his mother, who was separated from her husband, John Starchfield. He had been missing since the previous afternoon. Witnesses said they had seen a boy answering to Willy's description with a man on the previous afternoon, and the inquest brought in a verdict of wilful murder by the father.

But the witnesses were unreliable, and at his trial Starchfield was acquitted. He had no motive to kill his son – unless out of spite against the mother, which was never established. Not long before the murder, John Starchfield had been shot when he tackled a murderous maniac with a revolver, and he was awarded a 'hero's pension' of £1 a week. It has been suggested that someone killed Willy out of 'revenge' for his brave act, but this seems just as unlikely. The murder remains unsolved.

Another English railway murder occurred on March 13, 1929, when a Mrs. East was murdered when she was travelling between Kidbrooke and Eltham. However, the crime aroused little interest, and the murderer was never caught. Neither was the killer of a nurse on a London-Hastings train in January 1920.

America has had many rail murders, but most of them have been connected – as one might expect – with train robbery. The Rock Island Express murder of 1886 had, for a while, an interesting element of mystery. Kellogg Nichols was an Express Messenger, and on March 12, 1886, he was carrying over $22,000 from Chicago to. Davenport, Iowa. Somewhere between Joliet and Morris a train hand named Newton Watt gave the alarm after a masked man had held him up. Investigation of the mail car showed that Kellogg was dead, his brains beaten out.

The safe had been broken open. William A. Pinkerton, son of the famous detective, was called in. His suspicions soon fell on Watt, and on the brakeman, Fred Schwartz. Schwartz's hands were badly scratched, and the dead man had had skin under his nails, indicating that he had fought his attacker. Although no evidence could be found against the two men, Pinkerton was certain of their guilt – they had been several times overheard talking about large sums of money, and they talked of retiring from the railroad.

Finally, Schwartz made his mistake; he fell in love with an attractive young girl, Ella Washam, and married her. Since he already had a wife in Philadelphia, the police now had an excuse to arrest him, and while he was in jail, Pinkerton talked to Ella and got from her an admission that Schwartz claimed he had 'found' a large sum of money. Confronted with her husband, Ella said: 'Please tell them about the money you found . . .' Schwartz now alleged he had found $55,000 in a package under a seat in the train on the day after the murder. A jury did not believe him, and although the evidence was entirely circumstantial, he and Watt were both sentenced to life imprisonment.

Cold-blooded Shooting

Perhaps the most spectacular case of train murder in America took place in the autumn of 1922. Three brothers named DeAutremont – Hugh, Roy and Ray – held up the Southern Pacific mail train near tunnel 13 in Oregon. When E. E. Dougherty, the mail clerk, saw a man with a revolver approaching, he slammed the door, whereupon the gunman, Hugh DeAutremont, placed dynamite under the car and blew it apart, killing Dougherty. The driver was ordered to take the train into tunnel 13, but when it failed to move – because of the damaged mail car – both he and the foreman were shot down in cold blood.

When the bandits tried to get into the mail car, dense fumes drove them back, and they eventually fled. An envelope containing Hugh DeAutremont's name and address was found in a discarded pair of overalls near tunnel 13, and launched a manhunt for the brothers which lasted four years; Hugh was captured in the Philippines, where he was serving as a soldier; the twins Ray and Roy were captured in Steubenville, Ohio. All three brothers went to jail for life.

The name of Winnie Judd also deserves to be remembered in connection with railroad crimes, although her murders were not actually committed on a train. It was in October, 1931, at the Southern Pacific station in Los Angeles, that a baggageman noticed the strong smell emanating from two trunks which had been sent from Phoenix, Arizona. Blood was dripping from one. When a young man and woman came to claim the trunks, they were asked to open them; they said they didn't have the keys, and went off to get them.

When they failed to return, the baggageman forced open the trunks – and found the bodies of two women, one dismembered. By now, Mrs. Judd, to whom the trunks were addressed, had vanished. The young man, her brother, had simply been asked to accompany her to the station – although, it appeared, she *had* finally admitted to him that the trunks contained bodies, and asked him to help her throw them in the sea. Her husband, a doctor, knew nothing whatsoever about the murders.

It transpired that Mrs. Judd had been in Phoenix for her health, and the two victims were her ex-flatmates, Hedwig Samuelson, 23, and Agnes LeRoi, 30. When Mrs. Judd finally gave herself up, after a nationwide hunt, she alleged that they had quarrelled about men friends, and that Hedwig had tried to kill her with a gun, wounding her in the hand.

She had grabbed the gun, shot Miss Samuelson, then shot Agnes LeRoi when she attacked her, after which she dismembered Hedwig, packed both bodies in the trunks, and sent them by rail to Los Angeles. If Mrs. Judd had left them where they were, she would probably never have been suspected. As it was, she was found guilty but insane, and was not freed until December 1971.

When the train finally gives way to the aeroplane, no doubt we shall read books on train murders with the same nostalgia with which we now read the Sherlock Holmes stories. In the meantime it may be as well to remember that most of them were exceptionally stupid and brutal. Perhaps they deserve to be recalled with interest; but never with regret.

Killer Kids

The dictionary definition of parricide is 'someone who kills his or her parent'. It is a horrifying thought that an innocent child could be driven to such an atrocious act, but children who kill members of their families do so for a number of reasons. Some of these reasons are readily understandable to the adult mind, while others are seemingly just the working out of immature desires.

ACCORDING TO Freud, the crime of parricide – the murder of parents – is one of mankind's oldest established customs. He theorized that the earliest human beings lived in small hordes, consisting of one powerful male and several females. Naturally, the old male would want all the women to himself, and the only way the younger males could get their share was by rising up and murdering the old man. This, he said, is why man has always been haunted with legends of parricide.

He may have been right; but if so, he failed to explain why ancestor worship is among the oldest of mankind's religions. The ancient Egyptians, Chinese, Japanese, and Hindus worshipped their ancestors as gods, and many African tribes still do. Deep respect for the parents is the basis of Confucian religion – which is still, even in Mao's China, the foundation of morality. Since the earliest times, parricide has been treated as the worst of crimes. Take, for example, the grim and bloody story of the Cenci family.

The Perfect Murder

Francesco Cenci was one of the most vicious reprobates in history. The son of the Treasurer of Pope Pius V, he was the heir to an immense fortune that his father had accumulated by swindling. Francesco soon discovered that his money gave him immunity. If he wanted to sleep with a beautiful girl, he didn't have to go to the trouble of seducing her; it was easier to have her kidnapped, then rape and sodomize her. When arrested, he simply bought his freedom. Altogether, he paid out over half a million pounds in fines at various times.

Cenci had 12 children by his first wife, and he hated them all. When the eldest two boys died, Cenci remarked that he wouldn't be happy until the others were buried near them. But as his youngest daughter, Beatrice, began to grow up, he found reasons for admiring her more than the others; with her pale skin and auburn hair, she was very beautiful. Cenci was so jealous of her that he transferred her – and his second wife – to a lonely castle near Naples called La Petrella. Francesco now decided to extend his repertoire of crimes to incest.

When a young, rich noble named Guerra – an abbé – made several proposals for Beatrice's hand, her father finally told him the reason for his refusal. 'She is my mistress.' Guerra thought he was lying, and spent three days trying to see Beatrice. Finally, he got his interview – and she admitted that it was true. 'He deserves to die,' said Guerra.

Beatrice, who was disgusted by her father's ill-treatment and avarice, agreed with him. Beatrice's stepmother joined in the plot; so did her brothers Giacomo and Bernardo. It was Giacomo who hired two *shirri* – a kind of police officer – named Marzio and Olimpio. Marzio was infatuated with Beatrice, and Olimpio had already been her lover – and the keeper of the castle of La Petrella – before Cenci suspected and dismissed him.

On the evening of September 9, 1598, the two women mixed opium with the old man's wine. Always a heavy drinker, Cenci passed out and was carried to his bed. Then the two murderers entered. They took a large nail, hammered it through his eye and into his brain, and drove another nail deep into his throat. The writhing body was then hurled out of the high window, where it caught in the branches of a tree. When it was found the next morning, it was assumed that Cenci had leaned too far off the balcony when he was drunk, and fallen.

It looked like the perfect murder. Except that Cenci's death was a little too convenient. A few months after the murder, the wheels of justice began to turn slowly. The court of Naples sent a commissioner to investigate the affair. The only evidence he could find against the plotters was the deposition of a washer-woman, who admitted to washing a blood-stained sheet given to her by Beatrice – who claimed that the blood was menstrual.

Incredible Courage

No one really mourned the dead debauchee; but the crime of parricide was too horrible for the authorities to contemplate. If the Cencis were allowed to get away with it, the whole fabric of society might collapse. The court of Naples decided on its favourite means of extorting confessions – torture. The Abbé Guerra heard about these plans, and hired two more *sbirri* to dispose of the murderers. They succeeded in assassinating Olimpio at Terni; but meanwhile Marzio was arrested. Under torture, he confessed. Beatrice, Giacomo, and Bernardo were all arrested. When Marzio saw Beatrice – the woman he still loved – he promptly withdrew his confession.

So the inquisitors thrust the Cencis into the torture chamber. Alexandre Dumas, who tells the story in his *Celebrated Crimes*, goes into gruesome detail. Beatrice was subjected to the *strappado*: that is, she was undressed, her wrists were fastened behind her, and a rope was tied to them. Then she was hauled into the air on a pulley. The effect was to dislocate her shoulders. With incredible courage, she denied everything. Weights were attached to her feet, and every time she fainted, she was lowered to the ground. Then, as soon as she opened her eyes, she was hauled up again. Her brother Bernardo showed less fortitude; he confessed. So did Giacomo, whose flesh had been torn from his body with red hot pincers.

Relatively Law-abiding

Appeals were directed to the Pope, Clement VIII. He was sympathetic, and about to grant a reprieve, when news came of another case of parricide: the Marquis of Santa Croce had been stabbed to death by his son Paul. That settled it. Parricide was becoming an epidemic. The death sentences were confirmed. On September 11, 1599 – almost a year to the day after the murder – the Cencis went to the scaffold. Beatrice was the first to be beheaded, and the executioner displayed her head to the crowd. Next came Lucrezia. Giacomo was killed by having his head smashed with a mace. Only Bernardo received a last-minute pardon from the Pope, and a sentence of life imprisonment. (He was freed after a year.) Marzio had already died under torture. Guerra was the one conspirator who managed to escape; he fled from Italy, and was never heard of again.

The grim story has fascinated generations of historians, novelists, and playwrights; the poet Shelley made it the subject of his greatest play, *The Cenci*. Modern historians are inclined to reject the evidence that Cenci raped his daughter. But whether it is true or not, there can be no doubt that Francesco Cenci was guilty of far worse crimes than the one for which his children were executed.

Compared to the passionate and excitable Italians, the inhabitants of Britain are relatively law-abiding. Yet, surprisingly enough, England has produced a number of classic parricides. The case that invites comparison with the Cenci murder is that of Mary Blandy, executed in 1752 for the murder of her father. Ever since then, writers on crime have argued about whether she was guilty or not.

Mary was the daughter of Francis Blandy, an attorney of Henley-on-Thames. Her father was anxious that she should make a good marriage, and let it be known that she would have a dowry of £10,000 – a vast sum in those days. In fact, Blandy's total fortune was less than half that amount. The suitors came by the dozen, and were all rejected by Mr. Blandy. Time drifted by, and Mary was approaching 30. Then one day, at an aristocratic house, she met the Honourable William Cranstoun.

Gullible Girl

He was short and bandy-legged, but his manners appealed to the amiable and placid Mary. One day, Cranstoun confessed that he was in love with her, and added that he was entangled with a mistress who claimed to be his wife. Mary agreed to marry him as soon as this problem was sorted out. This time her father agreed. Cranstoun may have been poor, but he was the son of a Scottish earl. He returned to Henley-on-Thames as a house guest of the Blandys, and his intimacy with Mary ripened.

Then came a setback. One of the captain's

relatives wrote to tell Mr. Blandy that the 'mistress' about whom Cranstoun had confessed was actually his wife. There were harsh words; but finally Cranstoun convinced the family that he was unmarried. For the next six months he lived with them, and Mary became his real mistress. Then the abandoned wife took him to a Scottish court, which found the marriage to be legal. This time, Mr. Blandy turned against his prospective son-in-law and told Mary to forget him.

In truth, Mary adored her father, and had always been an obedient daughter. But she was in love with Cranstoun. They continued to correspond, and one day it struck Cranstoun that the answer to his problems would be to remove Mr. Blandy. Accordingly, he hit upon a cunning plan. First, he gave Mary a powder which, he said, would make her father altogether more amiable. Mary put it into her father's tea, and it seemed to work; for a few days, he was less bad-tempered. So when Cranstoun sent her more powder, Mary had no hesitation in putting it in her father's food and drink.

She seems to have been a singularly gullible girl. When she discovered that her lover had another woman in London, she forgave him. When one of the servants drank some of her father's tea, and immediately became ill, she still had no suspicion that Cranstoun's powder was to blame. She introduced the powder into oatmeal soup, and her father became ill as soon as he ate some. The cook tried the soup, and also became ill. The housemaid, Susan, had a small taste, and was sick for two days. Susan took the soup to the local chemist for analysis, and she warned Mr. Blandy that he was being poisoned.

Francis Blandy undoubtedly loved his daughter. He hinted at his suspicion so plainly that she was panic-stricken, and threw the rest of the powder on the kitchen fire. As soon as she left the kitchen, the cook rescued it, and took it to the chemist – who soon pronounced it to be arsenic. Mary drew the net more tightly around her when she wrote her lover a letter, warning him to be careful. She gave it to a clerk to post; he opened it, and handed it to the chemist.

On August 14, 1751, Francis Blandy died. He had told Mary that he thought she had poisoned him, and that he forgave her. When Captain Cranstoun heard of Blandy's death, he fled to France. Mary was arrested and charged with murder.

Love Potion

The trial was chiefly of interest because of the detailed scientific evidence of the poisoning. Mary's defence was that she believed the poison to be a love potion to make her father change his mind. In retrospect, this seems to be true: why, otherwise, did she fail to get rid of the incriminating soup and tea? The jury disbelieved her, and she was hanged – asking the executioner not to hang her too high 'for the sake of decency'. Cranstoun died in poverty just over six months later.

There is an interesting sidelight on the case. When she was in prison, Mary Blandy heard about another woman condemned to death; Elizabeth Jeffries had plotted with her lover to murder her uncle. The novelist Horace Walpole wrote in a letter that the motive behind the murder was that the uncle had debauched his niece. Mary and Elizabeth Jeffries entered into a sympathetic correspondence; but before her execution, Elizabeth finally confessed to her part in the crime. Mary was shocked, and wrote her a reproachful letter – which again seems to suggest that she was innocent.

In the present century, one of the most horrifying representatives of parent killers was undoubtedly John Gilbert Graham – who was responsible for the deaths of 43 other people as well as that of his mother. It happened when a DC-6B airliner exploded in mid-air shortly after its takeoff from Denver, Colorado, on November 1, 1955. The wreckage was spread over a five-mile area, and the smell of explosive convinced investigators that the crash had been caused deliberately.

Suicidal Impulse

The bomb, it was discovered, had gone off in No. 4 baggage compartment – into which four cases had been loaded at Denver. The passengers who had boarded at Denver were checked. One of them was Mrs. Daisy King, a lady of considerable wealth. Her son, John Graham, a 23-year-old married man with two children, had taken out insurance policies on her life before she left Denver, but had forgotten to sign them.

Detectives soon discovered that Graham had a police record for forgery, and his wife mentioned that he had put a 'Christmas package' in his mother's suitcase shortly before she left home.

Under intense interrogation, John Graham finally admitted that he had made a time bomb with dynamite, and hidden it in his mother's case. He was identified by a man from whom he had bought the timing device. Graham was found guilty, and executed at the Colorado State Penitentiary. He certainly ranks as the most spectacular and hard-hearted of all parricides.

Our own time has seen the emergence of another type of parricide who is both an immature and emotionally disturbed parricide. The central difference is this: while the criminal-parricide plots his crime with every intention of avoiding its consequences, the psychologically-disturbed parent killer shows a complete lack of realistic foresight, fundamentally driven by a distorted suicidal impulse.

This can be seen in the case of Charles Whitman, the mass-killer of Austin, Texas. On July 31, 1966, Whitman went up to his mother's apartment at midnight, stabbed her, and shot her in the back of the head. In a note he wrote: 'I love my mother with all my heart.' Then he went home to his own apartment, stabbed his sleeping wife three times, and wrapped her naked body in a sheet. After this he continued his note, describing his hatred of his father – whom his mother had left only a few months earlier – ending: 'Life is not worth living.'

This done, he took two rifles, a shotgun and three revolvers up to the observation tower of the University of Texas, and killed the receptionist with a blow from a rifle butt. A few minutes later, some people walked up the stairs. Whitman used the shotgun three times, slaying a 19-year-old youth and his aunt, and seriously wounding the boy's mother. Then, at 11.49 a.m., he began shooting from the top of the clock tower – shooting with a terrifying accuracy. The first victim was a pregnant woman, who collapsed with a bullet in her stomach; a classmate who bent over her was killed instantly. Six more people were shot, and many wounded, within the next half hour.

Police and Texas Rangers who surrounded the bell tower found the angle at which they had to aim impossible. The bullets only struck the walls. A light aircraft was chartered by the police, with a sharpshooter in the passenger seat; but Whitman's deadly fire drove it away. Finally, at 1.24 p.m., the police managed to burst into the observation tower, and kill Whitman. An autopsy revealed that he would have died anyway; he had a brain tumour. Sixteen people died as a result of his orgy of destructiveness.

Drug-induced Delusions

But perhaps the most typical case of the suicidal parent-killer is that of Miles Giffard, a 26-year-old native of Cornwall. Giffard hated his father, who was clerk of the court to St. Austell magistrates. The two of them were always quarrelling about Giffard's dislike of work. On November 7, 1952, Giffard asked his father if he could borrow the car to drive to London to see his girlfriend; his father refused. That afternoon, while his parents were out, Giffard stayed at home and got drunk on whiskey.

At 7.30 p.m. he heard the car returning. He went down to the garage, and beat his father to death with a piece of iron pipe. He then went into the kitchen, and smashed his mother to the ground. When he was sure they were dead, he took the bodies, one by one, in a wheelbarrow, and dumped them over the cliff at the end of the garden. He then got into the car, and drove to London to see his girlfriend.

The bodies were found the next day, the car quickly traced, and within 24 hours of killing his parents, Giffard was under arrest. At the trial, his doctor described him as an 'idle little waster'. And in spite of clear evidence that he was schizophrenic, he was sentenced to death and executed. A Cornish jury declined to accept the Freudian explanations of a psychiatrist called by the defence.

In recent years, there has been a marked increase in the number of parricides, particularly in the United States. This is due largely to the increasing use of drugs; in one recent case, a man suffering from drug-induced delusions decapitated his mother, and carefully placed her head on a church altar. Yet the increase is not great enough to support Freud's theory that the majority of people harbour some deep resentment of their parents.

If this was correct, the release of these inhibitions by drugs should have led to a staggering increase in parricide. That this has not occurred suggests that Freud was wrong, and that the Chinese philosopher Confucius was right: most people actually like their parents, and wish them nothing but health, happiness, and long and contented lives.

Lizzie Borden took an axe
And gave her mother forty whacks.
When she saw what she had done,
She gave her father forty-one.

KILLER KIDS: CASE STUDY

The Hatchet Woman of Fall River

Lizzie Borden was not a violent woman and, even though she hated her stepmother, she certainly adored her father. Yet who else had the opportunity to murder them both . . . ?

LEGEND AND folklore are the marginal notes of a good historical story, but the consummate enemies of historical truth. Lizzie Borden would testify to that. The actual charge against her was that she gave her stepmother – not her mother – 20 blows with a sharp instrument, and her father 10. And, since she was acquitted, she even stands unjustly accused in the popular doggerel.

For all that, Lizzie deserves her place in folk-song. Her life-style, her mute, brooding family and the tight little community of Fall River, Massachusetts – in which she lived – were like the perfect setting for a play by Eugene O'Neill or Tennessee Williams. Lizzie Borden typified gen-teel, small-town, nineteenth-century America – and, in that, was almost as fascinating as the terrible crime which thrust her life and back-ground under the microscope of history.

At 32, she did not rank among the beauties of Fall River. Her large, pale eyes protruded from a sallow complexion framed by curly red hair. She had few friends, although those few thought highly of her. Perhaps that was because Lizzie did not choose them for their social positions, for she was no snob, although she liked money. Unlike her father, she was generous and charitable, and her supporters were quick to point out all the good works with which she was associated as a Congregationalist.

Among the 50,000 New Englanders who lived in Fall River, the family of Borden was as cele-brated as were the Medicis in Florence. No street was without its Borden. Andrew Borden, Lizzie's 70-year-old father, was among the most pros-perous of the line; he had started his career as the town's undertaker, next turned property specu-lator, then invested his quick profits in the textile industry – whose mills provided Fall River folk with most of their work. By the time Lizzie was in her teens, Andrew Borden was worth half a million dollars, and was soon to be worth a lot more.

His meanness with money was a local legend. He took his own hens' eggs in a basket to market, and lived in a shabby, three-bedroom house at No. 92 Second Street that had hardly changed since the days of the Civil War. Curiously, he had two weaknesses that invariably caused his purse strings to open; they were his two daughters Emma, the elder, and Lizzie. Whatever else they might complain about, neither had reason to criticise the way their father kept their bank accounts healthy.

The reason for this was Andrew Borden's desperate anxiety to buy peace within his family. Lizzie had given him many troubled moments – particularly when she had her 'funny spells', which caused her to act totally unpredictably.

ONE OF HER TURNS

Once, during one of these turns, she had reported to her father upon his return from an outing that the bedroom of her stepmother Abby had been entered by a thief, who had ransacked the room and stolen a watch and trinkets. Mr. Borden called the police at once, and then dismissed them half-way through their investigations. His knowledge of the geography of the house, and the circumstances of the theft, had rightly convinced him that the burglary could only have been committed by Lizzie.

Then there was Lizzie's relationship with her stepmother. Whenever the two women were in the house, which was frequently, for Abby Borden rarely went out, the atmosphere was electric. It was obvious to all who knew them that Lizzie hated her stepmother, whom she called 'Mrs. Borden'. She never ate at table when Abby Borden was present, and spoke to her stepmother only when it was absolutely necessary to do so.

The breach between them had begun over a trifling incident – a decision by Andrew Borden to buy the house his wife's sister lived in and to put it in the name of his wife. It was an act which saved his sister-in-law from possible eviction. But in it Lizzie Borden saw a move on her stepmother's part to usurp her father's fortune.

In a small town like Fall River – where the affluent Bordens could afford to spend long, lacklustre summer days brooding in boredom over supposed injustices – the episode of the house was enlarged beyond all reason. And because the eye of envy distorts most vision, Lizzie Borden never forgave her stepmother for it.

Poor Abby Borden scarcely merited such fierce attention. She was a pathetic figure covered in rolls of fat, and had difficulty in moving her colossal boneless flesh around even her own house. Without friends, without ambition, and without avarice, Abby Borden was one of life's non-starters . . . only her husband had seen warmth and sympathy in her, and had married her because of it.

The year of 1892 provided a rare 12 months of total summer; a period when New England sweated and suffocated. As the hot sharp sun cut the symmetrical streets, and made stiff shadows from the whitewood houses, several strange happenings disturbed the tedious routine of the Bordens' lives in Fall River.

Twice intruders broke into the outbuilding at the bottom of the Borden garden, where Lizzie, an animal fanatic, kept her pigeons. 'They're after those birds,' Andrew Borden said shortly. His remedy against the intruders was effectively simple: as if by some clairvoyant symbolism, he took an axe and decapitated the pigeons.

SMALL DOSES

Lizzie Borden's reaction to this extraordinary act was never recorded. Perhaps she said nothing, brooding on it beside the window in her bedroom. Perhaps she made a scene. Perhaps she simply stored up all the emotion it generated for the day of its total release, three months later, on the hottest day of the year and the most momentous one ever in the town's history.

It was then, as summer scorched on, the local drugstore owners began to notice that Lizzie was asking regularly for small doses of prussic acid, a lethal poison. In fact, they noticed it so acutely that Lizzie was obliged to cut down on her drugstore shopping trips, and to make her inquiries more discreetly.

As none of the drugstores would sell the poison without a prescription, Lizzie's attempts to buy it cannot be related to the stomach sickness which afflicted the entire Borden household at the end of July in that year. But oddly, Abby Borden was convinced that she *had* been poisoned after a long bout of vomiting. She made one of her rare outings – to the doctor's house across the road – and was afterwards soundly reproached by her husband for her 'nonsensical' behaviour.

Andrew's view of it was supported by the doctor, who pointed out that the whole family seemed to be retching, including Bridget the maid. As July gave way to August the summer's events had already established the Borden attitudes: there was hate in Lizzie's heart, fear in Abby's, and a feeling of growing irritation in Andrew's.

August 4 was the hottest day of all that hot summer; at first light Fall River already simmered. It was also the last day that Andrew and Abby Borden were to spend alive on earth.

BORDEN MALADY

Fortunately for her, sister Emma was out of town. Uncle John Morse, a guest in the house for the past few days, was up early. The Irish maid, Bridget Sullivan, followed him down and as she busied herself with her early morning chores she had to stop to be sick – the Borden malady still lay heavily upon her.

By 7.30 a.m. Abby and Andrew had dressed and were sitting at breakfast with Uncle John. Just over an hour later Uncle John left to go into town. Lizzie then came downstairs for a light breakfast, and Bridget went outside to clean the windows while Abby got on with the dusting and housework.

At about 9 a.m. a young man walked up to the Bordens' front door, rang the bell, and delivered a message. The message, it was later assumed, was addressed to Abby, and indicated that she should leave the house to visit a sick friend. Either shortly before or shortly after this event, Andrew Borden set off for downtown. He waited outside the bank and then made up his mind to return home – where he arrived about 10.30 a.m.

While he was away, the arrival of another young man had been noticed by the neighbours. He was said to have hung about outside the Bordens' house, sometimes looking agitated. Then he disappeared, and was never identified.

Inside No. 92 Second Street horrific things had begun to happen. Someone crept up behind Abby Borden while she was dusting the guests' bedroom and, with a mighty, crushing blow, brought a hatchet down upon her head – a blow that killed her instantly. Abby's barrel-like body collapsed on the bed, where more blows were rained upon it. When the murderer had finished this frenzied work, the room was awash with Abby's blood.

No noise had occurred to bring anyone running, and, if Lizzie, who was alone in the house, is to be believed, no one knew of the blood-soaked corpse in the bedroom. Then, at half-past ten, the key turned in the front door lock and Andrew, hot and tired by his walk back from downtown, entered the house.

STARK HORROR

Again, Lizzie is the authority for what happened next. She helped her father settle himself for a rest on the sofa in the sitting room and then went outside to the outbuilding. She was away for 20 minutes; when she returned a scene of stark horror confronted her.

On the sofa lay the crumpled body of her father. Half his head had been cleaved away by blows from an axe and his blood, still piping from the hideous wounds, covered the floors and walls.

During the next few hours Lizzie was to summon up some remarkable resources of self-control, which could not fail to be missed when the day's events were later recounted in a hushed courtoom. She went first to a neighbour, who quoted her as saying, 'Oh, Mrs. Churchill, do come. Someone has killed Father!'

Lizzie stated then that her mother had received a note asking her to go out and visit a sick person – she said, therefore, that she did not know where Mrs. Borden was. Even when the police and a doctor arrived, the corpse of Abby still lay un-revealed in the bedroom. It was found only after Lizzie had suddenly 'remembered that she thought she had heard Abby come back from town', and an inquisitive neighbour went to look . . .

DOUBLE MURDER

Even with the hottest day of the year to constrain their movements, the people of Fall River flocked in droves down Second Street to the scene of the town's first ever double murder. While they gaped from a reverent distance at the hard wooden rectangle of the Bordens' front door, a man came up the street.

It was Uncle John, whose behaviour, like Lizzie's, was now remarkable. Instead of hurrying forward at the sight of the crowd surrounding his brother-in-law's front garden, he slackened to a loitering pace. When at last he reached the house he went first into the back garden, picked some fruit from a tree and munched it. With all the visible evidence of a disaster about him, Uncle John was in no hurry.

Once inside the house, however, his story gushed out like jackpot coins from a one-armed bandit. Uncle John remembered everything he had seen and done that morning. No detail, however insignificant, had escaped his suddenly prodigious memory. So perfect was his alibi that he became a leading suspect.

The swelling crowd around No. 92 Second Street, which had brought the town's traffic and work at the local mills to a standstill, had no doubts about Uncle John. When he ventured out a few nights later a thousand outraged citizens chased him back inside. After that, the police advised the family to stay indoors until they had decided whom to arrest.

Their deliberations were long and earnest before they plumped for Lizzie. For five days District Attorney Hosea Knowlton had resisted police requests for Lizzie's apprehension. 'You don't have any evidence against her,' he told the senior police officers. When he finally gave in the situation wasn't much better – it simply seemed more than ever evident that Lizzie was the only one who could have done the 'bloody deed'.

If the murders had been committed by someone outside the household, they reasoned, the murderer had relied upon an extraordinary set of coincidences to enable him to enter the house and get away twice. There was the unplanned absence of sister Emma; Uncle John's excursion into town; Bridget's morning spent washing the outside windows, and Lizzie's disappearance to the outbuilding long enough for murder to be done twice.

And where was this bloodstained axeman, if he existed? There was a large reward out for information leading to the arrest of a man who had presumably vanished into the shopping crowds of the closed Fall River community while stained red with blood from head to foot. No one came forward with even a hint of his existence.

Of the three connected with the household, Uncle John had an alibi which checked out, and Bridget had been seen by so many people while cleaning the windows that her every movement was accounted for. Lizzie had no corroboration as to how she had spent that morning.

'Why had she gone to the outbuilding?' she was asked. 'To look for a piece of metal with which to mend a window screen', she replied; also to get some lead suitable for fishing weights (Lizzie was a keen angler). But detectives searching No. 92

found no broken screens, and no lead that could be used for fishing.

Where exactly did she go in the outbuilding? 'Into its loft,' she replied. But a policeman searching the loft afterwards thought it unlikely that the dust on the floor had been disturbed.

How long was she in the loft? 'About 20 minutes,' even though it must have been stifling hot. And, although she had a queasy stomach from the Borden sickness, she remembered eating three pears while she was there.

NO FINGERPRINTING

There was still plenty in Lizzie's favour to disquiet the District Attorney. In Fall River, although Lizzie had made no secret of her hate for her stepmother, her deep love for her father was well known. Of all the people who lived in that town, Lizzie Borden would have been the last to be suspected of parricide.

Then there was the murder weapon. A newly-broken axe handle had been found in the house, and, on a high shelf, its blade – rubbed with wood ash which bore no resemblance to the dust in the box into which it lay – suggested that there was no need to look further. But fingerprinting wasn't allowed in Fall River in the 1890s, so the only thing which could connect Lizzie with the axe was that they both happened to be in the house.

Most puzzling of all was the absence of any bloodstained garment. If Lizzie killed her parents, she would have been soaked in their blood, not once, but twice, at an interval of 90 minutes. Yet when the house was searched, all Lizzie's clothes were seen to be clean and spotless.

Later, when a friend of the Bordens, Miss Alice Russell, had moved into No. 92 Second Street to keep Lizzie and Emma company, it was announced that there would be another search, for the police were now convinced Lizzie was hiding something from them.

Was she, in fact? At Lizzie's trial time months later, Alice Russell and Emma told an extraordinary story. They revealed how, before the second search was held, Lizzie began to tear up an old dress and burn it in the kitchen stove – 'Because it was all faded and paint-stained'.

But, Alice Russell testified later, she saw no paint on that condemned dress. Possibly with a deeper reason in mind for its destruction, she had declared, 'I wouldn't let anybody see me do that, Lizzie, if I were you.'

INNOCENCE WRONGED

In the right hands that was a story which might have demolished the case for Lizzie Borden. But when Alice Russell spoke at the trial, there had been a dramatic volte-face in public opinion on the Borden case. Instead of the mob howling for her blood – as it had been in the murder week – all America was now loving Lizzie Borden. From every part of the country flowers poured in for her. Suddenly, she was innocence wronged, a maiden cruelly mistreated, a demure and heartbroken girl racked by the State on a charge that tried to make her a fiend.

The burnt dress? It couldn't possibly have been stained with blood, snorted hot supporters, because no two people could agree what dress Lizzie wore on the day of the tragedy. The dress that she said she wore was unstained and un-marked.

By now Lizzie had a lot more going for her. The considerable fortune she had inherited from her dead father enabled her to brief the best lawyer in Massachusetts. He was George Robin-son, a former Governor of the State. One of the three judges, Judge Dewey, was a man whom Robinson had elevated to the bench when he was Governor; Dewey, therefore, owed the defence lawyer a debt and he was aware of it.

It was certainly lucky for Lizzie that Judge Dewey refused to hear evidence about her attempts to buy prussic acid before the murders, citing it as irrelevant. And when, with a nice sense of timing, Lizzie fainted half-way through her trial, the emotional newspaper-reading public cried hysterically for an end to her torture.

They got their wish. The court shook with applause when, after a ten-day trial, Lizzie was found Not Guilty. That night she was guest of honour at a celebration party and laughed joyfully over the newspaper cuttings of the trial that friends had kept for her.

If Lizzie was innocent, then who was the guilty party? No one else was ever arrested for the Borden murders; indeed, no one else was ever seriously suspected. Was there ever such a person who, in the words of one of Lizzie's lawyers, had 'a heart that was as black as hell'?

PECULIAR TURNS

Who was the agitated young man seen outside the house? Did he, or someone else, dart in from the street that morning, kill Abby, strike again and make off undetected?

The idea of an intruder stumbles and collapses under a mass of facts. The front door was double locked and bolted all that morning. Even if the intruder had overcome that obstacle, it would have been impossible, in the small house, for him to have gone unnoticed by Lizzie.

Overwhelmingly the evidence points to the crime having been committed by someone who was alone in the house that morning – someone who could have only been Lizzie. What could have happened on the murder morning, says a modern American writer, Victoria Lincoln, was that Lizzie could have had an attack of temporal epilepsy – the medical term for what her family called her 'peculiar turns'.

They occurred in Lizzie, asserts Miss Lincoln in her book A Private Disgrace, about four times a year and were accompanied by menstruation. She goes on: 'During a seizure, there are periods of automatic action which the patient in some cases forgets completely and in others remembers only dimly.'

There was, suggests Miss Lincoln, a catalyst for the double tragedy of August 4. It was the note delivered to 92 Second Street just before Abby died. Uncle John Morse had come to stay at the Borden house to help arrange the transfer of another property to Abby at the bank on the morning of the murder. Naturally enough, the last person anyone wanted to tell about the transfer was temperamental Lizzie.

If Lizzie killed twice that day in an epileptic fit and believed that she did not kill, it would be one way of explaining her peculiar post-trial conduct. For although she then had wealth enough to keep several permanent servants, and enjoyed travelling, she went right on living in Fall River until the day she died.

But it was a different Lizzie Borden. She gave up church-going and quickly lost all the local popularity she had won during her ordeal. At first Emma lived with her; then, as the years passed, they became incompatible and Emma left.

Lizzie lived on alone except for her servants in a big, old-fashioned house she had bought in a better part of the textile town – a lonely, elderly woman about whom other elderly folk still whispered to the new, unknowing generation, when she passed in the street.

KILLER KIDS: CASE STUDY

The Death of James Bulger

Denise Bulger described her son, James, as 'a very bright little boy'. He was a very friendly child who was not afraid of meeting new people. Sadly, this was probably his downfall because he showed no hesitation when he was approached by two older boys . . .

JAMES BULGER was a very bright, two-year-old boy, who had large blue eyes, a beautiful smile and sandy-coloured hair. He was a friendly child who loved to spend time with his mother, but what happened to him on February 12, 1993, is almost too evil to comprehend.

James's mother, Denise, was a proud mother and took her son with her wherever she went. On Friday, February 12, in the early afternoon she went shopping with her brother's girlfriend, Nicola, to the Bootle Strand Shopping Centre, near Liverpool. It was around 2.30 p.m. when they entered the modern two-storey shopping centre. Nicola had to exchange some underwear she had bought recently, and Denise waited outside the store minding the children. James was already beginning to get bored with shopping and for a split second disappeared from sight. James had wandered off looking for adventure, but as soon as he discovered that he had lost his mother, started to cry. Denise heard him cry and ran to his aid and picked him up and gave him a cuddle. She decided to buy the children something to eat in the hope that her son would settle down, but James was too full of energy and soon became restless once again. Denise decided that it was time to take him home, but before she did she had to make one more purchase. She needed something for dinner and stopped at the butcher's shop. James, who was being held by his mother, was squirming and wriggling and trying his hardest to break free from his mother's grip. Deciding James would be safe for a couple of minutes while she chose her meat, Denise put her son down. However, the butcher took a little longer to deal with her order than expected, and although Nicola last saw James playing by the door of the shop, when Denise went to pick him up he was nowhere to be seen. She immediately panicked and ran back inside the shop shouting, 'I was only in the shop for a few seconds. I turned round and he's gone!'

PLAYING TRUANT

Jon Venables was always playing truant from school and on this particular day he dumped his schoolbag in his favourite hiding place and ran off to meet his friend Robert Thompson. Robert was with his younger brother, both of whom were also playing truant. Neither Jon nor Robert enjoyed school and took every opportunity to escape classes. They had been kept behind a grade because of poor classwork and they were starting to feel like outcasts. Consequently they had both become expert at truancy.

Still wearing their school uniforms the two boys decided to go to their local shopping centre where they planned to go on a shoplifting spree, this was much more fun than attending school. They usually discarded much of what they stole, it was the actual thieving that was the fun part.

Each shop that Jon and Robert entered they were driven off by the shop assistants, realizing that they were up to no good. In one shop they kicked a can of enamel paint until it started to leak, and teased an elderly woman by poking her in the back and making fun of her. They went into McDonald's but were soon chased out when they started climbing all over the chairs.

The two boys soon became bored and decided it would be fun to kidnap a small child and they started looking around the shopping centre for a child who was not being closely watched by their parents. They went into the TJ Hughes stores within the centre and tried to attract the attention of two young children. The mother of the three-year-old girl and her two-year-old brother felt uncomfortable with the situation and called her children back to her side. However, as soon as her attention strayed the children wandered off again. When she had completed her purchase the woman called to her daughter, and, realizing that her son was missing, asked her where he had gone. She told her mother that he had gone out-side with the two boys. The woman panicked and ran outside to see Jon and Robert motioning to her son to follow them. When Jon saw the woman running towards them he froze, and told the little boy to go back to his mother. Jon and Robert quickly disappeared out of sight.

Next the two boys went off to try and steal some sweets, when they noticed a small boy in a blue anorak playing with a cigarette butt by the door of a butcher's shop. He was eating some chocolate and looked up when Jon called to him, 'Come on, baby'. James was delighted to have found some new friends and immediately took one of the boy's hands. The video camera in the shopping centre captured the trio leaving at precisely 3.42 p.m.

THE SEARCH

Denise Bulger was in a complete state of panic and was directed to the security office, where she described her son and what he was wearing in detail. Initially the security men weren't too alarmed as it wasn't unusual for small children to wander off. They announced the child's name and his description over the loudspeakers and asked shoppers to keep a lookout for the missing boy. No one responded to the request and Denise and Nicola frantically searched all the shops again and again, but still they didn't find two-year-old James. At around 4.00 p.m. they went to the Marsh Lane Police Station to report a missing child.

EVIL BEYOND BELIEF

Jon and Robert left the Bootle Strand and led

James into Stanley Road. By this time James was starting to cry for his mummy, and so the boys picked him and carried him for a while. Ignoring his cries, the two boys took their captive down to an isolated area next to the canal. Here they teased and joked with the child that they were going to push him into the water. It was at this point that Jon and Robert first injured James – they picked him up and dropped him on his head. Scared at what they had done, Jon and Robert ran away leaving James lying on the ground crying uncontrollably. Probably at this stage the two boys had no intention of killing James.

A woman who was walking by the canal saw the young child crying on the floor, but just assumed that he had been playing with his older brothers and had become upset. For some reason Jon and Robert returned to where James lay, saying, 'Come on, baby'. In his utter innocence, James, with a large bruise and a cut on his forehead, took the boys' hands and once again went off with his tormentors. Worried about the blood on the boy's face, Jon and Robert pulled up the hood on James's anorak so that his wound would not be so visible. Although they passed several people who must have seen the two-year-old with a tear-streaked face and a cut on his forehead, no one stopped them, and no one made an attempt to find out what was going on. I suppose in their heads it was inconceivable that two ten-year-old boys were leading a two-year-old boy off to his death!

After leaving the canal the two boys seemed

uncertain what to do with James and they just wandered around aimlessly past shops, halls, offices and beside busy roads. A motorist witnessed two boys kicking a younger boy in the ribs, but still no one thought to stop and find out what was occurring.

By now Jon, Robert and James had walked over a mile and the young boy was becoming very tired. It was late afternoon by now and Jon carried James by the legs, while Robert held him by the chest. They carried him this way for a while until they came to a grassy spot beside a reservoir. It was now getting dark and they rested in this spot, placing James between them. A woman passer-by noticed that the youngest of the boys seemed to be hurt and approached them to find out what the problem was. James was in tears and his face was bruised and red. When questioned Jon and Robert claimed that they had just found the young boy at the bottom of the hill and didn't know what to do with him. The woman told the boys to take him just down the road to the local police station and gave them directions. Believing that the baby would be OK, she left.

Of course, Jon and Robert had no intention of taking James to the police station and they continued to walk around the streets. It was now 5.30 p.m., they had walked approximately two miles, and night had fallen.

THE BITTER END

James was exhausted, hurting from all the kicking

Harvey Glatman took photographs of his bound and gagged victims before raping and killing them. His pictures were used in evidence against him at his trial.

Torture fantasies were acted out in real life by Donald Fearn, killer of student Alice Porter. On October 22, 1942, Fearn was executed in the gas chamber in Canon City.

Al 'Scarface' Capone certainly left his mark on Chicago, and more than anyone else he had demonstrated the folly of Prohibition – but in the process he also made a fortune.

'Lucky' Luciano was perhaps the biggest ever of the Mafia's bosses. His funeral was magnificently ornate as can be seen below . . .

The man you see here is the infamous Lord Lucan, the British aristocrat who disappeared in the Autumn of 1974, after his nanny had been murdered. His disappearance has never been explained despite a lot of speculation.

When they were younger Ron and Reg Kray made a vow that they would either be boxers or villains. Being called up into the Army ended their boxing career and put them firmly on the road to infamy as Britain's best known gangsters.

Three faces of a con-man . . . Horatio Bottomley seen (top to bottom) as a young man, a respected and successful politician, and after his spell in prison.

Horatio Bottomley was one of those larger than life characters who litter the stage of history. His career veered wildly from failure to success, and from fame to disgrace, ending in the grotesque sight of the

journalist who had proclaimed himself 'the soldier's friend' being sent to prison for defrauding thousands of ex-soldiers of what little money they had.

In February of 1970, things were going very well for Green Beret doctor Jeffrey MacDonald and for his wife Colette and their two young daughters. Over, finally, were the years of financial hardship and punishing long hours of work during medical school and internship, of living with parents, of getting along on a very tight budget.

Colette's parents, Fred and Mildred Kassab (seen here holding a doll belonging to Colette) were interviewed in 1970 and told Army investigators that there was no ice pick in the MacDonald home.

OLD TOOLS OF THE TRADE FOR SPIES

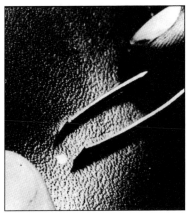

Microdots: The process which turned documents into punctuation-size points. Considered nowadays to be unsophisticated.

Private eye: This is a fully operational camera the size of a large wristwatch. Rather obvious compared with modern-day cameras.

Cuff link: This could be wired to a tape recorder concealed in a pocket and was virtually impossible to detect.

Conversation piece: The most useful of all spy equipment was the tape recorder, which is becoming smaller and smaller as time goes by.

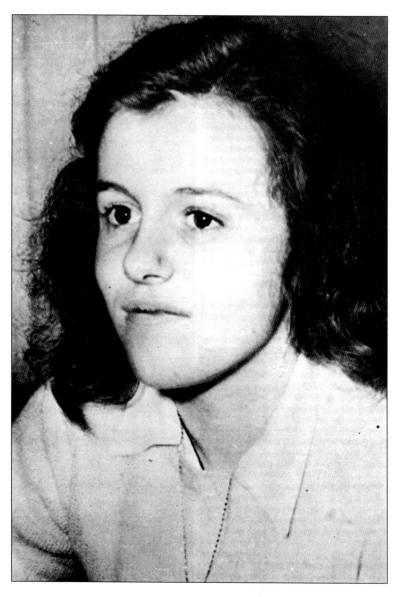

Jo Ann Kiger was acquitted of murder because the law recognizes the somnambulist's inability to control his actions or to distinguish right and wrong. The Kiger case was a classic example of sleep-walking which is rooted in deep insecurity . . . with sometimes fatal results.

and punching, and persistently crying. The three boys had spent many hours together, but quite why Jon and Robert took James up the dirt embankment to the railway, only they will know. They found a hole in the fence, pushed James through and then followed, kicking up white dust as they walked through the dusty shale.

The final attack and murder of James Bulger took place between the hours of 5.45 and 6.30 p.m. and started with them flicking paint into the young boy's face and eyes. Then they threw stones at him, kicked him, and beat him with bricks. Next they pulled off his shoes and pants, hit him with an iron bar and laid his body on the railway track. They covered his bleeding body with bricks and then left him there before the next train came along.

THE OUTCOME

Jon and Robert, who are now teenagers, were originally sentenced to eight and ten years for the murder of James Bulger. However, due to the public outcry at the leniency of the sentence, Home Secretary Michael Howard, increased their term of imprisonment to fifteen years. Defence lawyers were outraged that politicians were allowed to tamper with criminal sentences and took the case to the European Commission for Human Rights in late 1999. The Commission came to the conclusion that Robert Thomson and Jon Venables had not received a fair trail in 1993, and said that they should not have been tried as adults.

Jon and Robert were both released on Friday, June 22, 2001, and were given new identities and were rehoused in a secret location. Denise Bulger was completely outraged at this decision, and felt that the two boys had not been sufficiently punished for their unthinkable crime.

Deliberate Destruction

Explosions rock the night air, ships disappear in mid-ocean, mysterious fires spread death and havoc in factories and warehouses. It is all the work of a few relentless men bent on destruction . . .

IT WAS NEARLY noon on November 21, 1903, and the superintendent of the Vindicator silver mine, Cripple Creek, Colorado, set out on a routine check of the mine with his shift boss. They walked cautiously; for the past three months there had been constant trouble at the mine; the miners were on strike, the National Guard had been called in, and the night watchman had seen shadowy figures wandering around.

The two men reached the sixth level, and Charles McCormick gripped a handrail to steady himself. The sound of a revolver shot made them both fling themselves backwards; then there was a tremendous roar, and the mine collapsed around them, killing them both. Later, in the wreckage, investigators found the remains of a twisted revolver. Its trigger had been attached to the handrail with a fishing line, so that when anyone grasped the shaky rail, a bullet was fired into a bundle of dynamite sticks.

Union Clash

The Cripple Creek mine explosion was one of the first acts of industrial sabotage in American history. But in those days it was not known as sabotage. The word only came into general use after a French railway strike of 1912, when railwaymen cut the shoes (or 'sabots') of the railway lines to wreck trains. But sabotage, or industrial wrecking, had been preached by trade union organizations for more than 50 years; the first recorded instance of it occurred when Sheffield workers destroyed the tools of blacklegs (strike-breakers) in the 1860s.

That Cripple Creek mine explosion was not quite the first piece of industrial sabotage in American history. As early as 1892, there had been a clash between union and non-union miners at the Frisco mine at Gem, Idaho. Fifteen men died in the fight; then the strikers blew up the mine. Again, in 1899, a gang from Burke, Idaho, blew up the Bunker-Hill-Sullivan mine at Wardner, Idaho. These cases were not, perhaps, 'sabotage' in the modern sense. But an explosion that occurred soon after the Cripple Creek incident *was*. On June 6, 1904, 26 non-union men from a mine at Independence, Colorado, were standing on the platform at a train depot after finishing their day's work. A sudden explosion turned the depot into matchwood, killing 14 of the men and seriously injuring the rest – some were crippled for life.

On November 17, 1904, Fred Bradley, ex-manager

of the Bunker-Hill-Sullivan mine walked into the hall of his San Francisco home and lit a cigar; the next moment a discharge blew him straight out of the door. Although seriously injured, he recovered, and the San Francisco gas company subsequently paid him nearly $11,000 in damages, assuming the explosion to be due to a faulty gas main.

On December 30, 1905, Frank Steunenburg, ex-governor of Idaho, opened his garden gate, and was hurled into the air by a blast of dynamite. His wife rushed out to find the snow stained with blood, and her husband unrecognizable – and dying. The police acted quickly. All roads out of the city were closed, and the hotels were searched. They were in luck; the proprietor of the Saratoga Hotel thought that one of his guests had been acting suspiciously; when the police called the next day, the man was still there. In his room, the police found potassium chlorate, and other explosive ingredients. He was a small, cheerful-looking Irishman with a round, red face, and he gave his name as Harry Orchard. Many people at the time recorded the impression that he didn't *want* to get away – that he sought out the notoriety and publicity that he felt were his due.

Planted Bomb

He confessed to a whole series of crimes. He had personally lighted the fuse that blew up the Bunker-Hill-Sullivan mine; he had planted the dynamite and revolver in the Cripple Creek mine; he had planted the bomb that blew up the railway station at Independence; he had blown up Governor Steunenburg, *and* Fred Bradley. The explosion that blew Bradley out of his own front door was not gas; it was pure coincidence that it took place as he lit a cigar.

Having got himself arrested, Harry Orchard – whose real name was Albert Horsley – proceeded to wriggle his neck out of the hangman's noose. The first thing he did was to implicate several leaders of the Western Federation of Miners Union, including William Haywood, George Pettibone, and Charles Moyer. He then had a religious 'revelation', and declared himself to be a reformed man who had seen the light. He told reporters smugly that he had believed he was engaged in a class war, but that since God had enlightened him, he realized he had only been seeking revenge. His plan worked; he was sentenced to life imprisonment, and subsequently became a Seventh Day Adventist and a leading preacher in the penitentiary.

But if Orchard's conversion was unworthy of a revolutionary, his methods were an inspiration to labour saboteurs the world over. At the Independence railroad depot, a hundred pounds of dynamite had been placed under the floor. Detonating caps were placed on the dynamite. Above them, attached to a small wheel, was a bottle of sulphuric acid. A long wire fixed to the wheel meant that the acid could be tilted on to the caps at any time. Orchard was several hundred yards away when he tugged the wire that sent the station sky high.

He had got into Fred Bradley's home by becoming the lover of one of his servant girls. He used the same device – sulphuric acid on a kind of windlass. This time, however, the wire was attached to the door, so that the dynamite would explode when the door was opened. The same dynamite and acid-bottle device was used to blow up Mr. Frank Steunenburg.

There is one interesting point about Orchard's long confession. For all its pious expressions of repentance for his crimes, it is obvious that he enjoyed every minute of his strange manhunts. He had discovered a new sport that combined the adult's love of hunting with the child's delight in causing loud bangs. It is a characteristic that appears in many saboteurs.

Labour Hero

In spite of Orchard's confessions, the accused Union leaders managed to escape largely due to the brilliant efforts of the great advocate, Clarence Darrow. Darrow became the hero of the American labour movement, and Pettibone, Moyer and the rest were regarded as near-martyrs. In retrospect, it seems more than likely that the Union leaders *were* accessories. They were fortunate in that America's greatest criminal lawyer chose to defend them.

America suddenly discovered the full meaning of sabotage in World War I. The United States had a high population of immigrant Germans, many of them American citizens. Even before the

United States entered the war, in April 1917, it was supplying England with arms and food. And then the explosions began. It was on a hot June evening in 1916 that a guard in the great freight yards of Black Tom – the promontory of New Jersey that faces New York City – was startled to see a fire burning under a railroad wagon loaded with munitions. Then he saw another fire a hundred yards away. He rang the fire alarm, but a quarter of an hour later tremendous explosions sent a column of smoke and fire into the air.

The whole freight yard, full of munitions for the Allies, went off like a giant bomb. The concussion was enough to have destroyed the skyscrapers of Wall Street, but the force of the blast went upwards; only two adults and a child were killed. A landlady subsequently reported that her lodger, a Hungarian named Michael Kristoff, had been pacing his room all night after the explosion groaning 'What have I done?' An American agent actually got an admission of guilt out of Kristoff; then Kristoff disappeared. Ironically, he had been arrested for a civil offence, and put in jail, where he stayed for the duration of the war.

On the other side of the country, in San Francisco, a German reported to the authorities that he had heard of a plot to blow up the Mare Island Navy Yard. Before the authorities could act, the yard erupted in flames and suffered explosions as violent as those at Black Tom. This time 16 children were among the dead.

The solution of the Mare Island explosion came by chance, after the outbreak of war in 1917.

Although Mexico was neutral, there was much anti-Americanism there, and the Mexican police made no attempt to harass Germans who were obviously spies. Washington persuaded Paul Altendorf, a colonel in the Mexican army, to act as a counter-spy. In Mexico City bars, Altendorf made the acquaintance of Kurt Jahnke, who was suspected of being an enemy agent. Jahnke was a heavy drinker. One day, in a confiding mood, he told Altendorf that he was the patriotic citizen who had reported the plot to blow up Mare Island to the authorities – and also the man who had then blown it up. He had reported it because he knew that he would then be the last person to be suspected of the explosion.

Jahnke was an explosives expert, who worked in combination with Lothar Witzke, another of Germany's most skilled saboteurs. Altendorf, pretending to be as anti-American as Jahnke, offered his aid in future projects. Jahnke said that Witzke needed help finding his way back across the Mexican border into the United States. Altendorf said that he knew the country intimately and would be glad to help. The consequence was that when Witzke arrived in Nogales, Arizona, he found American Secret Service men waiting to arrest him. He was subsequently sentenced to death, but reprieved and later allowed to return to Germany.

Beautiful Spy

The end of the Witzke-Jahnke team was one of the triumphs that helped to put a stop to sabotage in World War I; the other was the capture of the beautiful German spy, Maria von Kretschman. This was due to a fortunate accident: a courier put two letters into the wrong envelopes. On the advice of British Intelligence, American agents were already watching an address on Long Island. A letter was duly intercepted, and the agents were puzzled. The envelope was addressed to a man – one of the German agents they were on the lookout for – but the letter inside was to a woman.

Chemical technicians tested the letter, and found another letter on the back, written in invisible ink. It was about the blowing up of munitions factories and mines. With excitement, the agents realized they had stumbled on a key figure in the sabotage network. But who was she? They traced the courier who had sent the letter – he had put his return address on the envelope – a sailors' lodging-house – but that didn't help much.

The man was simply a go-between who had agreed to post the two letters when he landed in New York. It was he who had removed the letters from their grubby old envelopes, and in re-addressing them, put them back in the wrong envelopes. He could even recall the address on the other envelope – but again the agents were frustrated. An old lady who lived there said she sometimes received letters for someone else, but she couldn't give any more information – except that she had once seen the name 'Victoria' on one of them.

That didn't seem much to go on. The agents managed to find another cache of unopened

'Victoria' letters at another *poste restante* address; but again the trail led nowhere. All they proved was that Victoria was involved in the series of explosions that were rocking American factories and dockyards every other week. The Secret Service then deployed dozens of agents to watch every person mentioned in the letters. They maintained their surveillance for weeks, and no one did anything suspicious. One weary agent reported to his chief that the young sister of one of the suspects seemed to be very religious – she never missed going to church. His chief looked up sharply, 'In that case, follow her, you fool!'

Prayed Briefly

His intuition proved to be correct. The next day, the agent saw the young girl kneel down in St. Patrick's Cathedral in Fifth Avenue, and place a newspaper on the seat; when she left, the newspaper was still there. Another man moved into the pew, prayed briefly, and left carrying the newspaper. The man went to a Long Island hotel, the Nassau, and sat in the lounge for a few minutes. Then he walked out, leaving the newspaper behind. A tall, beautiful blonde woman in her thirties then sat down and casually picked it up.

A few days later, she was under arrest, the elusive Madame Victoria – whose real name was Maria von Kretschman. Under interrogation, she confessed – and told the agents how she had used religion to aid her activities as a key saboteur. She persuaded Catholic priests to help her in ordering religious statuettes from Zürich, in Switzerland. When the statuettes arrived, they would be full of chemicals vital to the detonating of explosives. The nervous strain had been telling on her; now that she was arrested, she cracked. (She died, a drug addict, a few years later.) With her capture, and the break-up of the Jahnke-Witzke partnership, the United States had eliminated the sabotage ring that had been causing so much damage.

The damage might have been worse if one of Germany's master spies – and saboteurs – had not been hamstrung by jealousy from bureaucrats at home. Franz Rintelen von Kelist – usually known simply as Von Rintelen – got into the United States on a Swiss passport in the month America declared war. His speciality was sabotage.

A German-American, Dr. Schlee, had invented a new incendiary device, no bigger than a fountain pen. It was divided in half by a thin copper wall. One half contained picric acid, the other half, sulphuric acid. When the sulphuric acid ate through the copper, a brilliant, hot flame shot out of the device. It was called a Thermit pencil. Von Rintelen contacted Schlee, arranged for the manufacture of hundreds of Thermit pencils, and passed them on to Irish dock workers who hated the British – and who dropped them into cracks on munition ships about to depart for England.

Soon there were fires at sea, and the British realized that a new master saboteur was at work. Another German inventor named Fay produced a kind of bomb that would explode as the rudder of a ship moved from side to side; it was attached by a magnet, like a modern limpet mine. The mysterious fires at sea were then supplemented by mysterious explosions that destroyed the ship's rudder.

Von Rintelen's brilliance was his own undoing. Congratulatory messages came from high sources in the Fatherland, and passed through the Washington Embassy. Jealousies and resentments flared. To Von Rintelen's alarm, the men who should have been protecting him began to commit indiscretions; one day, he actually received a letter addressed to him with his correct name (he was under an alias, naturally) and military title. As American agents closed in, he slipped on board a ship. All might have been well; but the ship stopped at Southampton. Although his passport said he was a Swiss citizen, Von Rintelen was questioned. Suddenly, the interrogator tried an old trick; he yelled in German: 'Salute' – and Von Rintelen's heels automatically clicked together.

Greatest Saboteur

Even then, he succeeded in escaping from custody, and was finally captured in Leicester. The great British spy chief, Admiral 'Blinker' Hall, took advantage of his resentment about the German Embassy to get him to cooperate with British Intelligence. The man who could have been Germany's top saboteur of World War I was turned into a traitor by the petty envy and jealousy of his superiors.

The greatest saboteur of all time was also a German, although he devoted his life to working for Soviet Russia. Ernst Friedrich Wollweber was born in 1898, the son of a Hamburg miner. He was short, chunky, ugly, and driven by immense energy; later in life, he became an obese dwarf. It may have been some desire to compensate for his unattractive appearance that turned Wollweber into a revolutionary. In 1917, he joined the German navy; inspired by the Russian Revolution, he preached Socialism below decks. It was Wollweber's propaganda that helped stir the German fleet to mutiny in November 1918, and he personally hauled up the Red Flag on the cruiser *Heligoland* at the entrance to the Keil Canal – the signal for the revolt.

In Bremen, Wollweber led rioters on the Osleb-hausen prison, and saw the prisoners set free. He hoped for a swift Communist triumph in Germany – but he was disappointed. Even in defeat, Germany was not ready for revolution. The Weimar Republic was formed in 1919 and Woll-weber responded by leading another mutiny on board ship, and took the vessel to Murmansk, as a present for the Soviet regime. As a reward for this, he was appointed by Lenin as chairman of the International Seaman's Union. He sailed round the world, acting as an emissary of Communism in China, Japan, Italy, and the United States.

Undismayed

The Communists were shocked by the ease with

which Hitler destroyed the German Communist Party when he came to power in 1933. But Wollweber was typically undismayed. He chose Copenhagen as his headquarters, and settled down to a career as a master saboteur. Ships left Denmark loaded with supplies for the Fascists in the Spanish Civil War. Wollweber's agents mixed TNT with the coal, and many of the ships failed to reach Spanish ports, or had their cargoes destroyed by fire.

One of Wollweber's great triumphs was the destruction of the German troopship *Marion*, which left Denmark for Norway in 1940. A shattering explosion sank the ship, and badly burned corpses floated ashore for weeks afterwards – 4,000 of them. When the Nazis invaded Denmark, Wollweber moved to Sweden. Although he was promptly arrested, he had already succeeded in organizing a sabotage ring there. His agent, Jacob Liebersohn, had recruited two young waitresses, Erika Möller and Gunhild Ahman. They were ideal agents; no one suspected two women. They were responsible for the explosion that destroyed part of the freight yards at Krylbo, in central Sweden, on July 19, 1941 – and detonated truckloads of German shells. There were many more fires and explosions before the counter-espionage branch of the Swedish Statspolisen arrested the two women and their accomplices, and sent them to prison.

The Swedes kept Wollweber in jail until the end of the war, in spite of Nazi demands that he be handed over. As soon as it was clear that the

Nazis were losing the war, however, they allowed Wollweber to go to Moscow. There, he was treated as a Soviet hero, and entered Berlin not far behind Marshal Zhukov. Declining important political appointments, he went back to organizing an East German spy ring. He enjoyed undercover work. He may also have felt that a public appointment would restrict his sex life – for he was known as an insatiable satyr.

Again, there were explosions on British and American ships – the fire on the *Queen Elizabeth* in 1953 was almost certainly Wollweber's work. But that was one of his last achievements in sabotage; in that year, he was appointed Minister of State Security in East Germany. There was a point in 1961 when it looked as if Wollweber's luck was at last running out; after a clash with Walter Ulbricht, the Secretary of the East German Communist Party ordered Wollweber's arrest. Wollweber contacted Moscow, and a telegram arrived: 'Let Wollweber alone, he is a friend of mine.' It was signed 'Krushchev'. So Wollweber died a natural death after all, in 1962.

It is the fate of the saboteur to live in an emotional no man's land, with no place that he can openly call his own. His existence – and psychological condition – is one of constant uncertainty, fear, and suspicion. He is like a man who has betrayed his wife *and* the mistress whom he has set in her place. He is his own worst enemy.

Sleepwalkers

The steamy stillness of a midsummer Kentucky night is shattered. A madman, guns blazing, has broken into the home of 16-year-old Jo Ann Kiger. But it's all a dream: Jo Ann wakes . . . she has shot and killed her father and brother. The unconscious is no respecter of law.

ONE OF THE most valuable assets any detective can have is the ability to imagine himself in the position of the criminal he is hunting. 'What would I do if I were in his place?' That is the line of thought which brings success to so many crime investigations. 'If I wanted to rob that bank . . . if I intended to kill that man . . . how would I set about it?'

Many detectives commit the crime, time and time again, inside their own minds. Some become so absorbed that their lives are dominated by their current cases. They work on the cases through the day. They mull over them as they drift into the limbo-land of sleep. And, just occasionally, there is a danger of them becoming obsessed.

Robert Ledru, a brilliant murder detective, did become a victim of his own dedication. It began to manipulate his mind – and it transformed him into a Sleep-Walking Slayer.

Courts of law, on both sides of the Atlantic, have returned 'Not Guilty' verdicts on men and

women accused of a wide variety of crimes –
although the people concerned admitted the act
and were seen committing it. These have involved
allegations of dangerous driving . . . shop-lifting .
. . money thefts. And of first-degree murder.
Charges have been dismissed because the accused
have convinced judges and juries that, at the time
of the offence, they were fast asleep.

The Innocent Killer

Ledru provides one of the most dramatic examples of this phenomenon of somnambulistic crime,
for he is the only man in recorded history who
has tracked himself down as the innocent killer.
But, before considering his extraordinary case, let
us look at the broad picture of nightmares and
sleep-walking crime.

When a man is sleeping the defences of his
mind are relaxed; fears and violent emotions
which he has suppressed through the day – or
which he may not even know exist – are free to
roam out of their dark corners. The subconscious,
which still bears the imprints of our primeval
ancestors, takes control, and the shackles of
inhibition and convention are torn away.

That is why so many sleep-walkers display
such startlingly uncharacteristic behaviour – why
shy and respectable women wander naked
through busy streets, and why gentle and com-
passionate men become savagely brutal killers.
Sleep-walking, which usually starts an hour or
two after falling sleep, is far more common than

many people realize. Britain has half a million sufferers and America has two million. Children are more prone to it than adults, with 5 out of 100 sleep-walking at some time compared with the adult ratio of 2 in every 100.

Killings have been committed by sleep-walking children but, before we get to examples, let us look at a much simpler case – that of two-year-old Craig Welsh. In York he was recently seen walking in his bare feet between rush-hour cars and lorries on one of the city's busiest streets – wearing just his pyjama top and underpants.

Analysis of the sleep-walking state reveals that the sleeper is invariably grappling with some problem. But a child of only two? What sort of inner turmoil could provoke him into somnambulism? The most common reason is that the child wants to escape from some situation which, while appearing trivial to an adult, seems intolerable to him. Possibly he feels he has been scolded or punished unfairly.

In his sleep he dreams of escaping from the unfairness, and so urgent is the need that he really acts out the escape. In Lancashire there was a far more serious case. A seven-year-old boy climbed into the cot of his baby sister and lay on top of her. She was suffocated and the coroner, after hearing that the boy was sleep-walking at the time, recorded a verdict of misadventure. But what stimulated that misadventure? Unconscious jealousy of the newly-arrived 'intruder'? A burning desire, normally buried in the boy's subconscious, to return to his old place as the pampered baby of the family?

Parents have also been killed by their own innocently sleeping children. Carl Kiger, a successful local-government official in Kentucky, a typical victim, was shot five times by his 16-year-old daughter Jo Ann. On August 16, 1943, Mr. and Mrs. Kiger and their two children – Jo Ann and six-year-old Jerry – went to bed early. Soon after midnight Jo Ann, who had a history of sleep-walking, had a vivid nightmare; a huge madman with wild eyes was easing his way into the house. She saw him creeping up the stairs and she was convinced he was going to murder the rest of the family. It was up to her to save them.

There is a popular but completely false belief that sleep-walkers tend to walk slowly with their arms protectively extended in front of them. In fact, the sleeper usually sits up quietly, gets out of bed and starts to move about in a clumsy and confused way; soon his movements become more co-ordinated and complex and the only clue to his somnambulistic state is the blank expression in his eyes.

This is how Jo Ann Kiger was on that August night. She took two loaded revolvers belonging to her father and first went to the 'rescue' of her little brother; one bullet went into his head, two more went into his body. He never woke.

But the 'nightmare madman' was still amok in the Kigers' once-peaceful suburban house. Jo Ann chased him into her parents' bedroom and blazed away with both guns. Her father died almost immediately. Her mother, 49-year-old Mrs. Jennie Kiger, was shot in the hip. Suddenly Jo Ann woke up – still holding the guns and with the nightmare still lingering in her mind. She stared in horror at the body of her father and said: 'There's a crazy man here who's going to kill all of us.'

She was arrested on a charge of first-degree murder but, because of the sleep-walking defence, was acquitted.

Blemishes on the Mind

What *really* caused that tragedy? Our most deeply-rooted motivations, of which we may not even be aware, are a complicated legacy of the past – as it has impinged on us and on our ancestors. Anxieties and irrational dislikes are often buried deeply because they are mental blemishes, 'warts' on the mind, which people are too frightened or too inhibited to consciously recognize.

A man, for instance, may have repeated nightmares in which he is being strangled; this may not be a fear which worries him in the daytime and he may see no reason why it should haunt his nights. But, if it were possible for him to trace all his own history, he might well find that when he was a few days old he had almost suffocated in his cot. The incident has long gone into oblivion but the scar is still etched on his mind.

Legacy of Dread

The same applies to the illogical fears and super-stitions which we have unconsciously inherited from our long-dead ancestors; this is vividly demonstrated in the Fraser baby-battering case, described in detail in another article.

Our ancestors lived in terror of the beasts that prowled through the night. In their caves and rough huts they knew that death could be stalking them, that they might have to kill or be killed. Fraser, in a small and shabby house in 19th-century Scotland, wrestled through his sleep with that legacy of dread. The adrenalin surged through him in exactly the way it had done through his forebears. He jumped from his bed. He fought the monster and he killed it; and then he found it was his baby.

This common legacy of ours is still there, whether we realize it or not, and it forms a background tapestry to our thoughts; occasionally we make use of it and then we tend to talk about a 'hunch' or about 'acting on instinct'. The normal conscious mind, one not shadowed by mental sickness, is capable of keeping these mental blemishes in their proper perspective. But during sleep the conscious reasoning process is no longer in command – and so there are tragedies such as the one at the Kiger household.

The Kiger case was a classic demonstration of somnambulism being stimulated by insecurity, a motivation which psychiatrists know is immensely common among children. A child hears his parents quarrelling, perhaps, and hears them threatening to leave each other. This frightens him and the fear permeates his dream; he is going to lose one or maybe both of them, he is going to be robbed of their love and protection.

There does not have to be a row. This pervading sense of insecurity could be fuelled by a chance remark, by a wrongly-interpreted remark even, which festers in the sub-conscious.

Jo Ann Kiger deeply loved her family. The bond was so important to her that she had an obsessive fear that, in some way, she might be robbed of them, and although this fear may not have been in her conscious mind it was firmly lodged in her sub-conscious. She was an intelligent girl and, if she had been awake on that awful night and had really seen an intruder, she would probably have screamed and raised an alarm; it is most unlikely that she would have tried to tackle him single-handed. But, with reason suspended in her trance-like state, her response was purely emotional. She was going to lose her father, her mother and her brother. She alone was alive to the danger and she alone could save them.

Her brother was the smallest member of the family and so the most vulnerable. That was why her sub-conscious mental blemish took her initially to his room, and that was why he was the first to die. Children are more susceptible to sleep-walking than adults because they react more vigorously to most forms of mental stimulation. They have fewer inhibitions and have not learned the average adult's habit of self-control.

Their Lips may Tremble

There are ways to recognize potential sleep-walkers, even a day or so before they have set a foot out of bed. They often become quieter or more sullen, their lips may tremble a little or they may have unusual difficulty in pronouncing certain words. These are signs of some problem deep in the mind.

After a sleep-walking session the sufferer's heart usually beats faster than usual and the palms of his hands perspire more than normal. Most sleep-walkers, of course, wander harmlessly around. They may go downstairs or walk along corridors of blocks of flats and then return to their beds without realizing they have ever left them.

Some have killed themselves. One youngster, the son of a professor at Cambridge University, doused his clothing in turpentine and then set fire to himself. Another drank prussic acid. Many have fallen through windows or from great heights. In nearly every part of the world there have been cases of sleep-walkers who have woken up to find themselves in a state of acute embarrassment.

Back in 1954, for instance, there was a housewife who was found doing a Tarzan act, swinging completely naked from the branch of a garden tree. She had to be rescued by her husband and the fire brigade.

Many others find that in their sleep they have innocently broken the law. A 19-year-old apprentice bricklayer was charged with dangerous driving at Chesterfield, Derbyshire, and witnesses described how he was travelling at 60 miles an hour when he crashed into a car. The case was dismissed because the court accepted that he was fast asleep.

In Lymington, Hampshire, a 20-year-old girl admitted to having taken more than £3 belonging to fellow servants in a large house. She was also found Not Guilty because she too had been sleep-walking. In February, 1970, a 51-year-old housewife appeared at South West London sessions accused of stealing a case and a calendar from a store. A store detective said that he followed her outside and shouted after her but 'she didn't seem to hear'. Again the defence of somnambulism was accepted.

Psychiatrists agree that these cases of 'innocent dishonesty' again have their roots in our ancestry. Primitive man used to take what he wanted when he wanted it; to him this was absolutely natural. Through the centuries, for the majority of people, that sort of instinct has been repressed, and has become anti-social and unlawful, but the unconscious mind owes no particular allegiance to the laws of modern man.

The full potential horror of sleep-walking, however, is brought home most forcibly by the violent killings and the number of incidents which almost end in a violent killing. At Devon Assizes in February, 1952, consultant psychiatrist Dr. Hugh Scott Forbes emphasized the startling frequency of somnambulistic attacks. Giving evidence in the case of a 34-year-old Royal Navy lieutenant who was charged with attempted wife-murder, he described two other cases of som-nambulists attacking their wives which, to his personal knowledge, had taken place in the previous eighteen months. One had tried to

313

strangle his wife on two occasions and the other had injured his wife with his fists.

The lieutenant admitted that he had fractured his wife's skull with an axe and that he had woken up to find himself with his hands around her throat. His wife told the court: 'Our married life has always been perfectly happy – always. We have never had a serious quarrel. At no time, apart from that night, has he ever used any kind of violence towards me.'

The defending counsel, Mr. Dingle Foot, asked Dr. Forbes if a man in a state of somnambulism would have any conscious purpose.

The psychiatrist replied: 'No, he is living out a dream. He is not fully in touch with reality. He is incapable of forming any logical purpose.'

Dr. Forbes added that somnambulism was not a mental disease; it existed mostly as an entity in itself, without any other abnormality. It did not cause any form of mental deterioration and it never necessitated certification. It tended to recur. After a retirement of ten minutes the jury returned a verdict of Not Guilty, and the lieutenant left the court arm-in-arm with his wife.

Some legal experts feel that somnambulism, if it can be established beyond doubt, provides such clear evidence of innocence that it is pointless to put a man through the ordeal of a formal hearing in a criminal court. That was the attitude the authorities adopted towards William Pollard, a 24-year-old chicken farmer of Arkansas after he became a Sleep-Walking Slayer.

Everyone in the district knew that Pollard was

an habitual sleep-walker. One typical night, wearing his pyjamas, he loaded his wagon with chickens he intended to sell and started to make the journey to the nearby town of Little Rock; then he woke up, wondering why he was not in bed.

Nobody was very concerned about this type of escapade; his friends thought it was all a bit of a joke. 'Wait till he nods off,' they used to say. 'He always works best when he's asleep.' But in November, 1946, the joke exploded into horror.

Pollard had a nightmare in which he was being attacked by a strange man. He lashed out in self-defence and then awoke. That was all he could remember. Just a short and simple nightmare. But his four-year-old daughter was dead.

Strange and Vacant Look

Fuller details of that terrible night were given to a coroner's jury by Mrs. Pollard. She had been woken up by noises and had been aghast to see her husband, a strange and vacant look on his face, aimlessly playing a torch over an object on the floor; that object was their daughter Brenda and the back of her head had been crushed. Mrs. Pollard screamed hysterically but the child seemed beyond help.

Pollard had looked at her in a bemused way and shook his head hopelessly; he could not remember. He could not remember if he had dragged the child from her crib or not, he could not remember what he had hit her with or if he had hit her at all; he could not even remember where he had got the torch. All he could re-member was the nightmare and how he had lashed out.

When he had collected his senses, Pollard rushed to get his father from next door and the two men took the child to a local hospital; she died within minutes of getting there. The authorities felt that, as Pollard's reputation as a sleep-walker was so well-established, he was not to be held responsible for any crime, so no charges were made.

Some people may feel that the slaying of little Brenda Pollard was no more than a gruesome psychological accident, one of those freaks of behaviour which cannot be explained, and this view might seem to be endorsed by the fact that Pollard was undeniably devoted to the girl. How-ever, there is a strong line of expert opinion which indicates that the cause of the tragedy was Pollard's survival instincts and those to protect his wife and child.

His sub-conscious reacted to the 'nightmare intruder' and immediately propelled his body into action. Fright, in this raw and basic state, leads to one of two things, flight or fight. Pollard, aware of the need to defend his family, chose to fight.

The snatching of the child from the crib, even though he could not consciously remember it, could well have been a desperate attempt to pull her to safety. Then, if she had struggled in his arms, his imagination was almost certainly capable of transforming her into the person who was opposing him. So his daughter could become the enemy who was threatening the safety of the home and who had to be destroyed.

The Sleeping Strangler

A very different type of unconscious motivation would seem to have been behind the curious strangling of Jean Constable. The way she died, in England in 1961, is described in a separate article but here let us consider the psychological battle which must have raged in the mind of her sleeping strangler.

Staff Sergeant Willis Boshears had a marriage which was apparently normal and quite happy; but on New Year's Eve his wife and three young children were away visiting relatives and he was left all alone.

In the early hours of the following morning he was still asleep when he killed a girl who was sharing his bed. As he later explained to the jury: 'There was no quarrel or argument. At no time did I make any overtures or sexual advances to her, nor did I have any desire to kill her or harm her in any way.'

Other evidence seemed to confirm the truth of that statement; so why, then, did Jean Constable die? One of the most probable explanations is that Boshears's sub-conscious mind regarded her as a dangerous intruder. He wanted the company of his wife and this woman beside him had stolen his wife's place; there could be no hope of his wife and children returning to him while this girl was there. So the girl represented a threat to his marriage, and he had to get rid of her.

That may sound as if the killing had undertones of premeditation but this was certainly not the case; the sub-conscious cannot be indicted of premeditation.

The most bizarre case of a somnambulist killing was the one involving the French detective Robert Ledru. He was a man with a fine record of success which, to a great extent, he owed to his own lively imagination. He specialized in murder and he would try to put himself inside the mind of the criminal; so, in his head, he executed murder after murder, perfecting a small point here, a tiny detail there. He was conscientious, perhaps too conscientious, and in 1888 his long arduous hours brought him a nervous breakdown.

He went to convalesce by the sea at Le Havre and, because the nights were cold, he got into the habit of wearing his socks in bed; one morning, after sleeping for twelve hours, he was perplexed to find that his socks were damp. There seemed no explanation but, then, it was not all that important; he shrugged, put on fresh socks, and forgot the matter.

A Chill of Recognition

Later that day he received a message from his chief in Paris: the naked body of a man called André Monet had been found with a bullet wound on the beach at nearby Sainte Adresse. Ledru's vast experience might prove useful to the local police and, although he was still on leave, would he be interested in helping? Ledru was delighted and, naturally, flattered.

The dead man had been running a small business in Paris and he had apparently gone for a night swim; his clothing was found in a neat pile near the body. As far as could be established, he had no particular enemies and he was not a rich man. So what possible motive could there be? There were two clues to the identity of the killer but the local police did not consider them to be useful.

In the sand, quite near the body, there were distorted footprints which had apparently been left by stockinged feet. Then there was the bullet which, it was established by ballistics experts, had been fired from a Luger. It was so very little to go on; Lugers were such common weapons and, indeed, even Ledru himself had one.

But as Ledru examined the footprints through a magnifying glass he noticed a detail which sent a chill of horror through him; in each footprint there was something missing, the imprint of one toe. Ledru, as the result of an accident, had one toe missing from his right foot.

He pulled off his right shoe and pressed his foot into the sand; then he compared the prints and realized why he had woken with damp socks. His Luger was at his hotel and he found it had a discharged cartridge in the breech.

Robert Ledru had made up murders in his mind just once too often; they were fine and safe when his conscious mind kept his fantasies on a leash and made use of them, but when they percolated through into his unconscious mind they became a grim reality.

He surrendered himself to the authorities, but a court decided that he could not be held responsible. But, because doctors warned that he might kill again while asleep, he had to agree to report nightly to a Paris prison to be locked in. So until he died in his mid-eighties in 1939 he spent his days in freedom but, for the hours of darkness, he always submitted to captivity.

Nightmares in Harness

However, no one should imagine that nightmares, in themselves, are dangerous; they can, in fact, be blessings in hideous disguise. Those grotesque fantasy creatures which trespass through your sleep can actually be harnessed rather like cart horses to work for you.

They can, for example, give you advance warning of imminent illnesses. British psychiatrist Dr. J. A. Hadfield reports a typical example. He had a patient who repeatedly had the same frightening dream – that he was paralyzed in the mouth and one arm; months later he did become partially paralyzed in the mouth and in one arm.

This man, Dr. Hadfield concluded, had been suffering mild attacks in his sleep, for the unconscious can pick up tiny symptoms from the body long before they penetrate the conscious mind, and translate them into dream form.

The most important function of nightmares, and dreams in general, is that they release tension. They let us indulge in refreshingly different fantasies, in amazing adventures and even in crimes which real life denies us. Only in the minority of cases is this release function ever likely to develop into tangible physical action. But from that minority come the pitiful ones who, usually unexpectedly, are identified as Sleep-Walking Slayers.

Houses of Death

Number 10 Rillington Place was a crumbling terrace house in London's Notting Hill. For more than a decade, and unknown to the police, a steady trickle of young women entered that house and were never seen again. Then a new lodger found the bodies. They were stacked neatly in an old cupboard!

THE LATE Professor Francis Camps did not look in the least like a crime doctor. A cheerful, untidy man in baggy clothes, he might have been a farmer or auctioneer. He was, in fact, one of the most brilliant of English pathologists since the great Sir Bernard Spilsbury. On March 24, 1953, he became involved in an investigation into a death house murder case that received wider publicity than any criminal affair since Jack the Ripper.

Late that afternoon, he was contacted by the Criminal Investigation Department of Notting Hill Police Station in West London. They had received a five word message: 'Woman's body found in cupboard.' Camps packed his murder bag, and joined the murder squad detectives at a squalid, grimy-looking house at the end of a cul-de-sac. Its address, 10 Rillington Place, became as familiar to the British public as 10 Downing Street.

Earlier that evening the current tenant, Beresford Brown, had been tapping the wall at the end of the kitchen, looking for a place to put up brackets for a radio set. The wall sounded so hollow that he pulled of a strip of paper, and found a cupboard door with a corner missing. He shone a torch through the hole, and saw the naked back of a woman.

Well Preserved

When Camps arrived, the police had stripped the remaining paper from the door, and opened it. The seated woman was not quite naked. She was wearing a suspender belt and brassiere, and also a jacket and pullover. These had been pulled up so that a strip of blanket could be tied to her brassiere, then fixed to the wall to prevent her falling forward. When the police removed the body, they spotted another victim, shrouded in a blanket and propped against the wall. They took it out, and came across a third body, also standing upright and wrapped in a blanket.

When the corpses were laid out in the next room, they proved to be those of three young women, all in their mid-twenties. A further search of the house revealed yet another corpse under the dining-room floor – this time of a woman in her fifties. She was soon identified as a previous tenant of the flat, Mrs. Ethel Christie. Her husband, John Christie, had left the place only three days earlier.

The corpses in the cupboard were remarkably well preserved; a constant stream of air had started to 'mummify' them. Camps took vaginal swabs, and quickly established that the motive for the murders had been sexual; the girls had each had intercourse shortly before or after death.

But where was Christie? A nationwide alert went out for him. Surkov, head of the Russian writers' union, who was on a visit to England at the time, remarked contemptuously that the capitalist press seemed more interested in the bodies of women found in a cupboard than in political realities. But this was hardly fair. A mass murderer was apparently at liberty, and he might kill again. Camps recalled that there had been two other murders in the same house four years earlier – Mrs. Beryl Evans and her daughter Geraldine. The husband, Timothy Evans, had confessed to the crimes and been hanged. At one point, however, he had accused Christie of being the killer. No one had taken his accusation seriously, either in the police station or at the trial.

Now, as the police combed the death house, they discovered a human femur propping up the fence in the garden; digging uncovered two more skeletons – both female. Camps examined the other bodies at the nearby Kensington mortuary. The three bodies from the cupboard showed signs of carbon monoxide poisoning – coal gas – and they had been strangled.

The murder hunt for Christie ended a week later, when he was recognized by a policeman as he stood on Putney Bridge. He made no attempt to escape. He was a tall, thin, bald-headed man in his fifties. He seemed exhausted and confused; but he confessed to the murders.

When Camps examined Christie's shoes, he made a curious discovery; there were definite traces of semen on them. Christie had not only raped his victims; he had also masturbated as he stood above them. The enigma of Christie's mind began to fascinate Camps as much as the forensic details that emerged from his examination. And, as detectives slowly uncovered the evidence of Christie's past, he began to gain some insight into the motivations of this middle-aged, quietly-spoken monster.

The police investigation showed that Christie had committed eight various murders between 1943 and 1953 – including, most probably, that of the baby, Geraldine Evans. He had lured women to the house when his wife was away, killed and sexually assaulted them, and then concealed the bodies – except in the case of Mrs. Evans. He had disposed of his wife in December 1952, and followed this by a three-month 'murder spree', slaughtering the women whose bodies were found in the cupboard.

Traumatic Experience

Many sex murderers are subnormal men, who slay without considering the consequences of their acts. But Christie was a man who gave an impression of intelligence and control. He had appeared as a witness in the trial of Timothy Evans, and had been complimented by the Judge on the clarity of his evidence. What had driven such a man to an orgy of killing, for which he was almost certain to be hanged?

Little by little, Camps pieced together the evidence of the strange life of John Reginald Halliday Christie. He had been born in Yorkshire in 1898, the son of a harsh, stern father, a carpenter. Christie was a born 'loser' – weak, myopic, always ill. He was inclined to pilfering, and was usually caught; his father beat him brutally on these occasions. When he lost a job as a clerk through petty theft, his father threw him out of the house.

At some time during his teens, he had a traumatic sexual experience. He took a girl out to lover's lane, and she led him on to have intercourse; at the crucial moment, his nerve broke, and he failed. The girl repeated the story, and he became known in the area as 'Reggie-No-Dick', or 'Can't-Do-It Christie'. During the 1914 war he was mustard-gassed and blown up. How far he suffered a real disability is not known; but it encouraged his lifelong tendency to hypochondria. Periodically, he suffered from blindness and loss of voice due to hysteria.

At 22, he was married to Ethel, but it was two years before he was able to have sexual intercourse with her – the hysterical fear of failure remained. They had no children. Then, in 1934, he was knocked down by a car and suffered head injuries. Due to his handicaps, he earned low wages as an unskilled clerk. Yet he had a tendency to boast and show off. At one point he even became a member of the Halifax (Yorkshire) Conservative Association, and encouraged the rumour that he had been a rich man when he married, but had lost his money.

In 1939 he became a war reserve policeman. It was what he had always wanted – authority. But he abused it by acting as a petty tyrant, taking pleasure in issuing summonses for minor blackout offences. He was still a constable in 1943 when he invited a woman called Ruth Fuerst back to his London home. But he was incapable of sex with a fully-conscious woman, even if she was willing. So he devised a way to render his 'girl friends' unconscious. He claimed that he had an ideal remedy for catarrh and various nasal ailments – a mixture of Friar's Balsam and other ingredients, mixed with boiling water.

Sense of Peace

The bowl had to be covered with a cloth, to prevent the steam escaping, and the patient had to breathe in the vapour. Christie then connected a rubber tube up to the gas tap, and allowed the gas to bubble through the hot liquid. When the girl was dizzy or unconscious, he carried her to the bedroom, raped her, and then strangled her.

When he had satisfied his desires – in a kind of frenzy that came from years of frustration – he knew he had to kill the girl, to prevent her from charging him. In this way, he killed Ruth Fuerst in 1943, and Muriel Eady – a friend of his wife – in 1944 (also during his wife's absence). In 1949, his neighbour Timothy Evans who lived in the flat above, confided in Christie that his wife was pregnant again, and that he wanted to procure an abortion.

Christie immediately claimed that he was an expert abortionist, and agreed to do it one morning when Evans was at work. It seems fairly certain that when Christie saw Beryl Evans half-naked, he lost control of himself, beat her unconscious, and raped her. After this, he killed her and the baby Geraldine.

Perhaps the strangest feature of the murder is that Christie then somehow persuaded Timothy Evans that his wife had died during the abortion, and that he, Evans, would be blamed unless he fled. Evans did so and the police assumed he was the murderer. When caught he proved to be mentally subnormal, and later, after questioning, readily confessed. No one will ever know what went on in Evans's mind when he discovered that Beryl and Geraldine had been strangled.

In 1952, Christie's violent urges again reached a climax; but his wife was there to prevent him realizing them. In December, he strangled her and buried her body under the floor. Then, early in January, he invited Rita Nelson, a prostitute, to the house. He went through his usual procedure of persuading her to inhale gas, then raped and strangled her. In all probability, he kept the body around for several days before putting it in the cupboard. A few days later, he raped and strangled another prostitute, Kathleen Maloney.

During these murders, he was like a starving man eating his fill for the first time; in a confession he later described the enormous sense of peace that came over him afterwards. But the danger of being caught was growing keener. Ethel's relatives were getting worried; Christie had no job; he had sold his furniture. He was going to pieces. There was one more victim, Hectorina McLennan, the mistress of an out-of-work Irishman. Christie had allowed them to sleep in the flat overnight, then he lured the woman back the next day and killed her. His final act in the death house was to pack the bodies of his victims in a cupboard and cover it with wallpaper.

Mummified Body

Christie was executed for his crimes on July 15, 1953. Nineteen years later No. 10 Rillington Place was demolished together with the rest of the street (whose name had, by then, been changed to Ruston Close to discourage sightseers); it is now a truck park. But in the far corner of the park one can still see the outer walls and floor that once belonged to one of Britain's most notorious death houses.

In his posthumously published book, *Camps on Crime*, Francis Camps has described another case of a body-in-a-cupboard, which was investigated by his friend Dr. Gerald Evans of Rhyl, North Wales. In May 1960, a widow of 65 named Sarah Harvey was taken into hospital for observation; during her absence, her son decided to redecorate her house, 35 West Kinmel Street. On the landing there was a large wooden cupboard that had been locked for many years.

Mr. Harvey opened this, and recoiled. On the floor there was a hunched shape covered with a sheet; a discoloured human foot grotesquely protruded from one corner of it.

The police were at once called, together with Dr. Evans. When the rotting cloth was cautiously pulled from the body, they saw a brown, mummified body, whose skin was as hard as granite. It seemed to be a woman. The mummy was placed in glycerine, to soften it, and then examined. There was a mark around the neck which could have been due to a ligature, and there were fragments of a stocking stuck to it.

In hospital, Mrs. Harvey explained that the corpse was that of an old lady named Frances Knight, who had come to live with her in 1940. One night, she said, Mrs. Knight died in pain. Mrs. Harvey then panicked and pushed her body into the cupboard. She continued to collect £2 a week – due to Mrs. Knight as a result of a court order – for the next 20 years.

The presence of the stocking gave rise to suspicions of murder, and Mrs. Harvey was put on trial. The defence pointed out that many working class people have a custom of curing sore throats by wrapping an unwashed sock or stocking around the neck. Mrs. Knight could have done this, and accidentally strangled herself; or perhaps she had died of natural causes, and the neck had swelled after death, producing the mark on the flesh. The court gave Mrs. Harvey the benefit of the doubt. The trial was stopped after three days; but she was found guilty of obtaining £2 a week for 20 years under false pretences, and sentenced to 15 months in prison.

The Christie case and the Rhyl mummy case make it clear why 'murder houses' are so rare. It is true, of course, that many murders are committed in houses; but it is only under exceptional circumstances that the body is then kept in the house. It is not a wise thing to do, as Crippen discovered to his cost when he buried Belle Elmore in the cellar. When a man is suspected of murder, his house is the first place the police search. The consequence is that although horror stories are full of houses with corpses hidden under the floorboards and behind the walls, it very seldom happens in practice.

Really professional murderers understand the importance of disposing of the body as far as possible from home. The result is that not only were no bodies ever found at Landru's murder house in Gambais, but no bloodstains or other evidence was found either. Even the 'calcined bones' reported by *The Times* proved to be an unfounded rumour.

H. H. Holmes, the master of 'murder castle' in Chicago, discovered the most ingenious way of disposing of the bodies of his 20 or so victims. He hired a workman to strip off the skin, claiming that the people had died 'normally' and that their corpses were intended for a medical school.

The village of Cinkota, near Budapest, can claim to possess a genuine death house, at 17 Rákóczi Street. Its owner had gone to the war in 1914, and was never to be seen again. In May

1916, the house was put up for sale by the local authorities, to pay for its back taxes. It was bought by a blacksmith, Istvan Molnar. Molnar became curious about seven large tin drums concealed behind a pile of old metal in the workshop. A few days later he forced one open – and recoiled when confronted by the naked corpse of a woman. The other barrels also proved to contain female corpses.

Detective Geza Bialokurszky, in charge of the case, found it baffling. He looked through the files of more than 400 missing women before he found one who seemed to fit. She was a 36-year-old cook called Anna Novak, and her ex-employer was still resentful because she had left without giving notice. Her trunk was in the attic, and in it the detective found his first clue: a newspaper advertisement: 'Young man seeks female companion for walking tour in Alps; marriage possible.'

It gave a PO Box No. 717. A search of Budapest newspapers revealed that advertisements involving Box 717 had appeared 20 times in two years. The box was apparently owned by Mr. Elemer Nagy, but the address was – 17 Rákóczi Street, Cinkota. Nagy's handwriting was reproduced in newspapers, and a lady came forward to say that it was the handwriting of her fiancé. Bela Kiss; she had last received a postcard from him in 1914.

Baby Sitter

Kiss had apparently been killed in battle. The police obtained a photograph from his regiment, and showed it around Budapest's red light district; They discovered that Kiss was a man of boundless sexual appetite – in fact, a satyr. He was well dressed, a 'gentleman', and he paid well for his sexual pleasures. It was his physical desire which led him into the business of lady-killing; his advertisements lured spinsters with savings into his death house home. They ended up in metal drums, and their savings were spent on prostitutes. Kiss was never traced. He may have been killed in battle. One rumour has it that he changed identities with a dead soldier, killed in battle, and later emigrated to America.

In the United States the town of Plainfield, Wisconsin, also possesses a death house with a history as lurid as that of 10 Rillington Place or 17 Rákóczi Street, the residence of a gentle, quiet man named Ed Gein, whose obvious inoffensiveness made him a favourite baby sitter in the area. One afternoon in November 1957, a deputy sheriff, Frank Worden, called at the Gein farm. Worden's mother, who kept a grocery store in the area, had disappeared, leaving a pool of blood on the floor and a cash register showing that her last customer had been the mild-mannered Ed.

When Worden found that the farmhouse was empty, he looked into the woodshed – and saw the corpse of his mother, naked and headless, hanging upside down from the ceiling. The body had been 'dressed' like a carcass in a butcher's shop. He re-entered the farm and in the dining-room discovered a woman's heart in a dish; Mrs. Worden's head and intestines were in a box nearby. Gein, out at supper with a neighbour, was quickly arrested. He admitted committing the murder, but claimed he had been in a daze at the time.

Sexual Passions

Detectives made a full-scale search of the farmhouse – which was indescribably filthy and untidy – and found no less than ten skins flayed from human heads, and a box containing noses. Human skin had been used to repair leather armchairs, and even to make a belt. Gein had been living on his own at the farmhouse since 1945 and from his admissions, the police constructed an incredible story. His mother had been violently religious, convinced that God was about to destroy the world because women wore lipstick. She instilled into Gein a highly ambivalent hatred of 'scarlet women'. Gein's father died in 1940, his only brother in 1942. Old Mrs. Gein suffered a stroke in 1944, and Gein nursed her until she died a year later.

Then, alone in the house, he began to suffer from tormenting sexual passions. In 1942, he had called at a neighbour's house, and seen a woman wearing shorts; that night, a man had broken into the house, and asked the woman's son where his mother was. The intruder fled, but the boy thought he had recognized Gein. Not long after his mother's death, Gein saw an announcement in a newspaper that a woman was being buried. That night, he drove to the graveyard, dug up the body, put it in his truck, then replaced the coffin and buried it carefully.

Waistcoat

Back at home, he at last had a woman to share his bed. 'It gave me a lot of satisfaction,' he explained. He found the corpse so sexually exciting that he ate part of the body, and made a waistcoat of the skin, so he could wear it next to his body. At Christmas 1957, Gein was found insane, and confined for life in the Waupan State Hospital.

So the death houses – 'castles', apartments, farms – stay where and sometimes as they are until they are renovated or razed. People live in the buildings, in the bedrooms and lounges in which the murders were committed; frequently without knowing the previous bloody history of their homes. The death houses keep their secrets to themselves. Their walls may have ears, but they do not have tongues.

Blackmail and Extortion

When Sir Travers Twiss married his charming and
beautiful young wife, Marie, he accepted without
question that she was of 'respectable' social origins. He
reckoned without the insidious menaces of a
blackmailer . . .

'DO YOU FEEL a creeping, shrinking sensation,
Watson, when you stand before the serpents in
the Zoo, and see the slithery, gliding, venomous
creatures, with their deadly eyes and wicked,
flattened faces? Well, that's how Milverton
impresses me. I've had to do with fifty murderers,
but the worst of them never gave me the
repulsion which I have for this fellow.'

The speaker is, of course, Sherlock Holmes,
and the man he is referring to is the blackmailer,
Charles Augustus Milverton, 'the worst man in
London'. The story of Milverton was first
published in *Collier's Magazine* in 1904. The date
is interesting because the slithery Milverton was
probably the first blackmailer ever to make his
appearance in fiction.

In fact, the crime itself was relatively new; a
law against 'threatening to publish with intent to
extort money' was not passed until 1893, though

the word 'blackmail' dates back to the time of Queen Elizabeth I, when certain freebooting Scottish chieftains used to extort money from farmers along the Scottish border. This 'protection money' was called black-mail, or black-rent, to distinguish it from the rent the farmer paid to his proper landlord.

This was not actually a crime – the law taking the view that if a farmer chose to pay black-rent, that was his own business. It was not until 1873 that the British parliament decided that 'demanding money with menaces' was just as unlawful as pointing a gun at somebody's head and taking his wallet.

Medium Dominance

It may seem curious that English law – and this also applies to America – took so long to take account of blackmail, but the reason can be seen in *Charles Augustus Milverton*. Milverton makes a living by buying up 'compromising letters' written by ladies and gentlemen in high society, and threatening to send them to the husband or wife of the imprudent writer. Holmes is engaged to try to recover certain indiscreet letters written by a young lady to a penniless country squire; now she is about to marry an Earl, and the blackmailer threatens to send the letters to the future husband.

And, in fact, real-life Milvertons *were* making money in exactly this way. A century earlier, it would have been absurd; people in high society took mistresses – or lovers – all the time, and nobody gave a damn. Then Queen Victoria came to the throne, married a serious and religious German prince named Albert, and all that changed; in England, high society took its tone from the royal family. The Age of Respectability had arrived, and there were suddenly dozens of things that were just Not Done.

The 'breath of scandal' could ruin a man – and totally destroy a woman; Queen Victoria turned violently and passionately against her own son when she heard he was having an affair with an actress, whereas her predecessors on the throne of England would have thought there was something seriously wrong with a son who *didn't* fornicate with actresses, chambermaids and ladies-in-waiting. But the First Lady of England, being a woman of only 'medium dominance', was a romantic, one-man woman, who thought sex was rather dirty, and high society had to live up to her standards or else.

The case that made the Victorians aware of the curious legal problems involved in blackmail took place in 1872. The lady in the case was called Lady Twiss; the blackmailer was a London solicitor named Alexander Chaffers. Lady Twiss was the wife of Sir Travers Twiss, a well-known Victorian advocate, and a professor of International Law at King's College, London. She was regarded as thoroughly respectable – she had even been presented at Court to Queen Victoria. And now, to the horrified incredulity of British high society, she was accused by Mr. Chaffers of being a common prostitute.

Sir Travers Twiss had been a highly successful man of fifty when he had met a pretty Polish girl at his mother's house in 1859. Her name was Marie Van Lynseele, and she was the daughter of a Polish Major-General. Three years later, Sir Travers was in Dresden, and again met the pretty Pole. They fell in love, and married at the British Legation. On their return to England, Lady Twiss was presented first to the Prince of Wales, then to Queen Victoria.

One day, when she and her husband were walking in Kew Gardens, a man suddenly raised his hat and said hello. Lady Twiss introduced him to her husband as a solicitor, Alexander Chaffers. Chaffers congratulated her on her marriage, and not long after, Lady Twiss received a bill for £46 from Mr. Chaffers 'for services rendered'. She ignored it. He sent another letter, this time asking for £150. Lady Twiss showed it to her husband, and explained that she really owed Chaffers some money for legal work he had once done for a maid in her employment. Whereupon Sir Travers Twiss arranged a meeting with Chaffers, and paid him £50, asking for a receipt. This was marked 'in full discharge'.

But Chaffers was apparently not satisfied. He continued to ask Lady Twiss for money. He wrote a letter to the Lord Chamberlain – the Court official responsible for vetting the list of people who would be received by the Queen – telling him that Lady Twiss had been, to put it crudely, a French whore who had managed to worm her way into high society.

The Lord Chamberlain was baffled. Short of hiring a private detective, he couldn't think of any way of investigating the story, so he decided to treat it as a hoax and forget it. But he told Lord and Lady Twiss about the accusations. They were horrified, and confirmed his opinion that Chaffers was a madman. Chaffers certainly had the persistence of a madman. He had a writ for libel served on Sir Travers, claiming that Lady Twiss had been spreading all kinds of slanders about him, and then went to the Chief Magistrate at Bow Street to make a sworn statement of 'the truth about Lady Twiss'.

Made Public

This statement declared that she was actually a prostitute named Marie Gelas, and that she had been intimate with Chaffers on several occasions in certain houses of ill-fame in Belgium. Now, as much as he disliked the idea, Sir Travers Twiss had to take action. In May, 1871, Mr. Chaffers appeared at Southwark Police Court, charged with having 'published' various slanders against Sir Travers and Lady Twiss – in legal terminology, 'published' means simply 'made public'. Mr. Chaffers's defence was that the 'libels' were true.

Marie Van Lynseele claimed to be the daughter of a deceased Major-General, and that she had been brought up in Poland and Belgium as the adopted daughter of a Monsieur Jastrenski. Marie admitted that she *knew* someone called Marie Gelas; according to her, Marie Gelas had been her chaperone when she first came to England in 1859

– the occasion when she had first met Sir Travers.

During that visit, Marie Van Lynseele had fallen seriously ill, and Marie Gelas had decided that her employer ought to make a will; she therefore sent for Mr. Chaffers, whom she already knew, and got him to draw up a suitable document. This, said Lady Twiss, was the full extent of her acquaintance with Mr. Chaffers, and he had been paid his £50 professional fee after the meeting in Kew Gardens.

Mr. Chaffers replied that there never *had* been a 'chaperone' called Marie Gelas. Lady Twiss *was* Marie Gelas, and he had slept with her several times before she 'struck it rich'. Nowadays, this would be an open and shut case. Mr. Chaffers was admitting that he had tried to blackmail Lady Twiss by telling her husband about her past, and then, when that didn't work, tried to blackmail them both. But in 1872 there was no law against blackmail: only against libel.

Lady Twiss's problem was to prove that she was Marie Van Lynseele, daughter of a Major-General, not Marie Gelas. She called various witnesses to testify about her past, including a maid who swore on oath that Chaffers had tried to bribe her to support slanders against her mistress. Obviously Chaffers was a very nasty piece of work, and the judge made no attempt to hide his distaste.

Unsolved Mystery

And then, quite unexpectedly, Lady Twiss surrendered. On the eighth day of the trial she decided she had had enough. Her counsel appeared in court to tell the judge that his client had left London, and decided not to continue the case. The judge had no alternative but to discharge Alexander Chaffers. He told him that for the rest of his life he would be 'an object of contempt to all honest and well-thinking men'; but the fact remained that Chaffers had won.

A week later, Sir Travers Twiss resigned from all his various distinguished posts. His wife had vanished to the Continent, and, as far as we know, he never saw her again. The *London Gazette* published a paragraph saying that Lady Twiss's presentation to the Queen – which had taken place three years earlier – had been 'cancelled' – which was the Victorian way of saying that it hadn't really happened at all, and the case remains an apparently unsolved mystery.

But it is easy enough to read between the lines. If Lady Twiss *had* been Marie Van Lynseele, she would presumably have fought to the last ditch. The court was already inclined heavily in her favour. Her foster-father, M. Jastrenski, had testified that she was Marie Van Lynseele, and many other witnesses had declared on oath that they knew Marie Gelas, and that she was not Marie Van Lynseele. It was a foregone conclusion that Chaffers would be found guilty and sent for trial.

What probably happened is that Marie Van Lynseele – or Gelas – had bribed various people to appear in her favour, but that she realized a trial would be a more serious matter; perhaps her witnesses refused to testify at a criminal trial, because they were afraid of the penalty for perjury. She decided the game was up, and vanished. If she was innocent, why did she tell her husband that she owed Chaffers the £50 for legal fees contracted on behalf of a maid, when she later testified in court that it was *her* will that Chaffers drew up?

Homosexual Brothel

On the other hand, there remains the other possibility: that, persecuted by Chaffers, realizing that she had ruined her husband, no matter what the outcome of the case, Lady Twiss's nerve snapped and she fled. The case made upper-class Victorians aware how vulnerable they were to blackmail. A man like Chaffers didn't need any *evidence* that Lady Twiss was a prostitute. He only had to say so in court, and even if he was found guilty of libel, her reputation would never recover from the scandal.

It also made the Victorians aware that they needed a law to prevent people like Chaffers extorting money by threats: hence the state of 1873 against 'demanding money with menaces'. It cost Sir Travers Twiss his career, but his case had changed the law.

Unfortunately, a change in the law was not quite the answer. When a crime suddenly attracts public attention, criminals everywhere wonder whether this is not a new source of income. The Victorian poor had always been the prey of rich debauchees; there were few working-class girls who could refuse the offer of five shillings for the use of their bodies. Now the poor began to retaliate by exerting blackmail on the seducers.

Oscar Wilde was blackmailed by some of the working-class youths he slept with; when a homosexual brothel in Cleveland Street was raided by the police in 1889, the whole affair was quickly hushed up when they realized that one of the chief clients was the Duke of Clarence, the grandson of Queen Victoria. 'Eddie' – as the Duke was known – was packed off on a world cruise, and endless possibilities of blackmail were averted.

But it was not only the lower classes who indulged in blackmail. Aristocrats could play the game just as ruthlessly. One of the most famous – and notorious – of Victorian aristocrats was Lady Warwick, known universally as Daisy – the song 'Daisy, Daisy' was written with her in mind. The ravishingly beautiful Daisy married the future Earl of Warwick in 1881 and became mistress of Warwick Castle and a huge fortune. She soon found her husband's passion for hunting and fishing a bore, and began to take lovers.

Sexual Promiscuity

For several years she conducted a passionate affair with the dashing Lord Charles Beresford – in the Victorian age there was nothing to stop you having love affairs provided you were discreet about it, and avoided 'scandal'. When Lord Charles finally broke it off she went to his closest friend, the Prince of Wales, to beg him to help her get back a certain compromising letter.

Edward, Prince of Wales, was the son who had alienated Queen Victoria through his affair with an actress, and ever since that time he had devoted his life to sexual promiscuity with the energy of a Casanova. He took one look at Daisy, and dragged her towards the nearest bed. Daisy was willing enough; for although the Prince was no longer young or handsome – he was fat and inclined to wheeze – she saw he was a valuable ally. As for Prince Edward, he was genuinely in love with the delicious Daisy.

In 1893 her father-in-law died, and Daisy became mistress of a fortune. She immediately had War-wick Castle re-landscaped, filled it with expensive carpets and furniture, and gave huge week-end parties that were famous for their extravagance. The socialist press attacked her for wasting so much money when the poor were starving; as a result she went to see the famous left-wing editor, W. T. Stead, and immediately became converted to socialism. She had the double pleasure of being immensely rich and being known as the defender of the poor.

As the years went by, Daisy's beauty faded and her fortune dwindled. In 1912 she realized that she was close to bankruptcy. And then she had her inspiration. She would write her memoirs, make sure they were scandalously frank, and sell them to a publisher for some huge sum - £100,000 was her first estimate. In 1914, she contacted a journalist and writer named Frank Harris – now known chiefly as the author of the semi-pornographic *My Life and Loves*.

Harris was not only an editor, a novelist and a Don Juan; he was a completely unscrupulous blackmailer, and he instantly saw the enormous possibilities of her scheme. All she had to do was to make sure she included the love letters of the Prince of Wales – later King Edward VII, who had died in 1910 – and then ask the Palace how much it was worth to suppress the book.

Two years earlier a Tory Member of Parliament, Charles du Cros, had lent Daisy £16,000, and he now wanted his interest on the sum. Daisy also happened to know that he wanted a knighthood, and that he had an attitude verging on adoration for King George V, Edward's son. She sent for du Cros, told him about the memoirs, and mentioned that she had letters from the late King in which among more intimate and scandalous matters, he had given his opinion of such people as the Kaiser and the Czar of Russia.

Du Cros rushed to see George V's A.D.C. and his solicitor. The solicitor suggested that he had better ask Daisy how much she would take to suppress the book. Daisy said £85,000 – but told du Cros that he would have to see her 'partner', Frank Harris. Harris had fled to Paris, escaping his creditors; du Cros saw him at the Ritz Hotel, and was told that they would settle for a mere £125,000.

But the Establishment had its own way of dealing with blackmail. Instead of paying up, George V's solicitor asked for a court injunction to prevent Daisy publishing the late King's letters. Daisy at first found it incredible – to drag the affair into open court; but there she was mistaken. The Establishment co-operated admirably. The case was heard in chambers – a closed court. Edward VII's name was not mentioned; it was simply a matter of preventing the publication of 'certain letters'. The letters had to be handed over to the court. The injunction was granted, and the court also ordered that the letters were to be destroyed.

Two-way Mirrors

This was not quite the end of the story. Before the letters were handed over, Frank Harris went to stay with Daisy Warwick at her house, Easton Lodge – she had been forced by debts to move out of Warwick Castle. He asked to see the letters – and when Harris left for America, the letters went with him. In order to get them back, Daisy had to pay Harris for them. She was the loser all round . . . Her only consolation was that du Cros, feeling sorry for her, took over £50,000-worth of her debts.

Since Daisy's time the art of blackmail has been turned into an exact science – particularly by the espionage and counter-espionage services of all the major countries. In the West, we hear a great deal about the techniques of the Russian secret service, the K.G.B. – for example, how they blackmailed the American army sergeant James Harris, who appeared in the Rudolph Abel case, or of the pressure they brought to bear on the homosexual naval clerk, Vassall. But there can be no doubt that the C.I.A and Britain's M.I.5 are just as skilled in its uses.

A favourite technique with both sides is to lure a diplomat – or member of the government – into a sexually compromising position. The Russians are credited with the discovery of the use of two-way mirrors for this purpose – the English and American method was cruder, using a picture or photograph with tiny holes in it, usually in the pupils of the eyes, with the camera concealed behind it.

The invention of transistors enabled the C.I.A. to perfect a whole new range of 'bugging devices'. One of these was a tiny pill that emitted a radio signal. The girl who has been chosen as the decoy swallows a pill that makes a 'bleep' noise. Another pill – which emits a 'bloop' – is concealed in the food of the victim, so he swallows it. Agents are then able to follow the couple with radio receivers, and when their receivers pick up simultaneous bloops and bleeps, they can assume that the bellies of both parties are in sufficiently close contact to warrant a sudden intrusion.

Blackmail is the least documented of all crimes for an obvious reason: if a blackmailer is caught by the police, it is in everybody's interests to make sure that the case receives no publicity. And in most civilized countries, it is generally agreed that when a victim reports blackmail to the police, he will not lay himself open to criminal charges, even if he is being blackmailed for a crime he has committed.

BLACKMAIL AND EXTORTION: CASE STUDY

The Only Way Out

Captain Alfred Loewenstein was not accustomed to being crossed. He had made himself one of the richest tycoons in Europe by playing hard and winning. In fact there seemed to his enemies to be no weaknesses in his formidable armour . . . until a nameless blackmailer probed the secrets of his empire . . .

TO THE ENTOURAGE who followed him from his limousine, over the tarmac at Croydon airfield, near London, and up to his private, three-engined plane, there appeared to be nothing amiss with Captain Alfred Loewenstein. The tycoon – one of the best-known, yet most enigmatic, men in Europe – was his usual confident and aggressive self. He was flying to Brussels to conclude another of the deals which had made him a multi-millionaire, and his staff were prepared to work on documents on the plane.

Yet the night before – on July 3, 1928 – Loewenstein had learnt from a private detective in his employ that a blackmailer was about to publish a 5,000-word paper which would destroy his personal reputation and business career. The tycoon knew the identity of the blackmailer – a bitter rival he had refused to pay money to – and had told him to 'go ahead and do your worst'.

Now the man was going to do just that. Before

the day was out the world's newspapers would learn of the crooked inner workings of the International Holdings Company – the firm which handled his investments, stock market speculations, loans to governments, and his mining, hydroelectric, and artificial silk combines. They would learn that what they had long suspected was true: while the financial 'milk' remained within the company, the 'cream' was skimmed off and kept by Loewenstein himself.

CORRUPT PRACTICES

More than that, they would learn of the unscrupulous way he had disposed, or tried to dispose, of such reputable competitors as the Dreyfus brothers, who had legitimately defeated him in his ambition to control the firm they had founded, British Celanese . . .

They would learn that he had staged a large-scale jewel robbery at his palatial villa at Biarritz, on the south-west coast of France, and then collected some quarter of a million pounds-worth of insurance money. . . They would learn of the savings he had taken from the pockets of small investors and put in his own.

Worst of all, they – and every stockbroker and banker in Europe and North America – would learn that Loewenstein had no intention of ending his corrupt practices. He was too deeply enmeshed in his own double dealings for that. He could not stop, he could not retreat, he could only go on. And, once the truth about him was out, no one in power could allow him to do that.

Had he been able to confide in anyone – one of the aides or secretaries who entered the plane with him – he might have agreed to meet the blackmailer's terms. The money the man wanted, a half a million pounds or so, meant little to him. But pride, and the knowledge that once the first payment was made there would come another, and another, stopped him from taking the 'weak' way out.

He would sooner kill himself than give in to such a villian. He would sooner die than be exposed as a cheat, a criminal, and a fraud. Then, temporarily shrugging off such untypically pessimistic thoughts, he stood in the plane's cabin as the sun began its slow, evening slide towards the horizon.

PERFECT CONDITIONS

Everyone he needed for the trip was with him. There was Arthur Hodgson, his personal secretary and right hand, sitting at a table taking papers and files from the brief-case that was as much a part of him as his soft voice and unflappable manner. The two girl secretaries were at their tables, typewriters in front of them, ready to take dictation or type out letters he had already composed. Fred Baxter, his valet, was seated with his kit of brushes, combs, coat-hangers and shoe polish in a box by his side.

The plane – one of a fleet owned by Loewenstein – was commanded by his number one pilot, Captain Donald Drew, who had previously worked with Imperial Airways. He and co-pilot Robert Little had the important task of getting the millionaire safely to Brussels in time for a business dinner – one that could add further assets to his expanding empire.

Before the take-off commenced, Captain Loewenstein – who had been commissioned in the Belgian army during World War One – went forward to speak to Drew. A native of Belgium, and the son of a successful banker, Loewenstein had the accent and excitability of the 'continental'.

'Remember, I must be dining at my house by nine o'clock.'

'No problem, sir,' replied Drew. 'It's a two-hour flight and the conditions are perfect.'

'Even so,' continued the tycoon, 'I don't want you to fly high. If bad weather comes on you must fly straight through it – don't try to rise above. As you know, I have a fear of great heights.'

Drew nodded. 'You needn't worry, sir. I shan't take her above 4,000 feet. We'll not be out of sight of sea or land.'

GAMBLING SPLURGES

Satisfied, Loewenstein returned to the cabin with its thick, maroon carpet, luxurious armchairs, indirect lighting, and silk curtains. The plane – a Fokker VII – had been modified to his own specifications. One of its prides was the heated and well-equipped toilet – the door of which faced the entrance to the plane. The door – like many of the products of Loewenstein's mind – had more than one function.

When the plane was on the ground it was kept closed so that the lavatory was discreetly hidden from anyone entering or leaving the machine. During a flight, however, it was opened so that it shut off the rear of the fuselage from the cabin – so adding to the effect of exclusiveness and privacy.

Shortly after 6 p.m. – with the summer afternoon dying around it in an explosion of mauve, red, and gold – the Fokker taxied into the wind and took off in the direction of the Kent coast, then across to Dunkirk, and on to Brussels. As soon as the plane left the ground, Baxter the valet opened the toilet door. For the next two hours the world of Alfred Loewenstein was self-contained.

In the cockpit Captain Drew handed the controls over to co-pilot Little and relaxed with a thriller he was reading. In the cabin Arthur Hodgson shuffled papers and read through the voluminous and complicated memos which his employer had asked him to prepare for their forthcoming meetings. The secretaries clacked away at their machines. Baxter put his head back and dozed. Only Loewenstein had nothing to do but think, reflect, and brood.

Unlike some men with his influence and riches, he was not in constant need of sex and mistresses. A devout Roman Catholic, he was happily married and devoted to his wife and 18-year-old son. Living well had never been a problem to him. His main and family home was in Belgium, a mansion on the outskirts of Brussels. Whatever other capital he visited, he always took over an entire floor of one of the leading hotels – the Ritz in London, the George V in Paris, the Adlon in Berlin.

In Biarritz alone he had some 50 villas at his disposal, and filled them with friends whenever he went on one of his periodical gambling splurges at the casino there. It mattered nothing to him what he lost, for he was obtaining interest on the £12m. he lent to the Belgium government in 1926, and the £35m. he lent to France a few months later.

The basis of his fortune had been founded immediately after World War One. He invested the money left him by his father and reaped a rich harvest as inflation made paupers of some men and millionaires of others. His financial activities made him famous – or infamous – in banking and stock exchange circles. But the general public had still to hear of Captain Loewenstein – the man who boasted he had 'half Europe in my pocket and the other half clambering to get in'!

TANTRUMS

By the early 1920s, however, his name was appearing in the social columns and sports pages as well as in the financial sections of the Press. Rugged-looking and well-built, he disguised and made nonsense of his congenitally weak heart by becoming one of the leading amateur sportsmen of the day.

He boxed, he swam, he fenced, he played golf and tennis. He was trained and coaxed by his own team of professionals until, in the end, it was they who were learning from him. He was an expert gymnast, could ride a horse as if born in the saddle, and was a frequent competitor at horse-jumping shows held at London's Olympia.

He was a popular and much-followed race-horse owner, and in 1927 thousands of admiring punters backed Easter Hero – the favourite and owned by Captain Loewenstein – in its unsuccessful attempt to win the Grand National Steeplechase. Only one thing sullied his public image: his temper, which grew fiercer and more out of control each time he lost it.

His tantrums when losing on the golf-course or tennis-court made most sportsmen reluctant to play with him. And his rages were not confined to sporting spheres. In 1926 he assaulted one of his private secretaries (the man had had the temerity to alter the phrasing in a letter dictated by Loewenstein), knocked him to the ground, and hit him while he lay.

A few weeks later he and a friend drove to the Biarritz casino for a night's gambling. His companion – dressed in sports jacket and flannels – was refused admission and asked to return wearing evening dress. 'How dare you insult a friend of mine!' screamed Loewenstein at the bemused doorkeeper. 'Friends of mine are allowed in anywhere – dressed in any way they please!'

Bunching his fist, he struck the doorman on the jaw, breaking several of the employee's teeth. Charges were taken out against Loewenstein by both men, and he was fined at the local court for 'assault and conduct prejudicial to the general peace'. His self-esteem had received a beating, and that only made his disposition touchier, his frenzies more manic.

Perhaps it was looking back on all this that sent what his staff thought was a 'hot flush' running through his body. The English coastline had fallen behind when Loewenstein suddenly tore off his coat, shirt collar, and tie. Red-faced and seemingly gasping for breath, he opened the window on his left and put his head half-way out. The Goodwin Sands were just below him, and in anyone else it could be taken that he was admiring the view.

That was certainly the first thought that came to Robert Little as – while flying the plane – he glanced over his shoulder to inspect the people in the cabin. Through the glass panel in the cockpit door he saw that they were all busy with something – all except Loewenstein, who now put his head back in and slumped as if exhausted.

UNDUE EFFECT

Little then considered that, as the plane was flying so low, the millionaire was possibly suffering from the feeling of being 'too near the water or the ground'. Either that or the slight loss of oxygen content was having an undue effect upon him. But Loewenstein had given his orders, and Little knew better than to query them – let alone contradict them.

The Fokker flew on at 4,000 feet and Little returned to his duties as a pilot. If anything was wrong with the tycoon, then his valet or personal secretary could well take care of it. But those in the cabin – fearful of Loewenstein's growing bouts of fury – did not like to mention the fact that he seemed to be in discomfort. Until he raised the subject, they would let it safely and peacefully alone.

PARALYZED

Five minutes went by and Loewenstein suddenly got out of his armchair, strode down the cabin, and opened the door to the toilet and the rear of the plane. Again no one thought there was anything unduly significant – or ominous – about it.

A further 10 minutes passed before Loewenstein's absence caused the first flutter of panic. Looking up from his paper work, and seeing that his boss was still out of his seat, Arthur Hodgson went back to speak to Baxter. He shook the valet by the shoulder and asked him what could be keeping their employer.

Baxter muttered that he didn't know, but he'd go and take a look. He knocked, then reopened the door and peered inside the fuselage. For a moment he couldn't see anyone. There was no one standing by the wash-basin with a towel in hand, or combing his hair in the mirror. He looked again before the truth hammered him. It was starkly clear that Loewenstein was no longer on the plane!

He turned speechlessly to the rest of the entourage, his face the colour of the clean white shirt he was wearing. Hodgson hurried forward to confirm what the valet's expression told him. He then went back to his seat, sat for a moment with his mind paralyzed, and forced himself into action. Taking up a pencil he wrote three words in his notebook: 'The Captain's gone.'

With the others watching him as if he was about to throw himself under a bus, he hoisted himself to his feet and moved into the cockpit. Silently he gave the note to Drew, who was still deep in his murder mystery. The pilot read the three scribbled words, looked up, and said bewilderedly: 'How do you mean – 'gone'?'

Hodgson wrung his hands. 'He must have . . . fallen out.'

'But how?'

'The outside door – it seems to be open!'

It took Drew only seconds to see that Hodgson was not lying, that he hadn't gone mad. He ran through the cabin and into the toilet area. There the outside door – the one facing the lavatory seat – was slightly open and shaking in the slipstream. The gap was not more than a few inches – but the door could have been blown back once Loewenstein had fallen through it.

Or had he fallen? Had he thrown himself out deliberately? Or had he – incredible thought – been pushed? These possibilities raced again and again through Drew's head as he returned to the cockpit, took over the controls from Little, and brought the Fokker down almost to sea level.

There was no sign of the tycoon – no body lying spread-eagled on the flat grey surface of the sea. The three possibilities – accident, suicide, murder – again confronted Drew as he headed the plane towards northern France and landed on the beach near Dunkirk. There the crew and staff attempted to make some sense of what had happened – or what they thought had happened.

But with the secretaries weeping hysterically, and with Baxter and Hodgson in a state of shock, it was impossible to find any clues, make any sense, put forward any positive explanation. This difficulty arose again when the French police were called in, and the British Air Ministry sent a team of experts to examine the plane's outer door – which could be operated from the inside by a handle.

MORTAL SIN

The experts soon established that it would be possible for anyone to open the door in mid-air – to an extent of some two feet. That fact, obviously, ruled out two possibilities. It would be practically impossible for a man of Loewenstein's build to fall through such a narrow space. It would be practically impossible for anyone to have sneaked into the fuselage from the cabin and forced a man of Loewenstein's strength from the plane.

That only left suicide – and that answer was officially accepted when, two weeks later, the millionaire's body was found by a trawler off the coast of France. There was no sign of a struggle having taken place, and Loewenstein had been alive when he hit the water. In fact he had not been killed by the fall: he had drowned.

By his last action – the one mortal sin that a Roman Catholic can commit – Captain Alfred Loewenstein had defeated the man who was going to expose and disgrace him. To the tycoon, death was preferable to shame and dishonour. Whether it was weak or strong, he had taken what for him was the only way out.

The Case of Left Luggage

The suitcase was found at a London railway station. It contained the legs of a young woman whose severed torso had already been discovered. Pathologist Sir Bernard Spilsbury was called in to join the search for a killer who stored away his victim like pieces of unwanted property . . .

G. K. CHESTERTON suggested that the ideal place for a secret society to meet would be an open balcony overlooking a public square. The same kind of wild logic seems to inspire those murderers who use trunks for the disposal of the corpse. The ideal solution to the murderer's problem would be to make the body disappear into thin air; next on the list, to hide it where it could never be found. Putting it in a trunk, where it is sure to be discovered, is no way to conceal a murder.

The policeman and the pathologist, on the other hand, are bound to experience a certain satisfaction when a killer chooses this method of disposal. It gives them a sporting chance. For unless the murderer has the coolness and foresight of a master chess player, he is almost certain to have left a dozen clues that will eventually reveal his identity.

This was the view held by the Chief Constable of Brighton when, on June 17, 1934, he was called to the Brighton left-luggage office to examine the nude torso of a woman that had been found in a plywood trunk. Railway clerks could recall nothing about the man who had deposited the trunk there on Derby Day – June 6th – the busiest day of the year. But there seemed to be an abundance of clues.

Sir Bernard Spilsbury examined the remains. They were of a young woman in her early twenties. The head, arms and legs had been removed; but the torso suggested that the girl belonged to the middle or upper classes. She had a good figure, with no slack flesh, and the muscles were well developed, suggesting plenty of exercise. The golden brown of the skin also indicated that she spent much of her time in a warmer climate than England. At the time of death, she had been four months pregnant.

Important Clues

An alert sent out to all other cloakrooms in England led to the discovery of the legs in a case at King's Cross station in London. Each had been severed at the thigh and the knee, and they confirmed the view that the girl had been athletic and well-proportioned. The conclusion that the trunk had been left by a man was reached by weighing it; only a strong man could have lifted it without help.

There were two important clues. On a sheet of brown paper – in which the body had been wrapped – there was the word 'ford'. It looked as if it was the second half of a place name, like Guildford or Watford. In the trunk, there were two newspapers. The copies of the Daily Mail dated May 31st and June 2nd were of an edition that was circulated only within fifty miles of London. When a porter recalled helping a man to carry the trunk on Derby Day, it began to look as though a solution was near.

Secret Affair

For the man had travelled on the train from Dartford to Brighton. A girl who had travelled in the same third class compartment was able to give a rough description of him. But of the five cheap day return tickets that had been issued on that day, not all could be traced, and the police eliminated all those they were able to contact.

Although the police were able to trace the makers of the trunk and suitcase, they were unable to give any useful information as to where or to whom these had been sold. No shop owners came forward with any recollection of either piece having been bought from their shop in the weeks leading up to Derby Day. So here the trail petered out.

Spilsbury estimated that the girl had been dead since May 30, a week before the trunk was left at the station. The man obviously had plenty of spare time, as well as a home where he could conceal a body for a week without fear of discovery. That again suggested a man of leisure.

The fact that it had taken him a week to dispose of the body indicated that the crime was not premeditated. And so the police could reconstruct most of the story. A well-to-do man, strong and athletic, has a secret love affair with a girl of his own class. He lives in Dartford, which is on the south-eastern edge of London, part of the 'stockbroker belt'.

She gets pregnant; on May 30, she calls on him to ask him what he intends to do about it. There is a quarrel, perhaps a fight, and he hits her on the head with some heavy instrument – the head was never found, but the body bore no marks of violence – or perhaps fell on top of her against a piece of furniture. Her death shocks him; he spends several days thinking on what to do with the body, then decides to dismember it, and deposit the trunk in Brighton. He travels on a third class day return, so as not to attract attention. And, in all probability, he leaves the country as soon as he has disposed of the body.

Careful Searches

Sherlock Holmes would have had no difficulty solving the problem. He would have ordered a check on all ports, to establish which resident of Dartford had left the country immediately after Derby Day. He would have investigated the sports clubs in the Dartford area, and the riding stables. And the murderer would probably have been arrested boarding the *train bleu* to Cannes . . .

The British police had less luck. Careful searches

of left-luggage offices revealed the corpses of three children and much stolen property, but no further clue to the Brighton trunk murderer. And from that day to this, the crime has remained unsolved. This can be attributed to luck rather than careful planning. But the case remains the interesting exception that proves the rule: that a trunk is the worst possible place to hide a body.

Wishful Thinking

A study of the history of trunk murderers suggests that in many cases, the murderer has a sub-conscious desire to be caught. It can certainly be argued that the act of hiding a body in a trunk bears an interesting resemblance to the ostrich's attempt to hide by burying its head in the sand. In short, this is an example of Jean Paul Sartre's psychology of 'magic' – wishful thinking – that we have already encountered in the case of passion-killers. This can be seen clearly in one of the earliest cases of trunk murder in England: that of Arthur Devereux. It is a story of weakness, self-deception and wishful thinking that would have appealed to Stendhal, whose *Scarlet and Black* is based upon just a true-life murderer.

One warm summer day in 1898, a pretty girl named Beatrice Gregory was strolling in Alexandra Park, Hastings, when she fell into conversation with a polite and neatly dressed young man. His name was Arthur Devereux, and he was a chemist's assistant. Beatrice was on holiday with her mother, and the holiday atmosphere no doubt made her more susceptible to romance; she saw Arthur Devereux every evening for the remainder of her holiday. Her mother liked him too. Arthur Devereux was 'different' – imaginative and ambitious. When he talked about the future, it seemed marvellous and exciting, and she longed to share it. When he proposed, she accepted at once.

Pretty and feminine

Mrs. Gregory was less than happy about the engagement. There was something of the born loser about her, and she was afraid it had rubbed off on her daughter. She found it hard to believe that the future could be as glorious as Arthur painted it. And after a few months of marriage, Beatrice began to share her mother's misgivings. The truth was that, emotionally, Arthur was something of a child. He had wanted her because she was pretty and feminine; it never struck him that there is a practical side to marriage. He found the penny-pinching of married life on a chemist's assistant's wages less romantic than he had expected. He became gloomy and preoccupied.

Then a son was born. It made things more difficult for Arthur; yet oddly enough, he didn't seem to mind. He adored his son, whom they named Stanley. For a while, it looked as if the marriage was going to be a success after all. Then fate intervened, and Beatrice discovered she was again pregnant. The news plunged Arthur into depression. He spent more time than ever cuddling and playing with his son. When his wife produced him twin boys, Lawrence and Evelyn, it seemed the last straw. His affections were already fully engaged; he had no interest in the new arrivals.

Morphine Bottle

During the course of the next two years, the Devereuxs moved to a flat in Kilburn, north-west London. Beatrice was now undernourished. Arthur was still working as a chemist's assistant, but the wages were poor. He was an embittered man who felt that his wife had trapped him, and he daydreamed of how easy life would be without Beatrice and the twins. One day in 1905, he decided to do something about it.

The murder was carefully planned. First, he asked the landlord if, when the tenants in the flat below moved out, he could take over the extra flat. Then he brought home a large tin trunk. A few days later, on January 29, 1905, he brought home a bottle of morphine, and somehow induced his wife to swallow most of its contents – perhaps leading her to believe it was a medicine for her cough. Both she and the twins were dead by the next morning. Devereux placed them in the trunk, arranged for it to be taken to a warehouse in Harrow, then moved – with Stanley – to another part of London.

Mrs. Gregory called at the Kilburn flat, and found it empty. She succeeded in getting a letter forwarded to Arthur, but his reply was strangely non-committal. He said that he had sent Beatrice on holiday, and that he would prefer that her mother should not try to contact her. Mrs. Gregory's intuitions warned her of the worst. She heard about the furniture van, traced it to the depository in Harrow, and finally succeeded in getting an order authorizing her to open the trunk.

Twenty-four hours later, with the story of the discovery of the three corpses in all the newspapers, a worried Arthur Devereux prepared to move on again. This time, he went to Coventry, where he found another job with a chemist. Inspector Pollard, the man in charge of the case, had little difficulty in finding him; it was simply a matter of making a nationwide check on chemists who had recently hired a new assistant with a 6-year-old son. When Pollard called to arrest him, Devereux blurted out: 'You're making a mistake. I don't know anything about a tin trunk.' Pollard had not mentioned it.

Fantasy World

At the Old Bailey, Devereux's defence was that his wife had killed herself and the twins, and that he had lost his nerve and concealed the body in the trunk. But there was one fact that undermined his story. On January 22, 1905, he had replied to an advertisement for a job at Hull, with a telegram: 'Will a widower with one child, aged six, suit?' But at that time, Beatrice and the twins were still alive. On August 15, 1905, Arthur Devereux was hanged at Pentonville prison.

An alienist – which is what psychiatrists were called in those days – had found Arthur Devereux to be sane, but it is difficult to agree with the conclusion. Is it sanity to live completely in a world of fantasy, and to commit a murder without the slightest chance of escaping the penalty? Devereux adored his son; did it not strike him that, in killing his wife, he was risking leaving his son an orphan?

He knew his mother-in-law well enough to know that she would never rest until she had traced her daughter; and he must also have realized that a trunk containing three corpses will soon begin to attract attention by its smell. If he had been sane, he would have taken Stanley and simply left his wife. But he wanted Beatrice to vanish, to disappear like the lady in a conjurer's cabinet. Wishful thinking, to that extent, is surely a form of insanity?

Sexual Charm

The Monte Carlo trunk murder, which took place two years after Devereux's execution, raises the same question in an even more acute form. The killer was an adventuress called Maria Vere Goold, who had assumed the title 'Lady Vere Goold'. Her husband, an alcoholic and weak-minded Irishman, was in line for a baronetcy; but his wife was anticipating.

Maria's career had been even more remarkable than that of her fellow countrywoman, Maria Manning, hanged in 1849 for the murder of her lover. Both were hard, calculating women, who used their sexual charms unscrupulously. Maria Goold – born Girodin – had lost two husbands in suspicious circumstances when she met her third husband, Vere Goold, in London. Goold had little money, but that didn't worry the adventuress; she was used to living on credit and borrowed money.

Mumbled Answers

In their first year of marriage, Vere Goold exhausted the patience – and the purses – of all his close relatives. In Monte Carlo, in the early months of 1907, they tried gambling with what was left of their money, and lost it. Various dishonest expedients – like obtaining a ring from a jeweller 'on approval', and then pawning it – kept them going a little longer, until Maria succeeded in making the acquaintance of a rich old Swedish lady, Madame Levin, who was impressed by the aristocratic Vere Goolds. But she proved to be tight-fisted with money. She lent Maria forty pounds, but declined to part with any more. In fact, she pressed relentlessly for its return.

On Sunday August 4, 1907, 'Lady' Vere Goold invited Madame Levin out to the Villa Menesimy, where they were living in considerable poverty. And as the old lady sat talking to 'Sir Vere Goold', whose mumbled answers suggested he was drunk again, Maria crept up on her from behind, and dealt her a crashing blow with a heavy poker. Mrs. Levin collapsed, Maria produced a knife, and drove it into her tormentor's throat. Then she proceeded to hack off the head and limbs of the victim, and pack them into a large trunk. A niece who was staying with them returned later that evening and found the place covered with blood. Maria explained that her husband had had a fit, and vomited blood.

It is not clear what Maria had in mind. They left Monte Carlo for Marseilles that evening, taking the trunk with them. In Marseilles, the trunk was labelled 'Charing Cross, London', and a luggage clerk was instructed to dispatch it, while Maria and 'Sir' Vere Goold retired to a nearby hotel for breakfast and a sleep.

Cold Contempt

The clerk, a man named Pons, observed blood oozing from the trunk. The August heat was also causing it to smell unpleasantly. He went to their hotel, and asked them what was in it. Maria explained haughtily that it was poultry, and ordered him to send it off immediately. Instead, Pons called at the police station, where an Inspector told him that the Vere Goolds could not be allowed to leave Marseilles until the contents of the trunk had been examined by the police.

Pons returned to the hotel, and found Maria and her husband about to leave. He asked them to accompany him to the police station. With cold contempt, Maria agreed. She took along a carpet bag that had accompanied them to the hotel. In the cab, her façade collapsed, and she suddenly offered Pons ten thousand francs to let her go. He remained immovable. An hour later, the police had found the torso of Madame Levin in the trunk, and her head and legs in the carpet bag.

It was so obvious that Maria was the guilty party that it was she who was sentenced to death, while her husband received life imprisonment. The death sentence was not carried out. While she was in prison in Cayenne, Maria died of typhoid fever. Her husband, deprived of alcohol and drugs, committed suicide. Yet in retrospect, it seems that Maria also subconsciously committed suicide.

Copious Bloodstains

What could she gain from the death of Madame Levin? What was to prevent her flitting quietly out of Monte Carlo by night, as she had flitted from so many other cities? Or had a lifetime of crime and calculation finally loosened her hold on reality, as the murder suggests? Once again, the trunk is seen as the symbol of human inadequacy and self-deception.

As to the interesting question of who invented the trunk murder, there is no agreement among historians of crime. Possibly the honour belongs to a Herr Bletry, an innkeeper of Hegersheim, Germany. When the corpse of a woman was found in a yellow trunk at the Hegersheim left-luggage office, some time in the mid-1870s, the sheet in which the body was wrapped was quickly traced back to Herr Bletry's establishment.

If Bletry was the killer, he was singularly fortunate. Local gossip alleged that the corpse was that of his former housekeeper and mistress, Adèle Brouart, who had vanished some time before. Finally, it was positively identified as that of Adèle Brouart by various witnesses. But while Bletry was preparing to stand trial for his life, Adèle Brouart walked into the police station . . . The case collapsed, and the police were too discouraged to start all over again. If they had, Bletry would surely have been found guilty.

He tried to explain copious bloodstains in his kitchen with a story of a bleeding nose. The police were fairly certain that the trunk belonged to Bletry's present housekeeper, Franziska Lallemend, but because the other evidence seemed so strong, they had neglected to pursue this line of enquiry. Finally, a strange woman had been seen to arrive at the inn, and had not been seen subsequently. The motive for the crime was probably robbery; but since Bletry was allowed to go free, we shall never know.

A book called *Supernature* by the zoologist Lyall Watson mentions a curious fact that may be of interest to trunk murderers of the future. A Frenchman named Bovis, who was exploring the pharaoh's chamber in the Great Pyramid of Cheops, observed that although it seemed damp, the body of a cat, and various other litter, was apparently undecayed. It struck M. Bovis that perhaps the *shape* of the pyramid might account for this. He made an accurate scale model of the pyramid, and put a dead cat in it.

Cosmic Energy

The body mummified instead of decaying. Dr. Watson claims to have tested this himself with a home-made cardboard pyramid (made of four isosceles triangles with the proportion base to sides of 15.7 to 14.94). A dead mouse placed in the pyramid mummified, whereas a mouse placed in a shoe box decayed – and stank – in the normal manner. Even more strange, razor blades left in such a pyramid remain sharp even after much use – a Czech firm has patented the Cheops Pyramid Sharpener.

Dr. Watson's theory is that the pyramid acts as some kind of a greenhouse to cosmic energy, which dehydrates organic matter, and somehow affects the crystalline structure at the edge of a razor blade. So in theory, a trunk shaped like a scale-model of the Great Pyramid should preserve bodies indefinitely – even if dismembered – and prevent smell. On the other hand, it is true that the shape might arouse curiosity in railway cloakrooms. No modification is likely to alter the fact that the trunk is one of the least efficient means of disposing of human remains.

Hired Assassins

Is money the real motive? Or are there deeper reasons
why men offer their services as professional killers?
What kind of society do they reflect . . . ?

'I STARTED killing people for pure pleasure when I
was eight years old. Then I learned that you could
get good money for killing, and so I set myself up
in business . . .' The speaker was a 22-year-old
Mexican, Zosimo Montesino, whose murder record
certainly exceeded a hundred and fifty. His first
victim had been a 'witch' who had bewitched his
parents by giving them a strange brew.

Twelve years later Zosimo and his chief lieutenants, two brothers named Alcocer, set up an
ambush outside the town of Tepalcingo; they had
been hired by a local farmer to murder Mendoza
Omana, a politician. Mendoza happened to be
accompanied by his wife and 3-year-old son; but
that made no difference. All three were cut down
with shotguns and the father and son killed outright,
while the sobbing mother, lying beside the body of
her boy, begged two peasants passing by to help
her. 'We cannot interfere,' they said, and walked off.

Casual Brutality

Nearly seven weeks later, the killers were arrested

in a shanty town shack on the outskirts of Mexico City. They took their capture very lightly, treating it as something of a joke, and Zosimo casually admitted to his hundred and fifty or so contract killings, at prices ranging from £3 to £150. A week later, he alleged that the confession had been obtained from him by torture. 'I haven't really killed more than half a dozen people, and that was mostly in self-defence.'

Most of us find such casual brutality incomprehensible. It seems more frightening than the more familiar type of murder – the crime of passion or greed or anger. At least these have personal motives. To murder a stranger for money seems more depraved. Surely the existence of such monsters is a sign of some profound sickness in our civilization?

Not necessarily. It is a mistake to try to judge Zosimo Montesino in terms that would apply to the average citizen of London or New York. Mexico itself is a weird social paradox. It has the highest murder rate in the world; murder actually accounts for more deaths than disease; yet up to a few years ago it also had one of the lowest rates of juvenile delinquency in the world. In rural areas, the families were very close-knit; a Mexican teenager will put his arm around his mother in public without embarrassment.

On the other hand, because there is so much poverty, life is cheap. It is only in affluent societies that people treat illness and death as a catastrophe. All such societies have high murder rates – it is true of most tropical countries. And nowadays, as

Mexico becomes more urbanized – and prosperous – the rate of juvenile delinquency also
climbs steadily. It is hardly surprising that Mexico
seems to be caught in a spiral of crime.

The theories of the anthropologist Ruth Benedict
enable us to understand what is happening.
Among American Indians, she observed societies
in which there was a high level of kindness and
co-operation; she called these 'high-synergy
societies'; other tribes were naturally mean and
self-centred, and she called these 'low-synergy
societies'. Mexico is in process of transition from a
high- to a low-synergy society. This does *not* mean
that it will one day be wholly composed of mean
and self-centred people. Civilization may cause a
lot of problems; but it also produces a lot of people
who care about their fellow human beings. So
there *is* reason for optimism.

Most societies *start* as high-synergy societies –
when they are primitive – and then they drift
towards low-synergy, as they become more
sophisticated and civilized. As they slowly become
more civilized, there is a movement back towards
high-synergy, and this appears to be a kind of
social law. But when a civilization drifts from high-
to low-synergy, it is the poor who feel the effects
first – one cheerfully callous student of sociology
compared the process to the rats that die first in a
plague. *This* explains the existence of people like
Zosimo Montesino. It is clear from his confessions
that he felt he was living in a wholly vicious and
murderous society, where it was a case of kill or
be killed.

He told the police: 'I don't know why you're making such a fuss about me. I know people who have killed more. For example, the police captain Cosme Maldonado. He was a real mass murderer.' Zosimo then described at some length how he and one of his gang finally shot Maldonado. 'It took 13 bullets to do it, because he was so fat.'

Was Maldonado such a mass killer as Zosimo represented him to be? Probably. In the Argentine capital, Buenos Aires, a few years ago, the police got so sick of the crime wave that a special execution squad was formed; they rounded up known gangsters, took them for a 'ride', and dumped their bullet-riddled bodies where they would attract attention and serve as a warning to other criminals. Typically, this 'rough justice squad' got so out of hand that it had to be suppressed by the police themselves. The moral is a familiar one: in countries with a soaring crime rate and a high level of poverty, where the police are underpaid, they themselves are forced to out-do the criminals in brutality. So Zosimo may not have been exaggerating when he called the Mexican police captain a worse killer than himself. But all this adds up to a low-synergy society, where two farm workers can watch a mother and child cut down by shotgun blasts, and walk away saying: 'It is nothing to do with us.'

If Zosimo is by no means the rule among Mexican criminals, neither is he the exception. Martin Rivera Benitez, nicknamed 'Big Soul' in the state of Hidalgo, told police in 1972: 'I cannot count the number of people I have killed for money. My fame spread so far that I often had a long waiting list. In order to prove that the job had been done properly, I would cut off the head and show it to the man who had hired me.'

In his mortuary in the woods near Jazatipan, twelve headless corpses were found, but these are probably only a small proportion of the people Benitez killed between 1969 and 1972; police believe the victims total more than fifty. 'I didn't see anything wrong in killing for money,' said Benitez. 'If I hadn't done it, somebody else would. And it was better paid than working as a farm labourer.' The comment brings to mind the remark of Reggie Kray, the London gangster, to his biographer John Pearson: that in the society in which they were born, crime was the *only* way to get out of the social rut in which you were stuck.

Another vital aspect of the psychology of the hired killer emerges in the case of Nestor Mencias Alarcon, the 26-year-old youth who killed Isabel Garcia and her 9-year-old daughter Elvira with a machete. Alarcon claimed he was ordered to commit the murder by his employer, Señora Martinez Anguilar, who was jealous of a long-standing love affair between her husband and the victim. After paying a witch doctor £50 (1000 pesos) to bewitch Isabel out of her involvement, the impatient Señora Anguilar ordered Alarcon to kill her – or so Alarcon alleged. Alarcon was paid £55 – 'that's a lot of money for a man like me,' he said.

Señora Garcia's 9-year-old daughter was with her mother, the killer liked her 'because she was a nice polite little girl'. But as the child saw her mother hacked to death with a machete, she fought with Alarcon and was also killed. The murders, like so many others in Mexico, might have gone unpunished if, said Alarcon, his employer had paid up. But Señora Anguilar lost her temper when Alarcon admitted to killing the child, and called him a sadist. She refused to pay, and Alarcon made the mistake of going on the run, so that he became an automatic suspect.

The police had been convinced that Isabel and her daughter had been killed in a rape attempt. As soon as Alarcon was picked up, he confessed everything, implicating his employer. What is significant here is that Alarcon claimed he felt obliged to obey his employer's orders simply because she was his employer – his social superior.

Criminal Mentality

A psychologist who was asked to explain the hired killing of Olga Duncan by Luis Moya and Gus Baldonado pointed out that the killers were Mexicans of poor family, and that they found it easy to obey the orders of a white woman whom they felt to be their social superior. In other words, they felt *absolved* of the crime of murder, in the way that the soldiers at My Lai felt absolved because they were ordered to massacre Vietnamese civilians by a superior officer. Soldiers in war generally feel no guilt about killing; dispossessed persons of a 'socially inferior' group often feel they are at war with the non-synergic society that surrounds them.

The Mother Duncan case also raises the interesting issue of the psychology of the person who hires the killer. Elizabeth Duncan had the typical criminal mentality, the outlook that can be seen in murderers like Neville Heath, Marcel Petiot, and George Smith, the 'Brides in the Bath' killer; she was a plausible confidence trickster who could become so involved in her own lies that she came to believe them true.

She was also an example of a rarer phenomenon: the female counterpart of A. E. Van Vogt's 'right man' – the man with such a paranoid obsession with being 'in the right' that he will commit any violence rather than admit that he might be wrong.

Mother Duncan was a 'right woman'. When she set her mind on something, it seemed to her that it was one of the laws of nature that she should get it – a religious 'right man' would say that it was the 'will of God'. In her eyes, a woman who had married her son against her wishes had *no right* to be alive. It is tempting to declare that she was insane – and if the definition of insanity is to be out of touch with reality, she was. But if she was insane, it was by her own will, her own decision. She *wanted* to believe that her wishes were the will of nature, and she had always lived in such a way that she had got away with it.

The same may well be true of the principal figure in one of the most brutal cases of hired killing in America in recent years. The man behind the crime was a good-looking, smooth young lawyer named Joe Peel, who was a municipal

Judge at West Palm Beach, Florida. Peel was a 'go-getter' whose ambition was to become governor. In 1949, at the age of 32, he seemed well on the way to achieving his ambition. He was well-liked, a member of the social set, and the owner of a number of thriving enterprises such as night clubs. He also found vice profitable, but his neighbours knew nothing about this.

It was in 1949 that Peel met an ex-convict named Floyd Holzapfel. Holzapfel was also good looking and charming, and his criminal record was not too serious – a few incompetent gas station stickups, for which he had served terms in jail. Holzapfel was weak rather than wicked, with a feeling that fate had always dealt him a losing hand, and a strong desire to be liked and accepted.

The chief obstacle to Peel's plans for political eminence was another Judge, Curtis Chillingworth, who had had occasion to rebuke Peel for legal double-dealing. Peel had good reason to suspect that the Judge had learned about his rackets, and that he could not expect to remain a member of the Florida bench for much longer. To Peel's logical and ruthless mind, the answer was to murder Judge Chillingworth. When he explained the situation to his new right-hand man, Holzapfel was scared, and also shocked.

Social Respect

He was basically an easygoing, good-natured man, but his position as Peel's chief lieutenant also gave him the kind of standing and social respect that he had never had before. He allowed himself to be persuaded, but he stipulated that he needed an accomplice. Peel suggested a negro called Bobby Lincoln, who was involved in his rackets. Lincoln was also a non-violent man, with no criminal record, but when a Judge asked him a favour, he felt bound to agree.

On June 14, 1955, Holzapfel and Bobby Lincoln went in a boat to the beach below Judge Chilling- worth's house. They expected him to be alone that night – his attractive wife was supposed to be with relatives. Unfortunately for Mrs. Chilling- worth, she had changed her plans.

The hired killers knocked on the door, and the unsuspecting judge opened it in his pyjamas. Holzapfel asked if there was anyone else in the house; the judge called his wife. Holzapfel and Lincoln tied their hands with tape, and forced them into the boat. At one point, Mrs. Chilling- worth screamed, and was silenced with a heavy blow from the gun butt.

Undercover Man

Once at sea, they put weights around Mrs. Chilling- worth's waist. Her husband said: 'Remember, I love you,' and she answered: 'I love you, too'; then they tossed her overboard. She sank immediately, without screaming. At this point, the Judge man- aged to fling himself overboard, and began to swim with his feet. He was moving away from the boat when Holzapfel began battering him with a rifle butt. Then the anchor rope was looped around

Chillingworth's neck, and the anchor tossed overboard. The corpses were never recovered.

But in killing a man as distinguished as Judge Chillingworth, Joe Peel had over-reached himself. Police began an intensive investigation into his disappearance; it was a long job, and in the meantime, Holzapfel had a chance to commit another murder. This was of a crook named Lew Harvey, suspected of being an informer. Harvey was also forced into a boat, shot in the back of the head, and dumped in the canal with a block of concrete attached to his legs.

A few days later, the body floated to the surface. On the night he was 'taken for a ride', Harvey had felt nervous, and had given his wife the number of the car in which Holzapfel and Lincoln collected him. The police soon traced the car to Holzapfel; they now had a strong suspicion that this was how Judge Chillingworth had disappeared, and that Peel and Holzapfel were the men behind it.

An acquaintance of Peel's, an insurance saleman named Jim Yenzer, was hired by the police to act as an undercover man. Yenzer's inside information had soon got Holzapfel into so much trouble that he was sent to trial for an attempt to hijack arms from a group of Cuban revolutionaries. He was finally set free; but his faith in Peel's friendship – and his generosity – had been heavily eroded; Holzapfel began to mutter threats. Peel now approached the police informer Jim Yenzer, and offered him $2,000 to murder Holzapfel. Yenzer agreed, but kept putting it off.

Since the police were now paying constant attention to Holzapfel's affairs, his boss persuaded him to flee to Rio de Janeiro, with a promise to support him indefinitely. Shortly thereafter, Yenzer also went to Rio de Janeiro, commissioned by Peel to murder the hired killer of Judge Chillingworth – and by the police to try to get a confession out of Holzapfel.

He did not succeed immediately, but he did succeed in persuading Holzapfel it was safe to return to Florida, and during a two-day drinking session in a motel in Melbourne, Florida, Yenzer and another undercover agent finally got Holzapfel to describe the murder of the Chillingworths in detail, while other police agents listened in the next room with a tape recorder. It had taken five years of unremitting police work. As a result, Holzapfel was sentenced to die – although sentence was not carried out – and Joe Peel and Bobby Lincoln each received life imprisonment.

What emerges very clearly from the study of hired killers is that money is seldom the basic motive. In 1973, an American publisher brought out a book called Killer, the anonymous autobiography of a 'hit man', who is identified on the title page only as 'Joey'. According to Joey, he has thirty-eight 'hits' to his credit, and rates as one of America's top hired killers. Born in the Bronx, Joey became involved in the rackets from childhood. At the age of 16, he was asked if he would kill a man. He accepted the job, and shot the man in the back of the head in the street.

'Then the realization came to me that I was a

made individual. I was a force to be reckoned with. A lot of people who had looked at me as being a snot-nosed wise-ass kid would now be speaking of me in different tones. The job paid $5,000.' It is significant that he mentions the money last.

What is more important is the feeling of 'being somebody'. Joey's autobiography may or may not be authentic – an anonymous book is bound to be open to doubt – but there can be no doubt that these blood-chilling pages are an accurate reflection of the psychology of the hired killer. The money is only secondary, even in mob-killings.

All of which makes it clear that it is inaccurate to speak of 'hired killers'; it would be more exact to speak of 'cat's-paw killers'. In the great majority of cases, the true psychological motivation is to be found in one man's dominance over another. The murders committed by the Charles Manson family are an archetypal example of 'cat's-paw' murders, and the Manson case also raises one of the basic legal problems of the cat's-paw murder. Manson's defence – and the defence that his supporters have been making ever since – is that he did not order Tex Watson, Susan Atkins and the others to commit murder. They may have thought he did, but that does not make him guilty. In Manson's case, it is almost impossible to believe that he was not closely involved, because his 'family' committed at least three sets of murders, but in a more recent case, there is room for doubt.

On the night of February 19, 1972, the home of Black Power leader Abdul Malik – also known as Michael X – burned down near Port-of-Spain,

Trinidad. Police investigating what looked like a case of arson discovered the corpse of a man buried in the garden. It was Joseph Skerrit, a 25-year-old barber and disciple of Michael X. Further digging finally revealed the body of Gail Ann Benson, the pretty 27-year-old daughter of a British Member of Parliament. She had been stabbed 7 times, and buried alive.

Gail Benson, it soon transpired, had been the mistress of another of Michael X's close associates, Hakim Jamal. It was believed that she had disapproved of Michael X's influence over her lover, and had tried to cause a rupture between the two men. This, said the police, was the motive for her murder. Skerrit was murdered because he happened to witness it. Jamal was also subsequently murdered by Black Power members in the USA.

Disturbing Possibility

Michael X escaped to Guyana, in South America, but was arrested there on March 1, 1972. In Trinidad, three 'lieutenants' were arrested and accused of the actual murder. Of these, Edward Chadee and Stanley Abbott were found guilty, whereas the third, Adolphus Parmassar, turned Queen's evidence, and thus escaped conviction. It was his evidence that really convicted Michael X, who was sentenced to death as the man who gave the orders, although he claimed to have been at home at the time of the murders.

And it must be admitted that, on present evidence,

there is no clear proof that Michael X ordered the executions. He was hanged on May 16, 1975; his lawyers were given no time to appeal.

The 'cat's-paw killer' is a social phenomenon, the product of a painfully evolving society. If Ruth Benedict is correct, world civilization will one day become a unified high-synergy society. When that happens, the hired killer will be no more than a relic of the savage past.

HIRED ASSASSINS: CASE STUDY

Mother Duncan's Devotion

Elizabeth Duncan's love for her child was obsessive and this love somehow seemed to spiral out of control. She had been married eleven times and bore four children, three of whom she gave up for adoption. However, Frank was different!

MIDDLE-AGED Mrs. Elizabeth Duncan, an outwardly respectable divorcée, devoted mother of a successful grown-up son, went shopping in the downtown area of Santa Barbara, California. Like so many other women among the 59,000 people of this opulent Pacific coast city, careful spender Mrs. Duncan was keeping alert eyes open for a bargain. But her quest, that December day in 1958, was not for a new chic hat, a becoming housecoat or a memorable evening gown. She was out to buy the services of a killer who would 'eliminate' – as she delicately put it – her newly-acquired daughter-in-law.

Many women like to have the company of a friend on a shopping spree and Mrs. Duncan was no exception. With her as she bustled along Santa Barbara's State Street was her close friend and confidante, Mrs. Emma Short. To the casual passer by they appeared to be no more than two rather nice, mature citizens, Mrs. Duncan nearly sixty, her friend Emma in her seventies.

But their animated, low-voiced chat was about purchased death. Mrs. Short fully shared her friend's secret and for a homely old pensioner she was remarkably complacent about it. Her only reaction, as she could later recall it, was that, although she was keeping Mrs. Duncan company, 'I didn't approve of her plan to kill her daughter-in-law'.

TWISTED WOMAN

The 'market-place' to which their dangerous mission took them was a seedy, run-down beer parlour on State Street, called the Tropical Café, owned by an illegal Mexican immigrant, Mrs. Esperanza Esquivel. Wily Mrs. Duncan had chosen it carefully. Mrs. Esquivel lived in fear that the police would discover that she had no legal right to be living and operating a business in the United States; already, on a quite separate brush with the law over the alleged receiving of stolen property, Mrs. Duncan's lawyer son, Frank, had represented the Mexican family's interests.

As Mrs. Duncan saw it, Mrs. Esquivel owed her a

favour and, moreover, she seemed the likely sort of person to know drifting, café-haunting customers ready to offer their services as hired killers.

It was all incredibly cold-blooded yet it all fitted the psychopathic personality of Elizabeth Duncan. For, despite outward appearances, she was a dangerously twisted woman. In the course of her life she had had many husbands – probably 20 or more, but even she was not certain – some taken in legal marriages, others bigamously. She had married most of them in the hope of acquiring their money, for she was also a diligent, if not very skilful, confidence trickster.

The only man who had brought her any lasting joy was Frank Low who had fathered her son, Frank, in 1928. She quickly tired of Mr. Low and illegally 'married' a Mr. Duncan, whom she also deposed in favour of yet another 'husband', but she raised her son as Frank Duncan. Young Frank she doted upon and she wrapped him in a suffocating mother love, obsessed with the anxiety that he would one day leave her.

MAJOR QUARREL

'Frank,' she told her own doctor, who was concerned about the effects on the boy of her neurotic obsession, 'will never leave me. He would never dare to get married.' Surprisingly, in view of this crushing maternal weight, Frank Duncan showed remarkable independence. An intelligent, lively-minded boy, he did well educationally, made his way through law school and ended up as a successful lawyer with bright prospects.

Somehow he survived the embarrassment of being followed around from court to court by his energetic, clinging mother and listening to her vigorous and sustained applause every time he won a case. Lawyer-colleagues, gossiping together while juries deliberated, expressed the private view that the sooner Frank Duncan found himself a wife and escaped to complete personal freedom the better off he would be.

In the few quiet moments of meditation that he could snatch for himself, Frank began to think along similar lines. He was more than ready to throw off the yoke that bound him and, in 1957, he and his mother had their first major, stand-up quarrel. In his exasperation he ordered her out of their apartment. She, prepared to go to any lengths to remind her son of her permanent servitude, responded by taking an overdose of sleeping pills. Loving Mother Duncan survived, but her action was to have terrible and far-reaching results for herself and three other people. For she was taken to a nearby hospital and there given into the care of a dark-haired attractive nurse, Canadian-born Olga Kupczyk, a 29-year-old daughter of a railroad foreman.

Olga was one of the first people Mrs. Duncan saw when she emerged, pallid and shaken, from her coma. And Olga was almost the only person in the hospital, even including his mother, to whom Frank paid immediate attention on his first bedside visit to the patient. The attraction was mutual and the devastated mother, watching the alarming, affectionate glances between son and nurse, now saw there her worst fears were being realized. Her rival, long dreamed of with dread, had taken human shape and soon Mother Duncan would no longer be Frank's only and eternal love.

Within a few months the web that was being spun between the three principals in the drama tightened with the disclosure that Olga had become pregnant and a hesitant Frank found it necessary to inform his mother that he was considering marrying the girl. Mrs. Duncan, now restored to normal, angry health, was driven into a frenzy of range, saw the nurse and told her with vehemence: 'I'll kill you before you ever marry my son. You are not a fit person to live with my son.'

Determined as he seemed to lead his own life, Frank Duncan was nevertheless still too con- scious of his mother's vulnerability to make a decisive, precipitate break. Accepting the quite exceptional patience of his betrothed, he secretly married Olga but, from his very wedding night, left her at a late hour each day to return home and sleep at his mother's apartment. Later he remarked, ruefully, 'Quite frankly, I was going back and forth like a yo-yo.'

SCREAMING TIRADE

But it was impossible to under-rate a woman of such tenacity as Elizabeth Duncan. Within a day or so she had learned of the marriage and determined that it would not last. Her first move was to insert an advertisement into a local newspaper declaring:

'I will not be responsible for debts contracted by anybody other than my mother, Elizabeth Duncan on, or after, June 25, 1958. Frank Duncan.'

The advertisement came as a surprise to Frank but, still anxious to dampen the fires of fury, he felt it unnecessary to do more than to admonish his mother for interfering in his private affairs. As far as Mrs. Duncan was concerned, he had no private affairs and she presented herself, without warning, at Olga's apartment and launched into a wild tirade which was ended only when Olga summoned the help of her landlady who persuaded Mother Duncan and her son to leave.

Clearly, poor Frank had not launched himself upon wedded bliss but his mother was only yet in the early stages of her campaign to separate husband and wife. Her first improbable scheme was to kidnap Frank, while he was visiting his bride, and whisk him away to a hideout in Los Angeles. She even bought some rope with which to secure her rebellious son and confided her plan, inevitably, to her good friend, Emma Short. But in her more lucid moments even Mrs. Duncan was forced to acknowledge that the scheme was preposterous and she abandoned it.

What she could not, or would not abandon was her vitriolic hatred of Olga. She assured Mrs. Short that she would disfigure Olga with acid but then, on second thoughts, proposed that she should strangle Olga with Emma Short's assistance. The idea was that Mrs. Short should induce Olga to come to her home where Mrs. Duncan would hide in a cupboard. When Emma Short had invited Olga to take a comfortable seat, with her back to the cupboard, Mrs. Duncan would spring out and strangle the girl.

As the monumentally acquiescent Mrs. Short later explained: 'The idea was that she should then hang her up in the cupboard until the evening. Then she would put a blanket around her, tie her with a rope and put a stone to the rope and take her to the beach in a car and throw her over the wharf.' According to her own narrative, Mrs. Short's response was curious. 'Do you realize,' she told her bloodthirsty friend, 'what you are trying to do? She will never stay in my apartment all night!'

Faced with Emma Short's reasonable objection to being saddled with the annoyance of a corpse in a cupboard, Mrs. Duncan turned her mind towards more businesslike and better-organized methods of disposal. She would put the 'job' out on hire and, for a mutually agreeable sum of money, hand over the technical details of her daughter-in-law's death to a third party. And so it was that the two old ladies, Elizabeth and Emma, found themselves in the steamy premises of the Tropical Café on State Street.

APPRENTICE KILLERS

Mrs. Duncan turned her glib tongue to the immediate task of convincing the Tropical's owner, Mrs. Esquivel, of her problem – adjusting the facts to suit the situation. Her daughter-in-law, she confided, was blackmailing her and unless she could be removed, her son, Frank, might well be the victim of Olga's wrath. Perhaps Mrs. Esquivel had some friends who might not object to 'removing' a bothersome person?

Mrs. Esquivel, adopting the view that the customer, however eccentric, was always right, knitted her brows in thought and finally pronounced that there were 'a couple of boys' but whether they would be available or not she did not know. Perhaps if Mrs. Duncan could return the following day she would introduce them to her?

Mrs. Duncan duly returned with the imperturbable Emma still tottering in her wake, and was introduced to two unemployed young men, Luis Moya, Jr., 21, and his inseparable companion, Augustine (Gus) Baldonado, 26. Both were drifters, who had been in and out of the hands of the police, but neither of them had any history of violence.

Almost certainly they had never met any matronly old body with such a persuasive tongue as Mrs. Duncan before and they solemnly sat down at one of the café's grubby tables with her and discussed her proposition as others might discuss a real estate deal.

For once, Emma Short was excluded and left to sit on her own, sipping coffee at an adjoining table. But the trio of Mother Duncan and 'the boys' moved swiftly to the heart of the matter. As young Moya subsequently reported: 'After we got down to brass tacks we just started making suggestions of how much money it would be worth to her to eliminate her daughter-in-law, and when it could be paid and how much, and there were suggestions made of how to get rid of the body.

At first Mrs. Duncan just wanted to pay $3,000, but I finally boosted the price up to six . . . She agreed to pay $3,000 right away and then the remainder after Mrs. Olga Duncan was eliminated.'

Mother Duncan was full of suggestions for the actual commission of the 'elimination'. Once again, it involved rope, with the addition of sleeping pills and a final neat touch of acid 'to disfigure her in general and her fingerprints . . .' Finally, 'the boys' agreed to accept the assignment and promised to proceed as quickly as possible to fulfil it.

There remained, of course, the question of money. Mrs. Duncan omitted to mention that, far from having $6,000 at her disposal, she had not the remotest chance of laying her hands on the initial $3,000, or anything like it. But Moya and Baldonado were among two of the most gullible apprentice hired killers in criminal history. They listened to Mother Duncan's promises, finally accepted a ludicrous cash advance of $175 and naively agreed to receive the balance after the 'contract' had been completed.

Mrs. Duncan left the café in high spirits, informing reliable old Emma on the way back home, 'I think they are going to do it.'

Moya and Baldonado wasted no time. They hired a 1948 Chevrolet for $25, borrowed a .22 pistol from an obliging friend and bought some ammunition to fit it. Soon after 11 p.m. on Monday, November 17, 1958, they drove to Santa Barbara's quiet suburban Garden Street and parked outside number 1114, the house in which Olga Duncan lived.

They waited to ensure that all was quiet and then young Moya went into the building, up the stairs and knocked on Olga's door. She appeared in housecoat and slippers and politely Moya launched into the killers' well-rehearsed script. Frank, her husband, he said, was downstairs in the car. 'I met him in a bar and he's pretty drunk and has quite a large amount of money with him and he told me to bring him home. But I need help to bring him up.'

Immediately Olga offered that help and followed Moya back down to the street. Baldonado had meanwhile stretched himself out on the back seat of the car, face downwards, to simulate the drunken, passed-out form of Frank Duncan. Moya opened the car door and Olga put her head in, reaching towards what she took to be her inert husband. As she did so, Moya struck her a blow on the side of the head with his pistol and pushed her on to the car floor as the suddenly active Baldonado dragged her towards him. In a moment the car door had shut and Moya was driving fast away towards the beach.

But the two young hoodlums had not made a very professional start to their killer careers. Olga, who was only dazed, came to her senses, began to scream and struggled to escape from the fast-moving car. Baldonado grabbed at her and tried to quieten her but she was a well-built, strong young woman and she fought against him valiantly.

'I can't hold her,' the breathless Baldonado gasped and, as he was forced to brake at a stop sign, Moya leaned back across the front seat and struck viciously several more times at Olga's head with the pistol. Quiet at last, her blood spilling into the car, she slid to the floor.

DAMAGED MECHANISM

Now the second part of the makeshift plan worked out by the two killers began to go wrong. They had intended to dispose of the body somewhere around the Mexican border but, shaken by events, they changed their minds and decided instead to head for the mountains, south of Santa Barbara, and rid themselves of their victim with the utmost speed. Thirty miles down Highway 150 they found a darkened roadside culvert, parked beside it and, seeing that the road was deserted, dragged Olga Duncan out of the car.

She was still breathing and Moya drew his pistol once again, this time to put a final, despatching bullet through her head. But the use of the gun earlier as a club had damaged the firing mechanism and, while Moya struggled with it in vain, Baldonado bent over the reviving woman in the darkness, searched for her neck and strangled her. When she had ceased to move, Moya picked up a rock and used it to deliver the *coup de grâce*.

So pathetically inept were the two young murderers that they had brought no tools with which to dig a grave and conceal the body. Both jumped down into the culvert and began scrabbling the dirt away with their bare hands, gouging out, after much sweated effort, an insecure and shallow pit into which they slid their victim's bloodied body.

CRYPTIC QUESTION

Blood dominated their thoughts as, at last, they drove back to Santa Barbara, for there was blood everywhere. It saturated their clothes, it lay in thick pools on the car seats and it seeped and trickled between their feet. Back in the city they spent anxious hours getting rid of their bloodstained clothes and tearing out the blood-covered seat coverings. They had accidentally started a fire in the car with a lighted cigarette, they explained to the Chevrolet's owner.

For a time it looked as though the clumsy murder might escape detection. A distraught Frank Duncan, calling at Olga's apartment and finding lights blazing and doors unlocked, summoned the police, but their best assessment was that this was a missing-person case. No doubt Mrs. Olga Duncan would return, or be traced, before long. No one came forward to offer any useful information, not even Emma Short who knew the almost certain answer to the mystery.

Two days after the murder, Luis Moya telephoned Mrs. Elizabeth Duncan at her home and reported that the 'contract' had been duly carried out. 'You don't have to worry about her any more,' he said before coming to the principle reason for his call: 'Are you going to be able to accomplish your end?' Mrs. Duncan was in no doubt as to what that cryptic question meant. The labourers now wished to make it clear that they were worthy of their hire but, worthy or not, Mrs. Duncan had no money for them and no intention of meeting the full bill.

She had her story well prepared. 'The police have been up to the house asking about Olga's disappearance,' she explained. 'So I can't draw any money out of the bank.' She had a little money – around $200 – and that would have to suffice for the moment. A few days later she met the two boys, accompanied by faithful Emma Short, and handed over an envelope to Moya. On opening it later he found it contained only $120.

Infuriated by what was now clearly a rather nasty con-trick, the two killers began to pester Elizabeth Duncan for their pay-off to such a wearing extent that she decided to indulge in a piece of table-turning blackmail. She told the police that she was being blackmailed by two Mexicans, whose names she could not reveal but who were threatening to kill her and her son, Frank. Her theory was that once the killers heard of her action they would quietly leave town and she would be rid of them, just as she was now rid of her daughter-in-law.

It was Mother Duncan's last and clumsiest move. The police, by now aware of the bad blood that had existed between mother and daughter-in-law, began to look more closely at Mrs. Duncan's wide-ranging activities. They questioned Emma Short, because of her known close association with Elizabeth Duncan, and at last old Emma began to talk. Astonished policemen sat wide-eyed as they heard her tell of the 'contract' meeting at the Tropical Café and her explanation that she had not thought it necessary to pass on the information before murder was committed.

SIDE BY SIDE

From that point on, events moved swiftly to an inevitable climax. Baldonado and Moya were picked up and Baldonado dictated a confession which included precise details of the roadside grave of Olga Duncan. Mother Duncan's arrest followed as a matter of routine and by the time they came to talk to her at length the police were convinced that she was one of nature's pathological liars. Almost nothing she said rang true – except her blinding devotion to her son.

All three, the female instigator and the two hired killers, were found guilty and sentenced to death. Mrs. Duncan still had hopes of survival and her lawyer son repaid her distorted devotion by fighting after a long series of appeals, for a final stay of execution. But even his energy and skill could not prevail against the course of the law and the murder trio went to the gas chamber at San Quentin on August 8, 1962. Moya and Baldonado died together, strapped into death chairs placed side by side.

Mother Duncan died alone. Her son could not be with her for, up to that final, eliminating moment, he was still pleading her case. Her last words, as the door of the glass and steel gas chamber was opened, were: 'Where is Frank?'

Fearsome Families

She was young, delicate and beautiful. Yet she lived under the shadow of death. For her own mother was one of the "black" sisters who, like others before them, turned murder into a family business. One day, Mummy struck . . .

ONE OF THE most bizarre cases in criminal history is also the earliest British murder case of which there is a detailed record. And the details are so incredible that they sound like the plot of a horror film. Anyone who knows the highlands of Scotland realizes that there is something frightening about those great tracts of bleak hillside and boggy valleys – a touch of the emptiness of the Sahara Desert. In the year 1400, the whole of Scotland was like this, from John O'Groats to the border. 'Glasgow' means 'dark glen', and it was little more than that; even the city of Edinburgh, later the seat of the royal family, was hardly larger than a modern country town.

Reign of Terror

It was in the reign of James I of Scotland that the people of Galloway were subjected to a reign of terror. Travellers were vanishing – so many of them that the natives at first suspected packs of wolves. But there were no wolves – in that bleak country they would have starved to death. And even wolves would have left behind some sign of their presence – bloodstained clothing, or the bones of a horse. There were no such signs; the travellers had simply vanished.

Alarmed by the situation, the king sent his officers to investigate the natives. Several suspicious looking tramps were arrested, and hanged just to be on the safe side. A number of inn-keepers fell under suspicion, and were also executed. But the 'vanishings' went on. They continued for so many years that some people reached the conclusion there were supernatural forces at work – werewolves, or perhaps the Devil himself.

One day, a man and his wife were returning from a village fair, both riding on the same horse. Suddenly, a wild-looking man leapt out of the bushes at the side of the road, and seized the horse's bridle. The horseman was well armed; he pulled out his pistol, and fired. There was a yell, and suddenly the horse seemed to be surrounded by savages. The man drew his cutlass and slashed at them, spurring his steed. His wife screamed as she was pulled off from behind him. One of the creatures slashed her throat with a knife. The man was dragged to the ground. And, at that moment, rescue belatedly arrived.

A crowd of about 30 people, travelling from the same fair, came round the corner. What they saw stunned them. The woman's clothes had been torn off, and someone had disembowelled her. Others were tearing at her flesh, and apparently eating it. It was like watching a pack of hunting dogs tearing a deer to pieces. The husband was still holding off other attackers with his cutlass. Someone gave a shout. Within seconds, the cannibals had vanished at incredible speed.

The woman was dead, but her husband – and the horse – were alive, the first living creatures to survive an attack from the human wolves in twenty-five years. It now became clear why travellers had vanished without trace. The wife's body had already been dragged a considerable distance off the road. If any traveller had passed by the spot 24 hours later, he would have noticed nothing – for by that time the bloodstains would have been indistinguishable from the brown grass and heather.

The news was carried immediately to the king in Edinburgh. Within four days, he was in Galloway, with a troop of four hundred men. They went to the place on the road where the woman had been killed. There were plenty of rocks and thickets where the murderers could have hidden to waylay travellers. They then set out across the moorland, in the direction taken by the fleeing murderers.

In a short time, they arrived at the seashore. The scene was dominated by tall cliffs, and below them the sea pounded on the rocks. They waited until the tide went out, then rode along the beach, looking for any sign of habitation. There seemed to be nothing; they noticed some caves, but none of them big enough to shelter a large gang. Discouraged, they turned and went back.

Sickening Smell

At this moment, however, two of the hunting dogs began barking at a small crack in the cliff face. Someone clambered up to examine it; it hardly seemed wide enough to admit a human being. But the dogs had now gone inside, and were still barking and howling with excitement – as if they had sighted their quarry. The king sent some men to the nearest village for torches, while a few of his soldiers ventured into the rocky cleft, and called out that it seemed to go deep into the cliff. Finally, the torches arrived. Led by the almost hysterical dogs, the men squeezed through the crack, and followed the winding, narrow way. A sickening smell came from inside.

Quite suddenly, the tunnel opened out into a cave. In its recesses, they could see crouching human figures, dazzled by the torchlight. In the corners, there were piles of money and jewels. And, hanging from the ceiling, objects that were easily recognizable as parts of human beings – arms, legs, torsos.

Cornered in their den, the wild creatures were prepared to fight; but they were quickly overcome by the men in armour. The soldiers counted their prisoners and discovered that a family of 48 beings was crowded into the cave. It became clear why the cave-dwellers had flung themselves on the murdered women with such ravenous appetite. They were cannibals, and the unappetizing lumps of flesh were part of their larder. They ate it raw. It must have seemed a luxury for them to be able to eat fresh meat.

The soldiers buried the limbs and torsos in the sand. The savages were taken to the Tolbooth in Edinburgh (which is still standing), then to Leith. By this time it had been established that the head of the family was a man named Sawney Bean, who had been born in East Lothian, not far from Edinburgh. As a youth, he had run away with a woman, and for 25 years they had been living in the same cave. The woman had been fertile, giving him eight sons and six daughters; these, in turn, had produced eighteen grandsons and fourteen granddaughters.

Leith was their place of execution. There was no trial, 'It being thought needless to try creatures who were even professed enemies to mankind,' recorded the chronicler, John Nicholson, of Kirkcudbright. The barbarity with which the Beans were executed was typical of the period; the men's hands and feet were chopped off and they were left to bleed to death. The womenfolk, having been made to watch this, were then burned alive in three fires. 'They all in general died without the least sign of repentance,' wrote Nicholson, 'but continued cursing and vending the most dreadful imprecations to the very last gasp of life.'

In executing them without trial, the king recognized that they were wild beasts; it is a pity he could not have ordered them to be killed as cleanly as such. Civilized culture is only skin deep, and there are well-authenticated cases of human babies who have been brought up by wild animals; there have been several such instances recorded in India. In one of the most remarkable, a 'wolf-child' was captured by hunters at the age of two, and taken back to civilization.

Carnivorous Species

Like Kipling's Mowgli, he had been brought up by wolves since babyhood – presumably his parents were killed by them, and the baby acquired the smell of the animals, which would be enough to protect him. But the child remained a wolf for the rest of his short life. No amount of civilized training could make him behave like a human being.

There is a central lesson to be learned from the Sawney Bean family; it applies to all 'murderous families' – which explains why they are so rare in the history of crime. When people reach the extremes of desperation, they turn away from human society, and in so doing place a gap between themselves and the rest of humanity. They look upon other human beings as a farmer looks on his sheep and pigs – as a different species. It makes no difference whether they do this instinctively, as the Beans did, or intellectually, as Charles Manson's followers did. In a fundamental sense, they cease to be human.

It is shocking to read about Sawney Bean's family disembowelling a woman and eating her flesh in front of her husband. But it is no worse that what Manson's followers did to actress Sharon Tate and the LaBiancas. It is definitely not 'sadism', any more than the Jewish butcher is sadistic when he cuts the throat of a kosher animal and drains off its blood. It is basically the attitude of one carnivorous species to another. The same is true of the Bender family. They were not murderers so much as butchers.

There is a paradox in the idea of a family banding together to commit murder. Members of a family feel close to one another. They are aware of one another as human beings. In that case, they are bound to be aware of their neighbours as human beings. Unless they feel desperate – fighting with their backs to the wall against the rest of society – they are unlikely to combine together for purposes of slaughter. Families like the Beans, the Benders, the Mansons, are a million-to-one-chance accidents. In almost every case, the reasons for the accident are completely different. But they can be roughly classified into three groups: sadism, gain, and resentment.

Apart from the Beans, British criminal history has two cases of murderous families which fall into the first classification, sadism. They both occurred at the same time, and in the same place: London in the mid-eighteenth century. Elizabeth Brownrigg was a midwife who treated her servant girls – supplied to her from the Foundling Hospital – with such barbarity that one of them died from the beatings. She and her husband and son were tried for the offence, and Mrs. Brownrigg died on the gallows, to the howling of an indignant mob.

Badly Beaten

A few months later the London crowds had an even more sensational case to gloat over, when a mother and her daughter, both called Sarah Metyard, were tried for murder of two servant girls. Like the Brownriggs, the Metyards were given to sadistic ill-treatment of their hirelings. The mother was a milliner who lived in Bruton Street, and in 1758, five girls were handed over to her from various foundling hospitals; these included a sickly child called Anne Naylor and her sister.

Anne worked badly, and was beaten and half-starved. She tried to run away twice, and Sarah Metyard decided to tame her by cruelty. The girl was badly beaten, then made to stand upright, with her hands tied behind her back to a door handle so she couldn't sit down. After three days without food, she was allowed to crawl into bed – whereupon she expired of exhaustion. The other girls were told to go and wake her; when they said she wouldn't move, the younger Sarah Metyard, a teenager, flung herself on the body and beat it with a shoe. She soon realized that the child was dead.

For a while, the two women panicked. They decided that the best plan was to conceal the body. They locked the attic door –where the child lay – and told the other girls that Anne had run away again. That seemed to satisfy them – all except the younger sister, who had noticed that Anne's shoes and clothes were still in her room.

During the next two months, she voiced her suspicions. The Metyards, who were already half insane with worry about the decomposing body behind the attic door, decided she had to die too.

They duly strangled her and hid the body. After this, they set about the gruesome task of disposing of Anne's remains, chopping them up, and wrapping the members in two bundles. An attempt to burn one of the hands made so much smell that they took the corpse out into the street, and tossed it over a wall on to the grate of a sewer. The watchman found it there the next day, and the local coroner was called to look at the pieces. Since they were so decomposed, he gave it as his opinion that the body had been dug up from a churchyard. The pieces were buried, and no one suspected the Metyards. Presumably they disposed of the second body more efficiently – it was never found.

Psychological Question

Four years went by and young Sarah Metyard ceased to be her mother's favourite. All the evidence indicates that Mrs. Metyard was a violent, foul-mouthed old woman who felt the world had treated her badly. A lodger called Mr. Rooker felt sorry for the daughter, and invited her to come and be his servant. The girl accepted, in spite of her mother's objections; within a short time, she was Mr. Rooker's mistress. Her mother was enraged; she called at Mr. Rooker's house every day and screamed abuse through the front door. He tried moving out to the western suburb of Ealing; but the old lady traced him, and continued to make a nuisance of herself.

One day, he let her into the house, hoping to cajole her into a less hostile mood; but she flew straight at her daughter and beat her. Angry words passed – some of which puzzled Mr. Rooker. When they had got rid of the old lady, he asked Sarah what she meant about 'killing'. Sarah told him everything. Mr. Rooker decided this was the ideal way of getting his revenge on the mother. He assumed the daughter would not be brought to trial, since she was still under age. He was mistaken. The Brownrigg scandal had made the officers of the law sensitive. And both Metyards had taken part in the disposal of the body. They were tried together, and executed at Tyburn in July 1768, one year after Elizabeth Brownrigg.

It is a psychological question of great interest whether crimes like these should be labelled sadistic. The motive behind them seems to be less a desire to inflict pain than a need to inflict 'just' punishment; probably Mrs. Metyard, like Mrs. Brownrigg, would have been outraged if anyone had accused her of *enjoying* hurting Anne Naylor. The same is certainly true of America's worst case of calculated ill-treatment, the Ocey Snead affair, which involved three highly respectable sisters.

The sisters were Caroline, Mary, and Virginia Wardlaw, daughters of a Supreme Court Justice of South Carolina. Virginia, the clever one of the family, became head of Montgomery Female College in 1900. Her two sisters lived nearby.

Caroline was married to a Colonel Martin, and had a daughter named Ocey, a quiet, gentle girl; Mary, separated from her husband, had two sons, John and Fletcher. One day, John ran away with a pretty student from his aunt's college. He was pursued and dragged back. Two days later, there were screams from the Wardlaw house on the campus: John was found writhing on the ground, his clothing burning. He died shortly afterwards, and the coroner agreed that the death was suicide. But his mother benefited by an insurance policy worth $12,000.

Starvation

There was much local gossip about the incident, and the sisters decided to separate. Mrs. Martin went to New York with Ocey and was joined there by her husband. One day, the landlady heard groans; she burst open the door, and found Colonel Martin writhing on the floor, and Ocey – filthy and in rags – on a bed in the corner of the room. Colonel Martin died shortly afterwards; his death was assumed to be from natural causes – and the widow benefited from a policy for $10,000.

Virginia Wardlaw had now changed her job; she was principal of a women's college at Murfreesboro, Tennessee – where the other two sisters joined her. The women seemed to be dominated by a pathological meanness. They proceeded to starve Ocey to death. A doctor who called was shocked by the filth and bareness of the house. Another doctor quickly diagnosed

Ocey's complaint as starvation, and threatened to get the police. The sisters told him that it was none of his business – Ocey was now married to her cousin Fletcher. This turned out to be true. But the doctor still caused trouble, and the three sisters – who now habitually wore black – left the college hastily.

With the benefit of normal food, Ocey immediately revealed that she was no invalid – indeed, she blossomed and became pregnant. But then the three deadly sisters descended again. Fletcher was completely under his mother's thumb, and allowed himself to be sent to Canada. Once more, the sisters began to starve Ocey to death. When the baby was born, they immediately handed it over to a foundling hospital, telling Ocey it was dead. And on November 29, 1909, at a house in East Orange, New Jersey, the police were called in to another 'suicide'.

Ocey had drowned in her bathtub, in a few inches of water. As soon as the police discovered that she had been insured for $32,000, they arrested the 'sisters in black'. Virginia Wardlaw starved herself to death in jail. Ocey's mother was sentenced to seven years in prison, although the prosecution declared she was insane. The third sister was found not guilty. In jail, it soon became clear that Mrs. Martin was insane; she died in an asylum in 1913.

No account of family murder would be complete without a mention of the strange case of Russell Colvin, which took place in New England in 1812. Two brothers, Stephen and Jesse Boorn, hated their brother-in-law Colvin, not only because they suspected that their father meant to leave him his farm, but because he made excessive sexual demands on their sister Sally. Some time later, as they were clearing a field of rocks, Colvin and the brothers began to quarrel. Colvin's son ran back to the farm in a panic. Later, his uncles told him that his father had 'run away up the mountain', and threatened to kill him if he mentioned the quarrel.

Seven years after this, in 1819, Old Amis Boorn, the uncle of the brothers, had a dream in which Russell Colvin appeared and told him he had been murdered, and his body buried near the farmhouse (which had meanwhile been burned). Charred bones were found in a field; the brothers were arrested, and confessed to the murder. They were sentenced to hang. Then, to everyone's amazement, Russell Colvin turned up again. He had gone off up the mountain. No one has ever answered the question of why the brothers made such a circumstantial confession; it remains one of the greatest psychological puzzles in the history of crime.

In today's society the phenomenon of the lethal family – the family that stays together slays together – is not likely to occur. With the increase of social communications, and the 'shrinking' of the world, it is no longer so possible for families to hide in hills and backwoods – or in city tenements even – without their presence being known to the authorities.

Once they are officially on record their murderous activities (if indeed they plan any) are severely circumscribed. They have become part of the human family in general, and are guarded against turning on their kind.

FEARSOME FAMILIES: CASE STUDY

The Manson Family

Beautiful actress and film star Sharon Tate and six others had been savagely murdered during two nights of terror in Hollywood in the summer of 1969. Now three young girls and a 35-year-old man were on trial. But Manson and his 'harem' behaved as if they were on a Sunday picnic!

WHEN CHARLES Manson entered the Los Angeles courtroom for the first time his presence seemed to evoke, among the waiting newsmen and spectators, a strange mixture of misgiving and complete revulsion. Charged, along with three female members of his 'family', with the savage murder of Hollywood actress Sharon Tate and six others in August 1969, it was the revulsion which held sway in people's minds. But the disquiet was there too, as the memory of Manson's weird outbursts to the press invaded the courtroom. 'I'm at the other end of your society,' he had asserted.

Now, as the audience stared at this curious figure of horror and tragedy their fascination was not untinged with fear. When he turned to face them, a gasp of shocked astonishment went round the court. For 35-year-old Manson, pale but composed in blue prison denim, his dark hair flowing like a prophet's round his intense, wiry face, had branded in blood on his forehead the symbol of the outcast: an X, put there because 'I have X-ed myself from your world'.

Even before the nine-month trial began Manson provided reporters with plenty of headline copy. He clearly intended to be the star of the proceedings, and made an early attempt to be allowed to conduct his own defence so that no 'interfering' lawyer could come between him and his 'public'. Judge Charles Older, however, decided otherwise. Manson, it was argued, was incapable of safeguarding his own procedural rights and must, therefore, be represented by a defence team.

With stubborn perversity the defendant then proceeded to interview more than 60 hopeful attorneys before settling on three. It would be difficult to imagine a group of lawyers less likely to work well together than this strange, ill-matched trio.

First, there was Ronald Hughes, 35, a one-time conservative turned hippie who had flunked the bar exam three times before passing and had never tried a case in his life. In his favour was that he had met Mansion previously – and, at the latter's insistence, he agreed to appear in court wearing a beard.

Hughes did not see the end of the trial through. He disappeared suddenly while on a short camping trip in north California and was later found drowned. The trial had to be adjourned for two weeks while a replacement – Maxwell Keith – familiarized himself with the case.

Then there was Irving Kanarek, 52, whom Manson brought in. Kanarek was a well-known attorney in Los Angeles and he hoped that his legal skills would be able to reduce Manson's infamy in the eyes of the court and the general public. Not many people shared his optimism and even Manson himself must have had his own doubts and felt uncertain about the outcome.

The third member of Manson's team was Daye Shinn, 53, a former used-car salesman, who sometimes earned his living by arranging immigration papers for wealthy clients seeking foreign maids.

To Manson's fury, the public defender's office assigned a fourth defence lawyer to the case – in a necessary effort to ensure a modicum of sanity and competence in dealing with the complexities of what was obviously going to be a gruelling and lengthy legal ordeal. This was the young but highly skilled Paul Fitzgerald who, at 33, was soon to reveal how much better than his older colleagues he had mastered the art and science of courtroom crossfire.

Fitzgerald soon became the unofficial defence leader. But he often found himself aligned not only against the prosecution case – admirably led by Vincent Bugliosi – but also against Hughes, Kanarek, and Shinn – whose courtroom techniques frequently undercut his own efforts. Kanarek, in particular, sometimes seemed actually to assist incompetent prosecution witnesses, leaving them more confident and impressive than when they started.

'It's like living in a concentration camp,' Fitzgerald remarked. Even Prosecutor Bugliosi was dismayed by some of the defence 'tactics'. 'This isn't a trial,' he blurted at one point, 'this is a laugh-in comedy!'

There was nothing amusing, however, about the prosecutor's opening remarks on the first day of the trial, in which he referred to the full horror of the Tate murders. The quiet tone in which he outlined the case against Manson – and the three young members of his harem accused with him – belied the savage story of hatred and blood lust to which the jury of seven men and five women listened in awestruck silence.

Patiently and with commendable clarity, Bugliosi explained that two of the girls on trial – Susan Atkins, 22, and Patricia Krenwinkel, also 22 – had been involved both in the murder of Sharon Tate and house guests on the night of August 9, 1969, and in the murder of Mr. and Mrs. Leno LaBianca in Los Angeles on the following night. The third girl, Leslie Van Houten, 20, was on trial only for the LaBianca murders.

VIOLENT DEATH

Two others, said Bugliosi, were involved. One of these, Charles Watson, was in a Texas jail fighting extradition and would be tried later. The second, 21-year-old Mrs. Linda Kasabian, was the only defector from the Manson 'family' and would, later, give a detailed account of the events on the two murder nights.

First, however, Bugliosi wanted to implant in the minds of the jury his own version of what happened to the victims. He began with a brief account of what he called 'Manson's mind'. He told of the defendant's passion for violent death and his bitter hatred for the 'establishment'. Son of a prostitute, Manson seemed destined for some kind of career in crime. As a young boy, he was frequently in court for juvenile delinquencies and later he graduated first to car theft and then to pimping – which culminated in a ten-year jail sentence.

Armed, continued the prosecutor, with a grudge against society and a fanatical interest and belief in hypnotism and the occult, Manson began to see himself as a kind of messiah. A Messiah who, just as in the Bible, was the creator of a new way of life. The poor and the dispossessed – particularly if they were young girls – were offered a place where they could feel accepted.

But, Bugliosi added, Manson's messianic ravings were not about love but about hate, violence, lust, sexual depravity, and ritual murder.

Bugliosi talked briefly about the Manson 'family' and the quasi-hypnotic effect which he exercised over its members so that they would, apparently, obey his every wish with unquestioning devotion. Then he mentioned one of the most absurd – and for that reason frightening – of the influences which had motivated Manson's behaviour: his devotion to the Beatles, who spoke to him 'across the ocean'. One song in particular, called Helter Skelter, whose lyrics seemed unexceptional to the normal ear, had been given a weird interpretation by the defendant.

According to him, Bugliosi asserted, the words signified a black uprising against the whites. Manson would escape from it by leading his followers into the California desert – where they did have a hideout – and then recreate a paradise of sex and drugs. First, however, the family would precipitate helter-skelter by fostering the idea that it had already arrived. That is why they scrawled the words PIG and WAR in blood on the walls of their victims' homes.

The murders themselves, the jury were told, had not been directly conducted by Manson. Like some demoniac general he had sent out his troops to kill the pigs, the 'enemies'. To a tense courtroom Bugliosi spelt out the murderous happenings. He told of the approach to Sharon Tate's rented house in Hollywood and how Charles Watson, armed with a .22 calibre rifle, had led Susan Atkins and Patricia Krenwinkel into the house, leaving prosecution witness Linda Kasabian on watch outside.

In the temporary absence of her husband, film director Roman Rosemary's Baby Polanski, eight-months pregnant Miss Tate had invited round former boyfriend Jay Sebring, writer Voityck Frykowski and his lover, coffee heiress Abigail Folger. It was, said Bugliosi, a quiet, intimate evening of drinks and talk. The arrival of the Manson family signified not merely an end to the get-together, but an end to their lives. One by one the guests were brutally hacked to death.

Frykowski alone was shot twice, hit at least 13 times on the head with a blunt instrument, and stabbed no less than 51 times. Sharon Tate, the jury heard, heavy with her unborn child, was left until last. Then, to the 'music' of her pleas – as one of the murderers later described it – her frantic pleas to save the child, she too was stabbed repeatedly in her neck, breast, back – and womb.

The murder of Mr. and Mrs. LaBianca on August 10, in which Leslie Van Houten also took part, was of similar brutal savagery, said the prosecutor. Only Linda Kasabian, he stated, had balked. She, as a relative newcomer to the Manson family, was the only one who was unaware of the purpose of the August 9 mission – and only fear had led her to accompany the murderers on the second night's outing.

For Prosecutor Bugliosi, this was the crucial point of his case. Only if he could establish that Mrs. Kasabian – who was originally indicted but later promised immunity in return for her testimony – was not legally an accomplice to the murders, could this key witness be considered reliable and trustworthy. Otherwise his case would be seriously weakened. For it would undoubtedly be argued by the defence that Kasabian was merely trying to save her own skin and was as guilty as the rest.

GIRLISH FIGURE

Thus her story would be seen as presenting

421

tailored evidence designed merely to convince the jury of her own innocence. Ultimately Judge Older would decide the issue. Much depended on the young mother's performance in court, and it was a tense moment when, in July 1970, she stepped for the first time into the witness box.

She was a girlish figure in her simple blue and white dress and blonde pigtails. It was difficult to believe that someone who looked so unremarkable could have been involved at all in crimes whose bloodiness and cruelty had horrified the world. As Bugliosi approached her, she glanced nervously round the packed courtroom. For a moment her eyes rested on the three accused girls, each of whose foreheads now bore the X mark of the outcast. They grinned at her with a kind of unconcerned maliciousness. Then she turned to Manson, her lips set firm in determination as if trying to prove to herself that he no longer had control over her actions.

For seconds she held his fierce stare and only turned away when, in an obvious attempt to frighten her, Manson drew a thin forefinger across his throat. But Linda Kasabian did not falter, and her composure drew a quick smile of relief from Bugliosi. He knew from that moment that she would adhere to her evidence.

Under the prosecutor's questioning, Kasabian told how she had first joined the Manson clan shortly before the murders. 'I felt like I was a blind little girl in a forest. I took the first path,' she said. It was not a surprising statement from a girl who had run away from a broken home as a young teenager and by the age of 20 had had two husbands, two children, and lived in at least 11 drug-orientated communes. To her, Manson was the bountiful giver of life and happiness; she loved him and believed 'he was the Messiah come again'.

Then, as she began to reveal details of the Tate murders – which had been inspired by Manson's jealousy of the rich and famous – the courtroom grew silent. Audience and jury strained forward to hear every word of her narrative, and held their breath at peak moments as if in the presence of a great dramatic performance. She related how, left on guard outside the Tate home, she suddenly became aware of what was happening inside: 'Then all of a sudden I heard people screaming saying 'No, please, no!"

'What kind of screams?' snapped Bugliosi.

'Loud, loud.'

'How long did they last?'

'Oh, it seemed like forever, infinite, I don't know.'

She went on to describe how the dying Frykowski had crawled out of the house towards her: 'He had blood all over his face . . . and we looked into each other's eyes for a minute – I don't know however long – and I said, 'Oh, God, I am so sorry. Please make it stop.' And then he just fell to the ground into the bushes.'

UPRAISED KNIFE

Entering the house, the witness continued, she saw Watson beating one of the victims on the head. 'And then I saw Katie – Patricia Krenwinkel – in the background with the girl, chasing after her with an upraised knife . . .' Watson, she said, was screaming: 'I'm the Devil. I'm here to do the Devil's work!'

By the time Linda Kasabian had finished her testimony several members of the audience were in tears, and the jury looked suddenly fatigued and pale. Even Judge Older was visibly moved, and Bugliosi, whose probing, intelligent questions – continuously interrupted by literally hundreds of objections from the defence – had provided a framework for her story, was trembling with emotion and fury.

Mrs. Kasabian herself stood up well to the harrowing ordeal, though at the end of the testimony she, too, was clearly exhausted. The pressure on her had been enormous. For, apart from the extraordinary obstructionist antics of the defence, she also had to face continuous pressure from the four accused. Once, Susan Atkins fixed her eyes upon Linda's. 'You are killing us,' she breathed. 'I am not killing you,' came the reply. 'You are killing yourselves.'

Undaunted, Mrs. Kasabian continued, for ten days, to pour out her narrative and face the barrage of often absurd questions flung at her by the defence.

The latter's tactics were simple. Their whole method lay in attempting, by any means possible, to discredit Mrs. Kasabian as a reliable witness. Kanarek, in particular, was persistently belligerent. He made the witness go through her story detail by detail in a vain effort to secure an admission from her that she was involved in the killings – thus rendering her whole testimony suspect. When this failed he tried a new tack.

'Have you ever taken hallucinogenic drugs?'

'Yes.'

'LSD, for example?'

'Yes.'

'How many trips had she made on LSD?'

'Oh, about 50, I guess.'

At the time this looked like a rewarding line of questioning, and Kanarek followed it up by delving into her sexual life with the Manson family. Mrs. Kasabian admitted that drug-induced orgies were frequent – and pleasurable. What happened during an orgy? Kanarek wanted to know.

'Everybody made love to everybody else. We all shed our clothes and we were lying on the floor, and it was like it didn't make any difference who was next to you.'

Did she know who was the father of her second child – the one conceived during her time with the Manson family?

'No,' she replied, 'I couldn't be sure.'

It was more sensational material for newsmen, and exciting entertainment for the spectators – many of whom had come, no doubt, in anticipation of hearing just such confessions as these. But, in the end, Kanarek's probings and innuendos were in vain. Judge Older stuck to his ruling that Linda Kasabian's tesimony was in order and acceptable as evidence.

Even so, Bugliosi had never intended to rely entirely on Mrs. Kasabian. He then called a further 84 witnesses, and presented some 300 exhibits, in his effort to prove that Manson – in spite of the fact that he was not personally present at the killings – was 'as guilty as sin'; and he took four months to present the prosecution case. At the end of this marathon there came another unusual twist.

The four beleaguered and bickering defence lawyers finally managed to reach some kind of uniform agreement between themselves. Before a stunned court they promptly announced that the defence rested. In short, there would be no defence at all. The reasons for this curious procedure – or lack of it – were not, on examination, difficult to understand.

Manson had devised a curious and almost satanic means to escape the law. He had persuaded – the word seems totally inadequate – the three girls to take the stand, 'confess' that they were responsible for the murders, and declare their 'master' innocent. Manson would then confirm their story and proceed to tell the world about his divine 'missio'.

LIFE STORY

Appalled, the lawyers refused to let them do it. When the girls insisted – backed by the judge, who ruled that they had a right to testify – the legal team declined to ask any questions. The girls countered by demanding to tell their stories verbatim, whereupon the jury was removed so that they could later be presented with a written version with the inadmissible portions edited out. Then the girls objected once more, and refused to testify unless the jury was present. It looked like stalemate – and a difficult decision for the judge.

Unbelievably, the situation was rescued by Manson himself. He suddenly sprang up, asked to take the stand, and talked for fully 90 minutes about his origins, his 'family', and his beliefs. It was, possibly, the most remarkable testimony ever heard in a United States court. And though it did nothing to allay the horror of his actions, it did much to explain them. Occasionally, in tears, but more often restrained and seemingly sincere, Manson began with the story of his life, and ran it through to the 'end'.

'I have stayed in jail,' he stated, 'and I have stayed stupid and I have stayed a child while I have watched your world grow up. And then I look at the things you do and I don't understand. Most of the people you call the family were just people that you did not want, people that were alongside the road; I took them up on my garbage dump and I told them this: that in love there is no wrong.

'I have done my best to get along in your world, and now you want to kill me. I say to myself, 'Ha, I'm already dead, have been all my life . . .' What you want is a fiend. You want a sadistic fiend because that is what you are. You only reflect on me what you are inside of yourselves, because I don't care anything about any of you. If I could I would jerk this microphone off and beat your brains out with it, because that is what you deserve. You kill things better than you.

'I don't care what you do with me. I have always been in your cell. When you were out riding your bicycle, I was sitting in your cell looking out the windows and looking at pictures in magazines and wishing I could go to high school and go to the prom. My peace is in the desert or in the jail cell, I would be satisfied with the jail cell much more over your society.'

There was an almost tangible silence as everyone hung on Manson's words. For the next few seconds the weird, merciless killer held the whole court under his fanatical spell. Then as nothing more came from him, Bugliosi stepped into the gap determined to normalize the strained atmosphere with a blast of ridicule:

'You say you're already dead, don't you, Charlie?'

'As anyone will tell you,' Manson retorted, 'you are dead when you are no more.'

'You think you've been dead for close on 2000 years, don't you?'

This was an allusion to Manson's expressed belief that he was Christ incarnate, and the defence promptly objected. Judge Older sustained the objection, but Bugliosi pressed on.

'Just who are your children, Charlie?' he demanded.

'Anyone who will love me,' Manson replied quietly, and then stared fixedly at the judge for several seconds.

Finally he stepped down, shuffled over to the accused girls and whispered: 'Don't testify.'

They didn't. And neither did Manson when offered the chance to repeat his story before the jury. 'I've relieved all my pressure,' he told the judge.

In his summation, Bugliosi called Manson 'one of the most evil, satanic men who ever walked the face of the earth'. The jury agreed, and all four defendants were found guilty and later sentenced to death – which, in the legal situation of the time, meant they would be kept alive and waiting in Death Row.

As a murderous family unit they were no more. Whether they were eventually executed or not, the essential thing was that they were kept apart from each other. And that Manson – so named, he said, because he was the 'son of man' – was no longer the all-powerful, all-vengeful patriarch.

Vampires

Vampires have fascinated the so-called civilized world for centuries and doctors have even made efforts to discover if they exist. Why is man so attracted to these creatures? What kind of human fantasy do they seem to represent?

'WITHIN STOOD a tall old man, clean-shaven save for a long white moustache . . . His face was a strong – a very strong – aquiline, with high bridge of the thin nose and peculiarly arched nostrils; with lofty domed forehead, and hair growing scantily round the temples, but profusely elsewhere. His eyebrows were very massive, almost meeting over the nose . . . The mouth was fixed and cruel-looking.' Bram Stoker's description of his legendary Count Dracula is a remarkably accurate sketch of the original Dracula – the great Wallachian warrior whose terrible perversions earned him the name of Vlad the Impaler. After his murder in 1476, he was buried in the monastery of Snagov – now in Rumania; yet the grave has never been discovered. It seems to lend weight to the legend – mentioned by Irishman Stoker – that Dracula belongs to the legions of the undead and of vampires.

National Sport

Voivode Dracul – Count Dracula: the word is actually a title, derived from the Rumanian word *dracoul*, meaning devil (which, in this case, might be better translated 'the terrible one'). And there is no doubt that he was a sadistic psychopath and a national hero. When he came to the throne in 1456, Wallachia (today part of Rumania) was weak and divided. Rival noblemen kept the country this way by squabbling among themselves. Wallachia was menaced by Turks and Hungarians, and its trade was strangled by German merchants, who controlled all the custom posts. Added to this, the murder of its kings had become almost a national sport – there had been 20 of them in less than 40 years.

Dracula had seen his own father murdered and his favourite brother buried alive. So when he acceded to power, he acted with brutal decisiveness. His enemies among the noblemen were murdered, and their families systematically exterminated, in case someone contemplated revenge. The Saxon merchants were seized and impaled en masse. When Turkish ambassadors failed to show him the respect he demanded, he had their turbans and clothes nailed to their bodies – making sure the nails were short, so death would be slow.

All this may sound like the typical savagery of an uncivilized warrior. But there is definite evidence that he was a pervert who derived sexual satisfaction from torture. On one occasion, he invited all the poor and sick people of the area to dine in the palace of Tagoviste, then had it boarded up and set on fire, so they were all burned alive. He had men blinded, maimed, and boiled. When the Hungarians kept him prisoner, from 1462 to 1474, he vented his sadism on animals.

Victim's Blood

But his favourite method of torture was impalement on a long, pointed pole. The victim was placed on it so that his own weight and his death struggles gradually forced the point through his body. One print shows Vlad dining among the spiked bodies of men and women, and the positions of the victims reveal agonizing and ingenious variations in the methods of impalement.

The German chronicles that describe these tortures make particular mention of his practice of drinking the victims' blood. This was why Bram Stoker chose Vlad as the model for his own sinister Transylvanian nobleman. When Dracula speaks of the exploits of his heroic but cruel ancestor to solicitor Jonathan Harker, he is obviously speaking of himself – and of Vlad the Impaler.

How did the imagination of Bram Stoker come to transform the historic Vlad into the supernatural Dracula – the most famous vampire in world literature? This is an intriguing question, for Stoker – who put his inspiration for Dracula on a nightmare following a supper of too much dressed crab – was not a particularly imaginative man. A huge, gentle Dubliner, he became secretary to the actor Sir Henry Irving at the age of 30, and for the next 30 years worked like a drayhorse for his talented but eccentric employer. When Irving died a pauper, Stoker – already famous as the author of *Dracula* – churned out second-rate horror novels that reveal just how little imagination he possessed. On his death the death certificate bore the word 'Exhaustion'.

Stoker was a typical Victorian gentleman – courteous, chivalrous towards women, basically rather puritanical. And yet *Dracula* is a masterpiece of horror, full of instinctive insights into perversions and cruelties. Its author would have been shocked if someone had told him that his novel was replete with sexual overtones and rape fantasies; yet no one who reads *Dracula* can fail to be aware of them. Was this a case of Freudian repression – or was it something altogether more sinister?

Primeval Fear

The Swiss psychologist Jung believed that below the ordinary memory of each individual there is a deeper layer of the unconscious mind, the collective or 'racial' unconscious, which has been passed on to us by our remotest ancestors. This racial memory contains certain primordial images or symbols, which Jung calls 'archetypes' – for example, father-figures, mother-figures, giants. From the moment Dracula first made his fictional appearance in 1897, he exercised the same curious fascination.

The book has never been out of print, and in the form of plays and films, the story has been seen by millions. (Stoker would have been a very rich man if he had lived a few years longer.) All this suggests that Stoker had stumbled on one of the Jungian archetypes and given it a new life. But had he merely given shape to some primeval fear, some imaginary bogeyman? Or is it possible that there is some kind of reality behind the idea of the vampire?

There were stories about vampires in ancient Greece and Rome, but they were significantly different from the modern vampire. The Romans believed in a creature called the Lamia, a beautiful woman, who seduced men and then ate them. In his humorous classic *The Golden Ass*, Lucius Apuleius describes how the witches of Thessaly, in northern Greece, were in the habit of chewing pieces off newly dead male corpses. These legends obviously spring from man's ambiguous feelings towards women – a mixture of fear and masochistic desire. Being eaten alive – or having vital organs gnawed off – by women is a masochist's daydream.

But the later vampire is not a masochistic fantasy; it is definitely sadistic. Perhaps the strangest thing about it is that the legend swept across Europe like an epidemic during the early eighteenth century. It seems to have started at the village of Meduegna, near Belgrade, Yugoslavia. A young soldier named Arnold Paole had returned from active service in Greece in 1827, and he told the girl to whom he was engaged that while away he had been attacked by a vampire. The record does not specify whether this was a male or female vampire; but he said he had found its grave and destroyed it.

Some time after returning to his native village, he died after a serious fall. A month later, however, people began to see him around the village. Some of those who saw him died soon after; finally, there was a decision to disinter the body. It was found to be perfectly preserved, and there was dried blood around the mouth. Paole's corpse was burned – as were the bodies of four of the people who had died since his burial.

The reports of the 'walking dead' ceased for a time – six years. Then there was a fresh outbreak, which writers on the case attributed to the death of someone who had been bitten by one of the 'vampires', and who duly became a vampire after his (or her) death. There were further investigations, undertaken by three surgeons from Belgrade – Johannes Flickinger, Isaac Seidel, and Johann Baumgartner.

On January 7, 1732, these three, together with a lieutenant-colonel and a sublieutenant, signed a document at Meduegna in which they described the opening of several graves, and the finding of another 15 vampires – bodies which looked as if they had been freshly buried, with ruddy cheeks. Significantly, the majority of these creatures were young or fairly young women, and there were three children among them.

All this may have been pure superstition and hysteria; if so, then it induced a wave of similar panic in Hungary, Rumania, and other Slavonic countries. So many cases of vampires were reported that they began to attract the attention of European travellers, who brought reports back with them. Then in 1746 the French author Dom Augustin Calmet popularized the subject in his *History of Apparitions and Vampires*.

He cited a case which took place in the village of Haidam, on the Austro-Hungarian frontier, and which was investigated by a commission on the orders of the Emperor Charles VI. The Count de Cadreras, of the Alexandetti Infantry, made a deposition at Freibourg University in 1730 verifying his own part in the investigation – how he had ordered the corpse of an old farmer to be dug up, and had found it to be completely fresh.

Buried Alive

The farmer had been dead for ten years. Yet only a few evenings before, he had appeared to his family at their dining table, touched his son on the shoulder, and then gone out. The son, as though stricken by the plague, had died the next day. The Emperor's commission verified these facts by taking depositions throughout the village.

Rationally, what is to be made of these strange events? Some writers ascribe them to hysteria, which seems unlikely – the accounts appear too circumstantial. Others believe that the stories about vampires originate from a few genuine cases in which people had been accidentally buried alive, so their bodies were found in life-like positions when they were exhumed. This is obviously a possibility. However, serious students of the occult are inclined to accept another and more bizarre explanation.

There are, in occult literature, thousands of well-authenticated cases of 'apparitions of the living' – that is, of a living person who may be seen in a place many miles from where his physical body happens to be at the time. In many such accounts, the person himself is quite unaware that his 'apparition' has been seen miles away, although he may have been *thinking* about the place at the time.

There is also another phenomenon, equally well-attested, called 'projection of the astral body'. This occurs when a person feels himself to be leaving his physical body and floating around in the air above it – or even travelling somewhere else. This cannot be dismissed as mere super-stition; both the English and American Societies for Psychical Research have investigated hundreds of such cases, and found evidence for accepting them as genuine.

Scalding Liquid

Such findings have led some writers on vam-pirism to advance the theory that vampires may be some kind of 'astral projections', endowed with a malign power to suck vitality (rather than blood). Everyone has had experience of people who seem to 'drain one of energy'; perhaps vampires are disembodied forces who have the same enfeebling effects.

Whether or not vampirism is a supernatural phenomenon, there can be no doubt whatever that it is a sexual perversion, and one that has been encountered by most psychiatrists. And it *is* regarded by them as one of the most puzzling of all the sexual deviations. Most sexual perversion springs from frustration. Unlike animals, whose physical appetites are governed by natural cycles, human sexual desire is present all the year round. In certain people – particularly young men – it may become a kind of scalding liquid that causes the same kind of inner discomfort as a violent need to urinate.

The inner pressure becomes so great that it can be released by almost anything that has sexual associations; a sexually frustrated male may find female shoes or underwear as exciting as a naked woman. After a few experiences of experimenting with such objects, he may begin to find them *more* satisfying than a naked woman – or at least they become an essential element in his sexual experiences.

This is known as fetishism, and is fairly harmless and widespread. If a frustrated male brings himself to a sexual climax with fantasies of ill-treating his sexual partner, he may develop into a sadist; if the fantasies are of *being* ill-treated, into a masochist.

Dead Cats

It is easy to see how men who have access to the corpses of women might become necrophiles – lovers of the dead. In fact, most recorded cases of necrophilia concern mortuary attendants. But there have been cases in which a man has become a grave robber to satisfy this craving. British writer Montague Summers quotes the classic case of necrophilia in his book *The Vampire in Europe* – that of Sergeant François Bertrand, sentenced to a year's imprisonment in 1849 for robbing graves in and around Paris and violating female corpses.

Bertrand, who was 27, was known as an admirable soldier. He admitted that at an early age he had sexual fantasies which involved torturing and raping girls. He was, in fact, an attractive man, who had no difficulty finding mistresses, many of whom wanted to marry him. But 'normal' sex was never as satisfying to him as his fantasies.

At the age of 24, he began sadistically maltreating animals, and also cutting open the bodies of dead dogs and cats. A year later he happened to be walking through a cemetery with a friend, and saw a half-filled grave in which a young woman was buried. (In those days, many people were interred without coffins.) He later returned to the grave in a state of wild excitement, dug up the corpse, and proceeded to beat it with a spade in a kind of frenzy. Someone heard the noise and he ran away.

Two days later he dug open the same grave

with his hands, and tore open the belly of the corpse – at which he enjoyed intense sexual satisfaction. The experience convinced him that it was dead women he wanted, rather than live ones. He made a practice of digging up corpses – preferably of young women who had been newly buried – and of violating them, after which he often tore them to pieces. Afterwards he always felt ashamed and vowed never to do it again.

Obsessed Women

The curious thing about Bertrand – who once swam an icy pond in midwinter to get into a cemetery – is that he was not a violent or brutal man. He disliked obscene talk, always treated women with chivalry, and refused to have affairs with married women. His social personality was reasonable and presentable. Under the surface, however, there was another personality, a kind of vampire or werewolf, that took over when he was possessed by sexual desire.

This is what makes *Dracula* such a remarkable book. Written by a rather puritanical Victorian, who adored his wife and was never unfaithful to her, it reveals that, somewhere inside him, Stoker possessed an alter-ego that understood all the nauseating violence and perversion of Sergeant Bertrand.

What is, perhaps, even more surprising is that the literature of sexual abnormality is full of examples of women who have been obsessed by blood. Psychologist Wilhelm Stekel describes a woman who could only become sexually excited by making small cuts on her lover's body and sucking the blood, and cites in detail the case of another woman completely obsessed by fantasies of smashing her lovers to a pulp and drinking their blood.

On the other hand, it is equally clear that women recognize a sexual significance in the idea of the vampire. The legendary vampire is not brutal; he doesn't inflict pain or commit rape; but he masters her completely, and draws her soul to himself so that it eventually joins him in death. The masochistic element is always strong in a woman's sexual response. Psychiatrist Magnus Hirschfeld records the case of a patient who was normally sexually frigid, but whose favourite fantasy involved lying naked on a butcher's slab, while the butcher prodded her all over deciding where to cut.

At a certain point the butcher would insert his finger into her sexual organ; she would then achieve a violent climax. Here the masochistic element, the desire to be a victim, can be clearly seen. And, as in the case of Sergeant Bertrand, the woman's fantasies had made her incapable of normal sexual response.

It seems possible, therefore, that the concept of the vampire is a Jungian 'archetype', which lies concealed in the 'racial unconscious' of each of us. This in turn raises the question: why, in that case, should the idea be so relatively modern? It is true that there are recorded stories of vampirism dating back three thousand years; but the idea of the Dracula-type vampire has possessed the European imagination only since the strange epidemic of the 1730s.

Strange Cases

The answer to this may lie in the concept that the patterns and types of crime change slowly from age to age. When civilization was crude and barbarous, crime tended to be purely economic – committed for food, or money, or perhaps land. The eighteenth century, the age that saw the publication of Calmet's book on vampires, was also the age of Baroque civilization. And, from the criminologist's point of view, it marked the beginning of the age of modern crime – of sex crimes, crimes of jealousy and violence.

Suddenly, the criminal records are full of strange cases of sadistic violence: men like Sergeant Bertrand, like Andrew Bichel, a Bavarian 'ripper' who tore open the women he killed, like Vincenzo Verzeni, an Italian murderer possessed by a craving to eat women, or like the French sexual pervert Victor Ardisson, another necrophile, who slept with the mummified head of a 13-year-old girl – or like that almost symbolic figure of murderous violence, Jack the Ripper.

In all this disturbing history of ferocity there is one ray of comfort. Although Dracula remains as popular as ever – and there is even a revival of interest in the original dracoul, Vlad the Impaler – the typical murders of our time are crimes of self-esteem, like the Moors murder case, or the murders of the Manson clan.

They may often be sadistic, but they tend to be more cerebral than the overpowering urges that gripped Sergeant Bertrand. Whether this is an advantage is open to question. But from the criminologist's point of view, it is a significant change – perhaps even the prelude to an age in which men cease to be prey to urges of irrational violence. And in which vampires – traditionally without a mirror image, allergic to garlic, terrified of crucifixes, and unable to exist in daylight – will remain in their Transylvanian graves.

Only a stake through the heart, it was said, could kill them. But they can also die of rational thinking – leaving only their human imitators for the police and psychiatrists to contend with.

VAMPIRES: CASE STUDY

Richard Ramirez

Richard Ramirez was nicknamed 'The Night Stalker' because stalked peoples' houses at the dead of night, break in, murder, rape, sodomize and then leave his calling card by writing a message in his victim's blood.

IN THE AUTUMN of 1984 Los Angeles was shocked by reports of a sinister 'Night Stalker', a sadistic burglar who seemed to have a taste for violent mutilation.

The evil had in fact started a year earlier with the murder of a 79-year-old woman in her home at Glassell Park. Her body was discovered by her son who lived in one of the apartments above his mother's. Her body had been stabbed repeatedly and her throat slashed. It was June 1984 and the police scoured the house and garden for vital clues, but came up with nothing.

In February 1985, the unknown stalker abducted two young girls in separate incidents. The first one was a six-year-old girl who was snatched from a bus stop close to her school. She was carried off in a laundry bag, sexually abused, and her body dumped nearby at Silver Lake. Just two weeks later on March 11, another girl was taken, a nine-year-old, who was snatched from her bedroom in Monterey park. She was also raped and dumped by her attacker in Elysian Park.

The police were still baffled by the attacker's identity, but realized that this man was a depraved monster with a lust for killing.

On March 17, 34-year-old Ts Lian Yu was ambushed close to her home in Monterey park. She was dragged from her car and shot several times by her attacker. The following day he struck again. Waiting in the shadows outside an apartment Ramirez waited until pretty Maria Hernandez had pulled her car into her garage. Unaware that there was a man standing behind a pillar, Maria stepped out of her car only do be jumped on by a man holding a gun. She pleaded for her life but the assailant paid no attention and pulled the trigger. Maria dropped to the floor and, thinking she was dead, her attacker stepped over her body and left by the side door. However, Maria was lucky, the bullet had been deflected by the car keys she was holding and left her with only a wound to her hand. However, not so lucky was her roommate, Dayle Okazaki. Thirty-three-year-old Okazaki was lying in a pool of her own blood, her skull had been smashed by the force a bullet fired at extremely close range.

Now the police had a description of the 'Night Stalker'. Hernandez was able to describe her attacker as tall, gaunt, dark and possibly Hispanic. With very little to go on the police started a desperate hunt for more clues, but they didn't have to wait long before their man struck again. Ramirez certainly had a lust for blood and on March 27, 64-year-old Vincent Zazzara and his 44-year-old wife Maxine, were fatally beaten to death. Maxine's eyes had been carved out and her body cruelly butchered. Their bodies were not discovered for two days. Hunting for vital clues the police found footprints in the flowerbed outside the Zazzara home. There were no witnesses to the murders but it was apparent these crimes were being carried out by the same man, and what was even more worrying was that his attacks seem to be getting bolder and more frequent.

Just before dawn on May 14 Ramirez struck again. Sixty-five-year-old William Doi didn't hear the intruder slipping in through an open window. After the attack, although close to death from his wounds William Doi managed to crawl to the telephone and dialed the emergency services before finally collapsing. His actions had saved his wife from an inevitable attack by the intruder.

Two weeks later, on May 29, 84-year-old Mabel Bell and her 81-year-old sister, Florence Lang were savagely beaten in their home in Monrovia. This time the intruder paused to write messages in his victims' blood before leaving, some on Mabel's body and more on the walls of the house. Florence managed to survive the attack, but her sister died on July 15.

More and more killings occurred and his *modus operandi* were always consistent. With each killing Richard Ramirez seemed to grow stronger and stronger, like a vampire figure who thrived on the blood of his victims. By August the 'Night Stalker' had been credited with 14 separate murders in the Los Angeles area. The police had issued sketches of the night prowler. His downfall came about when he shot 29-year-old Bill Carns in the head and raped his fiancée before escaping in a stolen car. The car was recovered on August 28, and the police managed to obtain a set of clear fingerprints belonging to a 25-year-old man from Texas, named Richard Ramirez. He had police records and had already been arrested on numerous occasions for traffic and drug violations. Further enquiries revealed that Ramirez was a long-term drug user who was obsessed wth the mock-Satanic rock group AC/DC. Ramirez had actually adopted one of their songs 'Night Prowler' as his personal tune, and played it repeatedly, sometimes for hours on end.

His description was released by the police and his face appeared in the press and on television the next day. He was captured by a citizen's arrest in Los Angeles on August 31, when he was overcome whilst trying to steal a car. The police arrived before he was beaten to death and by September 29, Richard Ramirez was facing a total of 68 felony charges. These included 14 counts of murder and 22 counts of sexual assault.

Richard Ramirez, or 'The Night Stalker' is still sitting waiting on San Quentin's Death Row.

Deathly Doctors

Rapid advances in medicine made doctors powerful and respected men in the nineteenth century . . . but some used their high social position to gratify their lust and greed, like Doctor Deschamps whose misuse of twelve-year-old Juliette Deitsch horrified New Orleans.

THE NINE-YEAR-OLD girl was sobbing so violently that her father could not understand a word she said. He shook her impatiently: 'Where is Juliette?' The girl controlled herself for a moment. 'She's asleep, and the doctor says he's going to die.' The father, Jules Dietsch, rushed through the streets to the house where Doctor Etienne Deschamps was lodging. The door to his room was locked. Deitsch ran to the police station, and begged the police to help him to break in. 'I think my twelve-year-old daughter is in there.' She was. Juliette was lying naked on the bed. Beside her, also naked, lay a great hairy man with a beard. Blood was streaming from wounds in his chest, but he was still alive. The little girl was dead.

It was the beginning of one of the most sensational murder trials in the history of New Orleans. For when the body of Juliette Deitsch was examined, it was discovered that she was no longer a virgin, and that she had been carnally abused in other ways. There were even love bites on her body. And, as the evidence made clear, this had not happened just once, but dozens of times over the course of six months or so. Dr. Deschamps was obviously the worst kind of pervert.

How had the respectable carpenter, Jules Deitsch, come to allow his daughter to fall into the hands of such a monster? Deitsch had met Dr. Deschamps in 1888, when Deschamps had told him that he was an adept in the occult. He possessed hypnotic powers, and he intended to use them to discover the lost treasure of the pirate Jean Lafitte. All he needed, he said, was the help of a pure young girl to act as a medium.

Deitsch was so impressed by the fifty-year-old doctor that he had no hesitation in entrusting Juliette to his care – in fact, both his daughters – for Juliette's young sister Laurence was fascinated by the doctor, and didn't want to be left out.

Later, Laurence described the 'experiments'. Juliette would be told to undress and to climb into bed. She was an unusually well developed child for her age, although she had not yet reached puberty. The doctor would also undress, and climb in beside her. He would soak a clean handkerchief in chloroform, and place it over her face.

The doctor always made them promise not to tell their father what had happened. So things had continued until that afternoon of January 30, 1889, when Deschamps had suddenly begun to sob in French: 'My God, what have I done?' Then Laurence, who was terrified, was told to run home and tell her father that the doctor was going to die. But the doctor did not die. The stab wounds he inflicted on his chest were too superficial to endanger his life.

It was obvious to everybody that Juliette's death was accidental – to everybody, at least, but the prosecutor. He alleged that Deschamps had deliberately killed the girl because he knew that his sexual abuses would soon be discovered. This was obviously absurd, since killing her was the sure was to discovery. On the other hand, Deschamps was more cunning and calculating than he tried to make out. The police found letters in his room, written by Juliette and signed 'Your love forever', and 'your little mistress'.

Covering his Tracks

Juliette, however, was a backward child, and could not have composed them. Deschamps had written them, and got her to copy them out, so that he could claim she had been willing to be seduced. But if she was willing, why chloroform her, as he had on every occasion? Besides, the letters also mentioned a jeweller in the neighbourhood called Charlie, and implied that he had been the man who had originally taken Juliette's virginity. But 'Charlie' was proved to be innocent. Again, Deschamps was covering his tracks. Why should he, argued the prosecutor, unless he meant to kill her?

The Deschamps case – which ended with the doctor being hanged – gained nationwide coverage in the American press. This was not simply because of the sensational nature of the crime; it was because Deschamps was a doctor. It is a curious fact of criminal history that doctors who commit murder excite more interest than almost any other type of criminal. The usual explanation for this is that doctors are supposed to save life, not take it. But that supposes that the public are more interested in morality than they actually are. The true explanation is that the doctor is a symbol of middle-class respectability.

In earlier centuries, people felt the same morbid interest in priests who committed crimes – hence the excitement aroused by the trial of Father Urbain Grandier, burned alive in 1634 on a charge of having seduced and bewitched a convent full of nuns.

The great age of medicine was the nineteenth century. It was also the great age of the medical murderer. Yet the company of killers had one distinguished predecessor of the eighteenth century: Dr. Levi Weil, whose strange story helps to explain why the medical murderer was such a latecomer on the criminal scene. Dr. Weil, a Dutch Jew, came to London from Holland in the 1760s – the London of Dr. Johnson, the actor David Garrick and the statesman Edmund Burke.

London then was full of disease, and most doctors were constantly busy. But this Jewish doctor with a foreign accent encountered a certain amount of prejudice, and his practice remained small.

Brother's Gang

One day, a merchant asked Weil if he would travel out to Enfield, outside London, to attend to his sister – the regular doctor was ill. Weil drove to the village, attended the old lady – with some success – and then ate supper with her brother, who paid him in cash.

All the way home Weil thought about the house full of money and jewellery and determined to take some of it for himself. In the City, he said goodbye to the merchant – and promptly made his way back to Enfield. When he finally reached home at daylight, he was exhausted, but some £90 richer – more money than he had made in months.

Ironically, Weil's practice began to improve as his income from burglary soared up to £500 a month. He kept his surgery open, knowing it was his best disguise. He entered the houses of wealthy patients, 'cased the joint', and passed on the information to a gang run by his brother. On one occasion, he heard that an old caretaker who lived near St. Paul's Cathedral had his life's savings hidden in one room.

Other burglars had already broken in, but although they had prised up every floorboard and ripped plaster off the walls, they had been unable to locate the money. Weil was called to the old man's bedside when he was ill. He tried to persuade the caretaker to go into hospital; the vehemence with which the idea was rejected convinced Weil that the money was hidden in his room.

The floor and the walls had been explored – so it had to be the ceiling. A great beam crossed the room. Weil examined it when the caretaker was asleep, and found a cavity. Two nights later, as the old man slept heavily from one of the doctor's sedatives, Asher Weil and an accomplice took nearly £3,000 from the hiding-place in the beam. The old man never discovered the robbery. He died a few days later. This may have been Weil's first murder.

By then, the gang had swelled to eight. One of the members, a German Jew named Isaacs, tried to conceal more than his share of the booty, and was dismissed. That was Weil's first mistake. Not long after, he made his second.

In the autumn of 1771, the gang – including Weil himself – waited until after dark in the vicinity of a house in Chelsea Fields – in those days, Chelsea was a village outside London. When all the lights were out, they knocked loudly.

The servant who opened the door was over-powered. The lady of the house, a Mrs. Hutchings, fought strenuously, but was tied with her petticoats over her head. In the upper part of the house, the gang burst into a bedroom, and two servants who had been asleep started up, alarmed. One was knocked out; the other, as he struggled, was shot with a pistol.

After that, the gang fled with their loot. Unfortunately for them, the servant, John Slow, died. Now the authorities decided to offer a reward for the gang, and Isaacs, the man who had been dismissed, saw his opportunity for revenge.

He knew that if he turned King's Evidence, he would be safe. Weil was planning his most ambitious robbery so far – of a diamond merchant expecting a consignment of £40,000 worth of jewels – when he was placed under arrest by the

Bow Street runners. Six of the gang were tried; two were acquitted for lack of evidence – a proof that, even in those days, justice was impartial. But Weil and his brother were among those executed at Tyburn on December 9, 1771.

The next notable name in the roll of medical infamy is that of Dr. Edmé Castaing of Paris. At the age of 27, Dr. Castaing enjoyed the good life, and did not look forward to the lifetime of drudgery of a general practitioner. One of his patients was a wealthy man named Hippolyte Ballet, who had tuberculosis. Castaing became friendly with Hippolyte's younger brother Auguste, and learned that the brothers were on bad terms – so bad that Hippolyte had excluded his brother from his will. One evening, as they drank together, Auguste hinted that Castaing might hasten his brother's death, and gain possession of the will.

So, on October 22, 1822, Hippolyte quite suddenly died, to the astonishment of other doctors who had occasionally attended him. A month later, Castaing paid off all his debts, and lent his mother 300,000 francs. The following year, on June 2, Castaing and Auguste Ballet went for a drive in the country, and stopped at a hotel in St. Cloud, where they ate and drank. Then Auguste was suddenly taken ill, and soon died, attended by his friend Castaing and two other doctors. The other G.P.s recognized the signs of morphine poisoning, and they discovered that, even after Ballet had started to vomit, Castaing had gone to a local chemist and bought more morphine.

When it was discovered that Ballet had made a will in Castaing's favour, the doctor was arrested.

Castaing was relying on the fact that morphine was very difficult to detect. And he was proved to be right. Although the doctors agreed that Auguste Ballet had shown all the signs of morphine poisoning – vomiting, diarrhoea, heavy breathing, contraction of the pupils – no trace of morphine could be detected in his stomach. The prosecutor asked indignantly if all murderers who used morphine should be allowed to go free, just because medical science was unable to detect its presence. That swung the jury. Castaing was sentenced to death, and executed in December 1823, protesting his innocence.

The next medical murder of any note took place in the peaceful environment of Harvard University, in Cambridge, Massachusetts, more than a quarter of a century later. Like so many medical murderers, Professor John Webster, aged 56, was given to living beyond his means. He frequently borrowed money from a wealthy friend, Dr. George Parkman. But Parkman ceased to be friendly when he learned that Webster's famous mineral collection, which Webster had pledged to him as security for a loan, had also been pledged to another creditor. The angry Parkman threatened exposure. On November 23, 1849, Parkman failed to return home for lunch, and the river was dredged in case he had drowned.

In fact, Parkman had called on Webster in his laboratory, and as he turned to go out, Webster had struck him such a tremendous blow on the back of the head – with a piece of wood – that he died. Later on, Webster alleged that Parkman had been so insulting that he had hit him in a blind rage; but all the evidence indicates a cool head and careful planning. Later the same day, he told an agent who collected his lecture fees that he had repaid Parkman. And that night, behind locked doors, he proceeded to dismember the body and to burn it in his medical furnace.

Two days after Parkman's disappearance, Webster called on his family, and told them that he had repaid Parkman a few hours before his disappearance. Surely this proved that Parkman had been killed by a robber who had concealed the body . . . ? Unfortunately for Webster, the caretaker at the medical school, Littlefield, detested him. Littlefield wondered why the doctor worked all night in his laboratory, he took care to double-lock the door; but Littlefield had a plan. The furnace was built against a wall, and there was a passageway on the other side. With his wife standing guard, Littlefield broke through the wall with a crowbar, shone his torch through – and saw a bone which he recognized as a human pelvis.

At his trial, which lasted eleven days – and got national press coverage – Webster pleaded not guilty. He contended that the bones in the furnace were not Parkman's at all – just the remains of a body they had been using for dissection. But a dentist positively identified the false teeth as Parkman's, and Webster's defence collapsed. Before he was hanged, in August 1850, he confessed to killing Parkman 'in a fit of rage'.

Weak Characters

The murder of Parkman was the beginning of what might be called the great age of medical murderers. It lasted for about a hundred years – from approximately 1855, the year in which Dr. William Palmer of Rugely poisoned his race-track associate John Cook, to 1954, when Dr. Sam Sheppard of Ohio was found guilty of murdering his wife. Studying the killers, an interesting point emerges. A great majority of the medical murderers were weak characters, given to lying or boasting, and to living beyond their means. And this implies that many of them were drawn to the medical profession to satisfy vanity – the self-esteem urge.

This was perhaps most obvious in the case of the Glasgow poisoner, Dr. Edward William Pritchard. In photographs, he looks a typical Victorian paterfamilias, with his frock coat and bushy beard, surrounded by a respectable-looking family. In fact, he was an utterly weak character, a joke among his colleagues because of his incredible boasting and lying. He claimed to be a friend of the Italian patriot Guiseppe Garibaldi, although they had certainly never met.

A typical narcissist, he was fond of presenting people with photographs of himself – he even handed one to a stranger he met on the train. He gave lectures – mostly invented – in which he described himself as an intrepid traveller and hunter. He also regarded himself as a great lover, and seduced servant girls and anyone else who would have him. In 1863, when he was 38, a fire broke out in the room of the servant girl in his house; she was found dead, and it seemed clear that she had made no attempt to leave her bed during the fire. Pritchard was widely suspected, but he nevertheless won a claim from an insurance company.

In 1864, he made another servant girl – aged 15 – pregnant, but performed an abortion. And it may have been his desire to marry her that led him to start poisoning his wife Mary, to whom he had been married for nearly twenty years. In November, 1864, she became ill, vomiting and dizzy. A doctor called in by Pritchard suspected she was being poisoned, and wrote to Mary Pritchard's brother, suggesting she should be moved into hospital. The result was that Mary Pritchard's mother, Mrs. Taylor, decided to come and nurse her daughter. Soon, Mrs. Taylor was suffering from the same symptoms. She died on February 24, 1865, and Mrs. Pritchard followed her a month later.

Pritchard provided both death certificates, stating that Mrs. Taylor died of apoplexy, and his wife of gastric fever. Someone wrote an anonymous letter to the police, and Pritchard was arrested. When the bodies were exhumed, both were found to be saturated with antimony, which Pritchard was proved to have bought.

Since the 1880s, England has produced her fair quota of medical murderers, while America has produced many more.

Triangle of death

Caught up in the demands of his own perverted passions, Ivan Poderjay went from one bigamous relationship to another until he was finally led to murder. Freud was fascinated . . .

THERE IS ONE matter on which the professional criminologist and the general public simply do not see eye to eye; the so-called 'eternal triangle'. For the criminologist, most such cases are elementary, if not downright boring. But the general public has a voracious and apparently limitless appetite for them. And who is to say who is right? The 'triangle' murder may be of small psychological interest; but it often contains great drama.

Though it is rare for such a case to appeal equally to both public and criminologist, the murder of Agnes Tufverson achieved this unusual distinction. Her killers were described by Freud as one of the most remarkable examples of sexual perversion he had ever encountered.

'Captain' Ivan Poderjay was not, in fact, a Captain; nor was he, as he declared, a member of Yugoslav Army Intelligence. He was a confidence trickster and professional lady-killer – in every sense of the word.

Born into a poor Serbian family in 1899, Poderjay started his career as a fortune teller in Belgrade, then joined – and quickly deserted – the French Foreign Legion. In 1926, he was cited as co-respondence in a divorce case by a high government official; he subsequently married the ex-wife, got possession of her fortune, and vanished.

Up to the age of 33, Poderjay continued to live off seduction. He was short, plump and losing his hair; but he also had that essential quality of the professional Casanova, the ability to make a woman feel that she was the most fascinating person in the world. He was heartless; but at least his victims escaped with their lives, until, in 1931, he met Marguerite Suzanne Ferrand, a French-woman with a firm mouth and a school-mistressy face.

Jackbooted feet

She was a research assistant in the British Museum. As soon as their eyes met, each knew they had found something they had been looking for all their lives, for the 37-year-old Marguerite enjoyed chastizing men; and Ivan enjoyed being chastized. After crouching naked at her jackbooted feet, Ivan realized that he had found the ideal sexual playmate, a woman whose fantasies were as bizarre as his own.

This was another case of a 'catalytic' relationship. If they had never met, Marguerite and Ivan might have pursued their ways harmlessly for the rest of their lives. But together, they entered into a combination as deadly as fire and gunpowder. Marguerite was not shocked to find that Ivan was a confidence man who lived off women; on the contrary, the thought of causing pain to other women caused her deep pleasure. In March, 1932, they were married in London – although Ivan was, in fact, already married to several other 'wives'.

One year later, in the lounge of a cross-channel ferry, Ivan noticed an attractive woman of about 40 – Agnes Tufverson. She was well-dressed, and she looked distinctly sick. Ivan introduced himself as a Captain in the Yugoslav Army, and advised her to get some air on the deck, where he mentioned casually that he was a millionaire and an inventor.

In subsequent weeks, in London, they saw a lot of one another, and Ivan spent a great deal of money on her – well over £500. But this was not a source of concern to him, for he had persuaded Agnes to allow him to invest $5,000 of her money . . . Back in New York, Agnes returned to her job as an executive at the Electric Bond and Share Company, and she confided to her best friend that she was to marry a romantic Yugoslav millionaire.

A week later, she received a cable from her 'millionaire', declaring that he had a marvellous opportunity to invest another $5,000 for her, and asking her to wire the money. She decided against it, for she wanted Ivan to come and get her, and that is precisely what he did.

In November 1933, Poderjay arrived at her New York apartment with a huge bunch of flowers, and on December 4 they were married. Ivan explained that it was hardly worth cabling his bankers to send money from London; they would be returning to London in a couple of weeks. In the meantime, they could live on Agnes's money; Agnes agreed.

On December 20 Agnes and Poderjay prepared to leave New York. But instead of sailing as arranged on the Hamburg, they returned to their apartment late that night. The next day, Poderjay told the daily help that his wife had decided to sail on ahead, and that he was following her immediately. Their luggage had gone ahead on the Hamburg – all except one huge trunk, which had been delivered to the apartment the day before. Poderjay escorted this trunk to the docks himself, and insisted on staying with it until it was in his cabin on the Olympic. He had booked this cabin a week before – a single passage – with instructions that he must have a cabin above the waterline.

No one ever saw Agnes Tufverson again. Some months later, her family began to institute enquiries. These led to the arrest of Ivan and Marguerite Poderjay by the Vienna police, who were astonished to discover that their apartment was filled with instruments of torture and flogging. The police called in Sigmund Freud – the world's most famous psychoanalyst.

Lesbian affair

Freud found the Poderjays fascinating. Marguerite alleged her true 'personality' was a tyrannical sadist named Count John, although she had two subsidiary female 'personalities'. Poderjay in turn was psychically 'controlled' by a female called Ita, who was the mistress of Count John, and who was having a lesbian affair with one of Marguerite's female personalities; he was also controlled by another two 'spirit' girls who were tortured by Count John.

Poderjay admitted that Agnes had not sailed on the Hamburg; he told the police she had run off with another man, on the spur of the moment. Her luggage had arrived in Poderjay's flat in Vienna and was still there. The New York police had no doubts whatever as to what had happened to Agnes. On the day he bought the trunk, Poderjay had also bought 800 razor blades – explaining that they were cheaper in America. He had also bought large quantities of cold cream.

Once on board the Olympic, he had spent several days in his cabin. During that time, the police believe, he had carefully shaved the flesh from Agnes's bones until she was only a skeleton. The flesh had fed the fish who follow every liner. The skeleton, greased with cold cream, had also slipped out of the porthole.

Poetic justice

There was no body, and circumstantial evidence was not strong enough to hang Ivan Poderjay. Instead, he was sentenced to five years in prison for bigamy. While he was serving his time, an angry fellow convict, outraged by some bizarre proposition, beat Poderjay so badly that he lost his left eye and eight teeth. It sounds like poetic justice until we reflect that he probably enjoyed it. He returned to Marguerite, moved to Belgrade, and presumably continued to live a multiple sex life with Count John and his harem.

This is surely one of the clearest cases in all psychological literature of the 'catalyst effect' – that is, of two people, who would be harmless alone, inspiring one another to commit murder. Parallel cases – Snyder and Gray, Bywaters and Thompson, Brady and Hindley, Fernandez and Beck – have been discussed in connection with crimes of dominance.

This is only one type of catalyst effect; there is another, equally familiar to criminologists, that is also fraught with explosive possibilities. In this situation, the murderer and the 'catalyst' do not become partners in crime; the 'catalyst' inspires the crime, but takes no part in it. This happens when the 'catalyst' has a particularly yielding and gentle nature, inspiring a frenzy of desire and protectiveness that may explode into violence.

Violent man

It is illustrated perfectly in the relationship between Cesare Borgia and his sister Lucretia. Lucretia, with her gentle face and weak mouth, was a born 'victim'; it was inevitable that she should become her brother's mistress. But from then on, Cesare could not bear the thought of any other man possessing her; one suitor saved his life by fleeing; another became her husband, and was murdered on Cesare's orders.

Borgia was, of course, a 'violent man' in A. E. Von Vogt's sense – a man who would rather commit murder than ever admit that he was in the wrong. On the other hand, Crippen, who was also driven to murder by a 'gentle catalyst', was basically a non-violent man. His wife Cora was dominant, and Crippen accepted her as 'the boss'. His typist, Ethel Le Neve, was completely undominant: gentle, yielding, faithful; half a century after the murder, she told crime-researcher Pat Pitman that she was still in love with Crippen. In her company, Crippen felt like a superman. The result: the murder of Mrs. Crippen, and Crippen's execution in November 1910.

Eyeing a sparrow

The case of Dr. Philip Cross bears some basic resemblances to that of Crippen. A retired army doctor, 62 years of age, he lived comfortably with his wife and six children at Shandy Hall, near Dripsey, Co. Cork. His wife was 22 years his junior; they had been married 18 years, and it had been, on the whole, a satisfactory marriage. In October 1886, Mrs. Laura Cross engaged a new governess for the children, a 20-year-old girl named Effie Skinner. Effie, like Ethel Le Neve, was the catalyst type: not particularly pretty, but with something soft and yielding about her. As soon as he saw her, the military, rather forbidding Dr. Cross felt like a hawk eyeing a sparrow. For the first time, he realized that his marriage had been merely satisfactory, never ecstatic. It had never provided him with any real outlet for his male dominance.

One day, as Effie stood talking to him about the children, he bent and kissed her. He was afraid she would tell his wife or leave immediately. But she stayed, and his desire to possess her increased. His wife noticed it, and she took what seemed to her the sensible course: she sacked Effie. The girl was shattered, she went to Dublin, and when Dr. Cross visited her there, she finally gave herself to him. Possession did not cool his desire; he wanted to be married to her, living in comfort in Shandy Hall.

Early in May, 1887, Mrs. Cross began to suffer attacks of vomiting. Her husband told her she had a weak heart. She died on June 1st, and was buried three days later. Less than two weeks after this, he married Effie Skinner in London. At first, he decided that they had better keep the marriage a secret and live separately, but when he got back to Dripsey, he discovered the news had preceded him.

There seemed no point keeping Effie in London, so he moved her to Shandy Hall. Inevitably, there was gossip, and the police finally decided to act. Laura Cross was exhumed, and the coroner found 3.2 grains of arsenic in her body, as well as strychnine. There was no trace of heart disease.

State of shock

The police were also able to trace the firm from whom Dr. Cross had bought arsenic 'for sheep dipping'. Tried at the Munster Assizes in Cork, he was found guilty on December 18, 1887, and hanged in the following January. Effie was so shocked by the realization that she had been the cause of the murder that she refused to see him in the condemned cell, and Cross's hair turned white overnight.

Of more recent cases involving the 'innocent catalyst', the one with some of the most dramatic features is certainly that of Armand Rohart, mayor of Peuplinges, near Calais. In the early hours of May 24, 1967, the mayor of Escalles, near Peuplinges, was awakened by the sound of a motor horn. He found Armand Rohart, one of the district's richest men, collapsed over the wheel of his car.

Rohart seemed to be in a state of shock., and was taken to the Lille hospital. Back at Rohart's farm, his brother Jules mentioned that Rohart and his wife Jacqueline had gone off to the beach for a swim that afternoon, and had not been back since.

A search of the beach revealed Jacqueline's body, dressed in a pink bikini and covered in seaweed. Rohart's story – when he regained consciousness – was that he and Jacqueline – who was 45 – had waded into the sea up to their necks, holding hands, when a great wave had swept them away. Neither could swim. Rohart had struggled ashore, lost consciousness, and wakened after dark on the empty beach . . .

Dairy maids

Why had a middle-aged man and woman decided to go swimming on a chilly May day? Rohart was quite frank with the police. A few years before, he had had a love affair with the 14-year-old nurse of his children, Odile Wissocq, and she had borne him a child. He had sent the girl back to her parents, and ever since then had been trying to make his wife forget his lapse. They had decided to go to the beach because it was on just such a day, many years earlier, that they had made love by the sea . . .

The story sounded convincing. Certainly, Rohart's grief at the funeral seemed genuine. But the post mortem demonstrated that Jacqueline Rohart had not died of drowning; she had no water in her lungs. Further research into Rohart's background revealed that Odile Wissocq had not been his only lapse. For many years, the rich farmer had exercised a kind of droit de seigneur on dairy maids and farm girls. But the affair with Odile had been different. She was the sweet, yielding type, and it was not true that Rohart had broken off with her. They had been seen lying together on a blanket long after she had returned to her parents. But recently, Odile had talked of marrying a younger man; she was a girl who needed a protector, and her status as a mistress was wearing on her nerves.

There was still no reason to charge Rohart with murder. Then, on June 14, an ex-legionnaire named Jacob Kerbahay walked into the local police station with a tape recorder, and played the police a conversation in which Rohart asked him to murder Jacqueline. Kerbahay, who lived in a cottage on Rohart's land, said that Rohart had raised the matter with him earlier. At that point, Rohart's plan was to hide a needle covered with curare – the alkaloid used by pygmies on their darts – in her car seat, so it would penetrate her skin as she sat down; she would crash and perhaps break her neck . . .

Perfect plan

Kerbahay didn't like or trust Rohart, so when Rohart called on him again, he decided to tape the conversation for his own protection. Rohart noticed that the tape recorder was turning, but Kerbahay told him he was recording music from the radio, and played it back to prove it – switching to another track.

On Kerbahay's evidence, Rohart was arrested, and the police quickly uncovered the corroborative evidence they needed. On the day before her death, Jacqueline Rohart had been to the hairdresser, and had her hair set in a new style. The fixative would have been washed off if she had been in the sea for any length of time. The body was exhumed, and it was discovered that the fixative was still in place.

Her bloodstream, contained a large amount of alcohol, although she normally did not drink, and two weeks after the tragedy two bottles were washed up on the beach, one containing sleeping tablets, the other, traces of ether, Rohart's 'perfect murder' plan now became clear.

He had persuaded her to drink heavily, to celebrate their sentimental excursion to the beach. He had anaesthetized her with ether, then carried her body into the sea to drown her. She had woken up and fought him – he had shown the police scratches on his chest, which, he alleged, were made when Jacqueline tried to cling to him.

He had beaten her unconscious, dragged her

ashore, and suffocated her with a car blanket or cushion. She had been dead when he took her back into the sea to 'drown' her, so no water went into her lungs. Finally, the police discovered that Rohart had insured his wife's life for a million francs – £100,000 – not long before the murder. Their case was complete. Rohart was sentenced to life imprisonment.

Terribly injured

When a love triangle is complicated by violent Latin tempers, the result is almost inevitably violence. When Dr. Joseph DiFede was found murdered – apparently by a burglar – on December 7, 1961, the New York police sensed that this crime was less straightforward than it looked. The sobbing widow, 35-year-old Jean DiFede, told how she had been awakened by noises coming from her husband's bedroom. She had looked in, and found him dying, terribly injured.

It was the violence of the murder that troubled the police; someone had hit DiFede with a hammer, knocking out one of his eyes, then stabbed him again and again, covering the room with blood. This was surely no burglar, but someone who hated DiFede.

It seemed that there might be many people who felt like that. 38-year-old DiFede was not only a highly successful doctor; he was also an incredible lover, who made no secret of his voracious sexual appetite. His temper was so violent that his wife never dared to object; on one occasion he had been heard to boast that he had 15 mistresses. In the course of a thorough investigation of DiFede's patients, the police interviewed two Italian youths who lived nearby; one of them had only a temporary visa. What puzzled the police was that although neither of them had regular jobs, they lived in a comfortable apartment, and one of them, 19-year-old Armando Cossentino, ran an expensive car.

Eventually, investigation revealed that while the fiery Dr. DiFede was out with other women, Armando was comforting his plump, long-suffering wife, and clearly, she was his source of income.

The two youths were subjected to long interrogation. Armando, the stronger character, insisted he knew nothing; but his friend finally broke down, and told how he and Armando had gone to the doctor's house to murder him. Armando was only 19, but he was as hot-tempered and strong-willed as Dr. DiFede, and he felt it was time Jean was freed from her husband's domination.

Cossentino was sentenced to death, later commuted to life imprisonment. Jean DiFede, accused of being an accessory – the actual charge was manslaughter – was also sentenced to life imprisonment.

Cases like these lead to a strange but inevitable conclusion: where a 'love triangle' is concerned, it is a mistake to speak of the 'psychology of the murderer'. What is at issue is the group psychology of three people. And as absurd as this sounds, the ultimate responsibility for the murder lies with all three – including the victim.

Gangsters

Since Sodom and Gomorrah, it has been cities that
have bred gangsterism. It was violence, with Asian
roots in Hong Kong that first infected the United
States, but the Sicilian brand of gun law finally
prevailed. And the organized crime that was
spawned by Prohibition lives on today.

ON THE evening of July 22, 1934, people began to
emerge from the Marbro Cinema, on Chicago's
West Side. The plain clothes police who were
standing around the entrance were tense with
anxiety. They were hoping to arrest John Dillinger,
America's Public Enemy Number One. They knew
he'd gone into the cinema with a brothel madame
– who had tipped them off – and another woman.
What scared them was that some of the women
and children in the crowd might get shot if
Dillinger went for his gun. They had reason to
worry; last time the Federal agents cornered
Dillinger, in a Wisconsin farmhouse, they got so
nervous they opened fire on a car full of innocent
people, and killed several; Dillinger escaped.

Now, as Melvin Purvis and his agents waited
outside the cinema, a police car suddenly drew
up. The cinema cashier had noticed the plain
clothes cops, assumed they were planning to
stage a robbery, and rang the local police station.

A Federal agent rushed up to the car, showed his identification, and ordered the police to move on fast. A few minutes later, John Dillinger walked out of the cinema with the two women, one of them wearing a bright red dress, so the police could identify her. To Purvis's relief, Dillinger pushed clear of the crowd, and started along an empty stretch of pavement. Purvis yelled: 'Stick 'em up, John, you're surrounded.' Dillinger went for his gun; dozens of shots sounded, and he crumpled to the pavement.

Most criminologists agree that the death of Dillinger was the end of an era. Capone had been in jail since 1932; prohibition had been repealed in 1933. There were still a few notorious gangsters at large – for example, 'Creepy' Karpis and Ma Barker's gang – but never again would the hunt for a gangster produce the nationwide excitement provoked by Dillinger.

It was the notorious Volstead Act – better known as Prohibition – that plunged the United States into its greatest period of lawlessness, starting on January 16, 1920. The puritans and bigots who persuaded the United States Senate to ban all alcoholic drinks thought they were inaugurating 'an era of clear thinking and clean living'; in fact, they were allowing organized crime a stranglehold on the U.S.

The Irish and Italian gangs of New York City and Chicago seized their chance to move into the big time. It was the era of Dion O'Banion, Johnny Torrio, Al Capone, Joe Masseria, Salvatore Maranzano, Vito Genovese. On February 14,

1929, five Capone gangsters, disguised as policemen, walked into the garage owned by an Irish gangster, Bugs Moran, lined seven men up against the wall, and mowed them down with submachine gun fire.

The 'St. Valentine's Day Massacre' shocked the world; suddenly, the U.S. wanted to be rid of its gangsters. A tough but intelligent Sicilian named Charles Luciano – known as 'Lucky' – organized the killing of many of the old-style gangsters. He then called a meeting of the survivors, and warned them that the public was sick of gang warfare. In future, he said, there would be a policy of co-operation. Their common enemy was the law; their common prey was the public. A few of the older mobsters – such as Dutch Schultz – preferred to carry on in the old way. After Schultz had eliminated his chief rival, Legs Diamond, he himself was shot down as he sat in a restaurant in Newark, New Jersey, in October 1935. After that, America was more securely than ever in the grip of the mobsters – but the average American knew nothing about it.

Murder Incorporated

Quietly and efficiently, Luciano organized 'Murder Incorporated', a pool of professional killers who committed murder only when the gang bosses decided someone was stepping out of line. Instead of booze, this new syndicate – sometimes known as the Mafia, sometimes as 'Costa Nostra' ('Our Thing') – dealt in narcotics, gambling, prostitution, extortion, labour racketeering, and anything else that made money.

The general public became intrigued by its existence in November 1957, when the New York State Police stumbled on a business conference of more than 60 top racketeers near the village of Apalachin. All at once, 'Murder Incorporated' was world news. There was a national scandal, and a special commission to investigate crime, headed by Senator Kefauver, produced amazing revelations of mass corruption. A top member of the Mafia, Joe Valachi, decided to talk, in exchange for police protection. Some of the more notorious gangsters, including Luciano, were deported. A book about the Mafia, written in 1959, ends with a chapter entitled: 'Twilight of the Villains?' The years since then have shown that the answer is: Definitely not.

Soon after the immense success of Mario Puzo's Cosa Nostra novel *The Godfather* in 1971, there were further outbreaks of gang warfare in New York City. Gangleader Joe Colombo was shot and critically wounded at a rally in Central Park; the rival gangster responsible for this shooting, Joe Gallo, was himself murdered as he celebrated his birthday in April 1972; in between these shootings there were a dozen other Mafia executions. Now, almost seventy years after the death of John Dillinger, America is still firmly in the hands of its 'mobs'. Capone and Luciano have been replaced by another Mafia leader; but there is always a 'Godfather' ready to step into the shoes of his predecessor.

Will this ever change? An unprejudiced look at history suggests that the answer is: Probably not. If prostitution is the world's oldest profession, then gangsterism is probably the second oldest. Moreover, scientific investigation suggests that this is more than just plain wickedness; it is a deep-rooted animal instinct. An instinct that is activated and intensified by conditions of over-crowding – not only in present-day communities and cities, but in the living areas of long ago.

This gives an interesting insight into the beginnings of crime – and of gangs. It is known that most of man's earliest cities, some of which sprang up 5000 years B.C., contained overcrowded slums. This may sound strange; after all, the world of those days had a tiny population. So why didn't the people spread themselves out more? The answer is simple. Men built cities for mutual protection; they preferred to be huddled together. Moreover, these cities were often in river valleys where there was a limited amount of space to expand. The result was inevitable – crime on a large scale. To people from quiet country villages, the wickedness of the cities must have seemed terrifying – as is instanced in the Bible, with its stories of Sodom and Gomorrah, and those godless cities of Mesopotamia that were destroyed by the Flood (which actually took place about 4000 B.C.). The city, therefore, literally created crime – at least, large-scale crime. And, unfortunately, the pestilence soon overflowed into the surrounding countryside; travellers were robbed and murdered; small villages were overrun by robber bands who killed the men, raped the women, and burned the houses.

It can thus be said with some confidence, that the first gangsters appeared soon after the first cities. But at this point, an important distinction must be made. There are two distinct kinds of gangster which, for convenience, can be labelled the bandit and the 'true gangster'. Bandit obviously means the same as gangster (since a gang is a band); but their motivations are different. To put it simply, the gangster tends to be crueller and more vicious than the bandit. The bandit lives in rural areas; he has space. He may have taken to crime for a variety of reasons; but one of these is not overcrowding. He prefers to be a member of a band because being a loner in wide open spaces is a demoralizing business. (Criminal loners often commit far more atrocious crimes than 'bandits', because boredom and solitude make them lose their sense of identity.)

Emotional Damage

Apart from his criminal activities, the bandit may be a normal human being with normal human emotions. On the other hand, the man who becomes a gangster because of the pressures of an overcrowded slum, has often suffered permanent emotional damage. To begin with, as already noted, overcrowding produces bad mothers and brutal fathers. The true gangster is the product of the slum, and he sees the world as a place to be plundered – if he can get away with it.

The city of Hong Kong offers some gruesome examples of this dating from recent years. Trapped between the sea and steep hills, Hong Kong is one of the most overcrowded cities in the world, and its murder rate has always been high. After World War II, the population quickly rocketed from half a million to more than two and a half million. Consequently, there was a terrifying wave of gang murders – murders so atrocious that the police speak of them as the work of 'horror cults'.

In 1958, there were more than 900 murders – five times the American murder rate, and 150 times the English. These 'horror cults' are, in fact, Chinese 'tongs', or 'Triad Societies'. (The earliest tongs were called 'Three Harmonies Societies'.) Like their American counterpart, the Mafia, they operate prostitution, drugs rackets, protection, and extortion. But their methods of ensuring obedience depend upon terrorism.

For example, in 1958, a rich merchant named Ko Sun Wei, together with four of his family, were horribly murdered in his house in Kowloon. The victims were staked out, with their arms and legs spreadeagled. Three women – the merchant's two daughters and his daughter-in-law – were raped repeatedly, then tortured to death with knives. One woman was still alive when the police arrived, but was unable to speak – her tongue had been cut out.

These were only five among 350 murders that took place in Hong Kong in September 1958. Sergeant Arthur Ogilvie, of the Hong Kong Police, who gives these figures, also mentions that during the riots of 1956, Triad Societies took the opportunity to pillage more than $25,000,000 worth of goods. With a figure of this size involved, it can be seen that crime in modern Hong Kong is an even bigger business than it was in the Chicago of the 1920s. The interesting point here is the verification of observations about overcrowding. It produces true gangsters – men who are adepts in cruelty and violence, because they are unable to experience ordinary human emotions.

Bearing in mind this important distinction, it can be seen that many of the famous criminals and gang leaders of the past 200 years have been bandits rather than gangsters. For example, Australia's most famous criminal, Ned Kelly, was definitely a bandit. Kelly, the son of an Irish farmer and former convict, became Australia's Public Enemy Number One when he killed three constables at Stringybark Creek in 1877.

From then on, he lived the traditional life of the bandit on the run, moving around the countryside with his gang – which included his brother Dan – and robbing banks. He made himself head and body armour, weighing 97 lb., and was wearing it when the police finally ambushed his gang in Glenrowan. He was only 24 when he was executed in 1880. Asked why he had decided to confront the police at Glenrowan, Kelly made a reply that was to be echoed by many American gangsters of the Bonny and Clyde era: 'A man gets tired of being hunted like a dog . . . I wanted to see the thing end.'

The most significant feature about Kelly is that he was a man who thought he had a grievance against the law – and in this he resembles many of the famous 'bandits', from Billy the Kid to John Dillinger. Whether the grievance is real or not is beside the point; but it starts the bandit off on the road that leads to the gallows, or the final bloody shoot-out with the police.

Most Wanted Man

The story of South Africa's most famous 'gangster' may be taken as typifying the pattern. William Foster was born in 1886, and his family moved to Johannesburg in 1900. While still under 20, William decided to seek his fortune in German South West Africa. Plodding around in the desert one day, he met two companions who were driving a pack of donkeys. He joined them – and a few miles farther on, all three were arrested and charged with stealing the donkeys. The young men claimed they had found the donkeys wandering in the desert, and were driving them back to the nearest village. William lost his temper with the officious German magistrate. As a result of this he was sentenced to a month in prison, while his companions were allowed to go free. The injustice of this infuriated him. When he came out of jail, he was aggressive and inclined to drink too much. A series of minor offences led to further prison sentences – and a thoroughly resentful William Foster was ready to become a 'complete' criminal.

He fell in love, and wanted money to marry. His first major crime, therefore, was a well-planned robbery of a jeweller. He and two accomplices ran into bad luck and an efficient police force, and each received 12 years' hard labour. Foster's girlfriend Peggy married him while he was in jail, awaiting trial. Nine months later, Foster escaped. In a bank robbery a few months later, two clerks were killed, and Foster's career as a 'hunted dog' began. Like Kelly, he had an amazing ability to shoot his way out of tight corners; and, as the deaths piled up, he became South Africa's most wanted man.

Committed Suicide

Whenever possible, his wife – who now had a baby daughter – joined him. The tragic end came in September 1914, when Foster and two companions were cornered in a cave in the Kensington Ridge. One of the men committed suicide. Foster's parents, his sisters, and his wife Peggy were then sent for. They agreed to try and persuade him to give himself up, and bravely entered the cave. The parents and sisters came out, with Foster's baby daughter. Then three shots rang out. Peggy had decided to die with her husband.

In the United States, the gangster era began long before Prohibition. New York was America's first major city, and as early as 1790 it had slums that were as foul and miserable as any in the world. In the hundred or so rooms of the Old Brewery, human beings were packed like rats, and murders averaged one a night. When the district was demolished in 1852, the builders filled numerous sacks with human bones and remains. There were many tough and colourfully-named gangs: the Dead Rabbits, the Roach Guards, the Shirt Tails, the Plug Uglies (which referred to their huge plug or top hats). Then, during the 1840s, Tammany Hall politicians discovered that gangsters could be useful allies, threatening rivals and drumming up votes. And it was from this period that the real history of American gangsterdom began.

At the time, most of the gangsters were Irish – and, oddly enough, Chinese. The Chinese were accustomed to their 'Triad Societies' at home. When they came to settle in America – mostly on the West Coast – they naturally formed themselves again into 'tongs' for mutual protection.

The Chinese were also among the first to practise gang assassination. In 1897, a rich Chinese gangster, Little Pete – owner of several gambling houses – was sitting in a barber's chair in San Francisco. He had made the mistake of sending his bodyguard out to find the result of a horse race. Two men who had been trailing him for months, awaiting their opportunity, came in and literally filled him full of lead. The killers were never caught. A similar scene was to be repeated half a century later when, in October 1957, Albert Anastasia, one of Murder Incorporated's assassins, was shot in a Manhattan hotel barber's shop.

Black Hand Gang

In the early years of the century, most of America's most formidable gangsters were Chinese. By comparison, the Irish were relatively amateurish and badly organized. But another racial group was slowly achieving ascendancy – the Italians. Fleeing from the poverty of their homeland – and from its chronic political troubles – they also had their tradition of secret societies. The word 'Mafia' originally described a Sicilian outlaw who had taken to the hills, covered with low scrub (mafia), to hide from justice (either at the hands of the police, or of the family of someone he had killed).

The Mafia came to New Orleans – under the name of 'the Black Hand' in the 1880s. Almost without exception, mafiosi preyed upon their fellow citizens, who, in turn, were too terrified to appeal to the police of their adopted country. Similarly, the Irish gangsters tended to prey upon their fellow Irish, and the Chinese on the Chinese.

Escape from Slums

As the century progressed, the Chinese slowly lost their reputation as gangsters – perhaps because many of them succeeded, through hard work and intelligence, in escaping the slums – and the Irish, and their bitter rivals the Italians, took over. Then came the double-edged sword of Prohibition. Chicago's crime industry was run by men like the O'Donnell brothers, and the flamboyant Dion O'Banion, who was quoted as saying angrily: 'To hell with them Sicilians!'

On November 10, 1924, four men walked into O'Banion's flower store, and unceremoniously gunned him down. The man who arranged the murder commented ironically: 'O'Banion's head got away from under his hat.' His name was Al Capone. The United States had entered its third and most lethal era of gangsterdom. It is still in the midst of it.

GANGSTERS: CASE STUDY

The Kray Twins

During the 1950s and 1960s the Kray twins were greatly feared members of the underworld. They ran their own protection racket, committed fraud and blackmail and employed their own group of hard men to do much of the dirty work for them.

The Kray twins were born October 24, 1933. Reggie arrived into the world first, followed ten minutes later by his brother Ronnie. Charlie and Violet Kray had another son, Charlie who was already seven years old when the twins were born.

The Kray family lived in the East of London in an area called Hoxton, now known as Shoreditch, until 1939. At the start of World War II their father, Charlie, was conscripted into the army. Charlie didn't like the routine that the army demanded, and found it hard to settle into army life. It wasn't long before he deserted and spent many months in hiding from the military police. It was probably this fact, and that their father was away from home for a great deal of the time during this period, that the twins developed a hatred for the authorities and in deed anyone in uniform.

Violet Kray remained cheerful despite the fact that it was quite a struggle to bring up her family despite the apparent poverty. In 1940 the family were evacuated to a small village in the county of Suffolk, and the boys came to love the countryside. However, after a year their mother desperately missed London and her friends, and she brought the family back to Bethnal Green much to the twins disappointment.

As the twins group up in the East End they grew more more interested in sports including football, athletics and boxing and it wasn't long before they were making a name for themselves in the boxing ring. They loved all the attention they received although Ron was much more of a loner than his twin.

Their Notoriety Grew

By the time the twins were sixteen their notoriety had grown in the East End of London. They had formed a gang who were always causing trouble in the area, and it wasn't long before they were banned from the majority of the dance halls and cinemas in the vicinity. There were always fights between rival gangs in the East End and so it wasn't unusual for a young boy to be seen carrying some sort of weapon. The twins usually carried a knife, but kept many other useful weapons underneath their beds back at Vallance Road. During their sixteenth year the twins were arrested and charged with their first major offence – Grievous Bodily Harm – for an attack against a rival gang outside a dance hall in Hackney. However, thanks to their association with Reverend Hetherington who acted as a character witness for the twins, they were let off with a warning.

When the boys were seventeen they were in trouble once again with the police. The boys were standing outside a cafe when they were asked to move on by a policeman. Unfortunately the policeman pushed Ron in the back. Ron was not in the habit of letting anyone push him around and he hit the policeman before running off. Once again they were arrested and charged with assault. It was their old friend the reverend who came to their rescue for a second time.

By this time both Ron and Reg were boxing professionally, and had it not been for the fact that they were called up to serve in the Army, would probably have made a career out of the sport. Like their father before them, the twins did not take kindly to the routine inflicted on them by the army and they spent most of their time either on the run or locked up in the guardhouse.

Gangsters in the Making

When the boys were younger they had made a vow to each other that they would either end up as boxers or big-time villains. The army put a stop to their boxing and so they turned to the only other career they knew – violence and crime.

When they were eventually released from the army they some protection work for various small-time villains, but decided that they really didn't want to work for anyone but themselves. They raised enough money between them to buy a rather run-down snooker club in Bethnal Green. The club had always had a really bad reputation for fighting and was always in a state of repair because of the violence. The boys knew they could turn it around, and before long the Regal had a far-improved clientele and the fighting had ceased. It was at the Regal that a Maltese mob tried to obtain protection money from the Krays. One of the gang had a bayonet thrust into his hand and the others were lucky to escape without being hurt, consequently the Krays had no further trouble from the mob.

Their club was frequented by many other well-known East End villains like Jack Spot, Billy Hill, and Mad Frankie Fraser. The twins were well respected by the underworld and had a finger in every crooked pie. They hijacked lorries carrying anything from cigarettes to furniture, dealt in National Service exemption certificates and also forged tickets which allowed men to work on the docks for short hours for large remunerations. Reg and Ron Kray were now big time villains.

While Ron's Away

In 1957 Ron was arrested for causing grievous bodily harm to a man called Terry Martin outside a pub in Stepney. He was sent to prison for three years. During his absence his brother opened up another club called 'The Double R. Charlie'. The club flourished and it wasn't long before the Kray empire was growing at a rapid rate, owning or at least having a stake in at least 30 clubs and bars in London.

Without Ron around, Reg found that the business side of their 'firm' ran a lot smoother. The twins argued constantly about how to manage their affairs, and Ron being the dominant twin usually won the arguments. After the death of his favourite aunt, Rose, Ron seemed to lose his sanity. He was sent to the psychiatric wing of Winchester prison where he was diagnosed as being a paranoid schizophrenic. Slowly his health deteriorated, and it was then that Reg decided to get his brother out of prison. He wanted his brother to have a proper assessment outside of the prison environment, and so he simply swapped places with his twin. By the time the guards realised what had taken place, Ron was long gone and they had to release Reg as well.

Ron managed to elude being recaptured for five months, but it wasn't long before Reg realised he had made a terrible mistake. Ron really was very sick. He was reassessed and returned to prison where he remained until May 1959.

When he returned home he was prone to terrible mood swings and was paranoid that everyone was out to try and put him down. The family took him back to hospital for his own sake and he was told that he would have to remain on medication for the remainder of his life.

Working Together Again

By the start of the 1960s the Kray twins were back working together. Ron was starting to behave more like his old self and the Kray 'firm' had truly established itself in the underworld. By now the Krays were mixing with some very influential people and had also started to make inroads into the West End gambling scene.

Part of the reason for the eventual downfall of the Kray empire was their love of publicity. Unlike the Mafia who kept a low profile and let others do the dirty work for them, the Krays were always eager to be in the limelight. When they were arrested in 1965 for demanding money with menaces, it wasn't long before they were released and cleared of all charges due to their friends in high places.

Reggie Kray married his all-time sweetheart Francis Shea in April 1965. She was 21 when they married but unfortunately the relationship ended in separation just eight months later.

The Kray twins were now starting to make contact with the Mafia. They went to the United States to further reinforce their links, and although they did not manage to do as much busines as they would have liked, it did mean that they protected their gambling interests in the West End by entertaining the Mafia when they were in London.

The main opposition to the Krays in London was the Richardson gang from South London. In March 1966 the Richardson gang went to a club called Mr Smiths with the intention of wiping out the Krays. However, when they got there only one member of the gang was present, Dickie Hart, and he was shot dead. A man called George Cornell was thought to be responsible for the shooting, but he managed to get away before the police arrived. Ronnie Kray decided to take the matter into his own hands and on April 9, 1966, he walked into the Blind Beggar pub and shot Cornell in the head.

The End of the Krays

Jack 'The Hat' McVitie was a dangerous man and had no fear of the twins. He could often he heard running them down and on numerous occasions he had been warned by Reg to change his attitude. However, these warnings had no effect on McVitie and one evening he was invited to a party in Stoke Newington where he was stabbed to death by his rival Reg Kray.

This proved to be the undoing for the Krays and indeed their 'firm'. Although in the past the authorities had allowed them to get away with certain indiscretions, they had now stepped beyond the limit, and it meant they had to be stopped at all costs.

The twins were arrested on May 8, 1968. Their eventual trial in January 1969 lasted for a full six weeks. Ronnie Kray, then 35, was convicted of the murder of George Cornell and Jack McVitie, while Reggie was charged with the murder of McVitie. They both received life sentences with a recommendation that they serve no less than 30 years.

Lord Lucan Mystery

The disappearance of Lord Lucan is indeed a
mystery. Even after thirty years, despite various
rumours and theories, the police have no clue as
to his whereabouts.

THE BODY of 29-year-old Sandra Rivett was found
at the London home of Lord Lucan on the night of
November 7, 1974. The first clue to the murder
was when a woman in bloodstained clothing
rushed into the bar of the Plumber's Arms in
Lower Belgrave Street. She was crying and her
words were almost incoherent, but eventually they
understood that her nanny had been murdered,
and she had managed to escape the murderer
who was still in her house. The distressed lady
was no other than the Countess of Lucan. The
whole ordeal eventually took its toll and she
collapsed unconscious on the floor, and was
subsequently taken to a nearby hospital.

The police were called and were informed that
a lady had been the subject of a violent attack,
and that she had fled her house in panic leaving
behind her her three children. The police immediately went to the Lucan house, which turned
out to be a stately home with six floors and a
basement. They forced there way in and began a
thorough search. The children were discovered

upstairs in their bedrooms completely unharmed, but the breakfast room had bloodstains over the walls and a large pool of blood on the floor. The floor was covered in large footprints, and in a door that led into the kitchen lay a bloodstained sack. Inside the sack was the body of the children's nanny, Sandra Rivett, who had been bludgeoned to death with some kind of blunt instrument. She had severe injuries on the back of her skull.

The back door had been left open and lying in the hallway was a length of lead piping covered in surgical tape, it was very misshapen and covered with blood.

When Lady Lucan had recovered enough to make a statement to the police, she named her husband Richard John Bingham, the 7th Earl of Lucan, as the murderer. However, there was no sign of him and no trace to his whereabouts. Lord Lucan had been separated from his wife for more than a year, and even a search of his apartment in Elizabeth Street gave the police no clues as to what had happened to him.

In Lady Lucan's statement to the police she said she had been watching the television in their sitting room and was waiting for Sandra to return with a cup of tea which she had offered to make for her. After what seemed rather a long time, Lady Lucan went to look for Sandra and as she went downstairs to the ground floor she was brutally attacked from behind. A struggle ensued and it was then that she realized it was her own husband. He openly admitted to accidentally killing the nanny, mistaking her for his wife and it was normally Lady Lucan that made the evening tea. She tried everything she could to calm her husband, saying that they could hide the body and that she would not be missed. She feared for her own life, so Lady Lucan was submissive and agreed to do everything her husband asked. She told the police that she managed to escape from the house when her husband went into the bathroom to get some towels to clean her wounds, but had no idea why he would want to kill her.

After the Event

A friend of the Lucans, Mrs. Madeleine Floorman, lived only a short distance away from their home. She told the police that she had been dozing in front of her television on the night of November 7, when shortly after 10.00 p.m. someone started ringing insistently on her doorbell. Thinking that it was probably just some local kid playing a joke, she ignored it and dropped back off to sleep. A little while later she was woken by her telephone ringing, and she was convinced that the voice she heard was that of her friend Lord Lucan. His voice was very shaky, and his words incoherent. When she went out of her front door the next morning she discovered a few spots of blood on the concrete.

The same evening, around 10.30 p.m., Lord Lucan telephoned his mother and told her that something dreadful had happened, and that he wanted her to go to his house and fetch the children. However, when she arrived at the house she found it swarming with police. She told them that the Lucans had been separated for more than a year, and that the children had been made wards of court. She also told them the address of Lord Lucan's apartment which was nearby. The children went home with their grandmother, while the police continued to search the house for clues.

In Lord Lucan's apartment they found his car keys, passport, chequebook, driving licence, wallet and glasses, and outside was parked his blue Mercedes car which apparently had been suffering from a flat battery for some time.

On the night of the murder Lord Lucan had borrowed a car from his friend, a Ford Corsair, and apparently he had insisted that he needed it on that particular night. At around 11.30 p.m. Lord Lucan arrived in Uckfield Sussex at the house of his old friends Ian and Susan Maxwell-Scott. Although Ian was away his wife let their old friend in, but noticed his appearance was very disheveled, and that his trousers looked as though he had been trying to sponge off some stains.

The story that Lord Lucan told to his friend was that he had been walking past his house in Belgrave Street when he had just glanced into the basement window. He could see someone struggling with his wife and so he let himself in, ran down the stairs and subsequently slipped on a pool of blood. He had calmed Lady Lucan down by taking her upstairs to her bedroom, but when he went to the bathroom to get a towel to clean her wounds, she had run out of the house screaming 'Murderer!' He had panicked, realizing that things looked really bad for him, and he fled.

Susan Maxwell-Scott listened to his story and then tried to persuade him to go with her to the local police station. At this suggestion Lord Lucan became edgy and said he had to 'get back'. He drove away from her house that same night and he has never been seen since.

Lord Lucan's bloodstained car was found abandoned in the town of Newhaven, East Sussex, leading certain people, including his wife Lady Veronica, to believe that he had drowned himself.

Case Reopened

Although Lord Lucan was officially declared dead by the High Court in 1999, the investigation into his case has reopened almost thirty years after his disappearance.

Police are examining the original evidence and with the help of DNA are hoping that they can come up with a more satisfactory conclusion. There is new information coming into the police station every year and each call or piece of information is taken very seriously.

There have been several reports of sightings of the elusive Lord Lucan, but on further investigation they have turned out to be nothing more than a hoax or a misidentification. The search for Lord Lucan continues to this day.

The Alibis

They come in all shapes and sizes: iron-clad,
watertight . . . and dangerous. Like the alibi
concocted for sex killer Raymond Morris by his
trusting wife, 'to save him trouble' – and to free him
for more fiendish attacks on children.

A CASE THAT would have taxed the ingenuity of
Sherlock Holmes took place in Montana in
September 1901. The body of an old man named
Dotson was found in his cabin, near Helmsville,
with a bullet in the heart. On the opposite wall, a
gun had been rigged up in a wooden frame, with
the muzzle pointing at the dead man. A string ran
from the dead man's hand, through a metal ring
in the wall, to the trigger of the gun. It looked like
a clear case of suicide. A note beside the body
seemed to confirm this. It read: 'It warnt my son
Clint done that Cullinane murder. Clint lide to
save me. I done it.' It was signed Oliver Dotson,
and friends verified that it was in his handwriting.

The 'Cullinane murder' had taken place on
August 5, 1899. A prospector named Gene Cullinane
had been found shot dead in his cabin, not far
from Dotson's place. A few days later, sheriff's
officers arrested Clint Dotson, and two other men
named Oliver Benson and Ellis Persinger. Benson
and Persinger admitted robbing Gene Cullinane,

but alleged that it was Clint Dotson who had shot the prospector twice in the heart. Benson and Persinger were sentenced to ten years in prison; Clint Dotson received life.

Now it looked as if Dotson might have been innocent after all. He had what amounted to a double alibi. He was behind bars at the time of his father's death, so there could be no question that he might have forced his father to sign a false confession. Old man Dotson seemed to be offering his son a kind of posthumous alibi for the time of the murder . . .

A Strange Problem

Undersheriff John Robinson, the man who had sent Clint Dotson to jail, went to interview Persinger and Benson. Were they quite sure it was Clint who had killed the prospector? They insisted they were absolutely certain; they had seen him do it. That left the undersheriff with a strange problem. Why had the old man confessed to a crime he did not commit? He was certainly an alcoholic; but had never been weak in the head.

He checked with the prison governor at Deer Lodge jail, where Dotson was serving his sentence, and learned that one of Dotson's closest friends, a robber named Jim Fleming, had been released from prison only a few weeks earlier. Sheriff Robinson decided he had to talk to Fleming. But first he adopted one of Sherlock Holmes's favourite expedients, and put on the worst fitting clothes he could find.

Then he made his way to the distant ranch, fifty miles from Helena, where Fleming's girlfriend lived. He introduced himself as an ex-convict from Deer Lodge, and explained that he was looking for his old friend Jim Fleming. The girl believed him. She told him that Fleming would be back in a few days, and invited him to have a cup of coffee. They had a friendly talk, and soon she mentioned a matter of $50,000 that Clint Dotson had got when he robbed Union Pacific. It seemed that she was expecting a share of the money.

This is what Sheriff Robsinson wanted to know. Now he had his motive for murder. He rode back to Helena, and made intensive inquiries to find out if Jim Fleming had been seen with old man Dotson at any time; soon he found what he wanted – someone who had seen them together just before the old man's death. Robinson went back to the ranch, lay in wait for Jim Fleming, and arrested him.

Incredible Viciousness

The sheriff had nothing to go on but guesses; nevertheless, he played his suspect as a skilful angler plays a big fish. He told him that he had been talking to Clint Dotson in jail. He spoke as if he knew all about the Union Pacific robbery. 'Clint didn't do that stick-up. He didn't have anything to do with it. There ain't no fifty thousand dollars.' And then he hinted casually that he knew Fleming had been drinking with old man Dotson just before his death. He knew because Clint had told him . . . Suddenly, Fleming saw himself surrounded by pitfalls of treachery. So when Robinson said: 'Would you like to make a statement?' Fleming said: 'Yes, I sure would.' The story he told revealed such incredible viciousness that even the veteran sheriff was shocked.

Clint Dotson had deliberately planned the murder of his own father, in order to clear himself of the murder of Gene Cullinane. With promises of a share of the $50,000 he had persuaded Fleming to go to the old man's cabin, and get him drunk. When the old man was drunk, it was easy to persuade him to do anything; that was how Fleming had got the note. The old man did it ' for a joke'. Later, when Oliver Dotson was stupefied with the raw whiskey, Fleming shot him through the heart, and rigged up the shotgun to make it look like an accident.

Fleming was hanged on September 6, 1902, Dotson in April 1904; and the double-alibi murder has come to rank as one of the strangest cases in modern criminal history. Yet if you had asked Clint Dotson if he had an alibi for the murder of Gene Cullinane, he would not have known what you were talking about. It is only in recent years, since the rise of the detective story and the TV thriller, that the word has passed into the language.

The Latin word 'alibi' actually means 'elsewhere', so it is correct to say: 'The prisoner has an alibi; it should be 'The prisoner was alibi'. Oddly enough, it is only in the past fifty years or so that the criminal has given serious thought to the problem of alibis. In less sophisticated days, he committed his murder, and then did his best to be elsewhere when the crime was discovered. The modern criminal has discovered the advantage of persuading the police that he was already 'alibi' at the time the crime was committed.

On the whole, most of these attempts have been fairly crude. In The Three Musketeers, D'Artagnan puts back the clock half an hour, then draws the attention of his regimental commander to it, to establish that he could not possibly have been present at a certain fight. Real-life alibis have sometimes been as obvious – and absurd. George Joseph Smith, the 'Brides in the Bath' murderer, moved into rooms in Highgate, London, on December 17, 1914, accompanied by his new wife, a clergyman's daughter named Margaret Lofty.

The following day, the landlady heard sounds of splashing coming from the bathroom, and hands slapping the sides of the bath – then silence. This was broken by the sound of the organ playing in the sitting room; John Lloyd – alias George Smith – was establishing his alibi. A few minutes later, the front door slammed loudly; then he came back saying 'I've brought some tomatoes for Mrs. Lloyd's supper'. At this point, the landlady noticed water leaking through the ceiling. Lloyd rushed upstairs, burst into the bathroom, and shouted: 'My wife can't speak to me – go for a doctor.' Predictably, 'Mrs Lloyd' was drowned.

But Smith might well have got away with it, if a newspaper report of the death had not been seen by a relative of one of Smith's previous victims. And when George Smith finally appeared in court, and the story of that evening was told by the prosecutor, Sir Archibald Bodkin, the killer found out that a poor alibi is worse than no alibi at all . . .

Far more brilliant and elaborate alibis than George Smith's have proved just as ineffective. The classic American case – with all those features so dear to the heart of the lover of detective stories – took place just one year after the execution of the 'Brides in the Bath' killer. Frederick Small was an unsuccessful grocer of Portland, Maine, whose matrimonial affairs were pursued by misfortune.

His first wife died in childbirth; his second wife ran off with the president of a baseball team. Small was granted $10,000 damages. In 1911, when he was approaching the age of 45, Small married a third time, Florence Arlene Curry, a girl nearly 15 years his junior. The marriage was not happy; Small seems to have been a coarse and bullying man, who often beat his wife.

In 1914, Small decided that it was time to retire; they moved to a cottage near Mountainview, New Hampshire. It was on the edge of Lake Ossipee, and Small spent much of his time fishing. The Smalls were not poor, but neither were they as well off as the husband thought they deserved to be. In early 1916, he insured his wife's life for $20,000, and his cottage for a further $3,000. The outlay - $1,000 or so – was large, for Small's total fortune was less than $5,000. But he had plans for re-couping his losses.

The man who had sold him the life insurance was Edwin Conner, who was also principal of the local school. Unlike most of the residents of Mountainview, Conner seemed to find Small pleasant enough, and Small went out of his way to be nice to Conner. They even agreed to take a trip to Boston together, partly to look into some further insurance business, but mainly for pleasure.

On the morning of September 28, 1916, Small phoned his friend and asked him if he could make the Boston trip that day. This was short notice; Conner said it would be difficult. Small insisted. Finally, Conner said he would see what he could do. At two o'clock, a local wagon driver named Kennett was asked if he would collect Small at three-thirty, in time for the four o'clock train to Boston. Kennett deliberately arrived early, because on previous occasions Small had invited him in for a tot of rye whiskey. But this time he found Small all ready, waiting on the back porch. Small opened the door, shouted 'Goodbye' to his wife, and they drove off.

Everyone was Sympathetic

The two men took the afternoon train, arriving in Boston at eight. There they checked into a hotel, and went to see a play; afterwards they ate supper, and returned to the hotel. The desk clerk was waiting with a message for Small. There had been a fire back at Mountainview, and he was to ring the local hotel. A few minutes later a distraught Frederick Small asked Conner to take the phone and confirm the message. His house was in flames, said the hotel keeper, and he had better hire a car and return immediately; Small's grief seemed enormous and genuine. Everyone was sympathetic.

Back home, as the dawn was rising over the lake, Small viewed the smouldering ashes of his cottage. In a choking voice, he asked the local doctor if someone could search the ruins for his wife's body. An hour later, the doctor rang Small at the hotel. 'We've found the body. What do you want us to do with it?' For a moment, Small was nonplussed; then he asked with amazement: 'You mean there's enough to be buried?'

There was indeed. For the body had collapsed through the floor of the sitting-room, into the basement, and there were several inches of water in the basement. Mrs. Small still had a cord knotted tightly around her throat. She had a bullet wound in the skull, and the head had been bludgeoned.

Frederick Small was promptly placed under arrest. He insisted that his wife had been alive when he left the house, and asked Mr. Kennett to verify that she had come out on the back porch to say goodbye. The wagon driver replied that, as far as he could recollect, Small had called goodbye, but there had been no reply. The police found other evidence to indicate that the murder had been carefully planned. In the wreckage there was an alarm clock with wires and spark plugs attached to it. There could be no doubt that it was a timing device.

Small had been too clever. In order to make sure

that his wife's body was completely consumed, he used a quantity of a substance known as thermite, a powder made of aluminium filings, metallic oxides and magnesium. It is used in welding, because it produces such an intense heat. The heat was intended to incinerate Mrs. Small's corpse; instead, it burned a hole in the floor, and the corpse fell into the water in the basement.

The evidence suggests that Small killed his wife accidentally, or in a fit of rage. Various witnesses described his violent temper. It is just possible that he might have escaped the gallows with a plea of second degree murder; as it was, he was hanged on January 15, 1918.

It is an interesting question whether Small's ingenuity inspired another fire murder in 1933. On October 25 of that year, Richard Budde, a middle-aged lumberjack of Eagle River, Wisconsin, arrived home from work at six in the evening and found the doors all locked. As he shouted his wife's name, neighbours came over to see what was the matter. They forced their way in, and immediately smelled smoke; there had been a fire in the bedroom closet – a large wooden cupboard. It had burned through the floor, and the closet door had fallen through into the basement. So had the body of Virginia Budde, which had also been in the closet.

The Door was Unlocked

This was a baffling problem for Sheriff Thomas McGregor. Why had Mrs. Budde shut herself in the closet and set fire to it? Or was it possible that she had been put in there and set alight On the other hand, the key was still in the lock of the closet door – on the outside – and the door was unlocked. The theory of the coroner was that Mrs. Budde, who had recently been ill, had gone into the closet and committed suicide by setting herself on fire. Burning oneself to death is, oddly enough, a fairly common form of suicide.

Budde had a watertight alibi. He had left for work at eight in the morning – neighbours not only hear him calling goodbye to his wife, but also something about bringing a loaf and some sausages home with him. The local fire chief estimated that the fire must have started about two in the afternoon. If Budde had killed his wife, he must have returned home to do so. That was just possible – he worked alone in the woods. But a check on the amount of wood he had chopped revealed that he had done an exceptionally hard day's work; there would have been no time to rush home and kill his wife – a process that would have taken two hours. Besides, the neighbours would most certainly have seen him.

The pathologist's report seemed to establish Budde's innocence beyond all doubt. Presence of smoke in the lungs proved that Mrs. Budde had been alive when she entered the closet. The fact that the door was unlocked seemed to clinch it. If she had been alive and conscious, she would have simply walked out. The coroner's jury saw no reason to doubt Budde's innocence. His wife's death brought him no advantage; she had not been insured, and there was no rumour of another woman. It was true that the Buddes often fought, but that was nothing unusual. A verdict of death through causes unknown was returned.

At which point – as in the Small case – fate took a hand. The coroner, P. J. Gaffney, was sitting alone in his office after the inquest, with various items of evidence on his desk – Mrs. Budde's half-burnt shoes, fragments of clothing, and the lock from the closet door. By some chance, the lock fell off the desk.

Startled, Gaffney jumped up and picked it up. He noticed that the fall had made the lock spring out. He dropped it again. The lock went back. He tried it several times. Through some peculiar fault, each impact caused it to either lock or unlock. He sat down again, and began to think deeply. This didn't prove anything, of course. But if the closet door, complete with lock had fallen through into the basement, shouldn't it have been locked when it was found? The fact that it was unlocked suggested that it had been locked before it fell.

But if Budde had put his wife in the closet, how had he set fire to her six hours after he left for work? There was no evidence of a timing device. The coroner was a painstaking man. He bought wood, and constructed a closet of exactly the same size and design as the one in which Mrs. Budde had died. He lined it with a flame-resistant material of the same kind that had lined Budde's closet. He allowed the same quarter inch air gap at the bottom of the door. He filled it with old clothes, set them alight, and closed the door. The fire that began at eight in the morning took more than twelve hours to burn through the floor. The fire chief had made a mistake. Richard Budde could have started the fire before he left for work.

With this much evidence, Gaffney decided on an autopsy. It confirmed all his suspicions: strychnine was found in Mrs. Budde's stomach. It had been a murder of atrocious cruelty. Budde had given his wife the poison – a large dose, enough to make her unconscious after considerable suffering. Then he had placed her in the cupboard, set fire to her, and then left her to suffocate. There was not enough of the body left to allow the coroner to estimate the time of death.

Budde was tried, but there was one thing that the coroner had not been able to establish: a motive. The jury decided that Mrs. Budde could have taken the strychnine herself. They acquitted Budde, who proceeded to drink himself to death. A few months later, in a fit of delirium tremens, he also took poison, in the bedroom where his wife had died. He left a note confessing to the murder. There were many people in Eagle River who said that it was his wife's ghost who drove him to kill himself. Gaffney was not entirely sceptical. He always claimed that the lock had been in the middle of his desk.

In the long run, the most effective alibis are probably the simplest. Perhaps the most effective method of all is to get someone else to provide it: preferably a wife, who cannot give evidence against her husband in court. Raymond Morris, theEnglish sex murderer, persuaded seven-year-old Christine Darby to get into his car on August 19, 1967; her naked and misused body was found in nearby woods near Cannock Chase, Staffordshire. Morris was among those questioned by the police, because his car fitted the description of the murderer's car.

Morris's wife told the police that her husband had been at home at the time the murder was committed. She had no suspicion he was the killer; she only wanted to 'save him trouble'. In the following year, Morris tried to drag a ten-year-old girl into his car; a woman noted the number, and he was arrested; his wife's well-meant loyalty almost led to another murder.

This whole matter of alibis has undoubtedly been exaggerated by the rise of the detective story. Could you remember what you were doing on the evening of August 10 last year? Of course not. Neither could I. Fortunately, most criminals are too stupid to realize that nothing makes a detective so suspicious as a 'watertight alibi'.

Lethal Ladies

Most data about violent crime and criminal types
has centred on males, and that is attributed to the
idea that males are more aggressive, violent and
criminally versatile than females. However, some
females are just as cold-blooded as males . . .

ON December 1, 1996 Lee Harvey, a 25-year-old
unemployed bus driver, and girlfriend Tracie
Andrews went for a drink with friends at a public
house in Bromsgrove. On their journey home they
were followed by a Ford Sierra which flashed its
headlights and then chased them for several miles.
When they turned into Coopers Hill near Alvechurch they were overtaken by the chasing car and
both cars stopped. Mr Harvey got out to remon-
strate with the other driver. The passenger in the
Sierra also got out and attacked Lee, stabbing him
thirty times including a wound which severed the
carotid artery. The Sierra then raced off.

At least that is the story that Tracie Andrews told
officers. Initially her story was believed and a
nationwide manhunt was launched for the killers.
A small spring and tiny pair of tweezers had been
found at the scene of the crime and these were
identified as coming from a Swiss Army knife
which was suspected of being the murder weapon,
although there was no trace of the weapon at the

scene. Following the massive publicity that the killing generated, two witnesses came forward to say that they had seen Mr Harvey's car prior to the incident and that there was no other vehicle in pursuit.

Police attention then focused on Miss Andrews. Tracie Andrews, a 27-year-old with a five-year-old daughter by a previous relationship, had lived with Lee in Alvechurch, near Redditch, for about 18 months and they were engaged to be married. She denied any involvement in the killing. Forensic scientists examining the clothing that Tracie had worn at the time of the murder noticed a faint bloodstain in the neck of one of her snakeskin-effect boots. It matched the shape of a Swiss Army knife and showed how she may have removed the weapon from the scene of the crime.

Tracie Andrews maintained her defence of an attack by the tall, heavily-built passenger of a Ford Sierra at her trial for murder at Birmingham Crown Court. After a four-week trial the jury took five hours to deliver a guilty verdict and Mr Justice Buckley sentenced Tracie Andrews to life imprisonment.

The Predator

Aileen Carol Pittman was born in Rochester, Michigan on February 29, 1956 and has sometimes been referred to as America's first female serial killer. Although this may not be true she is probably one of the only female killers to act like a true predator. During a 13-month period Aileen violently killed strangers, all men, while she was working as a prostitute along the Florida highways.

Aileen had a very tough start to life, being abandoned by her mother at a very young age. Her mother and father were separated before she was born and her father, Leo Pittman, served time in Kansas and Michigan mental hospitals for child molesting. He subsequently committed suicide whilst he was in prison.

Aileen and her older brother, Keith, were brought up by their maternal grandparents, Lauri and Britta Wuornos, who legally adopted the two children as their own. Her grandparents were both very private people and did not like to associate with the neighbours. At the age of six, Aileen suffered severe facial burns while she and Keith were lighting fires with lighter fluid. Aileen later claimed that she had been having sex with her brother from an early age, but this was never proved and Keith, who died from throat cancer in 1976, neither confirmed nor denied this fact. At 14 Aileen became pregnent as the result of a rape, but she was forced to give the baby up for adoption.

Aileen's grandmother died on July 7, 1971 and the two children were made wards of court. Aileen dropped out of High School in the ninth grade and subsequently became a prostitute by the age of 15. She drifted from place to place and avoided being caught by using various aliuses.

In May 1974, using the name Sandra Kretsch, she was arrested and jailed in Jefferson County, Colorado for a string of offences, including disorderly conduct, drunk driving and firing a .22-calibre pistol from a moving car. She managed to run away before the trial took place and evaded being rearrested until July 13, 1976 in Michigan.

When her brother died she received a totally unexpected life insurance payment of $10,000, and with this she was able to pay off her debt – a fine of $105. The remainder of the money was squandered within a period of two months on various luxuries, including a new car which Aileen wrecked after a couple of weeks.

By late September she was penniless again and decided to hitch a lift to Florida. She started a new life in the sunshine but her bad ways toon caught up with her. She had one stroke of luck when a wealthy 69-year-old man by the name of Lewis Fell picked her up one night. He immediately fell in love with her and they were married in 1976. But Aileen could not be tamed and she was too wild and uncontrollable to realize that she had hit the good times. She treated her husband badly, continued to get into bar fights and was sent to jail for assault. Needless to say it wasn't long before Fell realized that he had made a very big mistake, and the marriage was annulled.

From here Aileen jumped from one bad relationship to another. She carried on with her prostitution, committed forgery, theft and armed robbery, and in between all this she tried to commit suicide. She was an emotional and physical mess using drugs and drinks as an emotional crutch. She was on the road to total self-destruction when she met 24-year-old Tyria

Moore at a gay bar in Daytona. It was 1986, Aileen was depressed, angry at the world, and ready to try something new.

For a little while everything was going really well. Ty genuinely loved her and didn't walk out on her like her other partners. She quit her job and allowed Aileen to support her on her prostitution earnings. However, money soon became short and their affection turned to anger. Ty stayed with Aileen and followed her from one cheap motel room to another. Aileen knew something had to change and she was soon to take drastic measures.

Yearning for Revenge

Aileen talked more and more with Tyria about her life and the problems in her childhood, and how she yearned for revenge. Richard Mallory was a 51-year-old electrician from Palm Habor, and was last seen alive on November 30, 1989. His car was found abandoned the next day with his personal possessions scattered close by, together with several condoms and a half-empty bottle of vodka. His body was not discovered until December 13 in some woodland near Daytona Beach. He was still fully clothed and had been shot three times in the chest at close range. Several months of investigation into his rather sordid lifestyle revealed very little, and the investigation went cold.

In June another body was found in the woods about 40 miles north of Tampa. This time the man was naked, and a used condom was lying beside the body. He had been shot several times with a

.22 pistol. The man turned out to be 43-year-old David Spears, a heavy-equipment operator from Sarasota. His truck was found a little later abandoned beside a motorway with the doors unlocked and the licence plate missing.

On June 6, just 30 miles away from the previous murder another naked body was discovered. This time the body was so badly decomposed that the forensic team were unable to determine the date or time of death, or get a reliable set of fingerprints. They did, however, discover nine .22 bullets in the remains, which made the Sheriff believe that there was the possibility that a serial killer was at large.

A missing person report was filed with the police on June 22. Peter Siems, a 65-year-old merchant seaman, turned missionary, had left Florida on June 7, 1990, to visit relatives in Arkansas. No trace was ever found of the man, but his car turned up wrecked and abandoned in Orange Springs, Florida. Witnesses described the occupants of the car as two women – one blonde and one brunette – who clambered frantically from the vehicle, throwing beer cans into the woods and cursing at each other. The blonde woman was bleeding and had left a bloody palm print on the trunk of the car. The police were able to make accurate sketches of the two women but they were not distributed until a further three male bodies were discovered that had all been shot with a .22.

Women Suspects

Soon the similarities between all the murders

could not be ignored and the police soon realized that they could very possibly be looking for a female killer as the people who picked up the hitch-hiker in the first place obviously felt no threat. The press ran a story about all the murders and suggested that the women were looking for two women – the two in particular who had wrecked Peter Siem's car. They also issued detailed sketches of the two women and it wasn't long before several leads came in. They had witnesses that identified the two women as a pair of lesbians that went by the name of Tyria Moore and 'Lee'. 'Lee' turned out to be a woman by the name of Aileen Wuornos and the police soon discovered that she had used several other aliases. The hunt for Aileen began in earnest.

She was eventually tracked down to a bar in Port Orange. She was already guilty of parole violation so the police were able to take her back to the station for questioning. Tyria Moore had no police records but they put pressure on her and she soon gave them the evidence they needed. Along with that evidence and a key they had taken from Wuornos herself, they were able to uncover some personal items that belonged to the victims. Under pressure, Moore confessed that although she had nothing to do with them, that her girlfriend was indeed a murderer.

After several phone calls from Moore pleading with Wuornos to give herself up because the police were going to implicate her, Aileen eventually gave in and admitted to the murders. She said that all the murders had been in self-defence, that she had been hitch-hiking and when the driver of the vehicle had become violent and aggressive she had shot them.

It certainly appeared that Aileen's background had made her paranoid against the male sex. However her prosecutors did not believe the plea of self-defence, and stated she simply acted like a predator, luring men with the possibility of sex and then killing them for their money and possessions. Their key witness was Tyria Moore who had known about the murders but nothing about the rape or self-defence. The Court rejected pleas that Aileeen was a borderline psychotic and she received six death sentences.

At the age of 46, Aileen Wuornos was executed by lethal injection in Florida on Wednesday, October 9, 2002. She claimed in her last hours of life that she was the victim of her life 'not a predatory prostitute'.

Bent Coppers

They are the men people go to for help in cases of robbery, rape, theft. But what if the police themselves are dishonest? Who then ensures that justice is done?

IN JANUARY 1728, a play called *The Beggar's Opera* became the rage of London. It was written by John Gay, and presented by a manager called Rich; it made Gay rich and Rich gay. What the audiences found so piquant about it was that it was not about tragic kings and queens, but about the thieves, highwaymen, prostitutes, and fences. The villain, Peachum, is a receiver of stolen goods who supplements his income by handing over some of his customers to the law. In essence, it was an amusingly realistic portrayal of crime and corruption in eighteenth-century London.

Only three years earlier, Londoners had crowded to watch the execution of the man who served as a model for Peachum – the 'thieftaker' Jonathan Wild. In fact, Wild may be regarded as the archetype of the crooked cop. He was *not* a cop – officially the British police force didn't come into existence until the end of the eighteenth century – but he was regarded as a valuable ally of the law. Arriving in London about 1710, at the age of 22, Wild quickly made the discovery that the man who makes most out of crime is not the thief, but the man who finances him.

At this time, there was an extraordinary loop-hole in the law: a receiver of stolen goods could not be prosecuted. Wild set up as a receiver, and soon became so prosperous that he was able to buy an inn. By the time an Act of Parliament changed the law on receivers, he had already devised a way to operate legally. He would approach men who had been robbed, and offer to buy the stolen goods back from the thief, for a small commission. This was so successful that he set up a shop where people who had been burgled could come to inquire about their property.

Jealous Friends

For five shillings, Wild would enter their names on his books; a few days later, in exchange for a reward, he would restore the goods. The peace officers – employed by the City of London – had no objection. Wild was one of their best informers. So long as he helped to send highwaymen and thieves to the gallows of Tyburn, they didn't care what he did.

Wild would probably have died comfortably in his bed if he hadn't overreached himself. He organized some of the robberies himself. Business was so good that he had to store some of the stolen property in warehouses. Jealous confederates finally betrayed him. The law had to act. In May 1725 he was taken to Tyburn – now Marble Arch – in a cart, pelted and jeered at by the mob; there he was hanged on the triangular gallows. It was probably his reputation for betrayal, rather than dishonesty, that prompted the crowd's hostility.

'Wild's system and methods have been copied many times since then, in America and on the Continent, as well as in this country,' wrote a biographer of Jonathan Wild in 1937. This was not quite true. Before you can have large-scale official corruption, you must first have a flourishing crime industry. In the London of Jonathan Wild, the crime rate was very nearly as high as in present-day New York – and for a rather odd reason.

Enormous Bribes

In the middle of the seventeenth century, a Dutch professor named Sylvius discovered how to distil a powerful spirit from juniper berries. It was called 'genièvre' – French for juniper – and then shortened to 'gin'. The English had always been beer and wine drinkers; but when William of Orange became king in 1689, Dutch gin began to flow into England. In 1690 an Act of Parliament allowed anyone to brew and sell spirits without a licence. Thousands of gin shops opened up; the sign 'Drunk for a penny, dead drunk for twopence, straw free,' became commonplace. The crime rate rocketed, and men like Wild flourished. He was the most notorious 'crooked cop' of his time – but there were dozens of others. Gin, crime, and crooked police officers went together.

However, it is not quite accurate to talk about

'police corruption'. It is seldom the uniformed man on the beat who gets corrupted. In all the major police scandals – from the 'trial of the detectives' in London in 1877 to the widely publicized Knapp Commission Hearings in New York in 1971 – the culprits have been plain clothes detectives. There was even a certain amount of corruption among the famous 'Bow Street Runners', the forerunners of the modern London police force.

These un-uniformed detectives were known for their high living, and at least two of them left fortunes of over £20,000. That kind of money is not made by honest thief-catching. But the detective has to spend part of his days in contact with crooks, because his job is to obtain information. When he is dealing with small-time crooks, the temptation is small. But the big crook can offer enormous bribes – and his 'success' lends him a certain aura of sophistication and authority that may induce a sense of inferiority in a detective earning less than £2,000 a year. As if these pressures are not enough, the detective may be induced to compromise himself, and then be blackmailed.

All three of these factors were at work in the events which led to the London police scandals of 1877. The crooks in this case were two highly successful confidence swindlers named Kurr and Benson. Both had mastered the art of seeming to be rich men. Benson, with an excellent French accent, played the part of an aristocrat; Kurr appeared to be a bluff country gentleman who might have stepped out of the pages of a novel by Anthony Trollope.

Their chosen field was sport. And their method of swindling had a certain classic simplicity and originality. Benson, who was living in luxury at Shanklin, Isle of Wight, under the name of Yonge, wrote a letter to the Comtesse de Goncourt, explaining that he was a brilliantly successful sportsman. As a result, he said, bookmakers always shortened the odds when he backed a horse – knowing it was almost certain to win.

All that he wanted of the Comtesse de Goncourt was that she should act as his agent, and place bets on horses for him. He would send her the money, and when the horse won, she would post him his winnings, upon which he would pay her a 5 per cent commission.

The Comtesse could see no harm in this arrangement. She forwarded the cheque to a bookmaker; in fact, the bookmaker was Benson himself. Soon, she received a cheque for £1,000 from the 'bookmaker' – Benson's winnings. She forwarded the cheque to Benson, who promptly sent her £50 for her trouble. Naturally, the Countess wanted to invest some of her own money in this apparently foolproof scheme. She gave Benson, and his accomplice Kurr, £10,000 over a short period. She was only one of their victims.

How did Scotland Yard detectives come to be involved with these swindlers? The full story is unknown, but the first one to accept bribes seems to have been Detective Inspector Meiklejohn of the Yard. Meiklejohn was a friend of a man called

Druscovitch, who was in charge of the continental branch of the 'fraud squad'. Druscovitch got himself into some extraneous financial trouble, and urgently needed £60. Meiklejohn introduced him to a 'perfect gentleman', who persuaded Druscovitch to accept the £60 as a present. The 'gentleman' was Kurr.

Meiklejohn's boss Clarke was then drawn into the web by the 'aristocratic' Benson. Benson sent him a message, claiming to have information about a gang that Clarke had recently broken up. He explained that he was too crippled to leave his home on the Isle of Wight; could Clarke call on him? (Benson had previously crippled himself in an attempt to commit suicide in jail by setting fire to his mattress.) This was good psychology. Clarke went to the palatial home at Shanklin, and was introduced to the exquisitely dressed gentleman who lay on a couch, and whose handkerchiefs had coronets embroidered upon them.

Benson explained that he was afraid Clarke was about to be blackmailed; rumours were circulating that he had taken bribes from the gang he had recently broken up. Clarke said indignantly that he had never taken bribes. Of course not, Benson agreed silkily. But unfortunately there was a letter that Clarke had written to one of the gang, arranging a secret meeting. Perhaps it *was* all police business, but it certainly read very suspiciously. Finally, Clarke was not so much blackmailed as charmed and dominated.

When a fourth Yard man, Detective Inspector Palmer, was drawn into the circle, the swindlers felt they were ready to face the world. And they very soon had to. Benson decided that it was time for a grand coup. He told the trusting Comtesse de Goncourt that he had a superb opportunity to invest £30,000 for her. It would bring a huge return. The Comtesse did not have that much ready cash, so she consulted her lawyer, a man named Abrahams. Abrahams was instantly suspicious, and checked with Scotland Yard on 'Mr. Yonge of Shanklin'. Druscovitch instantly warned Benson that the Comtesse's lawyer had 'smelled a rat'.

Used Notes

The conspirators launched into action. They hadn't expected to be discovered quite so soon. The loot – well over £10,000 – was drawn out of the Bank of England. But in a transaction of that size, the numbers of the notes were known – it would have excited suspicion to ask for the money in old used notes. The police reached the Bank soon after the cash had gone, and Druscovitch was ordered to telegraph the numbers of the notes to all banks in the British Isles.

He conveniently overlooked Scotland – which gave Benson time to get to Glasgow, and change his 'marked money' into £100 notes on the Bank of Clydesdale – which had the advantage of being difficult to change outside Scotland. Duly, the detectives were all given their 'rewards' – Meiklejohn receiving £500. However, he acted stupidly. He changed one of the notes with a wine merchant in Leeds, Yorkshire. The Leeds police soon found out that a Scotland Yard man had cashed a Clydesdale note, and wrote to another of Druscovitch's superiors, Williamson, at the Yard. Druscovitch intercepted the letter and burned it.

The Clydesdale notes were proving to be more trouble than they were worth. Benson went to Rotterdam and cashed one at a hotel; the Dutch police promptly arrested him. Druscovitch informed the other swindler, Kurr, who sent a cable to the Dutch police, signed 'Williamson' (Druscovitch's immediate superior), ordering them to release their captive. They almost did so, but decided to wait for confirmation by letter – which failed to arrive.

Ironically enough, Druscovitch was then sent to Rotterdam to bring Benson back. He was in a gloomy mood; he realized that the net was closing in on him and his confederates. Within a short while, Kurr was also arrested, and he and Benson were tried. Benson got fifteen years, Kurr ten. They then decided that their 'bent cops' had not lived up to their side of the agreement in allowing them to get caught – and in retaliation they denounced them.

The result was the 'trial of the detectives', which shook the English middle class to its foundation. If its members couldn't trust the renowned British bobby, who *could* they trust?

The feeling in favour of the police was so strong that Clarke was actually acquitted. The other three were put inside for two years. The two swindlers were also satisfied; their sentences were reduced by a third. Benson later committed suicide – after a spectacular swindle practised on Adelina Patti, the Spanish-born coloratura who appeared in concerts in New York from 1850 – by jumping from a high gallery in an American prison, where he had ended up.

Raw Material

The scandal created by the trial of the detectives indicates how strongly the British trust their policemen. And, statistically, they are right to do so. Britain has never suffered from the presence of major crime – its murder rate is still one of the lowest in the world. Where there are no large pickings to be made from such activities, there is unlikely to be undue police corruption. In the Scotland Yard affair, only Meiklejohn had the makings of a really dishonest official.

In the United States, however, graft has always been so widespread – starting with the local City Halls – that police corruption is accepted with habitual resignation. From the beginning, the United States had the raw material, the wide open spaces, and the vitality that makes for enormous wealth. Violence – together with the opening of the frontiers – was a part of the way of life. In the original Wild West, the distinction between robbers and lawmen was likely to get blurred. In fast-growing towns such as Chicago and San Francisco, the same thing was true; and there it was actively encouraged by the Horatio Alger 'Protestant ethic' of success, which is so basic to

American society.

Any society which attaches so much importance to wealth and gain is asking for corruption. One of the first big inquiries into police corruption in New York was in 1893 – inspired by the Rev. Charles Parkhurst, who had discovered that practically every member of the police force had paid 'contributions' to Tammany Hall for the privilege of getting his job.

One police captain had handed out $15,000 for his rank. Where did he get the money? From the keepers of gambling houses and brothels. The police chief, Alexander S. Williams, had shares in a brewery, and forced saloon owners to sell 'his' whiskey on penalty of being raided. Williams was unable to explain how he had managed to afford an estate on Long Island, complete with a yacht (and its own dock) on his police salary. Although no charges were made against him, he resigned a year later.

French Connection

Understandably, then, a deep-seated distrust of the law is a part of American life – particularly among oppressed racial and religious minorities. Herbert Asbury, historian of New York gangs, records that in race riots at the turn of the twentieth century – usually started by white youths – the police would join in on the side of the whites, battering the Negroes with their clubs and arresting them.

From 1894 onwards, there have been major

investigations into police corruption about every two decades. In New York, the most recent of these was the Knapp Commission of 1971. In spite of the sensational nature of the revelations, the hearings excited little coast-to-coast attention. The final report which came out in December 1972 colourfully divided 'bent cops' into 'meat-eaters' and 'grass-eaters'. Meat-eaters are policemen who 'aggressively misuse their power for personal gain'; the grass-eaters 'simply accept the pay-offs that come their way'. The vast majority of corrupt policemen, said the report, are grass-eaters.

In an area like New York's Harlem, with its illegal gambling, a bent cop could make $1,500 a month. If he were transferred to another command, this payment would continue for another two months – giving him time to adjust to his 'lower income'. It could explain how, when the police seized heroin, it was likely to find its way back into the drugs market – and how of $137,000 seized from drug traffickers, $80,000 went into the pockets of the arresting officers. In one police precinct, over 68 pounds of 'French connection' heroin had vanished from the police laboratory - $7 million-worth at current prices then.

The figures poured out regularly, and no one was very shocked or very surprised. Americans had heard it all before. They expected their police to behave like that. They might be roused to protest occasionally if the misbehaviour became too public – as when Mayor Daley's Chicago policemen were seen on television beating up anybody who looked like a demonstrator during the Democratic Convention of 1968. But generally speaking the feeling is that the police have got a tough job, and that a little brutality and corruption is inevitable – if not, occasionally, necessary.

When Tom Murton became Superintendent of the Tucker Prison Farm in Arkansas in 1967, he soon discovered that nearly two hundred convicts were listed as having escaped, and had never been caught – a far higher number than would have been expected. Seasoned inmates said openly that there were a hundred or so bodies buried in the prison grounds; men who, for one reason or another, had fallen foul of the 'wardens'.

Murton dug in an area where the ground had sunk, and quickly unearthed three skeletons. For a few weeks, the scandal drew nationwide headlines; then, suddenly, the authorities ordered that there should be no further digging. Murton was dismissed, and the scandal was allowed to simmer.

Dirty Hands

Where tensions have increased – in racially mixed areas in both the United States and Britain – charges of corruption and brutality against the police have also increased. In September 1973, a Detective Chief Inspector and five of his staff were charged at London's Old Bailey with manufacturing evidence of drug smuggling against a Pakistani family. The police were convinced that the family was guilty, but there was not enough evidence against them. The prosecution alleged the police strengthened the evidence. The father's five-year sentence was later quashed.

The most interesting feature about such a case is that the newspapers scarcely bothered to report it. For the most part, it rated a small paragraph on an inside page. The English public was apparently as blasé about it as the American public was about the New York scandals of 1971.

As long as there is crime, as long as criminals flourish, police officers will be needed to combat the evil. It is inevitable, therefore, that some of the graft, the corruption, will rub off onto them. You cannot put your hand in a sewer without it coming up dirty. In the words of the lyricist W. S. Gilbert, 'The policemen's lot is not a happy one.' It was true when he wrote it some hundred years ago; unhappily it is truer than ever today.

The Headless Corpse

The man who gave his name to the guillotine was only trying to be humane. Yet no method of killing strikes quite the terror into man's mind as death by beheading. Is it the finality of this fate that freezes fear icy-hard? Or does the thought of meeting out decapitation unlock the most raw animal spirit of the inner beast? Was Freud right in his brutally blunt analysis of human behaviour? Was this the key to Eliott Ness's greatest case?

AS THE DUKE of Monmouth was about to kneel and place his head on the block, he held out his hand to the notorious executioner, Jack Ketch. 'Here are six guineas for you. Pray do your business well. Don't serve me as you served Lord Russell.'

He had reason to be nervous. When Ketch had beheaded Lord William Russell – for his part in the Rye House Plot to kidnap Charles II – he had completely bungled the job. After several violent swipes with the axe, Russell was still twitching, and his neck was unsevered. Monmouth, now being executed for his rebellion against James II, was understandably anxious to die less bloodily.

He turned to a servant, and handed him a purse containing more guineas. 'Give him that if he does his work well.' Then he felt the edge of the axe, and said, sighing: 'I fear it is not sharp enough.' Ketch was unnerved by all this coolness.

He raised the axe, then threw it down, shouting: 'I can't do it.' The sheriff had to threaten him with dire penalties before he could be persuaded to make another attempt.

The Crowd Gave a Groan

Looking pale and ill, he raised the axe above his head, and brought it down. The crowd gave a groan, and Monmouth jerked with agony; but his head stayed on his shoulders. Now thoroughly demoralized, Ketch made three more attempts, but there was no strength in the blows. The neck was only lacerated. Finally, he threw down the hatchet, pulled out a knife, and sawed the head off. The servant holding the purse pocketed it and walked away. Meanwhile, the crowd booed and threw things.

It was no sinecure, being an executioner in those days. Ketch usually hanged his clients; but he wasn't very good at that either, and most of the condemned men died by slow strangulation. It was preferable, however, to being butchered with a blunt axe, and even when the headman *was* efficient, it was tiring work. In 1746, Jack Thrift had to behead two Jacobite rebels, Lord Kilmarnock and Lord Balmerino. He severed Kilmarnock's head with one clean blow, but it took him three swings of the axe to decapitate Balmerino. There were many officers of the law who felt that somebody ought to devise a swift and infallible method for taking a man's life.

Half a century later, it became an urgent

necessity. France rebelled against its rulers. The Bastille was stormed, and its defenders massacred, the king fled and was recaptured: the Terror began. The enemies of the new regime had to be killed by the hundred – by the thousand. How could it be done? The solution was found by a gentle, kindly man, well-known for his good works: Dr. Joseph Ignace Guillotin.

Dr. Guillotin was a freemason – in fact, one of the founders of freemasonry in France. The freemasons are a benevolent secret society, devoted to the improvement of mankind; but the Church regarded them as wicked atheists. And it was for this reason more than for anything else that Dr. Guillotin found himself in the Constituent Assembly, with an influential voice in the new revolutionary government of France.

Now this gentle humanitarian was horrified at some of the bloodshed he had seen. He loathed those barbarous and primitive instruments of execution, the wheel and the gibbet. He was sickened by the sight of a man swinging from a gallows all day, while the crowd underneath drank beer and made merry. Guillotin foresaw the mass executions that were coming, and he brooded on how they might be made painless and swift: a moral lesson rather than a sadistic spectacle. Some kind of 'machine' was needed. He consulted the public executioner, Charles Henri Sanson, and they looked over various old prints and engravings.

As early as 1555, the Italians had invented a beheading machine, in which a heavy axe blade was placed between two upright posts, so that it could be hauled up to the top with a rope, then allowed to fall down the groove on to the neck of a man kneeling underneath. These 'sliding axes' had also been tried in Germany, in Persia – even in Scotland. But they'd never really caught on. The blade often got stuck in the groove, or the rope caught. The old manual method was simpler and more reliable.

An Agonizing Eternity

And now occurred one of those supreme ironies of history. The man who solved the problem was none other than the king himself, Louis the Sixteenth. It was shortly before the flight that cost him his life, and precipitated the Terror. The Assembly had asked Dr. Antoine Louis, the king's physician, to look into Dr. Guillotin's plan. Dr. Guillotin was asked to call on Dr. Louis at the Tuileries Palace, and he took Sanson, the executioner, with him.

As the three men were engaged in examining the sketches of the machine, a stranger knocked and entered. It was the king, dressed in ordinary clothes. He asked Dr. Louis what he thought of the machine, and looked at the drawing. Then he shook his head. 'That curved blade wouldn't suit every kind of neck.' The king picked up a pencil. 'What you need is something more like *this*.' He drew a straight, sloping line on the underside of the axe blade. Guillotin looked at the drawing. 'Yes, of course, you're right . . .' A few weeks later, the first guillotine was tried out on three corpses. The king had been right: a curved blade failed to decapitate one of the corpses, but the sloping blade worked perfectly on the other two. Two years later, the king was decapitated by the machine he had helped perfect.

For the next two years – until the Terror ended with the execution of Robespierre in 1794 – the guillotine thudded with horrible, mechanical persistence, and thousands of heads rolled into the basket. As to the good Dr. Guillotin, he continued his humanitarian work. He was one of the earlier pioneers of smallpox vaccination, and his work on the extermination of smallpox undoubtedly saved more lives in Europe than his guillotine destroyed. But when he died, in 1814, he already knew that it would not be his medical discoveries that would immortalize his name, but that triangular blade, with all its association of horror . . .

This raises the interesting question: why is it that decapitation strikes us as so sickening and gruesome? Guillotin was right: as a method of execution, it is certainly more humane than hanging, electrocution or the gas chamber. Hanging is only about 95% certain; a slight miscalculation in the placing of the rope, and the condemned man strangles to death. Men in the gas chamber have been known to hold their breath for minutes before breathing in the cyanide gas. And the criminologist Nigel Morland, who once stepped on a highly charged electric grid, is on record as saying that the last seconds of an electrocuted man must seem to be an agonizing eternity.

Only the guillotine has never failed to carry out its work with perfect swiftness and efficiency. Yet Guillotin is remembered as a monster, because the idea of decapitation touches some deep chord of horror in the human psyche. It may be because the loss of the head is so final; men can lose an arm or leg and still survive; not the head. Or could it be, perhaps, because our earliest ancestors cut off the heads of their enemies in battle, and often ate the brains? Is the twinge of horror due to some deep racial memory?

Whatever the reason, there can be no doubt that crimes involving beheading always seem most cruel and brutal than other types of crime. And this is absurd. For sheer vicious cruelty, slow poison is probably the most inhuman method of killing. Then there are the murderers who get pleasure from the fear of their victims – like José Marcellino, Mexico's 'lover's lane killer', captured in 1973, who admitted: 'I liked it so much, to see the males squirm, and the women frightened and crying, that I'd make my threats last a long time . . . I enjoyed the fear of death in their eyes.'

By comparison, murderers like Crippen and Patrick Mahon seem decent and sane. Yet it is Crippen and Mahon whose cases are endlessly rehashed by crime journalists under titles like: 'Horror of the headless corpse.' Still, no matter what the general public may feel about them, Crippen and Mahon are of scant interest to the professional criminologist; he is concerned with the motivations behind a crime, and it hardly matters to him what the killer does to dispose of the body. On the other hand, he finds a criminal like Patrick Byrne, the Birmingham Y.W.C.A. killer, of altogether greater interest.

There is no need to ask why Byrne killed Stephanie Baird – that is perfectly obvious. He was drunk, and he wanted sex. When he had strangled her into unconsciousness, he undressed her and raped her. All that is straightforward, if horrible; but why did he then cut off her head, and commit further sexual acts on the body? Why did he, even then, go out and try to kill another girl by hitting her with a stone? Why did he write a note saying: 'This was the thing I thought would never come.'

In the course of his confession, Byrne said one thing that provides a key to his strange personality. He said he wanted to terrorize all the women in the hostel 'to get my own back on them for causing my nervous tension through sex'. This is a curious statement. Even the most stupid man must see that women are not to *blame* for making him sexually excited. A cat may as well blame mice for making it feel hungry.

But Byrne was not trying to be logical; he was trying to explain, in his own fumbling way, what dark forces had suddenly mastered him when he found himself in a room with an unconscious girl. He also admitted to a psychiatrist that he had been indulging for years in daydreams in which he cut up girls with a circular saw. This brings us altogether closer to the heart of the problem, for what we can see so clearly, in Byrne's case, is that when he made his way into the Y.W.C.A. that

December afternoon, it was not simply a girl he wanted – ordinary sexual intercourse. It was somehow *all* women, all the women in the world. He was expressing one of the savage, basic frustrations of man.

Craving for Gratification

In 1930, Freud published a book called *Civilization and Its Discontents*, in which he advanced a disturbing – and profoundly pessimistic – theory. He suggested that man is not made for civilization, or civilization for man. Man is a carnivorous animal, and his basic instincts are violent and aggressive. Whether we like it or not, it is 'natural' for him to go on a raiding party to another village, kill the men, and then drag off the women for his own pleasure, as natural as it is considered for a tiger to eat antelopes.

But this human tiger was also intelligent and gregarious. He learned to live with other human beings in communities, and to create civilization. Every step he has taken into civilization has been a violation of his basic instincts. Culture is another name for suppression of these instincts. The great basic conflict of all human existence, says Freud, is the conflict between the individual's craving for personal gratification and the claims of society. So how can man be happy? Unhappiness is a basic part of his condition . . .

Less pessimistic psychologists, like Abraham Maslow, have pointed out that this is a one-sided view. Happiness does *not* mean unlimited self-indulgence. The history of crime and violence reveals to us that the men who *could* indulge themselves without self-discipline – Caligula, Ivan the Terrible, Vlad the Impaler – were not particularly happy men. Long-term happiness must involve self-discipline. Nowadays, there are very few reputable thinkers who take Freud's arguments about civilization seriously.

Nevertheless, without fully intending it, Freud *had* expressed the basic psychology of psychopathic killers like Patrick Byrne, Jack the Ripper, Peter Kürten. These *are* men who feel that Man and Civilization were simply not made for one another. Consider, for example, the nature of the male sexual drive. Unlike most women, man is not basically 'faithful'. Particularly when young and virile, the average man would be perfectly happy to sleep with a different girl every night; even healthy men have their sexual fantasies.

Avenging Sexual Tensions

Surely, where sex is concerned, civilization is *intended* to torment males, as you might torment a caged tiger by poking it with a stick? Taking it a step further, is a man to blame if he seizes his opportunity to grab a girl and pull her into a dark alleyway . . . ? *This* is what Byrne meant when he talked about 'getting his own back on women for causing my sexual tensions', and he was almost paraphrasing Sigmund Freud.

But why the decapitation? This is also easy to explain. Once a man is possessed by this urgency

– like a fox in a chicken farm – he is subjected to endless twinges of desire, like electric shocks. He compensates for an increasing feeling of frustration and inferiority with daydreams in which he dominates the girl completely; and the longer the fantasies continue, the more violent they are likely to become.

Charles Melquist, arrested in 1958 for the sex-murder and decapitation of 15-year-old Bonnie Leigh Scott, near Chicago, admitted to years of fantasizing about naked women, and of tossing them into huge grinding machines. When such a man finally finds himself with his hands around the throat of an unconscious girl, sexual inter-course is not enough. It seems an anticlimax. His overheated desires crave some stronger satis-faction, some ultimate act of violation and possession. And here, the basic human revulsion at the idea of decapitation rises up from the subconscious – the ultimate act of aggression . . .

What is equally significant is that both Byrne and Melquist were horrified by what they had done. Byrne said he was glad the police had found him; the murder had tormented him for the past two months; Melquist also made his confession in a long, relieved babble, and admitted that he had been unable to sleep after the murder. Not only is their act of violence no solution to the cravings that produced it: the killer recognizes that he is *further than ever* from a solution. Many killers of this type commit suicide.

The pattern can be clearly seen in the case of Jack the Ripper. The early victims – Mary Anne

Nicholls, Annie Chapman, Catherine Eddowes – were mutilated in the area of the genitals, indicating that the Ripper's basic obsession was with the woman's sexual function – perhaps with the womb. The last murder took place indoors; this time, the killer had unlimited time at his disposal, and the victim – Mary Kelly – was not only disembowelled but almost decapitated. Then the murders ceased, and all the evidence suggests that the Ripper committed suicide.

The novelist Zola based a novel on the Ripper crimes – *La Bête Humaine* – the human beast. This goes to the heart of the problem. Such a man has decided to become the solitary hunter in search of prey, rather than a responsible human being. In doing so, he has retreated from society as deliberately as if he had decided to become a Trappist monk. But men like Byrne, Melquist or the Ripper lack the qualifications for becoming hermits; they need society. Hence the conflicting whirlpool of urges that may end in suicide.

'Mad Butcher'

The case that most clearly demonstrates the complex morbid psychology of 'the human beast' took place in Cleveland, Ohio, in the mid-1930s: the curious unsolved case of the Butcher of Kingsbury Run. Between 1935 and 1938, the 'mad butcher' killed at least a dozen people, hacking the bodies into small pieces, and removing the heads – several of which were never found.

On September 23, 1935, two decapitated

bodies were found in the area of Kingsbury Run and East 45th Street, a slum area. Both had been mutilated with a knife; both were men – one, a 28-year-old medical orderly, the other, a 40-year-old vagrant, who was never identified. The fact that both victims were male suggested that the killer was homosexual, and a sadistic pervert. But when, four months later, the headless body of a 42-year-old prostitute was found not far from Kingsbury Run, the police became less sure that they were looking for a homosexual; the woman's body had been hacked as if in a frenzy, and the head was never found.

At intervals during 1936, three more victims were found in the area; all were men, all were headless, and in one case, the head was never found. The killer was obviously possessed by some kind of frenzy; some of the bodies were little more than a pile of mangled pieces.

On February 23, 1937, the victim was again a woman – headless, and in pieces. In June, the dismembered body of a 30-year-old Negro woman was found in a burlap bag under the Lorain-Carnegie Bridge. The ninth victim, a man, was found in July; he had been decapitated and the body hacked in pieces. The head was never found. And in 1938, there were three more victims; a dismembered and headless woman was found on April 8, and on August 17, the 'Mad Butcher' (as the press called him) committed another double murder, a man and a woman. In each of these cases, the killer decapitated the victim, and in six of them, the heads were never found.

The man who was then in charge of Cleveland's police department was Eliott Ness – hero of T.V.'s 'Untouchables'. Ness recognized that the usual methods of detection were of doubtful value here. But he realized that the mad killer was finding most of his victims among prostitutes and down-and-outs. The latter congregated in a shanty-town area in the centre of the city, near the market. One night in August, Ness raided the place, forced its inhabitants to leave, and burnt it down. This had the desired effect of depriving the killer of his victims; there were no more murders.

Ness also reasoned that the 'mad butcher' must be of a certain type. He must be big and powerful to overpower his victims. He must own a car, to transport the bodies. He must live alone, and in some quiet area – perhaps an unfrequented *cul de sac* – in order not to arouse the curiosity of his neighbours. And in order to fit this pattern, he must be rich, or at least well off.

Ness's team made painstaking enquiries in Cleveland society and, according to Oscar Fraley, chronicler of the 'Untouchables', soon found a suspect who fitted. He was physically huge, homosexual, sullen and paranoid, and well-to-do. Ness had the man brought in for questioning, and for months played a cat and mouse game with him. The man, confident he was cleverer than the police, almost admitted the murders, and dared Ness to find evidence.

And, finally, while Ness was still searching, he had himself committed to a mental home, where he died a year later. Ness never doubted that this was the torso killer.

Ness's suspect was an intelligent, literate man; he may well have read Freud's *Civilization and Its Discontents*. If so, he could have added a final footnote; that the man who lives as a beast of prey will almost certainly die as one alone and unmourned by his fellow creatures.

A Case of Witchcraft

In the 20th century, a weird ritual killing sets one
of murder's most fascinating mysteries. A legend
comes to life . . . and claims as its victim a man
who seems to have been singled out for this fate.
In a haunted corner of England, scene of a horrific
St. Valentine's Day killing, the powers of witchcraft
seem to live on . . .

AT A TIME when the roll of those dying by another's
hand had mounted to millions, the murder of one
solitary, lonely individual seemed of little account.
So it was that few outside the tiny English village of
Lower Quinton paid much heed to the news that,
in the chill dusk of February 14, St. Valentine's Day,
1945, the mutilated body of 74-year-old Charles
Walton had been found beneath a willow tree.

In a world at peace, the discovery would have
warranted immediate front page attention – for the
manner in which the aged recluse had died was
both revolting and deeply mystifying. He had
been pinned firmly to the ground by his own
hayfork, driven savagely through his neck and
then down into six inches of soil. Across his throat
and chest had been crudely scratched the sign of
the Cross, and from the wound still hung Charlie's
own long-handled hedge-trimming hook.

At first the local police were bewildered by the

brutality of the killing, and its apparent lack of motive. Then a curiously sinister chain of events began to unroll. First, a heavy curtain of silence descended over the village. None of its 450 inhabitants would talk in any detail about Charlie or the circumstances of his death; none could offer any kind of lead except that 'it couldn't have been anyone here who did it'. Second, and most extraordinary of all, one word began to whisper its way under the thatched roofs and along the narrow, twisting lanes: 'Witchcraft!'

It was a word much used in the past in Lower Quinton. The village lies in Shakespeare country, between Stratford-on-Avon and Chipping Norton, in Warwickshire, and there is little doubt that William Shakespeare drew upon boyhood memories of local gossip about witches and black magic while working upon such plays as *Macbeth* and *A Midsummer Night's Dream*.

A Headless Woman

Lower Quinton, like several other medieval villages, had its own fearful legend – the legend of the black dog. Over the decades, it was said, this strange animal, larger than most dogs and with unearthly, burning eyes, appeared from nowhere and disappeared into nowhere. Few had doubts about what its appearance portended: someone was about to die.

One nineteenth-century student of the legend, a Warwickshire parson named the Reverend Harvey Bloom, had recorded a frightening story about the black dog in his book, *Folk Lore, Old Customs and Superstitions in Shakespeareland*. In 1885, he wrote, a ploughboy encountered the dog nine times on successive days at dusk. The boy told his tale to fellow farm-workers and they scoffed at his vivid imagination. On the ninth day, however, the dog turned into a headless woman who glided hair-raisingly past him with a faint rustle from her silk dress. The next day the boy's sister died.

That boy, identified by name in the book, was – Charles Walton. No wonder that the villagers, remembering the story of Charlie and the dog and drawing a straight connecting line between it and his brutal death, preferred to keep silent and lessen the risk of further visitations. This may have been 1945, and the climax of a war in which modern technology was playing a devastating part, but in Lower Quinton no march of history could dim respect for ancient and inexplicable powers.

Charlie Walton himself had fitted closely into the pattern of the shadowy world of the unknown. To the local inhabitants he was 'odd'. He liked the company of the birds that sang around the village and its meadows more than he liked the company of people. As he worked at his various field-labouring tasks, he would talk to the rooks and jackdaws, and he claimed he could follow the meaning of every sound they made. Quiet and withdrawn, he had spent his whole life in Lower Quinton, rarely going more than a mile or two away. In his final years, he lived in the centre cottage of a row of three where his niece,

Miss Edith Isabel Walton, looked after him.

He was never seen in the village pubs – and not to be at least an occasional caller at these two centres of village social life marked a man out as 'peculiar'. Not that Charlie Walton was a tee-totaller; far from it. He drank a great deal of cider and sometimes bought 12 gallons at a time. But he always took the cider home, often trundling his supplies in a wheelbarrow with as much speed as his rheumatism would allow, and drank alone behind closed doors.

Two-pronged Hayfork

The village thought he 'had money', not only because of the cider he bought but because he was known to have a bank account – a most unusual status for a casual labourer in those days. When he worked he earned only around 2s. 9d. (8½p or $0.20) an hour. Some of the local gossips assumed, therefore, that he was a sorcerer whose money came from 'fees' paid for magical services rendered.

Wednesday, February 14, 1945, was a surprisingly mild day, a forerunner of what was to be an early spring followed by a long summer. It was just the day, Charlie Walton decided, to make a start on some hedge cutting he had promised to do for one of the local farmers, Alfred Potter. Shortly after nine, he set off with his walking stick, his two-pronged hayfork and his trimming hook, and made his laborious way to the slopes of Meon Hill, a little over a mile from his cottage.

He told his niece he would be home at four to make his own tea.

That was the last that anyone, apart from his murderer, positively saw of Charlie Walton alive. Just after midday, Farmer Potter, making the rounds of his fields and inspecting his sheep and cattle, *thought* he saw Charlie slashing hedges about 500 yards away. Certainly it appeared to be a man working in shirt sleeves, and he could not think who else it could be, except Charlie. Although at that distance it was not possible to make out the old man's familiar flowing moustache and sun-varnished features.

At six in the evening Miss Edith Walton returned to the cottage from her war job in a neighbouring factory. She was immediately worried by the absence of her uncle, who was a meticulous time-keeper and never came home later than his announced time. Quite naturally, thinking of his unsteady, rheumatic legs, she feared he had suffered a fall. She called in at the cottage of a neighbour, Harry Beasley, and together they went to The Firs, Mr. Potter's farm.

Shock and Abhorrence

Alfred Potter – as puzzled as Miss Walton – took a flashlight and lit the way from his farm to the middle of a group of five fields on the lower slopes of Meon Hill where he had last seen Charlie.

Quite suddenly the sharp snapping of fallen twigs under the men's boots ceased, and the beam of light came to rest on a patch of ground by a willow. Then the light flashed back into Edith Walton's face and Potter's voice, trembling with shock and abhorrence, cried: 'Stay there! Don't come any nearer. You mustn't look at this!' Bracing themselves, the men brought the flashlight beam back to bear on the hideous sight of old Charlie Walton, impaled and bloodily marked with the Cross, his moustache-draped mouth drawn back in a final grimace of terror and desperation.

Leaving Potter to guard the corpse, Beasley took Miss Walton home and summoned the police. When they arrived it took the combined strength of two policemen to release the deeply-embedded hayfork from Charlie's body – which was then lifted on to a five-barred gate and carried down to the village. There a brief examination disclosed that the old man had not died without a struggle. His bony, tanned arms were scratched and torn, and there were large bruises and blood on his head.

Charlie's walking stick, found close to the body, was bloodstained. All the indications were that he had been felled by a blow from his stick, and then lain helpless on the ground, watching in agony as his assailant stood over him and delivered the pitiless death thrust. Disconcerted by the mysterious circumstances, the Warwickshire police asked Scotland Yard for assistance. They promptly received it in the person of Detective Superintendent Robert Fabian, one of Britain's finest detectives and so familiar to the public that he was known simply as 'Fabian of the

Yard'. With him came his extremely able partner, Detective-Sergeant Albert Webb.

Prisoners of War

A first move by Fabian and Webb was to implement a suggestion from the local police and arrange for the questioning of the 1,043 enemy prisoners of war being held in a camp at Long Marston, two miles from Lower Quinton. There, Detective-Sergeant David Saunders, a multilinguist from the Yard's Special Branch, was called in as interpreter for the interrogation of the men, who included Italians, Germans, and Slavs.

For a while it looked as though the murder hunt might quickly produce a quarry. Some of the prisoners, not averse to turning stool pigeon on a comrade, reported seeing an Italian frantically trying to wash blood from his jacket. The man was found and his coat sent to a forensic laboratory in Birmingham, some thirty miles away. The resulting report, however, brought police hopes to an abrupt end: the blood was from a rabbit and it seemed that what the Italian had been trying to conceal was the fact that he had slipped out of camp and gone poaching.

One of the many frustrating features of the case for Fabian and his partner was that, unwittingly, Farmer Potter and his little search party had churned up the ground in going to and from the body and obliterated what might have been crucial footprints in the damp earth. Less excusably, the local police had added to the disturbance of the murder scene in carrying the body away.

From the village itself came neither word nor hint. So, day after day, Fabian gloomily tramped the slopes of Meon Hill, looking for just that one sign that would point his investigation in a positive direction. Then, one evening as dusk was closing in, a large black dog scuttled past him and was lost in the darkening woods. A moment later a boy came walking over the hillside and Fabian asked: 'Looking for that dog, son?' The boy gaped: 'What dog, mister?' 'A black dog,' said Fabian, and without a word the boy raced off as though the Devil himself was at his heels.

That night in the Gay Dog the indefatigable Fabian attempted, as usual, to strike up a conversation with the silent 'locals' and mentioned the odd incident of the black dog. To his surprise someone answered and, for the first time, he heard the legend of the dog, the headless woman, and the ploughboy whose sister died. 'We don't talk much about it,' said his informant, grudgingly. 'Nobody has spoken about it for years; not since afore the war, anyway.' The rest of the farmhands in the bar sat tight-mouthed, and Fabian noticed that some looked embarrassed and turned back to their pints of beer and other subjects.

New and Sinister

A few days later Fabian mentioned the dog and the pub story to a colleague in the Warwickshire police force who was interested in local legends. The colleague showed him a book he had just acquired, the Rev. Harvey Bloom's book. Fabian was astonished when, idly turning the pages, he came across not only the account of the black dog legend, as the man in the pub had related it, but also the one important item the man had left out: the name of the ploughboy, Charlie Walton.

This opened up a new and sinister line of inquiry and, unreal as it would have seemed in other circumstances, Fabian felt he had to pursue it. In another book, entitled *Warwickshire*, by Clive Holland, he read of an actual murder, in 1875, which closely followed the pattern of Charlie Walton's killing. At Long Compton, a village only a few miles from Lower Quinton, and reputedly a centuries-old centre of witchcraft, John Haywood, a feeble-minded lad had killed an 80-year-old woman, named Ann Turner, with a hayfork.

At his trial Haywood declared that there were 16 witches in Long Compton at the time and he said of Ann Turner: 'Her was a proper witch. I pinned her to the ground before slashing her throat with a billhook in the form of a cross.' There had been many cases throughout the history of witchcraft in England, and particularly Warwickshire, of suspected witches being impaled by hayforks. It was, in some ways, the equivalent of driving a stake through the heart of one of those mythical creatures, the vampires, as in Bram Stoker's fictional story of Count Dracula. In England, too, February was a much favoured month for ritual killing, and probably bore some link with ancient blood-letting festivals which took place at that time.

Fertility Rite

The central purpose of such blood-letting – usually it was animals' blood – was to replenish the fertility of the soil. Subsequently a Birmingham woman claimed, in a newspaper interview, that she knew the name of Charlie Walton's killer and that the murder had, indeed, been part of a fertility rite. 'Three or four survivors of an ancient cult live in the locality, but the actual murderer was a woman who was brought by car from a different part of the country,' she said. Although she refused to be more specific the police did believe that there were 'black magic' groups active in and around the area.

Meanwhile, Fabian and Webb found that the barrier of silence in Lower Quinton effectively kept them from real contact with the villagers. They suffered some remarkably bad luck, or 'warnings' as some of the village people termed it. One of their police cars had the misfortune to run over and kill a black dog (normal size and 'natural') in one of the winding, concealed country lanes. That was enough to convince the villagers that any word from them to the police might bring far worse visitations upon their community.

Despite this, Fabian and his colleagues took 4,000 statements – from the P.O.W.s, passing tinkers and gypsies, Allied soldiers and airmen stationed in the area. The Royal Air Force shot aerial photographs of Meon Hill, and men of the Royal Engineers trudged through meadows and coppices with their mine detectors. They brought to light a great deal of metallic garbage, but no murder clue.

In fact all the detectives' endeavours were in vain. People in surrounding villages spoke darkly of a witches' coven, formed at the turn of the century and still active around Meon Hill. But in Lower Quinton the sullen opposition to the detectives hung heavily in the air. Fabian later wrote: 'When Albert Webb and I walked into the village pubs silence fell like a physical blow. Cottage doors were shut in our faces and even the most innocent witnesses seemed unable to meet our eyes.'

All this had a profound effect upon Fabian and Webb, whose inherent sense of duty would not normally let them rest until they had examined every possibility in an investigation. But, in the end, even they, with all their stamina, were forced to admit that they could make no progress. They were powerless against the solidarity of the picture postcard village, with its lovely Saxon-Norman church which displayed a sixteenth-century coat of arms prayer reading: 'God love our noble Queen Elizabeth. Amen!'

Along the grapevine – the only open line of communication – it was 'suggested' to Fabian that perhaps an outsider had killed Charlie for his money. After all, it was asserted, he carried a bulging money belt. But there was nothing to support this and, in any case, why would a thief risk time and capture by going through the hideous death ritual? Shaky old Charlie Walton could have been laid low by one swift blow from behind and, even if he survived, never have seen his attacker.

Primitive Island

Finally, and to their everlasting regret, Fabian and Webb called it a day. They returned to Scotland Yard and other crimes that lacked black magic undertones and overtones. Life in Lower Quinton returned to normal, and if the villagers had any concrete evidence they steadfastly refused to yield it up. Later, the adventurous and energetic American anthropologist, Margaret Mead, paid a visit to the village, no doubt rightly regarding it as a strangely primitive island in a sea of so-called Western civilization. But she, to whom other 'backward' peoples had readily opened their mouths and minds, went away unrewarded.

There was one person, however, who could not turn his back on the scene, and for whom the case held a totally absorbing fascination. He was Detective Superintendent Alec Spooner, of the Warwickshire Criminal Investigation Department, on whose 'manor' the killing had occurred.

Every year for nineteen years, on the murder's anniversary, he went to Meon Hill and there kept watch, not attempting to conceal his presence. His theory as he explained it, was: 'If the murderer is about, he wants the crime forgotten. My return shows him that it has not been forgotten and this may wear him down.'

In 1964 Alec Spooner retired from police work and was not seen again on Meon Hill. The Lower Quinton murder file was not closed but put away, awaiting a concluding paragraph. Almost certainly it will never be written.

WITCHCRAFT: TRIAL

The Witches of Salem

During early Colonial days in America all but a few men believed in the actual existence of demons and witches, and harboured many superstitions that had been handed down from the Middle Ages . . .

TODAY MOST people laughingly dismiss witchcraft as a superstition of the ignorant. But in seventeenth-century Europe and America, witches, defined by the English Judge Lord Coke as persons who had 'conference with the Devil to consult with him or to do some act,' were taken very seriously. Witches were women – the male equivalent was warlock – and as a result of their dealings with the Devil were commonly believed to be able to perform supernatural acts.

The penalty for being proved a witch was death, and in the few years of Oliver Cromwell's rule in England many unfortunates accused of witchcraft perished on the gallows – 60 being hanged in a single year in Suffolk, a county which the notorious witch-hunter Matthew Hopkins pronounced to be infested with witches.

The panic on the subject was the natural result of Puritanical teaching acting on the mind and predisposing the ruling authorities to see Satanic influences at work in the community, expressed through the supernatural phenomena of witchcraft.

The seeds of the superstition crossed the Atlantic with the Pilgrim Fathers, and at a time when it was beginning to disappear in England it flourished alarmingly in the state of Massachusetts – which in 1692 was the scene of the most celebrated witch-hunt and witch trials in history. It all happened in the small rural community of Salem Village, since renamed Danvers, situated near the old port of Salem a few miles to the northeast of Boston.

The Rev. Samuel Parris, a local preacher, had previously been engaged in trade in the West Indies before accepting a call to the parish of Salem Village. He had brought back a married couple with him from Barbados, slaves called John and Tituba, whose presence undoubtedly lent prestige to the parsonage. Tituba, who was half Carib and half Negro, spent a good deal of time with the two children in the household, the Parris' nine-year-old daughter Betty, and her cousin Abigail Williams, who was two years older.

During the winter of 1691-92, a group of eight girls, including Abigail and Betty, mostly teen-aged, used to meet in the kitchen premises of the minister's house in the company of Tituba. It was later assumed that Tituba had stuffed their impressionable heads with tales of African or West Indian magic, and had even practised it with them – although no credible evidence of this came to light in the subsequent trials which were documented in great detail.

Tituba's activities do not seem to have gone beyond fortune telling and possibly what another New England divine, the Rev. Cotton Mather – who had made a study of witchcraft and written a book about it – described as 'little sorceries', practised with sieve and scissors and candle.

These sessions ended by driving Betty, Abigail, and a 12-year-old girl named Ann Putnam into what was evidently a hysterical illness. Abigail and Ann, in particular, moaned and shrieked for no apparent reason, grovelling and writhing on the ground and occasionally acting as if they believed that they had been transformed into animals.

The symptoms soon spread throughout the child population in Salem Village, and as a result it was concluded by the adult community – led by Parris and other clergymen in the area – that the girls were bewitched. Eventually, in February 1692, Abigail and Ann were able to name three of their tormentors. The first of these was Tituba; the other two were an elderly pipe-smoking hag named Sarah Good, and a moderately well-to-do married woman named Sarah Osburne, who owned some property.

The two Sarahs seem to have been unpopular in the settlement and were certainly disapproved of by the Puritan leaders of the community –

Sarah Good, because she had become something of a tramp who begged from door to door, and furthermore did not go to church, and Sarah Osburne, because as a widow she lived in sin with her overseer before marrying him as her second husband.

The three women were now arrested and brought before two magistrates, John Hathorne and Jonathan Corwin, who were sent out from Salem Village to examine the accused in a public session at one of the local churches which had been borrowed for the purpose. Both the Sarahs denied everything. Asked why she did not attend church, Sarah Good replied that she had no suitable clothes. Further questioned as to what she said when she went away muttering from people's houses, she answered confidently: 'It is the commandments I say. I may say my commandments, I hope.'

As for the unfortunate Sarah Osburne, she had been dragged from her sickbed and had to be supported by two constables during her interrogation. She was obviously very ill, and the most the magistrates could get out of her was that she was 'more like to be bewitched than that she should be a witch.'

After the two Sarahs had been taken off again to prison, the extraordinary Tituba was brought in. She produced an imaginative confession in which she said just the kind of thing her Puritan accusers wished her to say. She talked about red cats and red rats. These cats and rats, she declared, could talk to her and in fact had said to her: 'Serve me.' She went on to tell of 'a Thing' which she could only describe as 'something like a cat' – it had a woman's face and it had wings, and it was Gammer Osburne's creature. These and other shapes, she said, told her to pinch Betty and Abigail, but 'I would not hurt Betty – I loved Betty.' They also told her to attack Ann Putnam with a knife. Ann and Abigail were then fetched into court in Tituba's presence and they began to moan and whimper.

'Who hurts the children now?' asked magistrate Hathorne.

'I am blind now,' Tituba cunningly answered. 'I cannot see.' Thus the slave made it clear that second sight was not for a witch who had repented and renounced her calling.

No doubt Tituba's confession saved her life, and she was never arraigned. Meanwhile the list of suspect witches quickly grew, largely on the accusation of Abigail and Ann – though other girls occasionally joined in, and some of the accused followed Tituba's example by confessing.

It is noteworthy that none of those who confessed and implicated others was executed. Only those who steadfastly protested their innocence in the event suffered. Among those in this category were George Burroughs, a minister of religion, Martha Corey, who was a church member in good standing, and Rebecca Nurse, an invalid of unsullied reputation.

Not even children escaped, since Dorcas Good, the five-year-old daughter of the pipe-smoking Sarah, was also hauled off to prison.

There were also a few old villagers – such as the tavern keeper Bridget Bishop and Susanna Martin – who had been suspected of witchcraft in the past, and they were likewise taken into custody.

The Governor of Massachusetts, Sir William Phips, appointed a special commission of seven judges, presided over by the Governor's Deputy, Chief Justice William Stoughton, to sit in Salem Village and try the suspects. It might be expected that the two Sarahs would be tried first, but this was not possible. Sarah Osburne died in prison before she could be brought into court again, while Sarah Good's case was put back until the delivery of her child – since she was pregnant at the time of her arrest.

Consequently the first to face a formal trial was Bridget Bishop, against whom there was already considerable local prejudice. Not only had she been suspected of practising sorcery in the past, but she was regarded as a flashy dresser and an unsatisfactory tavern keeper.

Her 'red paragon bodice' set her style, as did her 'smooth and flattering manner' with men, and it was a long standing complaint that she permitted young people to loiter at unseemly hours in her tavern, playing at 'shovel-board' and disturbing the sleep of decent neighbours.

Her trial, like that of most of the others, was a travesty of justice, since the record of the pre-trial examination before the magistrates was accepted by the court as consisting of proven facts, rather than something to be tested. In the words of Cotton Mather, describing the court procedure in

Bridget's case, 'there was little occasion to prove the witchcraft, this being evident and notorious to all beholders.'

Poor Bridget, who like all the other defendants in the subsequent trials was denied the aid of defence counsel, got off to a bad start. While walking under guard from Salem prison to the court she cast a glance at 'the great and spacious meeting house', and at once a great clatter arose within. Those sent to see what the woman's evil eye had done reported that 'they found a board which was strongly fastened with several nails transported to another quarter of the house.'

Four male witnesses testified that she haunted their beds at night, sometimes coming in her own form, sometimes like a black pig and in one instance with the body of a monkey, the feet of a cock, and the face of a man. Three children of these witnesses pined away and died, they swore, because being good men they had virtuously repelled her advances.

Testimony to the effect that Bridget's own husband thought she was a witch was given by a female witness named Elizabeth Balch, who described how she had once seen a quarrel between them. Bridget was riding pillion on horseback behind her husband when the latter spurred his horse to a pace that nearly threw her. Bridget thereupon lost her temper, and they had words. She was a 'bad wife', said her husband; 'the Devil had come bodily to her . . . and she sat up all night with the Devil.' What particularly struck Mistress Balch, who was riding beside them, was that throughout this tirade Bridget did not once open her mouth to defend herself.

Other witnesses, who had searched Bridget's house in Salem, found in the cellar some dolls made of rags and hog's bristles, into which pins had been stuck. When she was confronted with these objects, Bridget could give the court no 'reasonable and tolerable' explanation.

Both immediately before her trial and immediately afterwards, Bridget was physically examined for witch marks by a jury of matrons – who were equipped with pins which they stuck into any part of her body that looked at all unusual. On the first occasion the women discovered a 'witch's tet' between 'ye pudendum and anus'; on the second, three hours later, this 'tet' had withered to dry skin.

The court jury found Bridget Bishop guilty and the judges condemned her to death. Ten days elapsed before the sentence could be carried out, since it had to be legalized by reviving an old colonial law which made witchcraft a capital offence. Then on June 10, 1692, High Sheriff George Corwin took Bridget to the top of Gallows Hill and hanged her from the branches of a great oak tree.

The court did not sit again for nearly a month. The reason for the delay, which was kept from the public, was a difference which occurred among the Judges as to the credence to be given to spectral evidence. At least one member of the commission was impressed by the fact that, had such evidence been held inadmissible, Bridget

Bishop would have been convicted for little more than wearing scarlet, countenancing 'shovel-board' in her tavern and getting herself talked about – no doubt all offences, but hardly capital ones even in those harsh days.

Since witchcraft involved theological as well as legal considerations, Governor Phips referred the question to a committee of 12 ministers of religion in the Boston region. Unfortunately the committee, to which the historian Cotton Mather acted as secretary, equivocated. The committee 'humbly recommend the speedy and vigorous prosecution of such as have rendered themselves obnoxious.'

First to be tried was Rebecca Nurse, an old invalid lady, almost totally deaf. The jury had before them a petition signed by more than a score of respectable inhabitants of Salem Village, testifying to her unwitchlike character, piety and the extraordinary care she had lavished on the Christian upbringing of her children.

'I am innocent and clear and have not been able to get out of doors these eight or nine days,' Rebecca protested. 'I never afflicted no child, no, never in my life.'

One of the witnesses against Rebecca was a certain Deliverance Hobbs, who had herself confessed to being a witch and repented with the result that her life was spared. When Deliverance came into court, Rebecca was said to have turned her head towards her and exclaimed: 'What, do you bring her? She is one of us.'

However, after deliberating on these matters, the jury brought in a verdict of Not Guilty. Ann

Putnam, Abigail Williams, and several other girls were in the court house, and they immediately set up a howling and wailing, twisting their bodies as if convulsed.

When the din had subsided somewhat, Chief Justice Stoughton addressed the jurors. 'I will not impose on the jury,' he said, 'but I must ask you if you considered one statement made by the prisoner.' The Judge then repeated what the accused was alleged to have said to Deliverance Hobbs. 'Has the jury weighed the implications of this statement?'

Neither the foreman nor the other jurors could remember exactly what Rebecca had said. Rebecca was thereupon questioned again and asked to explain herself. Unfortunately Rebecca, as she herself put it afterwards, was 'something hard of hearing and full of grief', and consequently did not give a very satisfactory answer. The jury again retired and this time brought in a verdict of Guilty.

On trial with Rebecca Nurse were Susanna Martin, the pipe-smoking Sarah Good, and two other women who had been denounced as witches, Elizabeth How and Sarah Wild, the latter by the nefarious Abigail Hobbs and the former by a family named Perley from Ipswich who claimed that their ten-year-old daughter had been 'afflicted' by Goody How. 'Did I hurt you?' asked Elizabeth How, when she was confronted with the child and took her hand. 'No, never!' the little girl replied. 'If I did complain of you in my fits, I knew not that I did so.'

The tale of Susanna Martin's spectral misdeeds

was recited at length. A neighbouring farmer swore that she had cast a spell upon his herd of oxen because he refused to hitch his ox cart to haul her some staves. 'Your oxen will never do you much service!' Susanna was alleged to have said, with the result that the oxen took fright and plunged into the sea.

Another neighbour told an unlikely tale of a phantom puppy which sprang at his throat as a result of Susanna's witcheries. Like Bridget Bishop, Susanna was also said to have molested honest men in their bedchambers, 'scrabbling at the window', hopping down from the sill and boldly getting into bed.

All four women were found guilty, and along with Rebecca Nurse, they were hanged on Gallows Hill.

Four men were condemned in the immediately following trial. They included the Rev. George Burroughs who was charged with seducing girls to witchcraft by offering them 'fine clothes' and subsequently biting them. The girls had toothmarks all over their arms and Burrough's mouth was prized open when it was established to the satisfaction of the jury that his teeth were responsible for the marks.

Then there was the case of the octogenarian Giles Cory who had incriminated his wife Martha – though his testimony had amounted to little more than an expression of wonder that Martha should linger by the fire to pray long after he expected her in bed, and one of annoyance that when the examinations were going on before the magistrates she had hidden his saddle to prevent him from riding to court. ('Nevertheless,' she commented later, 'he went for all that.')

In due course he, too, was arrested and charged with witchcraft – having apparently been denounced by some of the girls in their fits. However, when brought to court he remained more or less speechless and steadfastly refused to plead to the indictment. 'I am a poor man and cannot help it' was all he would say.

Under English criminal procedure, an accused person who 'stood mute' and refused to plead was subjected to peine forte et dure – in other words he was tied to the floor of his cell and heavyweights were placed on his chest until he consented to plead 'Guilty' or 'Not Guilty'.

The result was that Giles Cory was pressed to death by the sheriff in an open field beside the jail. His only recorded utterance as rock after rock was piled on his chest was to cry out 'More weight!' Such a revolting punishment was never afterwards carried out in America.

Although only 19 people in addition to Giles Cory were executed for witchcraft in Salem in 1692 – a number small by contemporary European standards – about 400 people were arrested and crammed into the local jails.

The Body in the Belfry

She had been strangled and savagely mutilated by a sex-crazed monster . . .

WILLIAM HENRY Theodore Durrant did not look like a monster. Indeed, to all outward appearances, he was, at 24, a paragon of the kind of ostentatious virtue much in favour in his time. He was studying for the respectable profession of medicine, he was assistant superintendent of the Sunday School at Emanuel Baptist Church, San Francisco, and was particularly admired for such traits of filial devotion as always kissing his mother upon leaving and returning home.

He was a stall, slim young man, with a pale complexion that gave an extra luminosity to his blue eyes and made him noticeable in a crowd. He was, in fact, the kind of young man, apparently heading for a comfortable and secure future, whom most mothers of late nineteenth-century daughters would have welcomed as a prospective son-in-law.

But beneath the skin of Theo Durrant – who was so proper and polite at church meetings – stirred a darkly brooding, unstable, inner being. He was being tormented by sex to such an extent that, secretly, even the most perverted sexual relationships seemed tame to him. He once told a fellow student: 'I have no knowledge of women.' But he finally rectified that ignorance in a way that went beyond sadism.

Brown eyes

It was 18-year-old Blanche Lamont – born in Montana but living with her uncle and aunt on West 21 Street – who stepped out into San Francisco's swirling, misty air on Wednesday, April 3, 1895, to unwittingly offer herself as the monster's first victim.

She, like Durrant, was tall and extremely pale. But what most excited attention, and gave her an especially delightful feminine quality, were the incredibly long eyelashes that swept demurely over warm, brown eyes. When she left home that morning she seemed dressed for an outing. Above a full, black skirt she wore a basque jacket, much in vogue at the time, and a wide, floppy-brimmed hat, adorned with feathers and anchored under her chin with pink ribbon. To the casual observer she was the era's idealized portrait of young womanhood: sweetly innocent, desirable, and homeloving.

Strange actions

But Blanche was not as naïve and inexperienced as she looked. She knew Theo Durrant, and she was certainly aware that his interest in her was more than platonic. She also knew of the current 'fashion' for young people to meet for sexual encounters, in the daytime or early evening, in deserted church rooms. One elder of Emanuel Church had been moved to confide in a few select fellow members: 'I have heard stories of strange actions on the part of some of the young people of the church.'

At 8.15 a.m. Blanche met Durrant at the junction of Twenty-first and Mission Streets and, with his arm about her shoulders, he guided her on to an electric streetcar. They made a handsome couple, and it was not surprising that afterwards other passengers remembered them. Even the busy car conductor, Henry Shellmont, paid them so much attention that he could later recall: 'He was fooling with her gloves which she had removed. He seemed to be talking very sweetly to her.'

They rode some distance on the car, with Durrant talking continuously and quietly into Blanche's ear. Then, at Polk Street, they parted – Durrant to go to Cooper Medical College and Blanche to the Normal School, where she was studying to be a teacher. But that was only the prologue to their day. By two in the afternoon Durrant was back, impatiently waiting on a corner near the Normal School, carefully watched by old Mrs. Mary Vogel – who lived nearby and whose fear of burglars kept her attention riveted on any loiterers.

Full-bodied figure

Suddenly, Durrant spotted Blanche leaving the school and 'ran like a boy' towards her, as Mrs. Vogel remembered. They boarded a cable car, noticed this time by May Lannigan, one of Blanche's fellow students, who said: 'It was the man's hair which attracted my attention as it struck me as unusual to see a gentleman with such long hair.'

Later the two were observed walking purposefully towards Emanuel Church. By that time the wind had turned blustery and revealed Blanche's full-bodied figure or, as one middle-aged eye-witness, Mrs. Elizabeth Crosset, delicately put it: 'Her clothes blew considerably around her limbs – her form – her dress.'

Mrs. Caroline Leak, another elderly observer, saw Blanche enter the church first, followed by Durrant. Mrs. Leak was the last person to see Blanche Lamont alive.

Just before five o'clock, George King, Emanuel's 19-year-old organist, arrived for a brief practice session on the music for the forthcoming Easter service. But, before he had played more than a few introductory bars, he was interrupted by the sound of footsteps. Turning from the console, he was surprised to see Durrant coming from the direction of the staircase that led up to the belfy tower. Theo Durrant seemed paler than ever and, conscious of King's puzzled look, he hastily explained: 'I have been fixing a gas jet upstairs and breathing some escaping gas. Would you go to the corner drugstore and fetch me a Bromo Seltzer?'

When George King returned from his errand of mercy, Durrant looked and sounded much better, and the two men left the church together. A few hours later Durrant returned for the evening prayer meeting and the first person he met was an anxious Mrs. Tryphena Noble, the aunt with whom Blanche boarded.

'Ah, Mrs. Noble,' Durrant inquired, 'is Blanche here tonight?' Indeed, no, the aunt replied, she had not returned home to dinner and her absence was most worrying. 'Well, I regret she is not with us,' Durrant said. 'I have a book called The Newcomers, by Thackeray, for her, but I will send it to the house.'

Oddly, Mrs. Noble waited several days before she notified the police of Blanche's disappearance. Along with others known to be her friends, Durrant was questioned and volunteered the curiously un-gallant suggestion that perhaps she had wandered from the moral path and 'gone astray'.

A few days later he attempted to pawn some woman's rings. The offer was turned down by the pawnbroker, and a week afterwards there came by post to Mrs. Noble three of Blanche's rings, wrapped in newspaper. Across the margin of the paper was scribbled the name: 'George King'.

As the days of Blanche's disappearance pro-gressed, another member of Emanuel Church, 21-year-old Minnie Williams, began to show signs of agitation. 'I know too much about the disap-pearance of Blanche,' she told a friend. 'I think she has met with foul play.'

Mutilated body

At eight o'clock on the evening of April 12, a homeward-bound claims adjuster, named Hodgkins' saw Durrant and Minnie arguing outside the entrance to Emanuel Church. Mr. Hodgkins was so concerned about Durrant's aggressive manner that he intervened to restore the peace. As he walked on, however, he saw Minnie take Durrant's arm and the two of them enter the church. Once more, as in the case of Blanche Lamont, the church door closed upon a seemingly affectionate young couple.

At 9.30 Durrant, gaunt and dishevelled arrived at the house of one of Emanuel Church's members for a meeting of the Christian Endeavour group. Before the proceedings began he announced, distractedly, that he must wash his hands. By the time the meeting ended, at 11.25, he was chatting amiably with the rest of the devout gathering and appeared to be his normal, polished self. As the members left he excused himself, saying that he must return to the church, where he had 'left something'.

The following morning some of the members of the Ladies' Society – who were decorating Emanuel Church for the Easter service – decided to adjourn for a rest to a side room used as the church library. In the room was a cupboard which, for some reason, one of the women opened. As she did so she gave a spine-chilling scream and threw back the door so that her companions could share her terror.

Fearfully, they peered inside. There, on the floor, they saw the mutilated and half-naked body of Minnie Williams. Some of her underclothes had been forced far down her throat. She had been stabbed in each breast, and the arteries of her wrists had been slashed, causing her blood to cascade over the cupboard walls.

A necrophiliac?

On Easter Sunday the *San Francisco Chronicle* reminded the police – who had been called immediately upon the discovery of Minnie's body – that Blanche Lamont was still missing. So detectives returned to Emanuel Church and began a thorough search of the building. They found that the door to the belfry tower – a tower which had no bell, and which church officials rarely ascended – seemed to have been recently forced. They thrust the door open and piled up the staircase.

There, on the dust-covered floor of the southeast corner of the tower, lay Blanche's naked body. There were deep bruises on her throat and it was clear that she had been strangled. Her head had been placed on two wooden blocks to hold it in position – in the way medical students were taught to place the head of a body for postmortem examination – and her hands had been crossed on her breast, as if in preparation for burial. Her clothes were stuffed out of sight behind the belfry's wooden beams.

Medical investigation suggested that Minnie had been a co-operative party to sexual intercourse before her murder. But the findings in the case of Blanche were more ominous and horrifying. She had, it was stated, 'not parted with life and honour without a struggle', and a sexual outrage 'had probably occurred after death.' If that was so then her murderer was also a necrophiliac.

Once the dreadful news of the murders was out and capturing the daily headlines, it did not take long for all those observers of Durrant with Blanche and Minnie to hurry forward with their accounts. And, since Theo Durrant had almost gone out of his way to advertise his association with the two girls, he was swiftly put under arrest.

Once more, paler than ever, seemingly shocked that such allegations should be made against an ardent churchgoer, Durrant protested his innocence. But it was all in vain. On the grounds that there were more witnesses who had seen him with Blanche Lamont than with Minnie, the state decided to try him for Blanche's murder.

He was put on trial on July 22, 1895, and although the evidence was circumstantial, it was strongly so. It took the jury only five minutes to find him guilty – one of the swiftest verdicts ever returned in a major murder case. He was sentenced to death by hanging and, after long legal wrangling, the Supreme Court finally confirmed the sentence on April 3, 1897. The prisoner then announced that he would 'die like a Durrant'.